KING DOLLAR

KING DOLLAR

The Past and Future of the World's
Dominant Currency

Paul Blustein

Yale

UNIVERSITY PRESS

NEW HAVEN & LONDON

Published with assistance from the foundation established in memory of Philip Hamilton
McMillan of the Class of 1894, Yale College.

Yale University Press books may be purchased in quantity for educational, business, or
promotional use. For information, please e-mail sales.press@yale.edu (U.S. office)
or sales@yaleup.co.uk (U.K. office).

Set in Yale and Alternate Gothic type by IDS Infotech, Ltd.
Printed in the United States of America.

Library of Congress Control Number: 2024942615
ISBN 978-0-300-27096-9 (hardcover : alk. paper)

A catalogue record for this book is available from the British Library.

This paper meets the requirements of ANSI/NISO Z39.48-1992
(Permanence of Paper).

10 9 8 7 6 5 4 3 2 1

To my grandchildren,
whom I will always love unconditionally,
even if they grow up to like crypto

CONTENTS

CONTENTS

ABBREVIATIONS

ACH	automated clearinghouse
AML	anti–money laundering
ATM	automated teller machine
BDA	Banco Delta Asia
BIS	Bank for International Settlements
BRICS	Brazil, Russia, India, China, South Africa
BSA	Bank Secrecy Act
CARES Act	Coronavirus Aid, Relief, and Economic Security Act
CBDC	central bank digital currency
CDO	collateralized debt obligation
CFT	counter-financing of terrorism
CHIPS	Clearing House Interbank Payments System
CIPS	Cross-Border Interbank Payment System
CISADA	Comprehensive Iran Sanctions, Accountability, and Divestment Act
CNAS	Center for New American Security
CPFF	Commercial Paper Funding Facility
CPI	consumer price index
DC/EP	digital currency/electronic payment (China)
DPRK	Democratic People's Republic of Korea
ECB	European Central Bank
e-CNY	digital version of the Chinese renminbi
e-HKD	digital version of the Hong Kong dollar
ETF	exchange-traded fund

ABBREVIATIONS

e-THB	digital version of the Thai baht
FAIT	Flexible Average Inflation Targeting
FATF	Financial Action Task Force
FDIC	Federal Deposit Insurance Corporation
FEC	Foreign Exchange Certificates
FinCEN	Financial Crimes Enforcement Network
FOMC	Federal Open Market Committee
G-5	Group of Five
G-7	Group of Seven
G-20	Group of Twenty
GATT	General Agreement on Tariffs and Trade
GDP	gross domestic product
HSBC	Hong Kong and Shanghai Banking Corporation
ICC	International Criminal Court
IEEPA	International Emergency Economic Powers Act
IMF	International Monetary Fund
JCPOA	Joint Comprehensive Plan of Action
JPM Coin	JP Morgan Coin (tokenized deposit)
KYC	know your customer
M1	money supply measure (currency in circulation plus private checking deposits)
mBridge	Multiple CBDC Bridge
MIT	Massachusetts Institute of Technology
NFT	non-fungible token
NYSE	New York Stock Exchange
OFAC	Office of Foreign Assets Control
OPEC	Organization of Petroleum Exporting Countries
PAC	Political Action Committee
PDCF	Primary Dealer Credit Facility
QE	quantitative easing
QT	quantitative tightening
REIT	Real Estate Investment Trust
SAMA	Saudi Arabian Monetary Agency
SAR	suspicious activity report
SDN	Specially Designated National
SDR	Special Drawing Right
SEC	Securities and Exchange Commission
SPFS	System for the Transfer of Financial Messages (Russia)
STC	state trading company (North Korea)
SWIFT	Society for Worldwide Interbank Financial Transactions
TAF	Term Auction Facility
TALF	Term Asset-Backed Securities Loan Facility
TerraUSD	Terraform Lab's US dollar algorithmic stablecoin

ABBREVIATIONS

TSLF	Term Securities Lending Facility
UAE	United Arab Emirates
UBS	Union Bank of Switzerland
UPI	Unified Payments Interface
USDC	Circle's dollar stablecoin
USDT	Tether's dollar stablecoin
V-E Day	Victory in Europe Day
WLF	World Liberty Financial

CHAPTER 1

WITH GREAT POWER

Of all the logistical problems bedeviling businesses through the ages, the woes of New York City banks in the first half of the nineteenth century surely rank among the most vexatious. During that period the banks employed squads of "porters" who traveled on foot from bank to bank toting bundles of checks and specie — that is, gold coins — exchanging items at each stop depending on how much their employers owed or were entitled to receive. Laborious, risky, and prone to mishap as it may sound, this system was the best the banks could come up with for settling mutual obligations that arose from the burgeoning amount of their customers' payments and receipts.[1]

Every time customers wrote checks, new obligations would be created, with more gold-hauling work for the porters. Suppose, for example, a gentleman buying a new horse-drawn carriage paid for it by writing a check for $200. The carriage makers would deposit the check at their bank, which would send a porter to the gentleman's bank to present the check for exchange into $200 worth of coins. Each bank would then record the appropriate sums on their books — a $200 debit on the gentleman's account, and a $200 credit on the carriage makers' account. Such transactions oblige banks to calculate and pay the amounts they owe each other, and in America's financial capital, the method involved carrying

———

valuable articles through city streets for conducting in-person exchanges at tellers' windows.

Contemporaries had no difficulty recognizing how cockeyed this was. An account published in 1858 conveys the flavor:

> The sixty Porters were out all at once, with an aggregate of two or three hundred bank-drafts in their pockets. . . . [They] crossed and recrossed each others' footsteps constantly; they often met in companies of five or six at the same counter, and retarded each other . . . drawing specie at some places, and depositing it at others; and the whole process was one of confusion, disputes, and unavoidable blunders, of which no description could give an exact impression.
>
> After all the draft-drawing was over, came the settlement of the Wall street Porters among themselves. A *Porters' Exchange* was held on the steps of one of the Wall street banks, at which they accounted to each other for what had been done during the day. Thomas had left a bag of specie at John's bank to settle a balance, which was due from William's bank to Robert's; but Robert's bank owed twice as much to John's. What had become of *that!* Then Alexander owed Robert also, and William was indebted to Alexander. Peter then said, that he had paid Robert by a draft from James, which he, James, had received from Alfred on Alexander's account. That, however, had settled only half the debt. A quarter of the remainder was cancelled by a bag of coin, which Samuel had handed over to Joseph, and he had transferred to David. It is entirely safe to say, that the Presidents and Cashiers of the banks themselves could not have untangled this medley.[2]

A solution came from a bank clerk named George Dummer Lyman, who circulated an anonymous article in 1851 proposing to streamline the process, a key function in finance called clearing and settlement. Clearing involves calculating the amounts due to and from each bank — a process of adding, subtracting, and netting the amounts over a given period, typically a single day — and checking that sufficient funds will be available when settlement occurs. Settlement refers to the transfer of funds, which extinguishes obligations.

Fortunately for Lyman, he could draw on the experience of English banks, which had previously employed "walking clerks" to carry checks and specie through London. Their solution was to establish an institution in London's

———

financial district called the Bankers' Clearing House, where the clerks could gather in safe confines and conduct their transactions much more expeditiously during the course of a day as checks came in.

Lyman's proposal, which was enthusiastically welcomed by other New York bankers, led to an improvement on the London system. With Lyman serving as the first manager, the New York Clearing House began operations on October 11, 1853, in a building on Wall Street where 52 banks exchanged checks worth $22.6 million on the first day. An oval table about 70 feet long accommodated two clerks from each bank, one sitting on the inside and another standing on the outside (figure 1). Upon receiving a signal at 10 a.m. from the manager, the outside clerks would take one pace forward and conduct transactions with the sitting clerk of the bank they faced; the same procedure would then be repeated, with the circle of outside clerks advancing one step at a time to the next bank until they were back to their original position. The whole process could take as little as six minutes provided everyone did their sums correctly in advance; clerks guilty of arithmetical errors were subject to fines, which helped keep operations running with minimal disruptions. Similar clearing houses were established in Boston in 1856 and Philadelphia in 1858, and later in other major US cities.

Forward-thinking though he may have been, Lyman could scarcely have imagined the implications of his brainchild for the global mightiness of his nation's currency.

This is a book about that currency. The US dollar, far more than the currency of any other country, is used to make payments on world markets for goods and services, to invoice customers abroad, to borrow and lend in global financial markets, to hold in reserve for troubled times or emergencies, and for a host of other international purposes. It is the most important kind of money on the planet, and that greatly enhances the global power of the United States, which can use its control over access to dollars as a weapon for foreign policy goals. For all the chatter about America's decline, the dollar's dominance is one key respect in which US hegemony is undiminished.

The dollar's unique status among currencies has drawn worldwide attention, and plenty of controversy, since it played an essential part in the

Figure 1. Artist's rendering of the New York Clearing House in its early years (from James Sloan Gibbons, *The Banks of New-York: Their Dealers, the Clearing House, and the Panic of 1857* [New York: D. Appleton & Co., 1858], p. 306).

unprecedented economic sanctions against Russia following Moscow's February 2022 invasion of Ukraine. Of all the measures that the United States and its allies took to sever Russia from the global economy, the most dramatic involved cutting off Russian banks, businesses, and government agencies from the dollar-based system that is essential for a modern economy to thrive. A number of countries, which have either been targeted for sanctions by Washington in the past or fear they might be in the future, are trying to engineer financial mechanisms that will enable them to bypass the dollar in international commerce. All this has come at a time of dizzying monetary innovation in which visionaries contend that digital tokens circulating in mobile devices will become the payment and investment vehicles of the future — perhaps with governments or private companies as issuers, perhaps under a decentralized regime using blockchain technology. The upshot, some claim, is that the dollar is doomed to lose its supremacy; others scoff and point to evidence that the US currency is going from strength to strength. Some argue that a diminution in the dollar's

international ranking would be of minor consequence or even beneficial; others
warn that it would be catastrophic.

Even to well-informed laypeople, the subject is a source of perplexity. As an
introduction, the tale recounted above about the launching of the New York
Clearing House is ideal. Although those events took place well over a century
and a half ago, they help illuminate inner workings of money and finance that
are highly relevant to the dollar's current international role. And in retrospect,
Lyman's innovation can be seen to have spawned a key underpinning of the
greenback's use as a sanctions weapon.

The institution that traces its lineage back to Lyman, the Clearing House
Interbank Payments System (CHIPS), is headquartered in plush offices on the
17th floor of a mid-Manhattan skyscraper. CHIPS processes over 540,000
transactions worth $1.8 trillion on an average day, according to its most recent
public disclosures.[3] In the place of clerks in top hats pacing around an oval table,
its computerized network uses algorithms to match orders from financial institutions, a system that CHIPS boasts "has operated without incident, always settling payments and distributing end-of-day balances, even during financial
crises, the terrorist attacks of 9/11, the COVID-19 pandemic, and natural disasters."[4] Although CHIPS is headquartered in New York, its facilities in Texas,
North Carolina, and elsewhere house the computers and personnel handling the
massive transfers of data, along with backup installations. It's a private entity,
operated by a company owned by more than 40 large banks, but CHIPS works
closely with a public sector network called Fedwire, which is owned by the US
Federal Reserve System and also settles huge amounts of interbank payments.

What's the big deal? Clearing and settlement is all about financial plumbing —
it's mechanical, and downright boring now that porters aren't scurrying through
New York streets with bags of gold coins. Any country can have a clearing house,
and many do. CHIPS isn't even as big as Fedwire in terms of the numbers and
dollar amounts of transactions cleared and settled. Readers who have closely followed news about the sanctions on Russia will have heard a lot about the Society
for Worldwide Interbank Financial Transactions (SWIFT), and may wonder
where it fits into all this.

The big deal about CHIPS is that it's the main conduit for large-value
transactions in US dollars that cross international borders. It handles more than

90 percent of the world total of such transactions, and about 95 percent of the payments going through CHIPS either begin or end — and sometimes begin *and* end — outside the United States. Fedwire mostly handles domestic transactions from one American bank to another. As for SWIFT, it's a messaging system by which financial institutions communicate (more about this later) and doesn't clear or settle transactions.

Plumbing it may be. But when the stuff flowing through the pipes is the bulk of international movements in the dollar, and the pipes are located in a jurisdiction subject to US law, foreign banks and even whole governments need to take care lest they lose access to that plumbing. The clout the US government gains as a result is incalculable.

The bafflement expressed in April 2023 by Luiz Inácio Lula da Silva, the president of Brazil, spoke for multitudes around the world. "Every night I ask myself why all countries have to base their trade on the dollar," Lula said in a speech to an audience in Shanghai, which responded with enthusiastic applause. "Why can't we do trade based on our own currencies? Who was it that decided that the dollar was the currency after the disappearance of the gold standard?"[5]

The system that Lula deems confounding is a hierarchy of currencies, with a few at the top and many at or near the bottom. The Brazilian real, Armenian dram, and Malaysian ringgit may be essential for conducting business when both buyer and seller are located within Brazil, Armenia, and Malaysia, respectively, but such currencies are little used as payment for goods and services outside their borders. Unfair as it may seem, the people and companies who sell oil, wheat, computer chips, pharmaceuticals, and other products almost always expect to be paid in "hard" currency — the US dollar, euro, Japanese yen, British pound, Chinese renminbi, Swiss franc, and a handful of others commonly accepted in international transactions. This is not just because richer countries tend to be more stable than poorer ones; it is also because hard currencies are easy and cheap to trade, invest, and hedge against changes in their value.

The dollar stands at the peak of the hierarchy, well above the other hard currencies. Its use at the international level is greatly disproportionate to the US economy's size. Although US economic output accounts for about one-quarter of global gross domestic product (GDP), and US imports and exports account for only 8 percent of world trade, data show that the dollar figures widely in transactions that don't touch US shores or involve Americans at all.

In the news media, the dollar is often described as the world's "main reserve currency," which is true as far as it goes. The term refers to reserves of foreign currency and other assets that are held by governments and central banks such as the Bank of Japan, People's Bank of China, Bank of England, and Reserve Bank of India. Nearly 60 percent of official reserves consists of assets denominated in dollars, mostly US Treasury bills and bonds.[6] (To avoid confusion, note that those are securities held in electronic form, not cash piled high in vaults.)

But the reserve-currency statistic fails to do justice to the full extent of the dollar's global role. In international trade, exporters commonly invoice in dollars and are paid in dollars — one big exception being shipments from one European country to another, which is mostly conducted in euros — but apart from intra-European trade, more than three-fourths of the global total in recent years is invoiced in dollars, including 96 percent of trade in the Western Hemisphere. Much of this trade is between non-Americans; close to 90 percent of exports from countries such as South Korea and Australia are invoiced in dollars, even though only a modest share of the goods those countries ship abroad are destined for the United States (less than one-fifth for South Korea, and a little more than one-tenth for Australia). When companies and governments around the globe borrow in a currency other than their own national currency, they most frequently do so in dollars, which account for about 60 percent of all international loans and deposits and nearly 70 percent of all international bonds and other debt securities. In the immense market where foreign currencies are exchanged, the dollar is used in nearly 90 percent of all trades; someone wishing to convert, say, Chilean pesos into Jordanian dinars will typically sell pesos for dollars first, then exchange the dollars for dinars, because direct trading between the two non-US currencies is negligible.[7]

Put in more conceptual terms, the dollar performs — at the international level — the main functions of money. As pretty much any monetary treatise will tell you, the functions of money are threefold: it is a medium of exchange, a unit of account, and a store of value. The necessity of these three functions is easy to grasp by imagining how inefficient everyday life would be if, in the absence of money, people had to resort to bartering directly with each other. A classic illustration involves a fruit seller who wants a taxi ride, and a taxi driver who wants to buy apples. By serving as a medium of exchange, money enables them to avoid haggling over how many apples a ride is worth and vice versa; instead, each pays the agreed-upon price. As a unit of account, money enables both of them to know the value of what they are paying and receiving; each party understands how much, say, $10 is worth. As a store of value, money gives both parties confidence that they can accept payment because even if they delay spending until a future time, their money will be worth more or less the same.

By providing a vehicle for payment in much of cross-border trade, the dollar fulfills the medium of exchange function in global markets. As the currency used for a great deal of invoicing, it provides a unit of account function. As the main reserve currency for central banks and most common denomination for international investments and loans, it functions as a global store of value.

Moreover, the dollar's dominance in each of its functions amplifies its dominance in others. Economists use the word "complementarity" for this phenomenon. For example, exporters outside the United States who invoice in dollars will expect to receive flows of payments in dollars and will therefore find it most convenient to borrow in dollars, to ensure that obligations coming due are matched with incoming cash. Such exporters will also want to convert their dollar revenues back into their home currency to pay their workers—which leads to more trading of dollars on foreign exchange markets.

Further entrenching the dollar's status is its ubiquity, bolstered by "network effects," meaning that everybody has an incentive to use the greenback simply because so many others do. Living as I do in a Japanese town that attracts lots of tourists, I often see network effects at work in another sphere—language, specifically the commonality of English. I can't help pitying the Italians, Germans, Brazilians, Chinese, and other foreigners whom I sometimes overhear in shops and restaurants struggling to communicate in English with Japanese clerks and wait staff, but the parties in such conversations understandably feel they have no choice but to study the language that is likely to be spoken, at least a little, by so many around the world. Similarly, businesspeople operating in international markets tend to transact in dollars for the sake of ensuring smooth dealings with all their counterparties, who will presumably be using greenbacks as well. To come back to the example of exports, it's only natural for an individual exporter

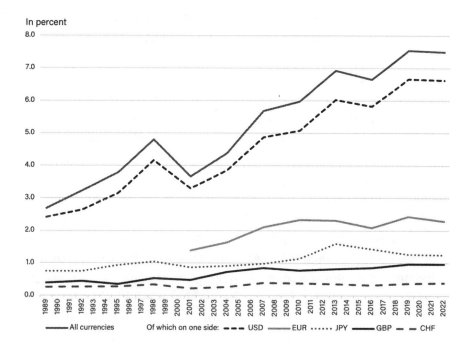

Figure 2. Foreign exchange swaps, scaled by world GDP (average daily turnover in the month of April, including spot and forward transactions). Sources: IMF, BIS Triennial Survey.

to invoice in dollars if customers are accustomed to paying in dollars; subjecting them to the inconvenience of using a different currency may be hazardous to the bottom line.

The complementarity and network effects go even deeper than those just listed. A graph provides a revealing illustration (figure 2). Drawn from data compiled by the Bank for International Settlements, it shows the turnover in a financial instrument called foreign exchange swaps, in which two parties trade a pair of currencies (say, dollars and Japanese yen) twice. First they trade at today's exchange rate, and then at some later time, they swap the two currencies back at a rate agreed at outset.[8]

Notice first of all that the US dollar dominates this market, as shown by the dark dashed line that's rising over time. That line shows swaps in which the dollar is one of the currencies being exchanged. Notice too that the lower lines, which are basically flatlined, are for swaps involving euros, yen, pounds sterling, and Swiss francs.

This is a market of staggering size; it isn't just a bunch of speculators trying to strike it rich by guessing the direction that the dollar or some other currency will go. The average churn in these swaps was close to $5 trillion per day in 2022, which is equivalent to the GDP of the entire world being turned over every 14 days or so. Rather than speculation, the purpose of this market is mostly for hedging — that is, protecting against currency fluctuations, making sure that the ups and downs of foreign exchange rates don't adversely affect the income that firms receive or the outlays that they make.

What's so significant about dollar dominance of this market? It reflects mutually reinforcing decisions among vast numbers of giant firms, mostly based in rich countries — multinational corporations, global banks, and other financial institutions — to use dollars for borrowing, lending, investing, and myriad other purposes. Swaps enable them to do so. Japanese life insurance companies, for example, invest their global portfolios heavily in dollar securities, and since they have obligations in yen to their policyholders, they typically hedge their currency risk using dollar-yen swaps. The same goes for, say, Swiss pension funds, which have obligations to beneficiaries that they hedge using dollar–Swiss franc swaps. The more money that such firms put into the market for dollar securities, the more they induce big manufacturers and other international companies to raise money by issuing dollar securities — and vice versa. Global banks are often the counterparties for dollar swaps, so they too run heavily on dollars. Dollar exporting begets dollar invoicing, which begets dollar borrowing and securities issuance, which begets dollar lending and investing, which begets dollar hedging, and so on.

No treaty or international accord formalizes the dollar's role — at least not anymore. The agreement struck among the Allies in 1944 at the famous Bretton Woods conference officially put the greenback at the center of the postwar international monetary system, but that pact broke down in the early 1970s. Instead, fundamental factors are at play in the dollar's supremacy. Most decisive is the unrivaled depth, breadth, and liquidity of US financial markets, which means that anyone wishing to buy or sell the most important dollar-based securities —

obligations of the US Treasury — can do so easily, in large quantities, without causing prices to move up or down, thanks to the wide range of instruments available for trading and hedging and the high volume of turnover. This feature of US markets has proven crucial during financial crises; in such circumstances, money managers attach enormous importance to being able to unload holdings in a hurry without incurring fire-sale losses. Also vital to the dollar's status is America's legal and institutional infrastructure, in which property rights are assured, contracts are enforceable, rule of law prevails, and government is relatively transparent. Although other hard currencies have similar features and are therefore used internationally to some extent, none can match the dollar; each has drawbacks that limit its global role.

The dollar's resilience has emboldened Democratic and Republican administrations alike to exploit it in the name of national security, especially during the past two decades, the main goals including fighting terrorism and isolating rogue states such as North Korea. Although dollar weaponization was widely welcomed when used in 2022 against Russia, it has evoked quite different reactions abroad on other occasions — a notable example being when the Trump administration imposed sanctions on Iran in 2018 and bullied other countries into compliance with US policy by threatening severance from dollar-based finance for any entity dealing with Tehran. Outraged by what they view as abusive US conduct, some foreign governments have taken "de-dollarization" measures aimed at loosening Washington's chokehold on flows of money, but these have generally proven ineffective.

Astute readers will have detected a glaring omission in the above analysis. It is all well and good to say that the dollar is rightfully higher on the totem pole than the euro, yen, and all other currencies issued by government authorities. But state-backed forms of money aren't the only kind. As cryptocurrency enthusiasts, libertarians, and all manner of deep thinkers like to point out, money is a social construct, a "shared fiction," the value of which depends on the willingness of society's members to accept it in the expectation that others will also do so in the future. At various times in history, items such as shells, beads, wampum, and animal skins have served as money, and people have a remarkable capacity for inventing money-like instruments for conducting exchanges under extraordinary circumstances — an example being cigarettes used for trading in prisoner of war camps. When Irish banks shut down for months in 1970 because of a strike, depriving their customers of access to cash, people managed to pay for things they needed by writing paper checks that were accepted, more often than not, on the basis of trust—a crucial element for any item with pretentions of serving as money.

From such examples and episodes, the conclusion may be drawn that money doesn't require the involvement of the state, and it certainly doesn't require state monopoly over its issuance. Thus the Brave New World of money toward which we are evidently hurtling raises a fundamental question: once technology gives us all sorts of heretofore unimagined ways of transacting with each other, why should the US dollar play much if any role at all? Put another way, in words similar to those often seen on social media, why should dollars be more worthy of serving as money than strings of software code cleverly designed by private individuals? A considered answer will provide insight, right off the bat, into what makes a dollar a dollar.

In the annals of monetary history, Kublai Khan stands out for his ingenious approach to the workings of money in his dominions. During his thirteenth-century reign, the Chinese emperor wanted to ensure widespread use of the paper currency, called *chao*, that was issued by his government, even though it wasn't backed by reserves of precious metal or commodities. So he decreed that any person refusing *chao* in payment would do so "at the peril of his life," according to the awestruck account of the Venetian traveler Marco Polo, the result being that all the emperor's subjects "receive it without hesitation, because, wherever their business may call them, they can dispose of it again" when they made purchases. Students of economics will readily identify "fiat currency"—the value of which stems purely from government authority rather than its intrinsic worth—as one of the concepts that the Great Khan was applying, albeit with a draconian twist.

The dollar is a fiat currency, having lost the last vestiges of its gold backing in 1971. Of course, nobody is threatened with bodily harm for refusing to accept it. But state power exercised by the US government does play crucial roles in instilling public confidence in the dollar. Some of these state powers easily come to mind with a little thought, while others require some specialized knowledge regarding the workings of modern monetary systems.

———

The power to tax is probably the most obvious. To be comfortable holding dollars, Americans need to be sure they can exchange the currency for real goods or services, and the knowledge that the government will accept dollars for tax payments is extremely important in that regard. Failure to pay what is owed to the Internal Revenue Service can be punished with fines or imprisonment, after all.

A related point can be seen by looking closely at a US dollar bill, where in small, capitalized letters are the words: "This note is legal tender for all debts, public and private." That means dollars will be accepted not only for tax payments but, under the law, for the discharge of private obligations. In other words, if dollars are used to pay the amount owed under a legally binding contract, courts will deem the obligation fulfilled; the same does not apply to, say, shells, beads, Bitcoin, or even gold ingots regardless of how valuable the payer may insist they are.

That helps a lot, but it isn't enough. Americans need to be reasonably certain that their dollars will maintain their purchasing power over time. That's the primary responsibility of the Federal Reserve, which is mandated by law to keep the overall price level stable, broadly speaking, while also fostering full employment. The Fed does its best to achieve these often-conflicting goals by moving interest rates up or down depending on whether economic conditions are weak or strong. The basic mechanics are well known to readers of financial news pages: When the economy is sluggish, the Fed tries to stimulate growth by opening the credit spigot and pushing interest rates down, using its influence over the rate banks pay for short-term borrowing from each other. When the economy is booming, and the Fed fears that prices will soar in response to excessive demand, it tries to dampen growth by closing the credit spigot and pushing rates up.

Beyond that, the state does much more. It ensures that a dollar is a dollar regardless of whether the dollar is public money or private money. This terminology may startle some readers who have never heard of the distinction between public money and private money, but it's important.

Paper currency — in the United States, dollar bills, which are the things most Americans think of as "money" — is one kind of public money. The words "Federal Reserve Note" printed on the top mean that it's issued by the Fed, and although it can't be taken to a government office to be redeemed into gold or silver it is

---

recorded on the Fed's books as a liability, which can be thought of as an implicit promise to maintain the note's purchasing power — its value against a basket of commonly purchased goods — or at least come as close as reasonably possible.

Most Americans don't want to keep a lot of their dollars in the form of cash, partly because of the risk of theft, partly because cash earns no interest, and partly for the sake of convenience in using modern payment systems. Instead, dollars get deposited in banks — and that's where they become private money. A deposit of, say, $100 takes the form of an electronic entry on the bank's books showing a $100 credit in the depositor's account, and that $100 becomes a liability of the bank — a private firm — to the depositor. Forget for a moment that, in the United States, a federal agency (the Federal Deposit Insurance Corporation, or FDIC) guarantees bank deposits up to $250,000 to help discourage people from yanking their money out in a panic. The $100 is merely a promise by the bank that it owes $100 to the depositor; it's no longer public money.

The vast bulk of the dollars used for payments in the US economy are private. And here's something that crypto fans find especially galling about this: private money can be created — as if by magic — by banks, when they make loans. A bank lending, say, $100 million to a company building a factory simply credits the company's account with $100 million. Just like that, the company has $100 million in deposits, and the amount of money in the economy has expanded.

Banks are regulated. However imperfect that regulation may be (and it is sometimes terrible), banks can't generate unlimited amounts of loans lest they run afoul of rules and laws designed to make sure they have a sufficient cushion to absorb losses. That's another way in which state authority helps protect the dollar's integrity. But there's an even more important thing the state does.

For a bank, a loan is an asset — a promise by the borrower to repay — which is legally binding. The company in the example above must repay the $100 million it borrowed, with interest, or it will be in legal difficulty. Sometimes loans are secured with collateral — a home, in the case of a mortgage — and if the borrower defaults the bank can institute foreclosure proceedings (or in the case of an auto loan, send a "repo man" to seize the vehicle). But even when no collateral is involved, a failure by a borrower to repay is a breach of contract, and the lender can pursue remedies, going to court if necessary, perhaps even forcing the borrower to declare bankruptcy.

Default, bankruptcy, and repo men are not the norm; most loans have happy endings, with full repayment. But the point is that the dollar is backed by much more than just the willingness of others to accept it. It's also backed by rule of law, with the state requiring contracts to be honored and courts standing ready to adjudicate disputes.

Finally, the dollar gets state backing in yet another way — obscure, but wondrous once it's understood.

Recall how New York banking worked in the 1850s: banks used specie to pay each other the amounts they owed. The wacky system of porters carrying gold coins through the street was eliminated when the New York Clearing House was established. But banks still needed to transfer funds among themselves — settling their obligations — when customers wrote checks, and in the 1850s specie was the "settlement medium."

In the modern world of fiat currency, banks pay each other with reserves, a special kind of public money that only they use. Reserves aren't shiny like gold, or even tangible like paper bills; they're simply electronic entries in accounts that banks have at the Fed. Also known as "central bank money" (a term that will come up again), reserves are the settlement medium when banks transfer money among themselves, reflecting transactions among their millions of customers who may be individuals, companies, nonprofit institutions, or a variety of other entities.

All of this takes place behind the scenes, with electronic data entries going up or down. When you make a payment — by writing a check, say, or tapping a debit card — it may look as if money moves from your account to the recipient's account. What really happens is: 1) your bank reduces the amount in your account, 2) your bank transmits the equivalent amount in reserves to the recipient's bank, meaning that your bank's reserve account at the Fed is reduced while the recipient bank's reserve account is increased, and 3) the recipient's bank increases the recipient's account.

The same process happens when you receive money, for example when your employer pays your wages. Your employer's bank transfers reserves to your bank, in an amount equivalent to your wages, with the transfer involving a simple debiting and crediting of the two banks' accounts at the Fed. Your account goes up, and your employer's account goes down.

Here's the wondrous part: all of these types of dollars — paper bills, bank deposits, and reserves — are interchangeable. You can go to an ATM and withdraw cash from your bank account, converting private money to public money with nothing more than the dipping of a card and entry of a PIN code. If your bank needs more cash to insert into its ATMs, it can ask the Fed to ship some, and the Fed will reduce your bank's reserves by a corresponding amount. At every step of the way, the dollars involved are dollars, with no restriction or loss of value, exchangeable at par, meaning exactly $1.00 per dollar, a state of affairs that academics call the "singleness of money," another term that will come up in later chapters.

Jon Cunliffe, who served as deputy governor of the Bank of England until recently, gave a brilliant speech on this subject in 2021,[9] and although he was speaking about the United Kingdom his words applied equally to the United States. He noted that even before the Covid pandemic, public money in the form of cash was used by British citizens for only about 23 percent of payments, and about 95 percent of the money they held that could be used for payments was in the form of bank deposits — private money.

"It is not clear to me to what extent the general public understand this distinction between public and private money — or even that most of the time they are using private money," Cunliffe said. "The fact that, unlike in some periods of history, we do not at present think much about these things and that people in the UK have a general confidence in the money they use regardless of its form and issuer is, I think, a good thing. It is not an accident. It is due to the credibility of the institutional framework governing money in the UK that tethers private money to the public money issued by the state."

This institutional framework can be abused, if those entrusted to run it choose to do so. Rulers with extravagant agendas have long used their power over money issuance in ways that erode the value of ordinary people's property, with deleterious long-term consequences. In the medieval era, princes seeking to finance unaffordable military adventures or luxurious castle-building ordered the debasement of gold and silver coins for distribution to soldiers and laborers. In modern times, powerful politicians twist the arms of central bankers to adopt monetary policies that will support profligate expenditure, low taxes, or both, regardless of the risks. Hyperinflations in Weimar Germany, Latin America, and

Zimbabwe are the most extreme manifestations, but prolonged bouts of even more moderate inflation can engender social and political upheaval.

Nevertheless, the main point stands about the fiat-currency dollar: it rests firmly on an edifice underpinned by a great deal of state scaffolding. But that only applies to the internal US economy. Internationally, the scaffolding depends on market forces. How durable is that scaffolding?

Centuries before the dollar rose to global preeminence, the currencies of other mighty powers — the Byzantine Empire's gold solidus, the Florentine florin, the Venetian ducat, the Dutch guilder, the Spanish silver peso, and the British pound sterling — reigned supreme in international commerce. Each one maintained dominant status until the clout of its issuing state faded. And now, it is the dollar's turn to follow those currencies into the dustbin of monetary history.

Or so we are often told. Predictions of such a turn of events resound with increasing frequency in books, in news articles and op-eds, and on social media. Cryptocurrency enthusiasts, only mildly discouraged by the crypto industry's many debacles, contend that Bitcoin or other blockchain-based monetary units will replace currencies issued by governments and ultimately overtake the dollar as the international standard. Foreign policy hawks warn that China's huge lead in developing a digital version of the renminbi poses a lethal threat to the greenback. Sound money zealots fret that the trillions of dollars pumped into the banking system in recent years by the Fed will result in ruinous inflation, eroding the US currency's value to the point where nobody will want to use it, at home or abroad.

"A Post-Dollar World Is Coming," proclaimed an op-ed by Ruchir Sharma, chair of Rockefeller International, in the August 28, 2022, edition of the *Financial Times,* and another, published in early 2023 by Zoltan Pozsar of Credit Suisse, was headlined, "Great Power Conflict Puts the Dollar's Exorbitant Privilege under Threat." Historian Niall Ferguson, citing the explosive growth of China's digital payment systems Alipay and WeChat Pay, wrote in the *Sunday Times:* "If America is stupid it will let this process continue until the day comes when the Chinese connect their digital platforms into one global system. That will be D-Day: the day the dollar dies as the world's No 1 currency and the day America loses its financial sanctions superpower."[10]

On CNBC in May 2021, investment magnate Stanley Druckenmiller railed thusly against the economic stimulus bill that Congress was enacting: "If we're going to monetize our debt and we're going to enable more and more of this spending, that's why I'm worried now for the first time that within 15 years we lose reserve currency status and of course all the unbelievable benefits that have accrued with it." A book titled *De-Dollarization* by Gal Luft and Anne Korin, co-directors of the Washington-based Institute for the Analysis of Global Security, portrayed the dollar's current path as "a train wreck in the making" and asserted that if its international role declines, "the impact would be felt not only in our pocketbooks, our retirement plans, our healthcare costs, the value of our homes and our bank loans but also in America's ability to preserve its superpower status." In a 2023 interview about the dollar on Fox News, Monica Crowley, who served as an assistant Treasury secretary during the first Trump administration, said the greenback was menaced by a "perfect storm" of "reckless policies," "Biden's weakness," and "America's enemies, led by China, forming an economic bloc" — which, if Saudi Arabia were to join, would lead to "sky-high inflation, just raging, Weimar Republic type of inflation. But more importantly, we would lose our economic dominance, and we would lose our superpower status."[11]

This book will show, *contra* the doomsayers' forecasts, that the dollar's global dominance is almost impregnable, and will remain so barring catastrophic missteps by the US government. The book will explain how Washington has used the centrality of its currency and the US financial system to devastating effect against adversaries, and make the case that this weapon can retain potency long into the future, even though some targets — notably Russia — have found ways to limit the damage. To further debunk alarmism about the dollar, the book will take the novel view that Americans shouldn't worry if another currency or two were to join the greenback atop the international monetary hierarchy. It's unlikely to happen to any great extent, and even if it did a more multipolar currency system could have many upsides.

But *King Dollar*'s message is not one of complacency — far from it. Note first of all the caveat "barring catastrophic missteps by the US government." The danger of such a misstep is hardly trivial; just a few months before these words were written, extreme right-wing members of Congress were threatening to force a default on US Treasury obligations amid a battle over the federal budget. Although that clash was resolved, it may be just a foretaste of a plunge into total dysfunctionality in Washington that could wreak havoc on the dollar-centered monetary system. Other havoc-wreaking scenarios can be conjured up, which will be spelled out later; suffice to say that the downsides would far exceed those involving the greenback.

More broadly, the overarching theme of the book is that the adage popularized by the movie *Spider-Man* — "With great power comes great responsibility" — applies to the dollar. Much is riding on the use of the great power held by the nation with the world's dominant currency. Whether it is wielded responsibly or not should be of profound concern to Americans and non-Americans alike. Here are some of the most important reasons why:

First, with so much leverage at their command, US officials will be tempted to resort to heavy-handed use of the dollar weapon. But thuggish, unilateral imposition of dollar-based sanctions — without broad backing from the international community — is likely to boomerang, with disastrous consequences. It risks infuriating other countries to the point where allies will be alienated and adversaries will be provoked into confrontation on other fronts. Even when sanctions are well justified and broadly supported, as in the case of Russia, they can inflict economic pain on the poor and on innocent bystanders (the rise in world energy prices in 2022 being a prime example), and they can draw retaliation. China has shown that it is no slouch at economic coercion, and may well use its own control over production of critical goods and materials to counter Washington's use of financial sanctions.

Second, the dollar's primacy puts a disproportionate obligation on the United States to foster and preserve global financial stability. Under the current regime, dollar shortages arise frighteningly often during bouts of turmoil, making the world heavily dependent on the Fed to prevent financial conflagrations from spreading and worsening. In other ways as well, the dollar's dominant status generates problems and risks for other countries and global markets that America must help ameliorate for the sake of its own welfare and the wider world more generally. One worrisome example was a near breakdown in the market for Treasury securities in 2020.

Third, the Spider-Man adage comes into play regarding the digitization of money. Claims that Bitcoin should replace the dollar may be balmy, but technological advances are undoubtedly going to transform the way payments are made and finance is conducted, with potentially disturbing implications for surveillance and control over financial transactions by the powers that be. (One meme circulating on the internet shows the following on the screen of an electronic credit card reader: "CARD DECLINED Please delete all tweets that violate your bank's hate speech policies to process payment"[12] — cartoonish, perhaps, but the idea is readily grasped.) As issuer of the world's leading currency, the United States shoulders a heavy burden for instilling the monetary system of the future with universal values that America has long championed, notably freedom of expression and protection of individual privacy, while also maintaining safeguards against abuse of the financial system for money laundering and other illicit activities. Some in US policymaking circles favor the development of a government-issued digital currency, as yet unnamed (e-dollar? Fedcoin?), while others contend that the private sector is much better suited to provide digital dollars in the form of so-called stablecoins. However that debate is resolved, Washington has a special obligation to take the lead in optimizing the difficult tradeoffs and influencing choices made in other capitals.

These responsibilities — especially those involving US allies — may not count for much in the mind of Donald Trump, who won back the presidency in November 2024, just before *King Dollar* went to print. But the gravity of these obligations merits wide recognition. With that aim in mind, the book addresses questions such as the following: Under what circumstances could dollar supremacy be threatened? Even if the dollar remains the dominant reserve currency, could the power of US financial sanctions be eroded by innovations designed to circumvent the dollar-based system? Must Washington use restraint in imposing financial sanctions, and if so why? Should America's central bank issue its own digital currency?

History is hugely instructive in elucidating the dollar's primacy and resilience as well as the implications for US power and responsibility. For that reason, chapters 2 and 3 delve deeply into the story of how the US currency attained and kept its international status. Chapter 3 might be called the book's Mark Twain chapter, since it shows how the dollar — like Twain, who famously stated, "The reports of my death have been greatly exaggerated" — maintained its dominance throughout the era following the collapse of the Bretton Woods system. During this period, as the chapter recounts, forecasts of the greenback's downfall repeatedly emanated from a chorus of prominent economists and commentators, especially as US inflation rose in the 1970s and US trade and budget deficits swelled in following decades. Time and again, however, the dollar defied obituary writers, most remarkably during the Global Financial Crisis of 2007–2009, which led to such frenetic demand for dollars all over the world that the Fed effectively had to serve as backstop for the global economy.

Chapter 4 might be called the book's anti-Twain chapter, since it tells the stories of the major currencies that have been envisioned to overtake the dollar; as the chapter shows, reports of their *dominance* have proved greatly exaggerated. The book then turns in chapters 5 and 6 to the dollar's use in sanctions, again using history to show both the potency of the dollar weapon and reasons for concern about its excessive use.

A natural segue from that topic is the digitization of money, which may provide the most effective means for sanctions busting. Chapters 7 and 8 therefore address the challenges that digital assets pose – and don't pose – to the dollar, by chronicling the development of new payment technologies, cryptocurrencies, Facebook's abortive foray into digital coin issuance, China's futuristic and ultra-convenient fintech systems, and the response from central banks.

Next, in chapters 9 and 10, comes a recounting of events in the 2020s that have provided "teachable moments" about the dollar. These include the Covid-related market crash of March 2020, when the world again depended on the Fed to keep the global financial system afloat. Also assessed, in chapter 10, are the sanctions on Russia – the desirable effect on Moscow's war-waging capacity, the weaknesses in the strategy that have allowed the Russian economy to remain resilient, and the undesirable fallout on the rest of the world. Conclusions and policy implications come in the final chapter.

Before examining the reasons for and implications of a mighty dollar, however, it is necessary to look back at a period – the first 150 years or so after the Declaration of Independence – when the international monetary system was quite different from that of today. A detailed retrospective of how poorly the dollar fared on the global stage during that period, and how far it rose thereafter, is crucial for understanding the US currency's current strength. That is the story of the next chapter.

CHAPTER 2

FROM HUMBLE ORIGINS TO KING OF CURRENCIES

Among nineteenth-century female journalists, who were almost exclusively confined to covering topics such as fashion and gardening, Nellie Bly was a pioneer, having published exposés about conditions in factories and mental institutions. Wracking her brains one Sunday in late 1888 for ideas to propose to her editor at the *New York World,* the 24-year-old Bly came up with a doozy: she would embark on a voyage modeled on the popular novel *Around the World in 80 Days* and chronicle her adventures for the newspaper's readers. After initially balking, on the grounds that such an assignment would be suitable only for a man, the *World*'s management assented, and on November 14, 1889, Bly boarded a London-bound steamship. Her aim was to circumnavigate the globe in a shorter period than the novel's hero – a goal she achieved, returning in 72 days – and in the process she also garnered vivid anecdotal information about the meagerness of the dollar's internationalization.

On the evening before her departure, Bly later recounted, she was given British money – 200 pounds sterling in gold and Bank of England notes – which was the dominant global currency at the time. She also took some US gold coins and paper bills "as a test to see if American money was known outside of America."[1] It was not until she arrived in Colombo, the capital of Ceylon (as

Sri Lanka was then known), that she first saw her country's currency, specifically $20 gold pieces strung on watch chains. "It is very popular in Colombo and commands a high price – as jewelry!" she wrote, but "it goes for nothing as money. When I offered it in payment for my bills I was told it would be taken at sixty per cent discount."[2]

Bly's observations reflected reality: the dollar was virtually absent from circulation outside the United States. (Canadian provinces were an exception, but even there use of the US currency ended shortly after the dominion government began issuing its own, following the 1867 confederation.) The puny status of US money abroad was not a result of economic size; on the contrary, production of goods and services by American factories, farms, mines, railroads, and other businesses expanded at such a torrid pace after the Civil War that US GDP surpassed Great Britain's around 1870. Although British output of manufactured goods remained No. 1 for a couple more decades, America was on the verge of taking the lead by that metric as well at the time of Bly's trip.[3]

How curious, therefore, given the brawniness of the US economic juggernaut, that a traveler like Bly would find her dollars so useless; and how disadvantageous for American companies engaging in international trade. Merchants seeking to import goods need credit to make their purchases from foreign sellers, and exporters need to extend credit to foreign buyers. But American firms undertaking such transactions had to rely mainly on banks in London that denominated their loans in pounds sterling, or (less often) banks in Paris or Berlin that did business in francs and marks.

For the currency of the world's biggest economy to be almost entirely unserviceable outside its borders was a striking manifestation of the nation's relatively primitive and disjointed monetary and financial system throughout the nineteenth century. (The bank porters mentioned in chapter 1 were just one aspect of this phenomenon.) That in turn was a function of Americans' strong sentiment for states' rights and widely held suspicion, especially in rural parts of the country, about the evils of big-city banks.

The Founding Fathers had intended a different outcome – or at least Alexander Hamilton had, and Hamilton's vision of a strong central economic authority prevailed in the Founders' initial divisions over monetary issues. The Constitution conferred upon Congress the sole power to coin money while prohibiting the states from doing so. As the first secretary of the Treasury, Hamilton also bore responsibility for legislation, enacted in 1791, establishing the Bank of the United States, which was based in Philadelphia and aimed partly at creating a common national currency that people would trust. ("Continentals" issued by the Continental Congress during the American Revolution had been printed in such voluminous quantities as to become almost worthless.) But Hamilton died in a duel in 1804, and the idea of a national bank endowed with money-creation powers became one of the hottest controversies in the young nation's politics. Agrarian interests in the south and west, distrustful of any entity that might favor urban financial and industrial elites, fought tooth and nail to sap the power of the Bank of the United States. Under the patrician Nicholas Biddle, who headed the Bank of the United States for 13 years starting in 1823, the institution made a commendable start on monetary unity; it issued its own notes that circulated nationwide as money, and exerted regulatory control over banks scattered around the country that also issued money-like notes. But sealing its fate was the 1828 election that bestowed the presidency on rough-hewn Tennessean Andrew Jackson, a quintessential elite-loather. Not only did Jackson withdraw the federal government's deposits from the Bank of the United States, he vetoed a bill that would have extended its charter past its expiration in 1836.

For more than a quarter century thereafter, in what came to be known as the "Free Banking Era," Americans contended with a multitude of currencies consisting of notes issued by hundreds of private banks.[4] These notes were redeemable for gold or silver if presented to the issuing bank, but they varied in relation to their par values — that is, the value printed on them — depending on the reliability of the bank, the state in which it was chartered, and the bank's distance from the bearer. A five-dollar note issued by the Quassaick Bank of Newburgh, New York, might or might not buy $5 worth of goods, and it might or might not have the same purchasing power as a $5 note issued by the Allegany County Bank of Cumberland, Maryland, which in turn might or might not have the same purchasing power as $5 notes issued by the Spicket Falls Bank of Methuen, Massachusetts, or the Bank of River Raisin of Monroe, Michigan. Such determinations had to be made by buyers and sellers in individual transactions, because although gold and silver coins minted by the federal government circulated, their scarcity necessitated the use of diverse bank-issued paper, which was adorned with a wide array of ornate engravings aimed at inspiring user confidence. Notes issued by banks in the Midwest often featured images of farmers harvesting wheat or other grain, while New England banknotes tended to be graced by imagery depicting industry (textile manufacturing, for example), and southern-state banknotes commonly portrayed the picking of cotton by enslaved African Americans – all in an effort to convey the vitality of the local economies where the banks were located. Portraits of the venerable, such as George Washington and Daniel Boone, were emblazoned on many notes, although a few – among them the $1 note of the Bank of Wisconsin, and the $5 note of the North River Banking Co. of New York – sported topless goddess-like figures in demurely relaxed poses, presumably in the hope of appealing to the easily titillated.

Wonderment, if not downright incredulity, is an understandable reaction to a look back at this kind of money. Present-day Americans take for granted that the dollar bills in their wallets are identical in appearance to the corresponding bills held by their fellow citizens and identical in value to the dollars held in their bank accounts. The banknotes of the mid-nineteenth century differed in fundamental and instructive ways. For starters, they were not legal tender, meaning they were imbued with no force of law as a means to settle debts or fulfill other payment obligations including taxes or contractual requirements. Rather, they typically bore promises by the issuing bank, printed in elegant script, to "pay the bearer on demand" the face value of the note in the form of precious metal coins or other valuable assets. In other words, they were strictly liabilities of banks, which issued them when they made loans to borrowers and maximized profit the longer the notes remained outstanding. State governments set the rules for the proliferation of such notes and banks, the result being no small amount of uncertainty about whether banks held sufficient assets to back the notes they issued. Notes bearing the names of well-known banks in New York, where state regulators were held in high esteem for their rigor, would generally change hands at face value or close thereto; the same would be true of notes from the biggest banks in, say, Boston or Philadelphia. But discounts would apply to notes issued by banks from states where the scruples of regulators and bankers were suspect (states on the frontier were particularly notorious). Some banks even employed men to carry bags full of their notes to distant states, the idea

---

being to reduce the opportunity for note holders to turn up demanding specie. Although a network of professional note brokers sprang up, which helped create a reasonably efficient national market for determining the discounts that should apply to each note, the overall system was prone to confusion that was hardly ideal for a monetary regime. Bank tellers and merchants had to keep large, published volumes handy to scrutinize the notes they were handed, not least because of pervasive counterfeiting.

The Civil War provided the impetus for imposing some degree of order on this chaos, because President Abraham Lincoln needed the means to pay for the battle against the Confederacy.[5] "Greenbacks" were part of the solution — paper currency issued by the government in Washington, with green printing on one side and the words "legal tender for all debts," a promise that made them suitable for paying soldiers. Members of Congress were initially loath to foist mere fiat money, totally unbacked by gold or silver, on the public; the idea "shocks all my notions of political, moral and national honor," declared William Pitt Fessenden, chairman of the Senate Finance Committee. But the near emptiness of the Treasury's coffers, which was obliging federal quartermasters to pay for military supplies with vouchers, left lawmakers little choice but to approve the necessary legislation. Although greenbacks invigorated the northern economy, they declined sharply in value relative to gold coins as more were issued, and inflation ensued, a classic example of too much money chasing too few goods.

Treasury Secretary Salmon P. Chase spearheaded a new approach, the National Banking Act of 1863, which established a network of tightly regulated, nationally chartered banks that would furnish credit to the Union by buying Treasury bonds. In return for accepting the conditions of national charters, these banks could issue notes engraved with a standard design plus the backing of a federal guarantee in case the issuing bank failed. By war's end, the system encompassed nearly 600 banks distributing identical-looking notes that changed hands at parity and served as money from Maine to California. By contrast, the monetary system in the Confederacy, where states'-rights dogma prevailed, consisted mainly of a hodgepodge of notes issued by individual states, cities, banks, and merchants. The resulting disarray contributed to the South's economic weakness and ultimate defeat.

All this bestowed a welcome measure of uniformity on the nation's currency as peace was restored. But it gave rise to a new problem, namely an artificial constraint on the quantity of dollars in circulation. Federally chartered banks were limited in the amounts of notes they could issue. That wasn't enough for bankers and leaders of the eastern business establishment, who wanted even greater assurance against any repetition of the wartime inflation that they viewed as inimical to prosperity. Their demands led to a decision by the United States in 1879 to join Great Britain and much of the rest of the world on the gold standard, meaning that paper currency issued by the US government, including greenbacks, could be redeemed for a fixed amount of the yellow metal, on demand. The legally binding tie between the dollar and gold sent a signal of financial rectitude; Washington was effectively forswearing any overuse of the printing press to cover shortfalls between federal outlays and revenue. Such was the ethos of the Victorian age, when the virtues of prudence drew quasi-religious devotion not only from bankers but from the world's growing middle class.[6]

The gold standard affords real economic benefits, the most obvious being confidence in the currency when it is backed by a tangible and valuable asset. Holders of wealth will be more willing to invest and lend if they feel assured that the returns they reap and loan repayments they receive will be in money of stable value. But the gold standard is deficient on another criterion, crucial for a well-functioning monetary system, namely the necessity for the supply of money to keep pace with the amount of transactions that an economy is capable of generating. Pegging the dollar at $20.67 per ounce of gold (the price set during most of America's gold-standard era) meant that the quantity of dollars available for lending and spending depended on the amount of gold in US government and bank vaults. If new gold was discovered and mined, money and credit would amply increase, but during periods when miners failed to extract additional gold, the money supply couldn't keep up with burgeoning US economic activity. When that happened, too few dollars were chasing too many goods, with deflation the result. And it did happen, with distressing regularity, during the last third of the nineteenth century, as the price level sank year after year, decade after decade, until the 1890s when new gold was discovered in South Africa.

Creditors benefited, but low-income people were squeezed, especially in the rural heartland, because farmers — perennial debtors that they are — received lower prices for their crops while the amounts they owed on their mortgages and other debts stayed constant in dollar terms. This was one of the chief grievances animating the late nineteenth-century Populists, who demanded the creation of new sources of money via greater coinage of silver — a much more abundant precious metal — most famously at the Democratic Party's 1896 convention when William Jennings Bryan, a Nebraska congressman, thundered "you shall not crucify mankind upon a cross of gold!" in the speech that catapulted him to the party's presidential nomination. (Bryan was defeated by William McKinley, who stoutly maintained that adherence to the "honest dollar" of gold was a matter of "duty" and "honor.")

Would the United States stick to the gold standard? Uncertainty about that question was one factor that helps explain the dollar's low international profile around the time of Nellie Bly's round-the-world trip. But the main reason stemmed from Americans' hostility toward concentrated financial power. Most banks' operations were legally limited to individual states, and even large banks were prohibited from establishing branches abroad. Some banks could not have any branches whatsoever. British banks labored under no such constraints; they had scores of branches in foreign countries, and the same was true of banks based in other major European capitals.

Perhaps most important, the United States lacked one monetary institution that Britain had concocted.

The founding of the Bank of England in 1694 stemmed from brutal national reversals, both military and financial. The Crown's credit was exhausted — a "Stop of the Exchequer," tantamount to debt default, had been called in 1672 — after decades of civil war, constitutional crises, and strife. Then a war with France led to crushing defeat. With debts piling frighteningly higher, the king's ministers glommed on to a proposal by William Paterson, a Scotsman who had made his fortune primarily on slave trading in the West Indies. A new bank, capitalized with gold bullion invested by wealthy Britons, would finance the sovereign's undertakings — and in exchange, the bank would be granted exclusive privileges to issue notes that would circulate as paper currency.

Thus was born one of the world's first central banks — that is, a bank that has been bestowed by a nation's government with monopoly powers over currency issuance, which enables it to regulate the money supply and interest rates. The Bank of England was not *the* first central bank; that distinction belongs to Sweden's Riksbank, which began operations some years earlier. But headquartered for nearly three centuries in neoclassical grandeur on Threadneedle Street in the City of London, the Bank of England enjoys pride of place for blazing trails that other central banks would follow. One episode in particular cemented its historic status, when the bank demonstrated its ability to serve as "lender of last resort" — a term that, as we shall see, figures prominently in the dollar's role today.[7]

It began on the afternoon of May 9, 1866, with the posting of a shocking notice on the London door of Overend Gurney & Co., a renowned financial powerhouse. Earlier in the nineteenth century, Overend Gurney had become the world's biggest broker of bills of exchange, a kind of IOU that merchants and industrialists gave each other when they wanted to buy or sell goods. But under new management that took control in the late 1850s, Overend Gurney was suffering ruinous losses on Caribbean plantations, railway shares, and a number of other speculative investments that were going sour. "We regret to announce that a severe run on our deposits and resources has compelled us to suspend payment," the note stated — the result being panic that caused a drying-up of available cash, as other bill brokers stopped dealing and crowds besieged every financial institution in the city clamoring to withdraw their deposits immediately. Their understandable assumption was that if Overend Gurney couldn't make good on its obligations, other banks would soon be similarly strapped. Overend Gurney was dumping bills of exchange and other securities in a mad scramble to come up with the money it owed, which was depressing prices and inflicting losses on even the soundest of banks. That intensified depositors' anxiety to obtain their cash promptly, before the banks' tills were empty.

Left to their own devices, banks cannot survive such situations. They are intermediaries between savers and borrowers; they amass the savings of many thousands of people, which they lend out to business enterprises, homebuyers, farms, and various other entities that need credit. And from the time they were first invented, banks have operated in one way or another according to "fractional-reserve banking," meaning that they keep only a fraction of their deposits in liquid, readily available reserves — that is, cash stored in their vaults or balances held in their accounts at a central bank. The potential problem is obvious: savers expect to be able to withdraw their deposits at a moment's notice, while borrowers expect to repay their loans only after an extended period; no bank can possibly satisfy demands for cash from all its depositors at the same time. A scene in the 1946 cinematic fantasy *It's a Wonderful Life* affords a dramatic illustration: George Bailey, played by Jimmy Stewart, is just about to depart for his honeymoon from the small town of Bedford Falls when he realizes that his family-run Bailey Brothers' Building and Loan is under siege from a throng of passbook-brandishing people intent on pulling out their savings. Rushing inside to the counter, he pleads for calm, telling one of the most vocal depositors: "You're thinking of this place all wrong, as if I had all the money back in a safe. The money's not here. Your money's in Joe's house — that's right next to yours. And in the Kennedy house, and Mrs. Macklin's house, and a hundred others."

Confronted with a cascade of runs on London banks, therefore, the Bank of England correctly diagnosed both cause and remedy: since depositors feared a dearth of cash, their frantic withdrawals would cease if assurances of ample supplies were forthcoming. On the days immediately following Overend Gurney's May 9 announcement, Bank of England officials did their best to furnish enough cash, for example by buying government bonds, bills of exchange, or other securities from bankers who flooded the bank's offices in search of funds. But the bank was running up against a legal constraint — a law prohibiting it from issuing banknotes that were unbacked by gold stocks. Henry Holland, the bank's governor, and his deputy, Thomas Hunt, sent an urgent letter on May 11 explaining their quandary to Chancellor of the Exchequer William Gladstone, who used his authority to suspend the law and permit the issuance of notes in unlimited amounts, regardless of whether the notes were backed by gold or not. This had the desired effect of quelling the panic; nobody had to worry about being last in the queue, because anybody wanting cash would be able to get it.

Controversy flared about the Bank of England's 1866 actions, but it drew praise in one of the most influential monetary treatises ever written, by Walter Bagehot, editor of *The Economist*. Not only was the bank right to have served as lender of last resort; it should be statutorily required to do so, Bagehot believed, in situations when the public lost faith in the safety of banks or availability of money. Uncertainty about the bank's readiness to provide liquidity would only make a panic catastrophically self-fulfilling. "Either shut the Bank at once . . . or lend freely, boldly, and so that the public will feel you mean to go on lending," Bagehot exhorted, adding that although the bank would be justified in charging some sort of penalty, such as a high interest rate, to discourage "idle" use of its resources during a crisis, it should lend "to merchants, to minor bankers, to 'this man and that man,' whenever the security is good."[8]

Another way for the Bank of England to nip the crisis in the bud would have been to rescue Overend Gurney. But Overend Gurney's request for a bailout was refused, for good reasons. Robert Bevan, a Bank of England staff member dispatched to examine Overend Gurney's books, reported that the firm was "rotten"—in effect, its problem was a matter of insolvency rather than illiquidity. This is a critical distinction: When prospects for a business enterprise meeting its obligations over the long run are so poor as to be negligible (as Overend Gurney's prospects were, in Bevan's judgment), lending money to tide it over a rough patch will simply delay the inevitable. But if a firm appears fundamentally sound—that is, capable of generating sufficient profit to meet its obligations in a sustainable manner—then a loan to ameliorate a shortage of cash (liquidity) makes perfect sense. The same principle applies to individuals, corporations, or even entire national governments that fall into financial difficulty. And when liquidity problems afflict a major bank, or a number of banks, it is all the more sensible to ensure that a short-term injection of cash will be forthcoming from a lender of last resort. A banking system that grinds to a halt for lack of liquidity can't furnish the credit that virtually every type of business enterprise needs to maintain operations; metaphorically speaking, the entire economy will be in danger of having its lifeblood choked off.

Nearly five decades would pass after Overend Gurney's failure before the United States would establish similar capabilities for addressing financial panics, despite its suffering debilitating ones in 1837, 1857, 1873, 1893, and 1907. But thereafter the dollar's heyday would come, fast and forcefully.

Staring into the eyes of John Pierpont Morgan Sr., according to a photographer who snapped his portrait, was like looking into the light of an oncoming express train.[9] The fierceness of Morgan's gaze helped him impose his will in numerous high-stakes confrontations during America's Gilded Age, including the mergers of major corporations and the avoidance of default by the federal government. His powers of intimidation were never more manifest than in the Panic of 1907, when at the age of 70 he used his status as the unrivaled king of Wall Street to stave off collapse of the nation's financial system.[10]

The trouble originated in a scheme by a coterie to corner the market in copper-mining shares — a failed gambit that, when it came to light, led to the downfall of the Knickerbocker Trust Co., New York's third largest trust bank, which had lent heavily to the speculators. In just a few hours on October 21, 1907, fretful depositors completely drained the Knickerbocker's coffers, and other banks across the nation — similarly beset by demands for withdrawals — hoarded every available modicum of cash, refusing to transact with each other for fear that more Knickerbockers were in the offing. With the official sector lacking any institution for managing such a state of affairs, Morgan summoned dozens of bank executives on the night of November 2, a Saturday, to his library on Madison Avenue where the walls and shelves were bedecked with medieval and Renaissance tapestries, paintings, and manuscripts. After finding themselves locked in the library in the wee hours of the morning — Morgan had pocketed the key — the bankers grudgingly agreed at 4:45 a.m. to his plan whereby the strongest among the trusts would back the deposits of the weakest, and the panic abated. Not that economic pain was averted; an ensuing recession sent unemployment soaring to around 8 percent.

Morgan's intervention prevented an even worse outcome. But the Panic of 1907 laid bare the need for a more sustainable, accountable, and institutionalized approach to sorting out financial crises. Depending on a private individual like Morgan, or even a few of his ilk, made no sense for a nation attaining economic modernity. The time had finally come to drop Jacksonian shibboleths and create an American central bank.

After several years of political wrangling over governance issues, the Federal Reserve Act was signed into law by President Woodrow Wilson on December 13, 1913.[11] Dollar bills with the words "Federal Reserve Note" printed on them (as they still are today) would be US government money, not private bank money. To avoid excessive centralization and afford some measure of control to regional agricultural and commercial interests, the law established a network of a dozen "reserve banks" based in major cities around the country, each with a board of directors representing banks, businesspeople, and the public from the district that the reserve bank served. But at Wilson's insistence a Washington-based board of governors, the members of which would be presidential appointees subject to Senate confirmation, would oversee the system.

The Federal Reserve was not yet the supremely powerful central bank that it would later become; for one thing, it was still constrained by the automaticity of the gold standard. By law, the amount of dollars it allowed to circulate in the economy had to be backed by ample reserves of bullion, to ensure that the $20.67 per ounce guarantee could be fulfilled. If its vaults were sufficiently full of gold, the Fed could make credit easier to obtain by lowering the interest rates that it charged on loans to banks, which would enable them to lend more cheaply to consumers and businesses and thereby pump money into the economy. By contrast, a depletion of gold reserves would oblige the Fed to raise the cost of credit, so that consumers and businesses would borrow less and the quantity of dollars in circulation would contract.

Still, by creating a US equivalent to the Bank of England, the Federal Reserve Act put New York on more of a financial par with London. And the act did so in other ways as well, by authorizing American banks of sufficient size to establish branches overseas.

American financiers took full advantage of this new right, which was bestowed just as history took a devastating turn that further tipped the geoeconomic balance in favor of the United States—the eruption of World War I and the associated laying of waste to Europe.[12] After branching into Latin America and Asia during the war, US banks barged into European capitals during the postwar period, positioning themselves as the new kingpins of the market for international finance of all kinds. The implications for the dollar's status as the Roaring Twenties dawned were, of course, salutary. Multinational companies seeking loans to establish overseas operations, or trade credits to finance individual transactions across national borders, increasingly did so in dollars furnished by New York–based institutions. Also enhancing the dollar's appeal was the fact that the United States easily maintained the gold standard after the war; other big powers, including Britain, had run short of gold and been forced by the exigencies of national survival to suspend the gold convertibility of their currencies, which oscillated as a result. Although gold backing for all major European currencies was restored by the late 1920s, the damage to their international standing was done.

The confluence of all these developments led to preeminence for the dollar even before the United States emerged in 1945 as the undisputed global hegemon. By the mid-1920s, central banks held more of their reserves in dollars than in pounds sterling, and the US currency surpassed the UK currency by other international metrics as well. But the dollar's link to gold, helpful as it may have been in elevating the greenback during the 1920s, contributed heavily to the US economy's undoing in the following decade.

The stock market crash of October 1929 might have dealt only a glancing economic blow had it not been for mistakes the Federal Reserve subsequently made by adhering too fervently to the gold standard's strictures.[13] When a wave of bank runs threatened massive numbers of banks in the American heartland starting in 1930, the Fed — instead of generating the cash that banks needed to meet depositor demands — adopted what it viewed as a virtuous policy of maintaining the dollar's peg to gold. At a time when the economy was in sore need of stimulus, gold standard–obsessed Fed officials kept a tight grip on the emission of money, the result being widespread bank failures that severely deepened the Great Depression. Deflation set in as spending power declined — prices of goods and services in the United States fell by 30 percent from 1931 to 1933[14] — making it all the more difficult for businesses and farmers to generate the revenue needed to make interest and principal payments. Debts, owed as they were in dollars tied to gold, became increasingly onerous. Defaults and bankruptcies proliferated, and the downward spiral grew ever more vicious.

Only in 1933, after Franklin Roosevelt assumed the presidency — with a quarter of America's workforce unemployed — did the federal government end the right of private citizens to receive gold for their paper currency, thereby taking the United States off the classical gold standard. (Although a new parity between gold and the dollar was fixed, it applied only to transactions between the US government and other countries' governments.) Economic historians regard this action, which Roosevelt took over the objections of a few horrified advisers, as a crucial turning point in the nation's revival.[15]

Which nation's currency held top rank was a matter of little consequence during the 1930s because the Depression choked off so much global trade. A decisive settling of the issue would follow the Second World War.

Three weeks after the June 6, 1944, invasion of Normandy, as Allied forces pushed toward victory over Germany and Japan, John Maynard Keynes and his wife, Russian ballerina Lydia Lopokova, arrived in Bretton Woods, New Hampshire, at a stately resort with octagonal towers and a 300-yard wooden veranda overlooking the White Mountains. The occasion was a conference of more than 40 nations on how to design the postwar economic order, and Lydia wanted to make sure that her husband, who suffered from a serious heart ailment, did not overtax himself, so she insisted that he skip cocktail parties in favor of joining her for dinner in their suite (although late at night she noisily practiced ballet exercises). She understood that demands on his time would be intense; he was, after all, internationally famous for his ability to foresee where the world was going catastrophically wrong.[16]

Keynes's warnings in the 1920s against the imposition of excessive German reparations and the maintenance of a rigid gold standard had proven particularly farsighted. The same was true of his admonitions about the need for governments to act aggressively in lifting their economies out of depression by spending money, as detailed in his 1936 classic, *The General Theory of Employment, Interest and Money.* His ideas were thus bound to play an outsized role at Bretton Woods. But Lord Keynes of Tilton, the title he now held by dint of a peerage, was attending as a British delegate, so although his arguments would hold sway on some major issues, he was obliged to yield on others to the Americans, led by Assistant Secretary of the Treasury Harry Dexter White, who was as ornery as Keynes was erudite. Among the points on which Keynes would lose to White was one of the most important of all—the dollar's place in the international monetary firmament.

Keynes and White shared common visions of creating a monetary system that, in addition to ending slavish devotion to gold (a "barbarous relic," in Keynes's words), would eradicate practices they viewed as the worst evils of the 1930s. During the interwar period, an epidemic of mutually deleterious actions had plagued the global economy, as countries adopted "beggar-thy-neighbor" policies aimed at boosting or protecting their manufacturers and farmers at the expense of economies elsewhere. For example, after the abandonment of the gold standard in the early 1930s, some governments had sharply lowered their currencies' exchange rates, one notorious instance being a tit-for-tat battle of devaluations between Denmark and New Zealand, both major butter producers, in a race to gain competitive advantage in the lucrative British butter market. In other cases, governments had erected high tariff walls and even engaged in outright trade wars. The pursuance of such policies had exacerbated the Depression, Keynes and White agreed, as had manic speculative flows of capital.

During two years of negotiations prior to Bretton Woods, Keynes and White reached broad accord on some of the postwar system's basic principles. Countries would fix their exchange rates while maintaining the ability to adjust them periodically as circumstances changed — a comparatively stable arrangement that would be aided by rules limiting movements of capital across borders.

But the two men differed dramatically in the approaches they favored. Keynes's plan, drafted while summering at his country home in Sussex, was much more ambitious — "complicated and novel and perhaps Utopian," as he admitted. A new global monetary unit, called "bancor," would be created, for use in all international trade — not as a currency that individuals or private businesses could actually spend, but rather as a unit for valuing exports and imports that would circulate only among the world's central banks. Bancors would be issued by another new creation, the International Clearing Union, which would control the overall bancor supply and increase or decrease the emission of bancors as needed, distributing bancors to each country in rough proportion to its share in world trade. Once bancors had been distributed, each country's central bank would have a bancor account at the Clearing Union for settling cross-border transactions. For each item a country exported, its Clearing Union account would gain bancors, and for each item it imported, its account would lose bancors, with the amount determined by fixed exchange rates between the bancor and countries' currencies. Using bancors, central banks would buy and sell their currencies with each other depending on what their exporters earned from sales to foreigners and their importers needed for purchases from abroad.

The important thing to understand about Keynes's plan is not the workings, which many readers will find bewildering. Rather, it is the aptness of his words "complicated and novel and perhaps Utopian" to convey the difficulty of devising a functional global currency. In any event, the plan had been shelved even before delegates arrived at Bretton Woods, because for a variety of reasons it contravened the interests of the United States. Above all, White wanted the dollar to be effectively as good as gold; one of his aims was to ensure that the precious metal, although continuing to play some part in the monetary system, would no longer constrain the Fed's ability to regulate the US money supply to the extent it had under the rules of the gold standard. And the United States held the whip hand, since its GDP would clearly comprise the bulk of the world's total postwar economic output, which meant that no global monetary system would work without American participation and active cooperation.

After about three weeks of meetings and conviviality, the Bretton Woods conferees approved a plan that was close to the approach White favored – that is, with no bancor or Clearing Union, but rather with a newly created International Monetary Fund (IMF), which would oversee a system of fixed exchange rates. And in a significant coup for the United States, the agreement enshrined the dollar's status as the world's preeminent currency.

The dollar was so firmly at the center of the new system that all other countries joining the IMF were to peg their currencies against the US unit, by setting "par values" (in the Netherlands' case, for example, it was 37.69 US cents per guilder, and in Mexico's case, 20.6 US cents per peso) around which their exchange rates were supposed to stay within narrow ranges. If a country's exchange rate rose or fell more than 1 percent from the par value, its financial authorities would be obliged to intervene – that is, buy or sell its currency to bring the exchange rate back into line against the dollar. Bigger moves in par values were allowed, with the proviso that IMF approval was required. And when countries ran into economic difficulties that might lead to an unwanted devaluation, they could borrow dollars from the IMF for use in propping up their currencies. This would tide them over until they could put their economies back on a sound footing under conditions agreed with the IMF, the hope being that the pain involved would be significantly less than the gold standard would have entailed. For its part, the United States would bolster confidence in the dollar by pegging it to gold at $35 per ounce. Not that Washington was returning to the classical gold standard; the pegged price still applied only to transactions between official entities such as governments and central banks, and American citizens still had no right to convert their dollars into gold. But White believed that some gold underpinning of the dollar was essential to the overall stability of the Bretton Woods system, which for this reason is often called a quasi–gold standard.

For all its boons, the Bretton Woods system was not entirely positive from the US perspective. In fact, the encumbrances would prove more than Washington was willing to bear — as one economist correctly predicted.

To Robert Triffin, there was something fundamentally wrong with an international monetary system that revolved around a single national currency. A butcher's son from a small Belgian village, Triffin was the first person in his family to go to high school and university, excelling to the point of winning a fellowship for graduate studies at Harvard, where he earned a PhD in economics. Having lived through World War I and the turmoil of the 1930s, he developed a passionate belief in the value of international cooperation, which led him to favor a global currency of the sort Keynes had proposed. The deeper he looked at the dollar-centered Bretton Woods arrangement, the more convinced he became that it would come to grief, a view for which he drew attention, both in the media and in top policy circles, in the late 1950s when he was a professor at Yale. A book he published in 1960 titled *Gold and the Dollar Crisis* was reportedly read closely by incoming president John F. Kennedy, and at a hearing of the Joint Economic Committee of Congress that year, Triffin called for "fundamental reform of the international monetary system" to avert an "imminent threat to the once mighty US dollar."[17]

Up to then, the Bretton Woods system had been working fairly smoothly at providing the capitalist world with a stable asset for conducting international commerce. Throughout most of the 1950s, when US manufacturers dominated global markets for a host of goods — automobiles, steel, appliances, machinery, chemicals, and many others — the dollar was in great demand from foreigners eager to buy American products, which had to be paid for in greenbacks. To ensure that America's war-battered allies had enough dollars to acquire the items needed to rebuild their economies, Washington provided about $13.5 billion in loans and aid to Europe via the Marshall Plan, and hundreds of millions of dollars more to Japan in a separate program. (Those sums totaled more than 5 percent of American GDP in the late 1940s, which would be equivalent to $1.25 *trillion* in current dollars.) At the same time, the United States' holdings of gold bullion in Fort Knox accounted for about three-quarters of the world total, amply justifying faith in the $35-an-ounce price. In short, the dollar's good-as-gold luster appeared merited, and the currency was serving its designated role in lubricating global trade, which was thriving.[18]

But as Europe and Japan continued to recover from war and their industries grew more competitive, the US economy—though still the world's biggest—declined as a share of global GDP, leading to a fundamental shift in the relationship between the dollar and gold. Foreigners needed fewer dollars to run their economies, which were becoming more self-sufficient, while at the same time American firms and individuals bought more goods from abroad, using dollars to pay for those imports. A global "glut" of dollars began to materialize, therefore, thanks also to heavy Cold War spending by Washington on the military and foreign aid. With so many dollars sloshing around the world, rumblings resonated about whether the gold in US government vaults was adequate to back all that currency.

In simplified terms, Triffin's analysis of this situation went as follows: On the one hand, the worldwide supply of US dollars must expand at a fast enough pace to fuel global trade; without that, commerce among nations would be deprived of sufficient amounts of the currency used for cross-border transactions, and stagnation would afflict the global economy. On the other hand, the creation of too many dollars would undermine faith in America's commitment to maintain the dollar's convertibility into gold at $35 per ounce. The "Triffin dilemma," as this contradiction became known, meant that sooner or later something had to give.

To resentful French officials, there was another profound flaw in the Bretton Woods system. "Exorbitant privilege" was the term coined in the mid-1960s by Valéry Giscard d'Estaing, who was then the French finance minister. Thanks to exorbitant privilege, the United States uniquely enjoyed the kind of power that derives from autonomy—the ability to act with scant regard for external constraints—in the economic sphere at least. Specifically, policymakers in Washington could afford to worry much less than their counterparts in other capitals about running deficits in their nation's balance of payments.[19]

———

To understand this important concept, which will come up repeatedly in this book, a brief detour into basic international economics is in order. Every country has a balance of payments, reflecting all transactions between its residents and those of foreign nations, with inflows consisting of revenue from exports and various inward movements of capital, and outflows consisting of expenditure on imports and various outward capital movements. When outflows exceed inflows, a deficit results and, if continued over a sustained period, eventually necessitates some degree of adjustment—typically, this means austerity-oriented policies such as high interest rates, government spending cuts, or tax increases. A good analogy is an individual who has been living beyond his means or loses a high-salary job; he can defer a downward adjustment in living standards by dipping into savings or running up a credit card tab, but the day of reckoning can't be postponed forever unless a new high-paying job or other financial windfall materializes.

Unlike individuals, countries can print their own money, so the analogy isn't exact. But printing money won't work for balance of payments purposes unless the currency in question is widely accepted internationally. Under the Bretton Woods system, the US dollar was pretty much the only currency used for cross-border transactions, and in any event the system's rules obliged countries to maintain their currencies' pegs against the greenback. For a country like France, therefore, running a balance of payments deficit (meaning a surfeit of francs circulating overseas) would eventually oblige the nation to undergo the pain of adjustment. The French government would have to constrain spending by its citizens and businesses, thereby curbing imports, so it could ensure that the Banque de France held sufficient reserves of dollars to defend the franc-dollar exchange rate.

The United States had no such concerns about where the dollars would come from for its consumers to buy imported goods or for its companies to purchase foreign businesses. Dollar creation, after all, was at the whim of the Federal Reserve. The United States could run "deficits without tears," as the French economist Jacques Rueff, an adviser to President Charles de Gaulle, indignantly put it.[20] De Gaulle himself called a press conference in 1965 to denounce the dollar and demand a return to the gold standard, arguing that international commerce "should rest . . . on an indisputable monetary basis bearing the mark of no particular country . . . on no other standard than gold – gold that never changes . . . that has no nationality and that is eternally and universally accepted as the inalterable fiduciary value par excellence."[21]

France's grievance was left to fester. The Triffin dilemma was not so easy to ignore. Soon after the publication of *Gold and the Dollar Crisis,* alarm bells for Bretton Woods began ringing when the price of gold shot up to $40 an ounce in October 1960 on the London gold market, where the metal was traded partly for use in jewelry and dentistry. Together with European central banks, the Fed used its financial muscle to push the price back down to the official $35 level and took a number of other measures during the 1960s to buttress the Bretton Woods system. Agreements were struck among central banks to pool some of their gold reserves and swap their national currencies (the swaps being in effect reciprocal borrowing arrangements). After the French government insisted on converting some of its dollars into gold, US officials pressured West Germany and Japan, which depended on the American nuclear umbrella, to refrain from following France's suit.[22]

But as the 1960s progressed, the measures that had been taken to shore up the dollar's $35-an-ounce price proved increasingly ineffectual.[23] President Lyndon Johnson was running a guns-and-butter policy, spending on both the Vietnam War and Great Society antipoverty programs while failing to finance the outlays sufficiently with new tax revenue. Inflation was kindled because, even with the economy growing robustly, the Federal Reserve maintained a fairly easy grip over the money supply; the consumer price index rose by more than 4 percent in 1968 and nearly 5.5 percent in 1969. (Annual increases in the index had never strayed above 2 percent in the first half of the 1960s.) The overhang of dollars reached increasingly glaring proportions the more foreign central banks bought up excess greenbacks for stockpiling in their reserves, while US bullion stocks dwindled by March 1968 to half the level of a decade earlier. In 1969, suspecting abandonment of the official price, speculators bid gold above $43 an ounce.

Even those steeped in the orthodoxy of the postwar regime were harboring doubts about its survival. One in particular was in a position of influence – the cigar-chomping, six-foot-seven-inch Paul Volcker, who was appointed in 1969 by President Richard Nixon as Treasury undersecretary for monetary affairs despite being a Democrat. In his previous career as an economist at the Treasury and Federal Reserve Bank of New York, Volcker had labored to preserve the stable currency principles at the heart of the agreement forged by Keynes and White, which he believed essential to postwar peace and prosperity. But he could hardly dismiss the strains on the Bretton Woods system, which grew increasingly acute in 1971 as the nation's balance of payments continued to erode, with imports exceeding exports for the first time in the postwar era. The more dollars Americans sent abroad to buy foreign goods, the more anxious governments in Europe and elsewhere grew about being left behind in the event that dollar holders rushed *en masse* to dump their greenbacks for gold.[24]

"None of us were ready to simply abandon the Bretton Woods framework of fixed exchange rates and convertibility of the dollar into gold," Volcker wrote in his 2018 memoir. "Our analysis did, however, reinforce the need for change. Our remaining gold reserves in mid-1969 were only 25 percent of foreign-dollar liabilities, down from almost 80 percent at the beginning of the Kennedy administration eight years earlier. The Triffin dilemma was apparent for all to see."[25]

Volcker wrote a memo to that effect for others in the administration. The Belgian's prophecy was about to come true.

Don't tell your wife where you're going, or your secretary either. So went the admonition to the 15 senior US economic policymakers — cabinet secretaries, agency heads, White House advisers, and the chairman of the Federal Reserve Board — who gathered at Camp David, the presidential retreat, over the weekend of August 13–15, 1971. "There are to be made no calls out of here," President Nixon warned the participants as their meetings began in his cottage overlooking Maryland's Catoctin Mountains, according to notes taken by White House speechwriter William Safire. "Everyone here is to button his lip."[26]

The need for secrecy was evident as Nixon turned the floor to John Connally, the silver-maned Treasury secretary who brought the force of his Texas politician's personality to economic policymaking. Connally ticked off a number of measures that the group would consider implementing in response to mounting market pressures on the dollar. On the list, to the consternation of some present, was this: "We close the gold window" — that is, stop converting dollars into gold at $35 per ounce, a price Connally said was no longer tenable even though it was a Bretton Woods keystone. "Anybody can topple us, anytime they want," he said, meaning that a demand for gold from a single large foreign government would trigger a run that would exhaust US supplies – and no less an ally than the British were signaling lost confidence. "We have left ourselves completely exposed."

Not completely; if the Nixon administration had truly prioritized maintaining the Bretton Woods system, it could have taken measures that would have enhanced the attractiveness of the dollar and preserved the $35-an-ounce peg. It could have raised interest rates, or imposed a tax hike to curb American consumption, thereby shrinking the trade deficit. But such a degree of austerity was anathema to the White House at a time when the US unemployment rate was already 6 percent and an election year was looming.[27] The president wanted to tackle the dollar's problems by announcing a comprehensive package that would show him taking charge rather than retreating. "I'm thinking of a speech of ten minutes – concise, strong, confident. Not a lot of stuff whining around that we are in a hell of a shape," he said.

Still, Nixon recognized the necessity of a thorough brainstorming before deciding on a package, and he was also concerned about securing backing from Arthur Burns, the pipe-smoking former Columbia University professor who chaired the Fed and was widely regarded as the nation's leading apostle of financial probity. Burns dreaded closing the gold window – "What a tragedy for mankind!" he wrote in his diary about the administration's inability to take the steps required for preserving the Bretton Woods system.[28] He deemed the discipline of gold essential to maintaining the dollar's soundness, and also worried about losing the "goodwill" of US allies in view of other measures that the group was considering, including a 10 percent across-the-board tariff on imports. "All the other countries know we have never acted against them," he protested to Nixon and the others at Camp David.

"So the other countries don't like it. So what?" Connally shot back with characteristic bluster, adding in the same vein that he was unconcerned about the possibility of retaliation by major industrial powers: "Let 'em. What can they do?" After further debate, Burns saw the futility of resisting, and he promised his "wholehearted support" to Nixon.

The weekend ended with a nationally televised address, interrupting the popular Sunday night show *Bonanza,* in which Nixon announced a "new economic policy" including the import surcharge, temporary wage and price controls, and the "suspension" of dollar-gold convertibility because, he said, "I am determined that the American dollar must never again be a hostage in the hands of international speculators." To soften the blow abroad, he added: "I give this assurance: The United States has always been, and will continue to be, a forward-looking and trustworthy trading partner. . . . We will press for the necessary reforms to set up an urgently needed new international monetary system."[29]

As Nixon promised, efforts were made to establish a new system—that is, a revised arrangement of fixed exchange rates at levels for the dollar that the United States could manage more easily. Volcker flew often to Tokyo, Bonn, Paris, London, and Rome—and his counterparts flew often to Washington—in pursuit of agreements. Negotiations were often testy, thanks in no small part to Connally's imperiousness; it was during this period that he jolted his fellow finance ministers with one of the most famous statements in international monetary history: "The dollar is our currency, but your problem."[30] But deals that were struck failed to hold, and the new system collapsed amid a new run on the dollar in the spring of 1973, leaving all major currencies to rise and fall against each other according to the laws of supply and demand as interpreted by foreign exchange traders in financial capitals around the world.

Bretton Woods was kaput. And the dollar was a pure fiat currency, its supply governed solely by what the Federal Reserve's policy-setting committee deemed appropriate. Dollars were created out of thin air when employees at the Federal Reserve Bank of New York, operating under the committee's instructions, bought Treasury bills from major banks and securities firms; the newly created greenbacks would be credited to the banks' reserve accounts at the central bank, enabling the banks to make more loans. And dollars would cease to exist when those same Fed employees *sold* bonds to major financial firms; the dollars paid to the Fed would essentially be extinguished, reducing the greenbacks available for lending. If all went perfectly, the Fed's additions and subtractions to bank reserves would increase the supply of dollars and result in a level of interest rates that would foster exactly the rate of expansion in the production of goods and services that the US economy was capable of generating without raising or lowering major price indices. Too many dollars resulting in overly easy credit would risk excessively rapid growth that would kindle inflation; too few dollars resulting in overly tight credit would risk job-killing recession. The Fed had operated in a similar manner since the early 1920s, but henceforth dollar issuance by its money-making machine would be completely liberated from the regimentation of gold.

Bretton Woods was kaput in another way as well, as governments loosened the restrictions on international capital mobility that Keynes and White had favored. Trade in goods was already well on the way to liberalization under agreements struck in the 1940s, '50s, and '60s, but only in the 1970s would the floodgates start to open for the transnational movement of loans, stock and bond issuance and purchase, and other financial flows. Instead of being confined within national economies, capital would become increasingly free to seek its profit-maximizing potential without regard to political or geographical boundaries.

In this floating world, so poorly did the greenback fare initially that Leonard Silk, the economics commentator for the *New York Times,* led a July 1973 article thusly: "The dollar is regarded all over the world as a sick currency." In the period since Nixon closed the gold window, Silk noted, the dollar had fallen 31 percent against the West German mark, 26 percent against the Japanese yen, and 23 percent against the Swiss franc. As a result, Silk continued, "Some American goods — such as soybeans and steel scrap — are so cheap to foreign customers that the United States Government has decided to clamp on export controls to prevent their leaving the country and worsening domestic inflationary pressures."[31]

Now that the pact formalizing the dollar's international role had disintegrated, and the greenback was both gyrating and sinking on global markets, dismal conclusions were echoed by a number of observers about US monetary leadership. Foremost among them was Charles Kindleberger, Ford International Professor of Economics at the Massachusetts Institute of Technology, who decried "the Crime of 1971" and flatly declared: "The dollar is finished as international money."[32]

That was an early example of the dollar's death being greatly exaggerated. The future would bring many more occasions and situations in which its demise would be prophesied — and overstated, as we shall see in the next chapter.

CHAPTER 3

MAINTAINING THE THRONE, THROUGH THICK AND THIN

A dilapidated, fly-infested building in Saudi Arabia's Red Sea port of Jeddah was the repository for the world's most spectacular cache of dollars during the period following the "oil shock" of 1973–1974, when petroleum prices nearly quadrupled. This was the headquarters of the Saudi Arabian Monetary Agency (SAMA), the nation's central bank, which in those years was poorly equipped for this role, with offices that typified the desert kingdom's detachment from modernity. Records of transactions were kept by hand in leather-bound books; an open-drain toilet was flushed once a day at 3 p.m.; newspapers from abroad arrived days late and only after censors had removed material objectionable to the royal family and elders of the fundamentalist Muslim establishment. International communication took place not on phones—voice calls abroad were impossible to complete—but on a single telex machine wedged into a tiny triangular room. "Making a call on the machine involved dialing the central operator somewhere in downtown Jeddah and requesting a number in New York, London, Tokyo or elsewhere," recalls David Mulford, who had been hired by SAMA from an investment banking firm in 1975 to serve as an adviser, in his memoir. "One then waited anywhere from ten to twenty minutes. Then all of a sudden, as we sat nodding in the heat, the machine would come to life and one was connected to someone in the outside world," with whom typed words could be exchanged.[1]

Incongruous as it may seem, this operation was tasked with investing an influx of cash the likes of which no country had ever seen. Saudi Arabia sat atop one-quarter of the earth's proven oil reserves, and revenue to the tune of $100 million a day was pouring into its coffers from exports of crude, which soared in price from less than $3 a barrel in the early 1970s to more than $11 a barrel by March 1974. Collusion among members of the Organization of Petroleum Exporting Countries (OPEC) was the main factor propelling prices upward, together with an oil embargo imposed by Arab nations following Israel's October 1973 war with Egypt and Syria. As Americans stewed in long lines at gasoline stations, their leaders wrestled with the conundrum of how to deal with the Saudis, whose willingness to use the oil weapon in support of Cairo and Damascus came as a rude surprise to US officials. The House of Saud had maintained a tight alliance with the United States since the 1940s, but the possibility that the kingdom might deploy its "petrodollar" wealth against American interests was a source of constant disquiet in Washington.

It was emblematic of the dollar's woes during the 1970s that this theocratic monarchy, with a population of only five million, should assume such influence as a holder of US currency. The dollar was facing its first major challenge of the post–Bretton Woods era — inflation, which was eroding the greenback's value to a degree that had seemed unimaginable in previous decades. The US consumer price index rose 11 percent in 1974, with petroleum products rising fastest in price but other items, notably food, also costing considerably more dollars than the year before; the inflation rate then subsided but remained relatively high at 9 percent in 1975, 5.7 percent in 1976, 6.5 percent in 1977, and 7.6 percent in 1978. The diminishing purchasing power of the dollar was an obvious threat to its use as a store of value. At the same time, the US trade balance was turning negative, in part because of the nation's sharply rising oil import bill, and the federal budget also went deeper into deficit as years passed in a decade infamous for "stagflation." Taken together, these factors drove the dollar's exchange rate down against other major currencies; from March 1973 to October 1978, the greenback depreciated 34 percent against the mark, 30 percent against the yen, and 51 percent against the Swiss franc.

———

How, then, did the dollar maintain its dominance as the international currency during this period? Therein lies a story that is partly about geopolitics, partly about the relative size of the US economy, and partly about the SAMA telex machine.

Fearful that the Saudis might lose faith in the dollar – or worse yet, try blackmailing the United States by joining an Arab initiative to switch funds into currencies of anti-Israel countries – Secretary of State Henry Kissinger and Treasury Secretary William Simon launched efforts in 1974 to ensure that Saudi and American interests were closely aligned. In his role as the chief official responsible for funding the US government's borrowing, Simon traveled to the kingdom to negotiate a deal giving SAMA a special, secret arrangement for purchasing Treasury securities. The Treasury normally uses open auctions to sell bills (short-term maturities, up to one year), notes (one- to ten-year maturities), and bonds (maturities of over ten years), with securities going to bidders willing to accept the lowest interest rates. Top-quality government bonds suited the hyper-conservative Saudis perfectly, but in exchange for promising to make substantial investments in US Treasuries, SAMA insisted upon being allowed to buy allotments directly, with the yield it received being an average of the interest rate set by the auction. And in view of Saudi sensitivity about being perceived as bankrolling US aid to Israel, SAMA had one other key condition, as spelled out in a memo written by a Treasury undersecretary that came to light years later: "The *sine qua non* for the Saudis in this arrangement is confidentiality and we have assured them that we will do everything in our power to comply with their desires."[2]

Kissinger, meanwhile, capitalized on the Saudi royals' insecurity about foreign or domestic enemies threatening their control over the kingdom. On a trip to Washington in June 1974 by Crown Prince (later King) Fahd, the two countries agreed to establish "joint commissions" that would coordinate policy in the economic and defense fields, which led to Saudi purchases of more than $100 billion worth of advanced American weapons, training of Saudi armed forces, and construction by the US Corps of Engineers of military bases and airfields on Saudi soil.

These interactions are sometimes portrayed as a cynical bargain in which the Americans pledged military protection for the House of Saud and the kingdom's oilfields, while the Saudis swore unwavering support for the dollar. Exactly what informal warranties may have been given is unknown; hard proof has never surfaced.[3] But more important, for purposes of understanding the US currency's continued primacy, is evidence about SAMA's reasons for keeping the overwhelming bulk of its holdings in dollar-denominated securities.

Mulford's memoir lucidly illuminates the Saudis' dollar preference. First of all, there were logistical constraints on SAMA's capacity for investing in a host of currencies: "We had a small team totaling only six professionals confronted by a mountain of work, no modern technology that enabled us to reduce hand-done clerical work, and a portfolio growing at $5 and later $10 billion every thirty days," he writes.[4]

Furthermore, as Mulford explains, in choosing markets to invest in, SAMA had to be concerned about liquidity, which in this context refers to the ability to buy or sell without causing prices to change significantly. With tens of millions of dollars coming in daily, SAMA had few attractive places outside of the United States to put its money.

"In order to buy government securities in other national markets that were very much smaller and less liquid than the US market we first had to buy the national currencies required," Mulford writes. "This . . . sounds easier than it was in practice. In most markets outside the U.S. in those days a currency trade of $5–10 million was enough to move markets, so there were practical limitations on the amount of currency diversification that we could achieve over a period of days. Add to this the fact that purchases of German Schuldschein (promissory notes), the most practical option for us in Germany, or Japanese yen bonds, or Dutch guilder bonds, or Swiss franc notes were just not possible in the sizes common in the U.S. market."[5]

SAMA did put some funds into non-dollar currencies. The Japanese government, eager to sell its bonds, struck an agreement with SAMA in early 1976 that was similar to the one Simon had negotiated for US Treasuries. Other opportunities were presented by bankers who mobbed Jeddah, staying in bug-ridden hotels in the hope of tapping the Saudi money spigot. They waited in lines at SAMA—sometimes trailing down two or three flights of stairs, according to Mulford—to seek the agency's participation in loans for all manner of public and private endeavors, many in Europe or elsewhere outside the United States.

But numerous bureaucratic procedures were involved in the lengthy discussions required to complete such deals, with SAMA's primitive telecommunications making each step an ordeal. By the end of 1977, only about 6 percent of SAMA's $60 billion in reserves was held in yen or deutsche marks; most of the rest was in dollars.[6]

There could hardly be a simpler and more straightforward illustration of the role that liquidity plays in the dollar's hegemonic status. And during the period that Mulford was based in Saudi Arabia, financial forces at work in the United States were making dollar markets even more liquid.

The limousine drivers knew who was making it big. "They'll tell you who rides the limousines out of the local saloons down on Wall Street," said John Eckstein, a trader in US government securities who ran his own firm, when I interviewed him in late 1976 for a *Forbes Magazine* article. "At one time, it was the equity boys; next it was the fund managers; next it was the over-the-counter stock traders; then the REIT [Real Estate Investment Trust] boys. And this year's big shots? The government bond people."[7]

Spectacular growth and profitability in the market for US Treasuries was indeed setting the pace for dealers and traders of all kinds of securities in the mid-1970s. The dollar value of Treasury debt changing hands on an average day in 1976 was running at $10.5 billion, triple the pace of 1973, just among the main dealers, which far outstripped the $631 million daily trading volume on the New York Stock Exchange (NYSE). Salaries and bonuses for bond traders and salesmen were skyrocketing, with banks like Morgan Guaranty and Bankers Trust being raided by Wall Street firms dangling six-figure annual compensation packages for promising traders in their twenties and early thirties — obscenely high by the standards of that era. Much of the action was taking place amid the hubbub of crowded, auditorium-sized trading floors at big bond houses such as Salomon Brothers, Paine Webber, and Aubrey Lanston, where traders shouted across rows of desks with colleagues about market rumors and barked over the phone with counterparts at rival firms to extract favorable terms. Not for nothing was the term "masters of the universe" applied (albeit sardonically) to bond traders in Tom Wolfe's 1987 bestseller *Bonfire of the Vanities.*

Who would have thought it possible? Even Wall Street's go-go 1960s had been dull for bonds, what with booming stock markets that made fixed-income investments look stodgier than ever. Things got so bad in bond alley that a trade publication, *Institutional Investor,* ran a cover story in 1969 showing a picture of dinosaurs with the question: "Can the bond market survive?" According to *Institutional Investor,* the bond market was an "anachronism . . . in the longer run, the public market for straight debt may become obsolete."[8]

Bonds, after all, are designed for investors seeking stable returns rather than big gains. A bond's issuer, whether a government or private firm, typically promises to make regular interest payments (annually or quarterly, in most cases) and repay principal when the bond matures. That's a much less risky but also much less exciting proposition than shares of stock, which provide no guarantee of return and can fluctuate significantly from day to day or even minute to minute based on news about prospects for the profitability of a company or its industry. For sound reasons, retirees put much of their savings in bonds, and the same goes for insurance companies, pension funds, university endowments, and other big institutions that need to buffer their portfolios against stock-market downturns. Of course, a bond issuer may default, so Treasuries backed by the full faith and credit of the United States provide the ultimate refuge.

But in the 1970s, several events converged to make the bond market boom — and to inflict sleepless nights and tension-filled workdays on its big-time operators, even as they reaped financial bonanzas.

The federal government was running deficits of previously unthinkable size (the budget gap of World War II being the only exception), which meant that the Treasury was raising cash by issuing hundreds of billions of new IOUs for investors to buy and trade. At the same time, advances in computerization imparted much greater efficiency to bond trading, which is conducted "over the counter" from offices scattered around a variety of locations, unlike the centralized trading floor of the NYSE. "We place our bets," said William Michaelcheck, one of the traders I interviewed for my *Forbes* article, "and then we watch this thing [a computer monitor displaying government securities quotations] very carefully."

Most important of all, interest rates were far more volatile during the 1970s than in the previous two decades. Inflation was corroding the returns that could

---

be expected from investing, so interest payments had to compensate. Reflecting fundamental axioms of bond trading, the ups and downs of interest rates caused bond prices to gyrate as well – and inversely to the direction of interest rates. For example, 1976 proved to be a bull market for bonds because interest rates fell sharply from their 1974 inflationary highs, with the yield on one-year Treasury bills dipping to 5 percent (meaning the interest payments would yield $50 on each $1,000 bond) from the earlier peak of 9¼ percent (when the yield was $92.50 per $1,000). Anybody would prefer to hold a Treasury security yielding more rather than a comparable Treasury security yielding less, so the prices of old Treasuries rose accordingly. Conversely, in 1973–1974, when interest rates went wild on the upside, red ink spurted all over the bond market; old bonds sank in price because new bonds offered better yields.

The bounties that Treasury bond traders were collecting when they correctly forecast market movements – and the losses they bled when they bet wrong – stemmed from the huge amounts they bought and sold with each transaction. Bond prices don't change very much during the course of a day; even if interest rates spike or dip by an unusual magnitude, the price of an individual $1,000 bond will go up or down by only a few dollars. But by buying and selling enormous quantities, traders could gain – or lose – many multiples of those price differentials. The "leverage" in the bond business is both dangerous and irresistible; in my *Forbes* article, I gave the example of a dealer with a mere $25 million in capital that might buy 20 or even 100 times as much in bonds – $500 million to $2.5 billion. To do so, the dealer would borrow from banks or corporate money managers seeking to earn a little interest on idle cash. Then the dealer would make profits or bear losses on any change in the bonds' price.

No less mind-blowing was the speed of the wheeling and dealing that traders recounted to me. Within minutes of acquiring hundreds of millions of dollars' worth of bonds, a dealer might sell some or all of them, earning the "spread" between the bid and offer price (that is, the differential that buyers pay and sellers get). Spreads were razor thin on government bonds, usually running between $\frac{1}{128}$ of 1 percent up to $\frac{1}{32}$ of 1 percent. But on a $100 million order – big, but not out of the ordinary – even $\frac{1}{128}$ of a percent amounted to a commission of $7,812.50, which in the 1970s would pay quite a few days' rent, heat, and light, to say nothing of clerical salaries.

So massive was the amount of churn in Treasuries that big bond houses like Salomon were often turning over their inventory twice a day. These firms happily handled the thin-margin, big-volume business; even though they might earn as little as $50 on each $1 million in bonds traded, that added up on volumes at the $1 billion level. When prices fell, these customer-oriented bond machines kept making markets — that is, buying and selling with all comers — although the spreads between bid and offered prices would widen sharply as they pitched their buying prices well below their selling prices to avoid being stuck holding the bag.

This sort of activity — which today involves dollar amounts many orders of magnitude greater — may sound like little more than high-stakes speculation. To some extent it is, but it serves a purpose. Holders of US dollars — whether they be investors, companies, financial institutions, central banks, or any other entity — can be assured of a smoothly functioning market to buy, sell, and park their assets in the world's safest instrument. And in the 1970s, the market for dollars was mushrooming as "petrodollar recycling" transmitted the US currency around the globe along new routes and in new ways. Dollars paid for oil to Saudi Arabia and other oil-producing states in the Middle East flowed into SAMA and other such institutions in the region, which often opted for the simple approach of depositing the dollars in large banks. Although some of these banks were based in the United States, others were based in different countries and operating in the rapidly expanding market for Eurodollars (a term that essentially means offshore dollars, not necessarily European ones). The Eurodollar market, which was centered in London, involved banks of many nationalities accepting dollar deposits and making dollar loans to borrowers all over the world. This gusher of lendable funds helped finance, at reasonable cost, the borrowing that nations including the United States needed to pay for foreign oil. (Billions of dollars in loans went to countries in Latin America and elsewhere that would fall seriously into debt difficulties in the 1980s, but that's another story.)

Thus, even in the absence of a formal agreement, the dollar remained perched high atop the international currency totem pole — and the United States was arguably garnering more benefits, at lower cost, than it had before the 1971 Camp David meeting. Those benefits were impossible to calculate precisely, but

———

they were indisputably significant; America alone could effectively use the money created by its central bank to pay for imported oil as well as other goods from nations that needed dollars to buy their own oil.[9] "To decide one August morning that dollars can no longer be converted into gold was a progression from exorbitant privilege to super-exorbitant privilege," wrote Susan Strange, the British scholar. "The U.S. government was exercising the unconstrained right to print money that others could not (save at unacceptable cost) refuse to accept in payment."[10]

In the closing years of the 1970s, however, the unconstrained printing of dollars reached a point that was verging on recklessness, severely testing the forbearance of the Saudis and other holders of US currency. Fingers pointed, with considerable justification, at the Federal Reserve.

Fed officials seemed incapable of keeping the greenback's debasement in check. Arthur Burns, who chaired the Fed from February 1970 to January 1978, used his professorial manner to good effect in presenting a stern face against inflation, but as he admitted later, he shrank from raising interest rates high enough to quash it given persistently high unemployment. His diaries show that in the leadup to the 1972 election he cravenly yielded to pressure for easy money from Nixon, who had appointed him, and he showed little more fortitude even after Nixon's resignation in 1974. Every time the Fed squeezed credit, Burns lamented, "it repeatedly evoked violent criticism from both the executive establishment and the Congress," which he feared might result in legislation stripping the central bank of its independence.[11] Burns's successor, William Miller, the former CEO of the conglomerate Textron Inc., was more ineffectual, albeit for different reasons. Showing little appetite or aptitude for monetary policy debate, Miller treated the Fed's policymaking arm, the 12-member Federal Open Market Committee (FOMC), like a corporate board—he used an egg timer to limit remarks—and tried mainly to forge the quickest possible consensus between "hawks" and "doves." (Hawks are those who favor tightening credit to fight inflation; doves prefer easier credit to spur economic growth.)[12]

Maintaining the dollar's stability became an even more daunting challenge in the wake of the January 1979 Islamic Revolution in Iran, which resulted in a second oil shock that lifted the price of crude oil higher still. Inflation in the

United States jumped to an annual rate of 10.75 percent in the first nine months of 1979, and the greenback plummeted anew against other currencies. OPEC member countries, sitting on huge declines in the value of their dollar portfolios, began to rumble ominously about moving out of the US currency.[13] Nothing much came of these threats; the size of the US market was still a decisive consideration. At SAMA, according to Mulford, non-dollar assets "never exceeded 15 to 20 percent of total holdings," even though operations had been moved in October 1978 to new headquarters in the desert capital of Riyadh with a "wonderfully equipped trading room, complete with push-button consoles that put us in direct contact via the Bahrain satellite with the money desks of the major banks." But Mulford adds that currency diversification was "a constant priority" for SAMA during this period.[14]

It is not hard to understand why. Anyone saving dollars in bank accounts or investing in US Treasury securities had to accept the likelihood that the interest earned would fall short of compensating for the effect of inflation – and for foreigners, the risk of exchange-rate depreciation. By the fall of 1979 investors were in full flight from the dollar, bidding up the price of precious metals, real estate, artworks, and other tangible assets to unheard-of levels. Gold, which had started the year at around $200 an ounce, leaped to more than $400 an ounce in late September as the annual meeting of the IMF and World Bank got underway in Belgrade, Yugoslavia.[15] Finance and monetary officials attending the meeting implored the US participants for drastic action to stem the rout in the world's reserve currency.

They would not have to wait long. The institution responsible for managing the supply of dollars was under new leadership.

Paul Volcker didn't drink much. But on October 5, 1979, when he was in his second month of chairing the Fed, two close associates talked him into a few glasses of wine over dinner at Chez Camille, a Washington restaurant. Volcker had seemed so tired and troubled that "frankly, we were worried about him," said Frederick Schultz, who was then the Fed's vice chair.[16]

After a while, Volcker began to relax and laugh at his friends' jokes. Then a powerful senator, Alan Cranston of California, entered the restaurant. The Fed chief's smile froze, according to Schultz, and he gently admonished his companions: "In view of what we're about to do tomorrow, we'd better be careful about the levity."

The next day, Volcker and his Fed colleagues launched a ferocious, protracted assault on inflation. Their campaign imposed a tremendous cost by driving interest rates to record levels and pushing the US economy into its worst recession in 40 years, with unemployment rising to nearly 11 percent. But it also yielded tremendous success. Double-digit inflation — a seemingly inescapable phenomenon in the early 1980s, bedeviling middle-class Americans whose paychecks couldn't keep pace with rising prices — fell to levels that no longer undermined faith in the nation's currency. By 1985, when the economy was expanding robustly, the consumer price index rose only 3.5 percent, and in ensuing decades the annual increase generally stayed well under 4 percent.

As a reporter for the *Wall Street Journal* in the mid-1980s, I spent months researching what went on behind the scenes at the Fed during this period. In addition to shedding light on the Fed's internal workings, one of the most surprising things I learned was about its interactions with other branches of government. My article, which was published in December 1984, reported: "One president, Jimmy Carter, objected to the Fed's strategy from the outset. He was all but ignored. A second, Ronald Reagan, lent crucial political support, but when his administration periodically complained, it often was rebuffed. Theoretically, Congress could have reversed the strategy at any time — but only theoretically, because few members of Congress clearly understood what the Fed was doing."

Thus did a handful of appointed officials, operating with extraordinary resolve, vanquish a once-frightful peril to the dollar. And by succeeding at their inflation-quelling mission, they imparted sanctity to a foundational principle of the dollar's international status — the independence of America's central bank.

Legitimate questions may be raised about whether the Volcker Fed was overly zealous in stifling the economy, and whether democratic norms were violated by its near-dictatorial power over the money supply and interest rates. But there is no debating the historic boost for confidence in the dollar that resulted from this series of events. Of all the policy actions taken in the post–Bretton Woods era that helped preserve the US currency's dominance, this was by far the most important, and the lessons remain highly relevant in the 2020s, because inflation is often cited as a grave risk to the dollar in the future. If prices continue to zoom upward, as started to happen in 2021, how would – and should – US economic policy respond? No well-informed answer can be given without due awareness of how the last serious bout of inflation was handled, in particular the autonomy with which the Fed acted, shrouded in its mystique of data, jargon, and Volcker's cigar smoke.

Much of the story is about deft maneuvering by Volcker, whose appointment to the chair by Carter in July 1979 was intended as a signal of determination to maintain the dollar's soundness. Volcker had firmly established himself as a hawk during a five-year tenure as president of the New York Fed, when he had one of the 12 votes on the FOMC and cast several key votes in favor of higher interest rates than the level supported by the majority. Markets responded with relief to Volcker's replacement of Miller (who became Treasury secretary), just as the president hoped – but the White House had not fully realized how hawkish the new chair would be.

In the weeks leading up to the dinner at Chez Camille, Volcker began to conclude that the Fed's approach to combating inflation needed a thoroughgoing overhaul. Ratcheting up interest rates step by step, he feared, would be insufficiently forceful at responding to the spiral in wages and prices. He moved forward in late September with a proposal of such huge ramifications that he took the unusual step of quietly lobbying fellow board members and consulting top officials of the White House and Treasury. Under the scheme he envisioned, the Fed would stop manipulating the federal funds rate, a key interest rate charged by banks on overnight loans, that the Fed had long controlled by injecting and withdrawing reserves to and from the banking system. Instead the Fed would concentrate on slowing the growth in the money supply – specifically, it would keep M1 (a weekly measure of currency in circulation plus private checking deposits) within a target range. That would cause interest rates to rise and swing violently, at least initially, as Volcker knew, because the Fed would steadfastly limit the supply of money regardless of how interest rates responded to market forces.

Such an approach had long been advocated by "monetarist" economists, who believed that slow, steady growth in the money supply is the key to low inflation and economic stability. Although Volcker wasn't a monetarist, he figured that firm money growth targets would signal the Fed's anti-inflation doggedness and impose internal discipline on its policymakers. The plan would also shield the Fed from political flak because the Fed could contend that in emphasizing control over the money supply, it was giving up its control over interest rates.

On September 29, amid a frenzied market atmosphere, Volcker boarded a plane to attend the IMF–World Bank annual meetings in Belgrade and presented his plan to Treasury Secretary Miller and Charles Schultze, Carter's chief economic adviser, who were also on the flight. Miller and Schultze expressed strong misgivings, urging that the Fed stick to conventional inflation-fighting methods. Miller later told Volcker that Carter was also opposed.

But the trip included a stopover in Hamburg, at the request of West German chancellor Helmut Schmidt, whom Volcker knew and respected from Schmidt's days as finance minister. "For almost an hour he harangued us about how waffling American policymakers had let inflation run amok and undermined confidence in the dollar," Volcker recalls in his memoir. "I sat there quietly. There could be no more persuasive argument for why I had to act."[17] Upon returning to Washington, he summoned the FOMC to an emergency meeting on Saturday, October 6.

A Fed chair can't simply impose his or her will on the FOMC, whose members – the seven Fed governors and five reserve bank presidents – include trained economists. But the chair controls the agenda and directs the Washington-based staff, which prepares policy options for each meeting. Above all, the chair's power flows from the institutional loyalty and collegiality that permeates the panel; members who frequently dissent, repeat dogmatic arguments, or promote political agendas tend to become isolated and lose influence. It helps, too, that the Fed is steeped in an ethos, bordering on self-righteousness, that central bankers stand above the petty fray of politics and are motivated purely by the nation's long-term interests.

Volcker's proposal to target money-supply growth was unanimously accepted at the emergency meeting, with the doves insisting only on assurance that interest rates could move down as well as up. As expected, borrowing costs soared; the prime rate, commercial banks' base rate on loans to their best customers, jumped six percentage points in six months. When prices continued to rise in months

---

thereafter, Volcker and his colleagues decided in the fall of 1980 — just weeks before the presidential election — that another tough anti-inflation message was required. Although the Fed generally tries to avoid taking election-year moves that might smack of interference in politics, the board raised the discount rate (the benchmark fee that the Fed charges on loans to member banks) by a full percentage point, on September 25. White House aides were furious, and from the campaign trail a wounded Carter blasted the Fed for "ill-advised" policies, but he was powerless to change the central bank's course.[18]

Reagan came to office proclaiming himself favorably disposed toward taming inflation with slow money growth, but his administration's relations with the Fed soured as tight credit continued to impede the economy. When tax cuts that Reagan pushed through Congress in 1981 failed to produce a promised boom, administration officials often blamed the Fed for sins such as "erratic" control over M1. The Fed paid scant heed, however; FOMC members were convinced that they were responding to a higher political authority, namely that of a majority of Americans sick and tired of constantly rising prices. By that time, Fed policy had devolved into what one staffer called a "game of guts ball," probing the limits of society's tolerance for unemployment in an effort to break the inflationary spiral. Interest rates stayed high even amid howls from the worst-affected sectors, such as auto dealers who sent the Fed keys to cars they could not sell and farmers who circled the Fed's headquarters on tractors.

Only in October 1982, when some economists were warning of depression and the US banking system was under severe strain, did Volcker relent. By that point he was becoming uneasy about the possibility of congressional action — Henry Gonzalez, the top Democrat on the House Financial Services Committee, was calling for impeachment proceedings against him — and Volcker understood that his independence was not absolute. Departing from his custom of speaking last at FOMC meetings, he surprised his colleagues by opening with remarks that came to be known in Fed circles as "the doom and gloom speech," stating: "There is a substantive need for a relaxation of pressures in the private markets. . . . We haven't had a parallel to this situation historically except to the extent 1929 is a parallel."[19] Well aware that the Fed's most historic blunder had been failing to halt the Great Depression, the committee voted 9 to 3 in favor of a more flexible, stimulative policy.

A new level of confrontation with the Reagan team arose when the economy began to recover. A strong rebound in growth would likely cause inflation to revive, Fed officials believed, so they took a series of measures aimed at ensuring that this didn't happen. Lyle Gramley, a Fed governor who prided himself on his forecasting record, argued at a May 1983 FOMC meeting that the consensus among most economists for a weak, low-inflation recovery was wrong, and despite worries about cutting the expansion short, the panel voted in favor of a tightening move. Gramley proved correct; growth soon surged, generating fears of inflationary bottlenecks and shortages. Later in the year, when a few signs of slowing emerged, administration officials – anxious to see healthy growth during the 1984 election year – publicly called for the Fed to ease at the December 1983 FOMC meeting. Instead, Volcker and his colleagues, persuaded that inflationary pressures were still lurking, tilted policy toward another modest squeezing of credit, roiling markets and outraging the administration. In an ironic twist, the result was a perfect year for Reagan to run on his slogan of "Morning in America," as unemployment was down, inflation was quiescent, and even interest rates had declined.

Solving one problem for the dollar, however, gave rise to another.

Lest there be any question about his certitude that the dollar was headed for a nasty tumble, Stephen Marris put his money where his mouth was. A British economist with a PhD from Cambridge who worked at Washington's Institute for International Economics, Marris kept the funds he was saving for retirement in West German marks. "They are parked in Frankfurt," he told a *New York Times* reporter, "ready to be converted into pounds to buy a 34-foot cruising catamaran."[20]

That was a logical investment decision for Marris based on the conclusions of his 1985 book *Deficits and the Dollar: The World Economy at Risk*, which focused on gaping shortfalls in both the US trade balance and the federal budget. "[On] present policies a hard landing has become inevitable for the dollar and the world economy," Marris argued. "The dollar will, over time, go down too far and there will be an unpleasant world recession."[21] Although Marris was one of the most outspoken exponents of this view, he had plenty of company.

The United States was learning that "exorbitance" could apply not only to the privilege but also to the pain involved in high dollar demand.[22] In the first half of the 1980s the US currency, lifted at times in seeming defiance of the laws of economic gravity, gained nearly 30 percent against the yen and more than 60 percent against the mark. As the greenback's exchange rate skyrocketed, imported goods became more and more of a bargain in US markets, while US exporters struggled to compete abroad. Although the abundance of cheap foreign products in American stores and showrooms – shoes, clothing, appliances, vehicles – was a blessing for US consumers, heartland industries that competed with foreigners were suffering. Among the most vociferous complainers was Lee Morgan, CEO of Caterpillar Tractor, who led a well-organized lobbying campaign in Congress. Morgan cited the dollar-yen rate as the reason for Caterpillar's loss of sales overseas to Japanese rivals such as Komatsu; the result, he said, was the layoff of 15,000 Caterpillar employees. At a time of massive unemployment in the American "Rust Belt," such figures resonated on Capitol Hill.

Dollar strength was, of course, an objective the Fed had aimed to achieve with its tight money policy; high yields on Treasury securities combined with low inflation made the greenback an attractive investment. Trouble was, this was strength with a vengeance.

The widening gulf between imports and exports provided new grounds for concern about the dollar. By 1985 the trade deficit, based on the broadest measure, the current account (which in addition to goods and services includes income flows such as interest and dividend payments) was running at nearly $120 billion annually, close to 3 percent of GDP, and as a result the US economy's health was dependent to a historically unprecedented degree on capital from foreigners. When Americans bought imported goods such as German autos or Japanese electronics, dollars would flow abroad, and to the extent those dollars were not used to buy made-in-America products, they would remain in foreign hands. Many of the dollars held by foreigners were invested in ways that benefited the US economy – purchases of US Treasury securities being the most common. But what if, at some point, the superabundance of greenbacks stashed in accounts around the globe led to a selling stampede of US assets? That scary scenario was the source of Marris's dire warnings, which were echoed to some extent by Volcker. Not only the trade deficit stirred alarm for this reason; so did its twin the budget deficit, as reflected in statistics showing the mounting percentage of Treasury debt that foreigners held.

Ordinarily a country running such a large trade gap would undergo a corrective weakening of its currency, which would enhance the competitiveness of its exports and make imports more expensive. Instead, the dollar's exchange rate reached giddier and giddier heights in early 1985 as investors worldwide loaded up their portfolios with greenbacks. Amid burgeoning support in Congress for protectionist tariffs on countries that were running large trade surpluses with the United States, Treasury Secretary James Baker and his deputy, Richard Darman, recognized that the international trading system might fall apart if the US currency continued to rise unchecked.

A man who had worked at one of the world's most secretive financial institutions, for whom missions requiring stealth came naturally, was dispatched to rectify the problem. In mid-1985, David Mulford, having left his job at SAMA, was in a new post as assistant secretary of the Treasury for international affairs, carrying out an assignment for his superiors that obliged him to exercise utmost discretion. His destinations were four foreign capitals, where his interlocutors were the Japanese, West German, British, and French officials who, together with Mulford and a handful of US colleagues, managed the Group of Five (G-5) finance ministers and central bank governors – the global economy's effective steering committee at that time. Mulford's task was to negotiate a deal that would change the course of the world's major currencies.

His pitch to his G-5 counterparts was for a coordinated effort to shock markets into pushing the dollar down. This entailed clandestine discussions; such a move would be most effective if it came out of the blue. To minimize any chance of leaks, participants at meetings among G-5 officials worked from a US draft communiqué that Mulford distributed at the beginning of the session and collected at the end. Agreement did not come easily – officials in other countries, notably West Germany, put the blame on US overspending and under-taxing – but the deal took shape in the late summer and early fall of 1985.

"The element of surprise was complete," Mulford crowed in his memoir, when "the world's best-kept secret" was unveiled on September 22.[23] On that Sunday, the G-5 finance ministers and central bank governors appeared together at New York's Plaza Hotel to announce an agreement, known colloquially as the Plaza Accord, the centerpiece of which was a call for an "orderly appreciation of the main non-dollar currencies against the dollar." (The word "orderly" had been inserted at the insistence of Volcker, who feared a free fall in the green-back leading to financial discombobulation of unpredictable dimensions.) To effect that goal, the G-5 ministers and governors said that they "stand ready to cooperate more deeply" — a strong, though carefully phrased, commitment to intervene in markets using their foreign currency reserves, which they began doing the following day as their central banks unloaded billions of dollars. The Japanese went the furthest with plans for substantive policy action, suggesting that the agreement would help guide the Bank of Japan's decisions about inter-est rates and the money supply; Tokyo committed to "flexible management of monetary policy with due attention to the yen rate."[24]

In accordance with the G-5's pronouncement, the dollar went into a steep, steady decline, without the convulsive fall of Volcker's or Marris's nightmares. By the end of October 1985, the greenback was down some 13 percent against the yen and more than 10 percent against the mark; its total depreciation during the two years after the agreement was nearly 40 percent against the yen and 36 percent against the mark. How much of that movement was due to the Plaza Accord, and how much would have happened anyway, remains a matter of de-bate. In any event, the dollar's weaker foreign exchange rate helped rebalance US trade somewhat, as the current account deficit shrank as a percentage of American output in the late 1980s and early 1990s.

But respite from worries about the dollar — and the US trade gap, and the associated dependence on foreign capital — would be temporary. "Declinist" sen-timent about the United States took hold among the world's chattering classes in the late 1980s amid the ascendancy of Japan, especially once America's cumu-lative foreign liabilities surpassed its claims abroad in 1986 — an economically inconsequential event by itself, but often described in shorthand as the point at which the United States shed its status as a "creditor nation" to become a "debtor nation." Even after America's triumph in the Cold War and the bursting of Japan's financial bubble in the early 1990s, Cassandras highlighted the persis-tent failure of US industry to export nearly as much as the nation imported.

"The Fall of the Dollar Order: The World the United States Is Losing" was the title of a 1995 *Foreign Affairs* article, published during a period of prolonged dollar weakness, in which Diane Kunz, a Yale historian of US economic policy, wrote: "V-E Day marked the beginning of the dollar era. If the administration

—

[of President Bill Clinton] does not change its laissez-faire dollar policy and cut the budget deficit, boost savings, and take a hard line on trade, the 50th anniversary of V-E Day will signify its collapse."[25] In a like vein, *The Economist* declared that "the dollar's dominance is waning," because its depreciation meant that it "no longer fulfills the classic function of an international reserve currency. . . . America was the world's biggest creditor until the 1980s. But it is now the world's biggest debtor and so likelier to succumb to the temptation to let inflation nibble away at the real value of its debt, or to devalue in order to narrow its trade deficit."[26]

That was only a foretaste of what was to come in the next decade. Anxiety about America's financial improvidence – and its currency – was going to reach a new crescendo.

Majestic columns adorn the front entrance of the US Treasury building on Pennsylvania Avenue in Washington, DC, looming over a statue of Albert Gallatin, the fourth Treasury secretary. It is understandable that Jin Renqing, China's finance minister, would assume he should use this entrance when he arrived on the evening of October 1, 2004, to attend a dinner of Group of Seven (G-7) finance ministers and central bank governors – the first time Chinese officials had been invited to a G-7 gathering. Unfortunately, someone had mixed up the directions; Jin was supposed to use a different entrance, on 15th Street, and when Secret Service agents refused to admit him, an uproar ensued. Serious diplomatic repercussions were averted only when Treasury Secretary John Snow, alerted to the problem, authorized emergency measures so that Jin could be cleared to enter, and rushed to the front gate to welcome the Chinese minister personally. To the relief of Treasury officials, Jin calmed down, and the news media never found out about the indignity that had been inflicted on the Chinese.[27]

The happy ending notwithstanding, this episode signified a major fault in the global economy. China's invitation to a meeting of the world's advanced powers was a belated recognition of its economy's burgeoning size and importance. Beijing's cooperation was essential to help manage an economic development that was stirring an increasing amount of concern, head-scratching, debate, and antagonism around the world – an enormous imbalance in which the United States imported, consumed, and borrowed while Asian nations exported, saved, and lent.[28]

US imports exceeded exports in the early 2000s by a much greater amount than in the 1980s, both in absolute terms and as a proportion of the economy. Whereas in the previous period the nation's current account deficit peaked in 1987 at 3.4 percent of GDP, the deficit had surpassed $600 billion – nearly 6 percent of GDP – by 2004, and it continued to swell even further thereafter. On the other side of the Pacific, by contrast, surpluses of similar proportions were being racked up by South Korea, Japan, China, and Taiwan.

Benefits flowed to both sides: Asians got jobs in firms that manufactured goods for export, while American customers got high-quality, inexpensive products in greater abundance than ever before. The United States also got cheap capital from Asia because the dollars that Asians earned from their exports often ended up invested in the bonds of the US Treasury and mortgage finance companies such as Fannie Mae and Freddie Mac. These purchases of US securities helped keep US interest rates low, which in turn contributed to a boom in housing.

Here was privilege at its most exorbitant. In exchange for handing foreigners pieces of paper with dollar signs that the US government and federally sponsored agencies could print voluminously, Americans were enhancing their lifestyles to the hilt with low-cost products and low-interest loans. But it was only natural to wonder how long this arrangement could continue before a day of reckoning in which the quantity of paper Washington was printing would be greater than the market could bear. It was only natural to believe, too, that US citizens would deserve comeuppance for their profligacy, as evinced in the personal savings rate (that is, savings as a percentage of disposable income), which fell to approximately zero in 2005 and hovered there for three years.

"Bretton Woods II" was the term often used to describe the workings of the global economy at that time, by observers who believed it to be sustainable. It reflected the view that the United States and the world's export powerhouses were maintaining a healthy co-dependency that could remain stable for many years, just like the monetary system established after World War II. The countries with large trade surpluses, after all, had ample incentives to continue supporting American spending habits. Their export industries were major job creators, and their governments took comfort from the dollars that their export-ers were earning, which were being socked away in their central banks' reserves. Memories were still fresh and raw of financial crises that struck in the 1990s, when a number of countries — including, notably, South Korea — ran short of the dollars needed to keep their economies functioning, necessitating rescues by the IMF, which imposed distasteful conditions in return for emergency loans. Government officials knew that their countries would be better protected against market meltdowns the more dollars their central banks could accumulate.

Moreover, in an echo of the old Bretton Woods arrangement, a number of Asian currencies were loosely pegged to the dollar, none more firmly than China's. The exchange rate of the renminbi had been fixed since 1994 at 8.28 per dollar, and Beijing maintained that rate even as the Chinese current account surplus mounted in 2005 to more than 7 percent of GDP, a higher proportion of its economy than either Japan or Germany had achieved. Instead of allowing its currency to appreciate, which would normally happen in a country with a huge surplus, China held it down, one reason being that even a modest rise in the exchange rate might lead to large-scale unemployment in an export sector full of low-margin business. The predictable result was an outcry among US industries — auto parts, furniture, and textiles, for example — that were taking a beating from Chinese competition, and that saw the fixed-rate renminbi as a classic manipulation of market forces to benefit Chinese workers at the expense of American workers. Indignant members of Congress introduced bills to im-pose tariffs on Chinese goods aimed at countering the renminbi's undervalua-tion, but US options were extremely limited. Slapping tariffs unilaterally on Chinese goods would have egregiously violated international trade rules and would have risked economic warfare between Washington and Beijing, a disas-trous scenario under almost any sensible estimation as far as the administration of President George W. Bush was concerned. China allowed the renminbi to rise a little in 2005, but only a little, and as the Chinese export machine relentlessly augmented its share of global markets, the nation's reserves of foreign currency swelled to $1.7 trillion in 2007, a quintupling over five years.

The sanguine appraisal of Bretton Woods II was not universally held; on the contrary, many economists, both in academic and policymaking circles, feared that the US deficit would lead eventually to a crash in the dollar and worldwide dumping of US securities. It was only a matter of time, they reasoned, before foreigners would wake up to the fact that they were collectively overexposed to dollar risk. The mountain of US bonds that foreigners were amassing meant that the nation was going deeper into debt to fund its import binge.[29]

"The world is set to jump off the top of a waterfall without knowing how deep the water is below," said Kenneth Rogoff, the IMF's chief economist and co-author of a paper projecting that the dollar would have to decline by about 35 percent to get US trade back into balance.[30] In a front-page article in the *Washington Post,* William Cline, an economist and the author of a book titled *The United States as a Debtor Nation,* stated: "Sooner or later, the rest of the world will decide that the United States is no longer a safe bet for lending more money." (Full disclosure: the byline on that article, published in November 2005, was mine, and I expressed similar views in other writings.)[31] Even more dire was the forecast of Nouriel Roubini, an economics professor at New York University, who was co-author, in February 2005, of a paper asserting: "There is a meaningful risk the Bretton Woods 2 system will unravel before the end of 2006," meaning there would be "a sharp fall in the value of the US dollar, a rapid increase in US long-term interest rates and a sharp fall in the price of a range of risk assets including equities and housing" that would in turn lead to "a global[ly] severe economic slowdown, if not an outright recession."[32] That prediction, in addition to red flags Roubini waved in the media about inflated real estate prices, earned him the moniker "Dr. Doom."

Little noticed amid all the attention accorded the trans-Pacific imbalance was another giant set of flows, potentially even more pernicious, crossing the Atlantic. Banks in the United Kingdom and continental Europe were pouring hundreds of billions of dollars into the US housing market, attracted by the juicy yields on offer for securities backed by mortgages that Americans had taken out on their homes. From financial titans in London and Zurich to *Landesbanken* in the German industrial heartland, European bankers placed huge bets on some of the riskiest securities that would later become infamous for their "toxicity," and they did so in a particularly dicey way. Since they were buying dollar-based assets, and didn't have deposits of dollars from American savers to draw on, they had to borrow the dollars they needed in financial markets. In some cases they directly obtained short-term loans of dollars from US banks, and in other cases they issued dollar-denominated commercial paper — that is, IOUs typically in the 30- to 180-day maturity range — which they mostly sold to US money market funds. One way of appreciating in retrospect the hazards of this business model is to note which Wall Street firms were doing pretty much the same thing, namely funding real estate gambles by borrowing short term. The most prominent names on that list were Bear Stearns and Lehman Brothers.[33]

The elements for crisis were now in place. Among the many stunning developments that were about to unfold, the ones involving the dollar would rank high on the astonishment scale.

Who could blame Gisele Bündchen, the Brazilian supermodel, for preferring to receive pay in euros rather than dollars in late 2007 for her work promoting Pantene hair products and Dolce & Gabbana fragrance? The greenback was hitting all-time lows against the euro and the Canadian dollar at that time amid waves of trouble besetting the US financial system. Markets had been unsettled for several months following the failure in the summer of four hedge funds that had invested heavily in securities backed by subprime mortgages, and the Fed — correctly surmising that further setbacks might be in store — was slashing US interest rates in the second half of 2007, which was causing the dollar's exchange rate to sink. Billionaire investor Warren Buffett professed bearish sentiment about the dollar, as did Bill Gross, manager of the world's biggest bond fund, who said he was advising clients "that if you only had one idea, one investment, it would be to buy an investment in a non-dollar currency." The worldwide publicity accorded Bündchen's partiality for euros (she wasn't *insisting* on them, her agent stated, despite news reports saying she was) indicated that dollar-shunning was spreading well beyond the realm of finance professionals and currency experts.[34]

The Wile E. Coyote moment, it seemed, might finally be at hand — when the dollar, like the cartoon character who runs off of cliffs, would succumb in a flash of horror to the force of gravity and plunge to the fathoms below. If that had happened, it would have vindicated Dr. Doom and others who predicted the "unraveling" of Bretton Woods II. But as we now know, this period was the early phase of a much different sort of crisis. The further it progressed, and the worse it got, the more the consequences for the dollar would diverge from that forecast by the Dr. Dooms of the world.

The causes of the Global Financial Crisis have been explained in countless books, reflecting its complex origins. Some of these books are devoted to shenanigans in the US housing market, exposing how unscrupulous mortgage brokers earned rich fees by arranging loans to overstretched homebuyers. Others recount what Wall Street did with those mortgages – bundling them together for sale as investments, typically in the form of collateralized debt obligations (CDOs), with the payments divided up into "tranches" of riskiness. As readers of these books know, the fees and profits generated by this sort of activity fueled greater demand for the creation of still more shaky mortgages, and the Triple-A ratings that many of these securities received from complicit ratings agencies helped lull investors into believing that they could reap higher returns without sacrificing safety. Still other books chronicle the downfall of individual Wall Street firms such as Lehman and Bear Stearns, showing how financial engineering theoretically designed to make those firms safer ended up doing the opposite, as bonus-hungry traders relied on models that drastically underestimated the likelihood of large losses on CDOs, derivatives, and other financial instruments. The scrambling by policymakers at the Fed and the Treasury to keep the crisis from wrecking the entire financial system is the focus of other authors. Virtually all of these crisis books are united by one theme – the lapses by regulators who turned a blind eye to market excesses, either because of their "capture" by the financial industry or their zealous faith in laissez-faire.

A full rehashing of those horror stories is not necessary here. For this book, the important point is that the bulk of the misfeasance, nonfeasance, and malfeasance stemmed from problems in the United States – the crisis was "Made in America" – and yet money rushed into the dollar. During the most severe months of the crisis, from April 2008 to March 2009, the dollar rose by more than 15 percent against an inflation-adjusted index of other currencies. Call this counterintuitive, call it paradoxical, call it unfair, call it confounding, call it perverse, but the "safe haven" became the currency of the country where the epicenter of the crisis was located. Notwithstanding Wall Street's abject failures at generating high-quality financial instruments, and Washington's abject failures at financial governance, the appetite of the world's investors for the dollar helped

—

insulate the US economy from the worst ravages of panic, conferring exorbitant privilege upon the United States yet again, in a new form.

In large part, the reasons for the dollar's allure during the crisis were similar to those that impelled SAMA to favor dollar-denominated investments in the 1970s – the liquidity of US financial markets. Just as the Saudis found US Treasury securities to be practically the only investment they could buy in quantity without affecting prices, so did investors during the Great Crisis crave Treasuries as the most liquid securities available anywhere. Almost by definition, after all, a financial crisis means that liquidity evaporates, and markets "seize up" as participants become unable to conduct the sorts of transactions necessary for day-to-day functioning, such as banks borrowing cash from each other overnight to cover obligations imminently coming due. In 2007–2008, seizing-up happened because revelations about shady mortgage finance practices made banks mistrustful of one another; for one thing, they couldn't be sure how much the mortgage-backed securities they received as collateral for loans were really worth. In circumstances like this, when each party fears that a counterparty may run short of cash, and the pervasiveness of such fears makes all parties anxious to ensure that they have enough cash to make payments on time, liquid assets become prized. Everyone seeks and hoards assets that can be transformed into cash easily, quickly, and at minimal expense; nobody wants to risk ruinous losses by unloading non-liquid assets at fire-sale prices or – worse yet – defaulting for lack of sufficient liquidity. The most sought-after and hoarded assets, therefore, were Treasuries.

But to fully grasp the incongruity of the dollar emerging from this made-in-the-USA crisis with its leading role intact, it is necessary to delve into another crisis phenomenon, namely the urgent need of foreign banks – European ones in particular – for dollars, and the Fed's rescue of them. In the process, the Fed, under chair Ben Bernanke, would play an unprecedented role – lender of last resort not only for the United States but for the rest of the world. The operations involved were so politically sensitive that the Fed tried to keep many of the key details under wraps for as long as possible, revealing them only after being legally compelled to do so several years after the fact.[35]

It will be recalled from the previous section that the balance sheets of European banks were loaded with liabilities owed in dollars (the amount was later estimated at over $2 trillion), because they had borrowed roughly that amount to make what they thought were lucrative bets on American mortgages.[36] When seizing-up started in the second half of 2007 they had to scramble, like banks everywhere, to obtain the cash needed for paying obligations coming due. They got some help from their own central banks – the European Central Bank (ECB), the Bank of England, and the Swiss National Bank – which were fulfilling their duties by pumping out plenty of money. But those central banks could furnish only euros, pounds sterling, and Swiss francs in unlimited quantities; they could not print the currency the banks most acutely required – that is, dollars.

This was where the Fed came in. It alone could print dollars and funnel them to where they were needed. One way this was done was indirectly, with deals between the Fed and foreign central banks to swap currencies. The first such pact came on December 12, 2007, when the Fed announced an arrangement with the ECB, Bank of England, Swiss National Bank, and Bank of Canada. The swaps involved straight trades of the respective central banks' currencies, at prevailing exchange rates, for fixed periods of time – for example, the Fed might send $5 billion or $10 billion to the ECB in exchange for an equivalent amount in euros, with each central bank promising to return the other's currency at the end of 90 days. During that period the ECB would lend the dollars to banks in the eurozone that were starved for greenbacks.

That was just the start. Bernanke and his Fed colleagues opened their dollar spigot wider for financial institutions – foreign and domestic – as market turmoil intensified in the spring of 2008. And a veritable gusher of dollars was forthcoming after the stupefying events of mid-September, which included the bankruptcy of Lehman, the emergency takeover of Merrill Lynch by Bank of America, and the bailout of the insurance giant AIG. Recognizing that the conventional approach of simply cutting interest rates and expanding the money supply would be far from adequate, the Fed established a number of programs for dispensing liquidity directly to private financial institutions that all told ran into the trillions of dollars. These were designed to avoid catastrophic breakdowns in various sectors of the financial system's plumbing such as the commercial paper market, the asset-backed securities market, and the "repo" (repurchase) market; the programs' dizzying array of names included the Term

Auction Facility (TAF), Primary Dealer Credit Facility (PDCF), Term Securities Lending Facility (TSLF), Term Asset-Backed Securities Loan Facility (TALF), and Commercial Paper Funding Facility (CPFF).

The dirty little secret about these programs was that foreign institutions were taking advantage of them, in some cases absorbing a majority of the funds on offer. The best-known European beneficiaries included the United Kingdom's Barclays and Royal Bank of Scotland; Germany's Deutsche Bank, Dresdner Bank, and West LB; Switzerland's UBS and Credit Suisse; and Belgium's Dexia. This information, known only to a handful of Fed insiders at the time, was withheld from the public until its release in late 2010 and early 2011 as the result of congressional legislation and a Freedom of Information Act lawsuit brought by Bloomberg News, which the Fed fought all the way to the Supreme Court.[37]

Not that there was anything improper or untoward — much less illegal — about the Fed's assistance to banks headquartered abroad; the word "dirty" is being used here only because Bernanke and his colleagues knew that controversy would flare, especially in Congress. It was in the enlightened self-interest of the United States to minimize the possibility of a global firestorm that would have resulted if a foreign megabank had defaulted to its US creditors for lack of dollar liquidity. In pursuit of that enlightened self-interest, Fed officials dispensed aid in a manner consistent with the principles established by Bagehot nearly 140 years earlier for how a central bank should act in a crisis. The Fed wasn't giving money away; a lender of last resort, as the term implies, is a lender, charging interest and providing cash only upon receipt of adequate collateral (typically securities that, although presumably valuable in the long run, could only be sold at fire-sale prices in the short run). Furthermore, the foreign banks that participated in the Fed's liquidity programs were, strictly speaking, not foreign but rather the US branches of foreign financial institutions and therefore fully entitled under law to the same treatment as domestic institutions.

But even within the Fed, all this lending to foreigners evoked some handwringing, notably when the scale and breadth of the currency swaps expanded dramatically, with the swap total surpassing $500 billion, in the weeks after the September 2008 Lehman bust. The central banks of more countries — Australia, Denmark, Norway, Sweden, and New Zealand — were added to the list of countries with swap lines; then four other major central banks – the ECB, Bank of England, Bank of Japan, and Swiss National Bank – got unlimited authorization from the Fed to swap for all the dollars they wanted. Finally, in late October 2008, the Fed announced that it had agreed with the central banks of four "systemically important" emerging markets – Brazil, Mexico, Singapore, and South Korea – to currency swaps, with a limit of $30 billion for each of the four.

Bernanke encountered pushback from some of his colleagues at an FOMC meeting where he sought approval for the swaps with the four emerging-market central banks. "I don't know where we draw the lines," fretted Charles Plosser, the president of the Philadelphia Fed, according to the meeting transcript.[38] Others asked whether any requests for swaps had been rejected – the answer was yes; some central banks had been turned down partly because their economies lacked the "systemic importance" of the four countries under consideration.[39] Even so, Plosser wondered whether all such countries ought instead to approach the IMF, which was reportedly planning to establish a new type of loan for countries with liquidity problems. "Why not just say that everybody else goes to them first?" he demanded.[40]

Ah yes, the IMF. In important respects it seemed ideally suited for the role of emergency dollar-emitter; as seen in chapter 2, the IMF was established to provide dollars to crisis-stricken countries. (In fact, three of the countries seeking swap lines from the Fed that day – Brazil, Mexico, and South Korea – had all gotten rescue loans from the Fund at various points over the previous 15 years.) One of the IMF's great advantages, from the US point of view, is that it provides bailouts multilaterally, sparing Washington from the burden and political strain of doing so on its own.

Plosser's argument was rebutted by Bernanke and the Fed's top international staffer, Nathan Sheets, who contended that the IMF lacked the financial clout for the task at hand. They were right; the Fund wasn't anything like the institution that Keynes had envisioned at Bretton Woods, with powers to create an international currency out of thin air. Its financial war chest, although substantial, was capped by the amounts its member countries contributed in the form of dollars and other hard currencies usable in international transactions. "Just to put some numbers on IMF lending capacity – [it] is about $250 billion," Sheets said. "So the $120 billion that we're proposing today [in swap lines, with $30 billion for each of the four emerging markets] would be essentially half of what the IMF could do." The IMF needed to save that money to ensure it would have enough for other countries that might fall into danger, Sheets asserted.[41]

The momentous step the Fed was taking was put into perspective at the FOMC meeting by Timothy Geithner, then president of the New York Fed. "The privilege of being the reserve currency of the world comes with some burdens," Geithner told his colleagues. "Not that we have an obligation in this sense, but we have an interest in helping these [countries] mitigate the problems they face."[42] Put another way, the central bank that printed dollars was the only institution equipped to serve as international lender of last resort, and fulfilling this heavy responsibility would avert calamity in foreign financial systems inextricably intertwined with the US system.

In the end, Plosser acquiesced, but the objection he raised—"I don't know where we draw the lines"—was profoundly vexing. In future crises, where *would* the world's sole international lender of last resort draw the line? Which countries' financial systems might be deemed unworthy of its aid, especially if political or foreign policy considerations came into play? In view of the Fed's reluctance to disclose the names of foreign banks receiving liquidity assistance, mightn't it be even more skittish about providing such assistance the next time similar circumstances arose? How might the Fed be inhibited if—hypothetically speaking—an "America First" president occupied the White House?

Small wonder that, in the aftermath of the crisis, a chorus of demands resounded for change in the dollar-centered regime. America's irresponsible exploitation of its exorbitant privilege was held liable for the world's misery, and foreign policymakers were galled by the idea of remaining so exposed to the US currency's vicissitudes.

In a March 2009 essay posted on the website of the People's Bank of China, Governor Zhou Xiaochuan wrote that the crisis showed "the inherent vulnerabilities and systemic risks in the existing international monetary system."[43] Without referring to the dollar, he asserted that the world should adopt an international reserve currency "disconnected from economic conditions and sovereign interests of any single country." It was a pity, Zhou said, that Keynes's bancor proposal had been rejected at Bretton Woods, but now Special Drawing Rights (SDRs), a quasi-currency administered by the IMF, could serve a similar

———

function. (More on the SDR in the next chapter.) Several months later, a UN commission of experts tasked with proposing post-crisis reforms agreed: "A global reserve currency whose creation is not linked to the external position of any particular national economy . . . is an idea whose time has come."[44]

European leaders, paying scant regard for the Fed's role in saving their banks, vowed to fundamentally alter the monetary hierarchy. "The United States will lose its superpower status in the world financial system," German finance minister Peer Steinbrück predicted, and with characteristic bombast, French president Nicolas Sarkozy declared, on the eve of a November 2008 summit hosted by President Bush: "I am leaving tomorrow for Washington to explain that the dollar — which after the Second World War under Bretton Woods was the only [international] currency in the world — can no longer claim" its lofty status. "What was true in 1945 cannot be true today."[45]

A number of scholars chimed in. "Although dollar doomsayers have cried wolf repeatedly in the past . . . the financial crisis of 2008 has further weakened the dollar's footing, a deterioration that will be more salient when the global economy recovers," wrote Jonathan Kirshner of Cornell University.[46] Across the Atlantic, Antonio Mosconi of the Einstein Centre for International Studies called the crisis "the last convulsion of the international role of the dollar."[47]

Was the dollar's culpability in the crisis so great as to merit such denunciation? Indeed it was, according to several prominent analysts — including Americans — who have contended that, in hindsight, the United States was harmed more than helped by having the world's reserve currency. Michael Pettis, a professor of finance at Peking University, has been on the forefront of those advancing this argument. "The preeminence of the U.S. dollar meant that Americans were the ones who absorbed the bulk of both the excess capital inflows and the excess manufactured goods from the rest of the world," Pettis asserts in a book he co-wrote. "The consequences were the housing debt bubble and a displaced manufacturing base. Rather than an exorbitant privilege, the dollar's international status imposed an exorbitant *burden*."[48]

That indictment of the dollar is more than a trifle overstated. Even in the absence of foreign capital, US housing prices would have shot up in the early 2000s. Unscrupulous lenders would have encouraged property owners to buy bigger houses than they could afford, Wall Street would have sliced and diced mortgage-backed securities, and ratings agencies and regulators would have given their stamp of approval. Money from abroad reduced interest rates on US government bonds by somewhere between 0.5 and 0.9 percent prior to the crisis, economic studies indicate — not enough, by itself, to have caused the bubble in property prices or the associated knavery.[49] As for America's "displaced manufacturing base," competition from imports is far from the whole story, and an even smaller part of the story is competition from imports attributable to dollar strength. Manufacturing employment has fallen steeply in all major advanced nations over the past five decades — even industrial powerhouses such as Germany — the main reason being rising productivity (output per worker) stemming in large part from advancing technology and automation.

But there is plenty of validity to the argument that the dollar's primacy and associated imbalances made the crisis worse than it would have been otherwise. US interest rates were lower, the granting of credit was more reckless, and the market was less effective in disciplining excesses than it would have been in the absence of high foreign demand for the US currency. Although US manufacturing would have suffered a "China shock" in the early 2000s simply by dint of China's low wages and export prowess, the cheap renminbi exacerbated the impact. In this sense the burden identified by Pettis was, if not exorbitant, at least substantive.

This much is indisputable: the crisis laid bare serious drawbacks in a system dominated by a single currency. But what was the alternative? For all the post-crisis talk about the desirability of replacing the dollar with a better international reserve currency — and there was discussion aplenty, at academic conferences, in scholarly journals, in the news media, and in policymaking circles — those seeking or expecting change were bedeviled by the question of which among the dollar's challengers stood a reasonable chance of success.

The four most plausible candidates for leading international reserve currency are examined in the next chapter. Each of the four, at various times, was either predicted to replace the dollar or championed as preferable to it, as we shall see. But each suffered from shortcomings, which sometimes materialized so rapidly as to leave their cheerleaders red-faced. In fact, the post-crisis world was about to get a lesson in just how problematic the dollar's main rival was.

CHAPTER 4

PRETENDERS TO THE THRONE

The Euro

The new kind of money that Greeks were using was a source of delight to the people I met on a reporting trip to Athens in 2002. Notes and coins denominated in drachma were no longer in circulation starting that year, the same as for many other European currencies including the German mark, French franc, Italian lira, Spanish peseta, Dutch guilder, and half a dozen others. Henceforth the money used by the majority of Europeans would be the euro, and my editors at the *Washington Post* wanted an early assessment of how things were going with the novel common currency of a huge economic area.

Greece was an ideal place to find out. Its leaders were hoping that joining the eurozone (the Economic and Monetary Union of the European Union, as it's formally called) would put an end to frequent bouts of instability that had long plagued the Greek economy. Their bet was that sharing the same currency as all 12 countries that were then in the union, with the money supply controlled by the Frankfurt-based European Central Bank, would give the nation a much firmer economic underpinning. At the time of my visit, their gamble appeared to be paying off.

One of the business executives I interviewed, Dimitri Papalexopoulos, remembered the pre-euro Greece he encountered when he returned to Athens from the United States in the early 1990s to help run a major building-materials

---

company founded and controlled by his family. During the two decades ending in 1994, inflation averaged 17 percent a year and the drachma experienced repeated sinking spells, fueling sky-high interest rates that hobbled business spending on plant and equipment and kept the country's economic growth creeping along at an average annual rate of less than 1 percent, adjusted for inflation, since 1980.

Papalexopoulos recalled asking people at the company what "hurdle rate" — acceptable borrowing cost — they used to evaluate investments, "and they asked me, 'what do you mean?' " That was because "there were no long-term fixed interest rates at that point — just one-year rates. So it was very difficult to fund any sort of long-term projects in Greek drachma."[1]

With Greece in the eurozone, by contrast, Papalexopoulos's company could borrow in a currency managed from Frankfurt — just like Germans, Dutch, and Finns. "As unbelievable as it sounds to Greek ears, we have a cost of capital roughly equal to that of the US," Papalexopoulos told me, adding that "this has made a tremendous difference" to his company's ability to finance expansion as well as sparking demand for cement and other products the firm made. For similar reasons, a market for mortgages and consumer lending, which barely existed in the country before, had burgeoned and was generating an explosion in home buying.

With the benefit of hindsight, we know that Greece would be the first of several countries to be stricken by a crisis that nearly ripped the eurozone apart. Looking back at how Europe fell into such difficulties shows why the world's No. 2 currency, for all its allure, has poor prospects for becoming No. 1. This train of events is especially worthy of retrospection because until the crisis erupted in 2010, the euro's potential for rivaling the dollar was a topic of lively conjecture.

Driving the euro's creation was a variety of motivations, which boiled down to a desire for Europe to have a currency commensurate with the region's economic heft. Inspired by the vision of a giant single market that would foster economic dynamism and end bloody conflict, European policymakers had dismantled countless customs and tariff barriers as they progressed from the six-nation European Coal and Steel Community to the European Economic Community to the European Union. Their aim of fuller integration was im-

———

peded by the multiplicity of European currencies, especially after the breakdown of Bretton Woods when sharp fluctuations in foreign exchange rates added a significant element of risk for companies and banks seeking to invest, lend, and trade across national borders. A monetary union would eliminate such incertitude at a stroke for the countries that joined, and by the 1990s European officials were moving forward in earnest toward this goal.

Sharp questions arose, from American and British economists in particular, about whether a common currency for such a disparate group of countries made sense. Among the most vocal were some of the biggest names in the field, including Nobel laureate Milton Friedman, Harvard's Martin Feldstein, MIT's Rüdiger Dornbusch, and future Nobel prizewinner Paul Krugman. Beneficial as it might be in promoting trade and other economic exchanges within the European Union, and noble as it might be to bind former wartime enemies more closely together, joining a currency union requires a sovereign government to relinquish control over some enormously important tools for influencing the health of the national economy, notably the money supply, interest rates, and the currency exchange rate – all of which would now become the responsibility of the ECB. So Friedman, Feldstein, and others warned that countries in the eurozone would risk serious trouble by embracing a unified monetary policy when so many other aspects of their economies and societies – their fiscal and regulatory policies, their financial systems, the competitiveness of their industries, and, of course, their languages – were so different. The obvious comparison was the United States, where a common currency and monetary policy are practical in part because of labor mobility; if one region of the country is suffering from high unemployment, the jobless can move to more prosperous areas, better enabling the Federal Reserve to decide on money supply expansion and interest rate levels based on the aim of keeping the overall economy on a stable, low-inflation path. In Europe, by contrast, people are much more loath to seek work by moving many hundreds of miles away, where they may not be able to communicate with their neighbors or relate culturally to them. If one European country (or group of countries) underwent a severe slump while others boomed, the slumpers – lacking control over their own money supply and exchange rate – would have very limited ways of generating recovery, the euro-skeptics pointed out.

—

Their concerns were not assuaged by the Maastricht Treaty, signed in February 1992, when the eurozone's prospective members agreed to a number of "convergence criteria" that would be required for membership, most importantly including low inflation, low interest rates, and budget deficits below 3 percent of GDP. Nor did euro-skepticism abate much following the "Stability and Growth Pact" agreed in 1997 to boost enforcement of the rules by threatening sanctions against violators. The rules didn't cover enough crucial areas, naysayers said, and wouldn't be enforced anyway.

Europe forged ahead with monetary union nonetheless, with the German and French governments in the lead. And as the finishing touches were being applied to the euro, ringing endorsements came from a few North American economists who maintained that their colleagues were not only underestimating Europe's strengths but disregarding the new currency's likely global appeal. Fred Bergsten, director of the Institute for International Economics in Washington, predicted in 1997 that the euro would attain "full parity" with the dollar in as little as five to ten years. "The euro's rise will convert an international monetary system that has been dominated by the dollar since World War II into a bipolar regime," Bergsten wrote in *Foreign Affairs*.[2] Adding his prestige as a Nobel prizewinner, Canadian economist Robert Mundell of Columbia University contended that "the introduction of the euro will challenge the status of the dollar and alter the power configuration of the system."[3]

Pessimism about the euro receded in the early 2000s as the old national currencies disappeared from circulation. The most striking sign of confidence in the new currency was the way financial markets increasingly treated member countries of the eurozone as if their creditworthiness was almost identical. Now that investors no longer had to worry about, say, a Spanish bond falling because of a decline in the peseta, they were more eager to buy. This was the phenomenon that so enthralled Papalexopoulos; in Greece, where in the early 1990s borrowers had had to pay roughly three times as much in interest as German borrowers did, during the euro's first decade funds could be raised at close to the same rates. In 2007, for example, the Greek government issued ten-year bonds paying 4.29 percent per annum, versus 4.02 percent for the German equivalent.

Exaltation over the euro swelled in volume as celebrations for the tenth anniversary of its launch began in late 2008 and early 2009 — coincidentally, just as the dollar was drawing castigation for having contributed to the Global Financial Crisis. At conferences, in scholarly publications, and in the news media, Europe's common currency was hailed for bestowing stability and prosperity on the 15 countries that had adopted it,[4] and for affording shelter from the havoc that was then embroiling Wall Street and the City of London.

"The euro has been a resounding success," declared Lucas Papademos, vice president of the European Central Bank, at a conference titled "The Euro at Ten," and the *Wall Street Journal* editorialized: "The single European currency, born on New Year's Day in 1999, is a rare economic shining star of the past decade." Gloating was irresistible for those who recalled that the euro's conception had been the target of derision by outsiders. "Perhaps the most significant flattery as the euro turns ten comes from that Euroskeptic nation par excellence, Great Britain, where some commentators are now wondering aloud whether adopting the euro (and ditching the age-old symbol of British financial prowess, the pound) would be a boon to the country's economic future," wrote a columnist for Germany's *Die Welt*.[5]

In its first decade, the euro had attained a solid No. 2 position globally, comprising 25 percent of the foreign exchange reserves held by the world's central banks, versus about 65 percent for the dollar. Attraction to the euro was attributable partly to the sheer economic size of the eurozone, the output of which exceeded 16 percent of global GDP. But also crucial were monetary and financial factors, starting with the sound policies of the ECB, whose president, Jean-Claude Trichet, was renowned for his rectitude and deep experience in central banking. Inflation in the eurozone was low; trade and investment flows among the zone's countries had significantly increased; and European financial markets operated at world-class levels of sophistication, with transaction costs for purchases and sales of securities roughly equal to or even lower than those in US markets. This record raised the obvious question of whether the euro might be on a trajectory to match or even surpass the dollar.

For some tenth-anniversary celebrants, the answer was at least a tentative yes. "The euro's first decade has been marked by incremental, yet noticeable, steps toward becoming an equal to the dollar as an international currency," wrote Elias Papaioannou of Dartmouth College and Richard Portes of London Business School in a report published by the European Commission. Even bolder was a 2008 paper by Menzie Chinn of the University of Wisconsin and

Jeffrey Frankel of Harvard, stating that "there now exists a credible rival for lead international currency, the euro." Citing the US economy's "25-year history of chronic current account deficits," Chinn and Frankel envisioned a scenario by which "the euro could overtake the dollar as early as 2015," and although that scenario was based on pessimistic assumptions about US policy, they concluded: "If the euro were to overtake the dollar in a few decades, it would be a once-in-a-century event. But it happened to the pound in the last century, so who is to say it could not happen to the dollar in this?"[6]

Exemplifying the zeitgeist, an article in the *New York Times Magazine* titled "Waving Goodbye to Hegemony" portrayed the euro's record as signifying a shift in geopolitical tectonic plates. "Many Americans scoffed at the introduction of the euro, claiming it was an overreach that would bring the collapse of the European project," wrote the author, Parag Khanna. "Yet today, Persian Gulf oil exporters are diversifying their currency holdings into euros, and President Mahmoud Ahmadinejad of Iran has proposed that OPEC no longer price its oil in 'worthless' dollars. President Hugo Chávez of Venezuela went on to suggest euros. . . . Meanwhile, America's share of global exchange reserves has dropped to 65 percent. Gisele Bündchen demands to be paid in euros, while Jay-Z drowns in 500 euro notes in a recent video."[7]

Within months of the euro's tenth anniversary, however, its major flaws would become glaringly evident.

The Greek government had taken advantage of low interest rates to borrow its way into deeper and deeper trouble — more than €300 billion of debt by 2010, roughly equal to the nation's GDP — while skewing statistics to give a misleadingly favorable picture. A related problem was diverging trade imbalances among member countries of the eurozone. Whereas Germany ran substantial current account surpluses (6.1 percent of GDP in 2006) and the Netherlands' surplus was even bigger (8.2 percent of GDP), current account deficits were running between 8 percent and 11 percent of GDP in Greece, Spain, and Portugal.[8]

These figures effectively meant that the surplus countries of northern Europe were helping to finance a binge of consumption and housing purchases in deficit countries such as Spain and Ireland, as well as a binge of government spending in Greece. Capital was pouring from the thrifty, ultra-competitive north into the peripheral countries of the zone; among the most enthusiastic funders were German regional banks (the same sort that invested heavily in US mortgage-backed securities). This flood of money made it much easier for governments, businesses, and individuals in the periphery to borrow – and in many cases, to borrow excessively, as the world would eventually learn to its sorrow.

Signs began materializing in the spring of 2009 of the crisis that would dash the euro's prospects for eclipsing the dollar. A bout of financial turmoil struck the weakest eurozone countries, as a sell-off in the government bonds of those nations caused a sharp rise in the yields demanded by investors, with a commensurate rise in the rates those governments would have to pay on new borrowing. Yields on ten-year bonds of the Greek government, for example, spiked above 6 percent at one point in early 2009, and the "spread" on those bonds – the difference in yield with German bonds, which are regarded as the safest European investment – widened to above 300 basis points, or three percentage points. (A basis point is 1/100th of a percentage point.) Spreads on Ireland's bonds swelled to about 250 basis points, Italy's and Portugal's to about 150 basis points, and Spain's to about 125 basis points.

In October 2009 came the shocking revelation that Greece's budget deficit for that year would be upward of 12.5 percent of GDP, more than triple previous estimates – and with that, the country began its slide toward the financial abyss. With the government obliged to pay much steeper interest rates on new bonds than it had previously, heavy debt payments coming due, and the economy hobbled by recession (thereby diminishing tax revenue), Athens was caught in a vicious cycle. It couldn't pull out of the slump by increasing government spending or cutting taxes, since that would only intensify market fears about its debt burden, which would cause interest rates to rise further; nor could it pump up the money supply or depreciate its currency, since those policies were under ECB control. By the spring of 2010, previously unthinkable outcomes for Greece, including a default on government debt payments, became the subject of speculation in market analyses and media reports.

The endgame that inspired the most dread was abandonment by Athens of the euro, because of the hellish chaos that would ensue both for Greece and economies elsewhere. A handful of economic commentators argued that Athens ought to leave the eurozone and bring back the drachma to regain control over its monetary levers, but the overwhelming consensus was that the costs of divorce would far outweigh the benefits. Contracts and other financial obligations would have to be redenominated in drachma, triggering fierce and convoluted legal disputes. And once the taboo of quitting the monetary union was broken, other vulnerable countries might be forced to revert to their national currencies too, as terrified citizens shipped their money to safe havens. A full-blown economic crack-up in Europe, far-fetched though it might seem, no longer seemed beyond the realm of possibility.

Only after a marathon series of meetings over the weekend of May 7–9, 2010, involving heated negotiations spanning three different countries, did Europe's political and economic potentates agree on a strategy. Greece would avert default thanks to a €110 billion package of loans, the bulk of which came from Greece's eurozone partner nations, whose leaders grudgingly overrode the so-called "no bailout clause" of the Maastricht Treaty. (This provision states that neither the European Union nor its member states shall "be liable for or assume the commitments of" other governments.) In return, Athens had to accept extraordinarily onerous terms including the slashing of government spending, hiking of taxes, and structural reforms such as revision of laws protecting workers from layoffs. A "firewall" would be erected to protect the rest of the eurozone, in the form of a new stabilization fund that could lend money to other member countries in distress. And the ECB would selectively buy the bonds of such countries, with the IMF also playing a role.

The ensuing calm was short lived. Markets were again in an uproar a few months later, this time over Ireland, which had a much more disciplined fiscal policy than Greece but was bedeviled by a banking system full of rotten property loans. On September 30, 2010, dubbed "Black Thursday" by the Irish commentariat, Finance Minister Brian Lenihan confessed that the losses in one go-go bank, Anglo Irish, were much deeper than previously acknowledged. And he announced additional news that, to use the Irish vernacular, was even more gobsmacking: since Dublin had given a two-year guarantee on all deposits in the nation's banks during the Global Financial Crisis, the rising bank-bailout cost to the government would cause the budget deficit for 2010 to swell to 32 percent of GDP. The nation's debt-to-GDP ratio, which had been just 25 percent in 2007, was officially projected at 98.6 percent of GDP.

Ireland's rescue package of €85 billion was followed by another, slightly smaller one for Portugal in the spring of 2011, which was followed by a second rescue of Greece in 2012 that included the biggest restructuring of a nation's debt in history, and crises in Italy, Spain, and Cyprus that required significant intervention by eurozone authorities at both the national and trans-European levels. Among the most alarming manifestations of the region's woes was a phenomenon called the "doom loop," in which the financial weaknesses of governments exacerbated fragility of banks and vice versa. Unlike the United States, where federal agencies in Washington hold responsibility for bank regulation and handling bank failures, Europe had left such powers in the hands of individual member states. As a result, a self-reinforcing, malign chain of causation was at play: banks were losing the confidence of depositors and creditors due to worries about whether their governments could support them; governments were suffering from fears that the cost of bailing out one or more banks would be too much for taxpayers to bear.

A chilling series of doom-loop-related events in mid-2012 finally prompted ECB president Mario Draghi to pledge "whatever it takes to preserve the euro." Seeing what he later called "the risk of a complete collapse of all credit markets," Draghi vowed – over the objections of some high-ranking German policymakers – that the ECB would buy unlimited quantities of bonds from crisis-stricken eurozone countries, provided the countries agreed to strict conditions set by European agencies and the IMF. This move ended the most virulent stage of the region's crisis, and by the time it was all over, Europe had accomplished a great deal to shore up monetary union. New rules were agreed, vulnerabilities were reduced, and a major new firefighting institution, the European Stability Mechanism, was established so countries using the euro could be assured that they would not be left entirely on their own if future conflagrations should occur.

But it was impossible to unsee what had happened, and equally impossible to ignore the implications for the euro.

The crisis exposed the mismatch between the eurozone's monetary commonality and the diversity of its sovereign member states. Without a central authority that wields power equivalent to the federal government in Washington, the euro suffers from the lack of a single security issuer like the US

Treasury. The *bunds* issued by the German government may be as safe as Treasuries, but the same can hardly be said of bonds issued by other large euro-zone nations such as Italy or Spain. Even though all those bonds are denominated in euros, the riskiness of holding them varies according to the creditworthiness of the individual government. It is only natural that investors and central bankers around the world, weighing what sort of securities to keep in reserve for emergencies, will tend to favor the ones that are both the safest and most liquid of all, meaning those of the United States rather than eurozone nations.

The Yen

Kaiseki dinners featuring multiple courses of delicacies, exquisitely presented on hand-crafted ceramics and lacquerware, served by kimono-clad waitresses, washed down with free-flowing sake and other alcoholic beverages, followed by karaoke sessions with geishas simpering over the singing performances — that was the sort of hospitality accorded US Treasury officials who traveled to Tokyo in the 1980s for "yen-dollar talks." Their hosts held senior positions in the powerful Ministry of Finance, which gave them entrée to the capital's most exclusive dining establishments and nightspots, all costs covered by Japanese government expense accounts.[9]

For all the delights of their evening entertainment, however, the Americans generally found these visits frustrating. Their goal was to persuade Japan to internationalize the yen by removing heavy regulations over the nation's financial system and allowing money to move freely in and out of the country. This point bears repeating to ensure that it sinks in: the US government wanted to make the yen more like the dollar; Treasury officials were not only willing to countenance another currency playing a global role similar to that of the greenback, they were insisting on it.

But progress was glacial. Their Japanese counterparts were skilled at parrying US proposals with painstaking explanations of why Tokyo couldn't take the measures Washington wanted or why, if implementation were to proceed, it would have to go "step by step" over a number of years. It didn't help that the negotiations were typically conducted in a stilted atmosphere, with each side sitting opposite the other at long tables while dozens of junior Finance Ministry officials hovered along the walls and in nearby rooms to provide their superiors with logistical support.

US impatience with Tokyo's "step by step" approach was manifest at one session when Treasury Undersecretary Beryl Sprinkel, an ardent free marketeer with a stentorian voice, rejected the argument offered by the lead Japanese negotiator, Vice Minister Tomomitsu Oba. "I grew up in Missouri on a dirt farm," boomed Sprinkel, who recalled that when piglets were born, "we had to cut their tails off. When we cut them off we didn't cut them off one inch at a time! This would just hurt them more. We just hacked them off once up at the top and that was the end of it." The translation, which took a few seconds to transmit, evoked shocked silence at first on the Japanese side of the table, until Oba laughed, which led to peals of laughter among his subordinates as well. The next day, Oba declared that he had understood Sprinkel's story and henceforth Japan's approach would change from "step by step" to "stride by stride."[10]

As the story suggests, US officials, who were actively encouraging a competitor currency to assume some of the dollar's international status, were up against a government that had no interest in mounting such a challenge. Japanese officials saw a low-profile yen as a crucial element in their nation's postwar economic miracle, and they were loath to mess with success.

That miracle was then in full swing. Toyota, Nissan, and Honda had invaded the US auto market in the 1970s and found it ripe for plucking; similar conquests had been achieved in consumer electronics by Sony and Matsushita Electric, in computers and integrated circuits by Fujitsu and NEC, in power generation and heavy machinery by Toshiba and Hitachi, and by other ultra-competitive Japanese firms in a host of sectors ranging from steel to construction equipment to machine tools. Books with titles such as *Japan as Number One* and *Trading Places: How We Allowed Japan to Take the Lead* explained to Americans how this resource-poor island nation, having rocketed to second place in the world's GDP rankings and accumulated the world's biggest stash of foreign exchange reserves, was on course to challenge the United States as the dominant economic power.

To attain such supercharged growth, Japanese policymakers had adopted a development model based on what economists call "financial repression," the idea being to use the financial system for the benefit of the nation's manufacturers and exporters. In the first quarter century after the war, these policies were draconian, with dollars and other foreign currencies carefully husbanded for allocation by bureaucrats to obtain machinery, technology, and other inputs from abroad needed to build industrial strength. So tight were restrictions on cross-border money movements during this period that as late as 1970, almost no Japanese trade was invoiced in yen. These regulations were loosened somewhat in subsequent years, but even in the 1980s, Japanese banks and savers were strictly limited in the amounts of money they could send abroad; government planners wanted a big pool of capital kept at home so that industrial firms could obtain the maximum amount of funding at the lowest possible interest rates. Another facet of this policy involved discouraging foreigners from buying yen in unlimited quantities lest that cause the exchange rate to rise, which would render Japanese goods less competitive on world markets.[11]

Washington's tolerance for these policies was at an end by the 1980s. As noted in the previous chapter, US manufacturers were in a lather about the handicap they faced as a result of the dollar's strength vis-à-vis the yen. Moreover, American banks, securities firms, and money managers were clamoring for access to Japan's protected financial markets. Under heavy US pressure to shift away from its mercantilist practices, Tokyo agreed to a yen-dollar pact in 1984 that liberalized its financial system somewhat, and during the 1980s the percentage of Japanese exports denominated in yen rose from less than 30 percent at the beginning of the decade to nearly 40 percent by 1991.[12] The yen-dollar deal was followed in 1985 by the Plaza Accord, which explicitly called for the yen to rise against the greenback.

Although those agreements helped address US grievances, Japan's economic muscularity only grew more formidable than before. To counter the effects of *endaka* (yen appreciation) on exports, the Bank of Japan cut interest rates to historically low levels, which drove prices on the Tokyo Stock Exchange and property in major Japanese cities to stratospheric heights. Japanese multinationals adroitly coped with soaring costs at home by shifting much of their labor-intensive manufacturing overseas — to North America and Europe, where their customers were; and to East and Southeast Asia, where they could export their premium-branded goods from low-cost production bases. This process firmly entrenched Japan as the top trading partner and foreign investor for most of its Asian neighbors, giving Tokyo a degree of influence that Japanophobes found disconcerting. One oft-cited piece of evidence was how the 17,000 workers at Matsushita's Malaysian plants donned Matsushita uniforms and started their days with the company song and calisthenics, just as employees did at Matsushita's Osaka headquarters. "Japan has established a presence in the region so rapidly that talk of a 'coprosperity sphere' is already a cliche," reported *Newsweek* in an August 1991 cover story, which was titled "Sayonara, America" and lamented that US companies were falling far behind amid an unprecedented burst of dynamism. "This year, for the first time since the Organization for Economic Cooperation and Development began keeping statistics, the Asian nations of Japan's yen bloc will generate more real economic growth than either the European Community or the combined economies of North America."[13]

That phrase – "yen bloc" – was widely bandied about, referring sometimes to a trade zone that Tokyo would presumably control but also to the prospect that the Japanese currency, liberated from the shackles of financial repression, would dominate Asia to America's detriment. The yen's share of reserves in East Asia topped 17 percent by 1990,[14] and the borrowing of yen surpassed the borrowing of dollars by those in Asia seeking foreign credit during this period. In 1995, in her *Foreign Affairs* article "The Fall of the Dollar Order" (mentioned in chapter 3), Yale diplomatic historian Diane Kunz foresaw grave consequences: "As the yen area solidifies and the yen becomes the common Pacific currency, Americans will need to sell dollars for yen to conduct business with any Asian nation," she wrote. "The death of the dollar order will drastically increase the price of the American dream while simultaneously shattering American global influence."[15] Later that year in another *Foreign Affairs* article, titled "Dominance through Technology: Is Japan Creating a Yen Bloc in Southeast Asia?," Price Waterhouse consultant Mark Taylor warned that "U.S. firms may soon find themselves excluded from a Japan-centered regional economic bloc."[16]

This ballyhoo about the yen was as poorly timed as the speculation about the euro's unbounded potential on the eve of the eurozone crisis. By the mid-1990s the Japanese economy was mired in deflation following the bursting of its stock and property bubble. Among the authorities' many desperate efforts to revitalize the economy was a "Big Bang" reform package in 1996 ending all remaining capital controls and including other steps aimed at turning Tokyo into a financial hub, much as London had done a decade earlier. But Japan could not overcome its legacy of financial repression. The nation's banks, accustomed to being cosseted by the Finance Ministry, were saddled with bubble-era loans that neither they nor their powerful regulators wanted to recognize as unpayable. Seeing the banking industry struggling to stay afloat, foreign financial firms downsized their Tokyo operations and headed for other, more vibrant centers of Asian finance such as Hong Kong, Singapore, and Shanghai.

Even after further liberalization policies were adopted in 1999, the yen remained a distant also-ran as an international currency. It accounted for 5.5 percent of foreign exchange reserves in 2001, declining by 2016 to around 3 percent, and played a modest part even in Japan's own trade, where it was used in only about 37 percent of Japanese exports and 26 percent of imports.[17] Although Japan enjoys enviable wealth, its growth has remained anemic, stunted by a rapidly aging society and dwindling population, so its gravitational pull has never again come close to that which it exuded during the 1980s. The Bank of Japan has bought such vast quantities of the government's bonds in its effort to stave off deflation that there has been very little trading in those bonds in recent years — yet another reason for the yen's relatively low ranking in the currency league tables.

Perhaps if Finance Ministry officials had taken the moral of Beryl Sprinkel's piglet story to heart and dismantled their controls much earlier, dollar users would have had strong motivation to shift to yen. But the opportunity was missed.

The SDR

Every workday, hundreds of economists hailing from dozens of countries arrive at the IMF's headquarters in downtown Washington, swiping their ID badges to pass through electronic security gates at the entrance before boarding elevators that whisk them to their offices. Most of them work on monitoring the economic conditions of nations or regions, or on rescue loans for countries in financial distress, or on economic research. But in one 12th-floor office is the unit responsible for overseeing one of the IMF's most esoteric functions —

creating, distributing and administering Special Drawing Rights (SDRs), the closest thing the world has to an international currency.

The office looks pretty much the same as others at the Fund, with a modern desk and small conference table made of light wood. There are no minting machines, no giant mainframe computers or other pieces of equipment that might be imagined as essential for an operation producing something akin to money. That's only natural, since the SDR's relationship to real money is tenuous and hard to comprehend. When I asked Olaf Unteroberdoerster, chief of the SDR Policy Division, how he tells friends and neighbors what he does, he chuckled and said, "It's not something I volunteer to talk about, but I do get the question. I've tried to explain it to my sister in Germany. It's not an easy subject."[18]

Many descriptions of the SDR emphasize what it's *not*. It isn't a currency that individuals or private companies can spend; it isn't something that can be used to buy goods and services. Nor is it a claim on the IMF, nor is it usable by central banks for intervening in foreign exchange markets or for financing imports.

As for what the SDR *is,* many of the definitions in the literature are bound to perplex the uninitiated. It's a "supplemental reserve asset," "a unit of account used by the IMF," "an IMF unit based on a basket of leading currencies," "a potential claim on the freely usable currencies of IMF members," "a composite accounting unit in which the IMF issues credit to its members," an instrument "used in balance of payments settlements among governments and in transactions with the IMF," and my personal favorite — "a composite digital pseudo-currency."

The theory underpinning the SDR, namely that the world would be better off if the main reserve currency were truly international rather than that of a single nation, is the same high-minded idea that inspired multilateralists like Keynes and Triffin when the Bretton Woods system was in its formative stages and early years. One obvious drawback to a single-nation reserve currency like the dollar is that developing countries are obliged to hold the securities of a wealthy country, which effectively means that the poor are lending on cheap terms to the rich. But a look back at the SDR's disappointing history helps illuminate why fantasies of an international currency remain exactly that.[19]

SDRs were first issued in the late 1960s, as a response to mounting doubts about the dollar's suitability for the task of anchoring the Bretton Woods system. World trade was expanding at a rapid clip, demand was on the rise for dollars to pay for the increased amount of international transactions, and to maintain the fixed exchange rates of their currencies against the dollar, countries needed more and more reserves — which meant they needed either dollars or gold (the only two assets that central banks could usefully hold as reserves at the time). But would the worldwide supply of dollars grow at an appropriate pace? As Triffin had warned, there was a potentially fatal dichotomy. If the United States failed to send enough dollars abroad — for example, if Americans didn't buy a sufficient amount of foreign goods — global commerce would be squeezed for lack of liquidity. Alternatively, if too many dollars were circulating, confidence in the currency's gold backing would ebb, leading eventually to the system's downfall. A solution, agreed in 1967 after much wrangling, was for the IMF to issue SDRs, which were popularly dubbed "paper gold," with each SDR valued at 1/35 troy ounce of gold (or $1), to all its member nations. The hope was that pressure on the dollar would ease as central bank coffers began to fill with SDRs.

Too little, too late — the first allocation was only 9.3 billion SDRs, and Nixon pulled the plug on the Bretton Woods system soon thereafter. Now that the dollar was no longer the official anchor of the international monetary system, the SDR was changed to a basket of major currencies, the value of which fluctuated depending on the exchange rates of its components — the greenback being the main one along with others including the yen, pound, French franc, and West German mark. (The euro replaced the franc and mark in 1999.) When the IMF allocated SDRs, it would dole them out to countries in rough proportion to their economic size, and the recipient countries were entitled to exchange them for any of the component currencies they wished. If, for example, Paraguay or Bangladesh wanted dollars, they could take their SDRs to the IMF and receive dollars in exchange.[20]

Amid the turbulent 1970s, all sorts of ideas percolated for how to use SDRs, and another allocation was approved at the end of the decade. But 30 years passed before the next accord for SDR issuance. One reason was that with widespread adoption of floating exchange rates, countries had less need for reserves to defend their exchange rates. Another major factor was US opposition. Although the IMF can create SDRs out of thin air, it can do so only after receiving approval from countries representing 85 percent of members' votes — which means the United States, with its 16.5 percent voting share, has veto power. American policymakers, especially in Congress, dislike the way that SDRs fall like manna from heaven on all IMF member countries including the likes of Iran, Syria, Venezuela, and Zimbabwe.

Only after the Global Financial Crisis did SDRs stage a comeback – a modest one. To alleviate strains on developing countries, many of which were undergoing panicky withdrawals of capital, the Obama administration led a move resulting in a 2009 agreement for the allocation of 161 billion SDRs, worth about $250 billion. More significant were calls by prominent figures for an overhaul of the international monetary system. As noted in the previous chapter, the reformers decried the role played by the dollar-centric system in causing or exacerbating the crisis; the American housing market, after all, would not have gotten as bubbly as it did without the low interest rates afforded by international holders of US securities. The plan mooted by Chinese central bank governor Zhou Xiaochuan was among the most ambitious, proposing that the SDR, "which is now only used between governments and international institutions, could become a widely accepted means of payment in international trade and financial transactions."[21]

In the speech outlining his scheme, Zhou acknowledged that implementation "may take a long time." That was putting it mildly. It deserved respectful consideration, a number of economists contended,[22] but making it work "presupposes deep and liquid markets" in SDRs and "a critical mass" of them, as Berkeley's Barry Eichengreen pointed out in a paper published a couple of months after Zhou's speech. That in turn would be complex and expensive for a "currency" that, in addition to being a composite of other currencies, lacked any private market whatsoever. Perhaps the IMF could serve as market middleman, buying and selling SDRs at sufficiently attractive prices to make large transactions as quick and seamless as they are in the market for US Treasuries, Eichengreen suggested – but how, he wondered, would countries agree on splitting the substantial cost of subsidizing such an operation? Assuming the United States would be unenthusiastic, would China foot the bill by itself? Numerous other practical obstacles were cited.[23]

Unteroberdoerster and his colleagues are by no means idle. Every morning, the SDR must be revalued according to the exchange rates of its component currencies, which expanded to include the Chinese renminbi in 2015. When countries wish to exchange their SDRs for one of those currencies, the SDR Policy Division handles the transaction. And when member countries approve a big SDR allocation, as they did in 2021 to help the developing world cope with the Covid-19 pandemic, the division's staff transmits messages to central banks and finance ministries around the globe conveying word about the amounts credited to each nation's SDR account.

But their work is a far cry from Keynes's vision for the "bancor," and it should come as no surprise that the SDR, which has accounted for a minor percentage of world reserves in recent years, remains a pale imitation of the dollar.

The Renminbi

Foreigners who spent time in China in the early 1990s, as I did, were obliged to use a peculiar kind of money called Foreign Exchange Certificates (FEC), which had some Chinese printed on them but also lots of English, including the following: "This certificate can only be used within China at designated places." FEC came in various denominations, the highest—bearing an engraving of the Great Wall—being 100 yuan. (Although Chinese currency is called the renminbi, which means "the People's money," the unit of account is the yuan.) The good news was that, after exchanging my US dollars or Japanese yen for FEC, I could use FEC at high-class hotels and restaurants and at "Friendship Stores," which were off-limits to Chinese and were virtually the only purveyors of luxury goods from abroad such as wine, chocolate bars, peanut butter, and Western-style toiletries and cosmetics. The bad news was that I couldn't legally hold ordinary renminbi; although the law wasn't rigorously enforced I was warned that I would risk unpleasant consequences if caught with renminbi in my wallet. One major reason for the system was to limit the types of establishments foreigners could frequent and places where they could travel, so it was a relief when Beijing phased out FEC in 1994. But FEC merit remembering. They serve as a potent reminder of China's long-standing penchant for using its monetary and financial system as a tool of economic, social, and political control—a policy approach hardly conducive to the renminbi's international appeal.

In those days central planning still permeated many facets of the Chinese economy,[24] notably state-owned enterprises, a classic example being the No. 1 Auto Plant, which I visited in 1993. Built in the northeastern city of Changchun during the 1930s, the factory employed 100,000 people who assembled Liberation trucks, Red Flag limousines, and other vehicles, wielding wrenches and blowtorches as they bolted engines and doors into place – more like a scene from Charlie Chaplin's 1936 comedy *Modern Times* than like automated plants I had seen in Japan and the United States. The sprawling grounds encompassed a cradle-to-grave social welfare system, called the "iron rice bowl," for workers and families, including tens of thousands of apartments and dormitories, a hospital, 22 elementary and secondary schools, dozens of stores, and a theater. Protected from foreign competition by steep tariffs, the plant was heavily subsidized thanks in no small part to a continual flow of credit from state-run banks, which obediently dispensed loans according to official directives issued by state planners. This was a form of financial repression that went far beyond the version practiced in Japan.

Drastic change came a few years later when reformers led by Premier Zhu Rongji privatized many such enterprises and dismantled much of the state's apparatus for intervention, culminating in China's entry into the World Trade Organization in 2001 under market-opening terms largely dictated by US trade negotiators. But even as exports and imports soared and Chinese manufacturers were exposed to the rigors of global competition, Beijing kept a relatively tight rein over its financial sector. Foreign capital was welcome if it came in the form of direct investment – that is, the building of plants and equipment or other commercial facilities. Not so, however, for speculative purchases of securities that might be dumped, or bank loans that might be called, at the first sign of trouble. Having seen the crises that struck Thailand, Indonesia, South Korea, and other neighboring countries in the late 1990s, China's rulers structured their financial regulations to maintain stability by banning inflows of short-term capital and strongly discouraging domestic firms from borrowing from foreign banks. In 2002, the government allowed foreign financial institutions to purchase securities in Chinese firms that had previously been available only for domestic investors, but the scheme involved strict licensing requirements aimed at selecting institutions with long-term investing horizons. At the same time, as noted in the previous chapter, the renminbi's exchange rate was kept fixed against the US dollar at a low level, which gave a huge boost to Chinese exports.

Financial repression continued, albeit in modified form. In 2003, banks came under the purview of a government agency, Central Huijin Investment Ltd., that held majority shareholdings in four giant banks – the Bank of China, the Industrial and Commercial Bank of China, the China Construction Bank, and the Agricultural Bank of China – along with a number of smaller financial institutions. These banks were listed on major stock exchanges, operated branches worldwide, vied with one another for profitable lending business, and were under pressure to generate high returns. But their control by Central Huijin provided the means for the state to direct their loans for national policy purposes when it chose to do so.[25]

Although this arrangement was not nearly as *dirigiste* as the post-Mao period when banker-bureaucrats mindlessly shoveled subsidies to state-owned enterprises on orders from above, it was also a far cry from a pure free market. Government-set interest rates virtually guaranteed that the banks could earn comfortable spreads on their loans, and bankers knew that lending to government-backed, state-owned enterprises or projects favored by the Communist Party was a relatively risk-free proposition. Top bank chieftains owed their jobs to the party and often held party leadership positions, further cementing ties to the Beijing hierarchy. Underpinning the arrangement was the nation's banking law, which states: "Commercial banks shall conduct their business of lending in accordance with the needs of the national economic and social development and under the guidance of the industrial policies of the State."[26]

The Global Financial Crisis took China's currency policy in new directions, reflecting deepening concern over the dollar-centric system. Seeing no progress for Zhou's proposal to replace the dollar with the SDR, Beijing began elevating the renminbi's international role – tentatively at first, then with increasing boldness. In 2009, a pilot program was launched to allow renminbi to be used for settlement of transactions between firms in mainland China and their customers and suppliers abroad. Initially covering five mainland cities together with Hong Kong, Macao, and Southeast Asia, this program was expanded to all Chinese enterprises in 2012. To give overseas users of renminbi attractive investing opportunities for their Chinese currency, China expanded a program for corporations to issue renminbi-denominated bonds in Hong Kong – "dim sum bonds," they were called, a landmark issue being the McDonald's August 2010 bond of 200 million yuan yielding 3 percent per annum over three years. A host of other measures followed, liberalizing both inflows and outflows – not fully by any means, but much more so than before. Centers for settling renminbi transactions were set up as far away as London and Frankfurt; the People's Bank of China negotiated currency swap arrangements with dozens of central banks around the world; the renminbi's exchange rate, though still carefully managed, was allowed to gradually appreciate, by 25 percent against the dollar from 2005 to 2015.[27]

These steps, combined with the dazzling advance of China's economic juggernaut – Chinese GDP quadrupled in the first decade of the twenty-first century, becoming the world's second largest in 2010 – inspired some excited commentary about the renminbi's prospects.

"We could be on the verge of a financial revolution of truly epic proportions," Qu Hongbin, the chief China economist at HSBC, declared in the *Financial Times* on November 11, 2010. "Given China's economic and trade power . . . it will become increasingly natural for the renminbi to be seen as a reserve currency. The world is slowly, but surely, moving from greenbacks to redbacks."[28] The following year, in a book titled *Eclipse: Living in the Shadow of China's Economic Dominance,* the economist Arvind Subramanian wrote: "The renminbi could surpass the dollar as the premier reserve currency well before the middle of the next decade."[29] Fueling such speculation was a narrow brush with default by the US government in 2011 amid brinkmanship between the White House and Republicans in Congress over raising the limit on federal debt.

In 2015, the renminbi's international profile rose even further when the IMF approved its inclusion in the basket of currencies comprising the SDR. The Fund had rejected the idea in 2010 on the grounds that the renminbi was not a "freely usable" currency of the sort that developing countries might wish to receive in exchange for SDRs. But in years thereafter China's influence and assertiveness on the global economic stage reached dimensions that IMF managing director Christine Lagarde and her colleagues could hardly ignore. Bestowing the prestige of inclusion in the SDR basket was more symbolic than substantive, and when

Chinese financial regulators committed to additional easing of restrictions on cross-border flows and lifting caps on interest rates for bank deposits, the IMF staff issued a paper in August 2015 assessing the renminbi's internationalization in favorable terms.[30] With Beijing making clear in public statements that a negative decision by the IMF's executive board would constitute a grievous insult, the board formally voted on November 30 to add the Chinese currency to the exalted list, as follows: the renminbi's share of the revamped SDR basket would be 10.92 percent, lower than the dollar's 41.73 percent and the euro's 30.93 percent, but higher than the yen's 8.33 percent and the pound's 8.09 percent.[31]

Even as Beijing was celebrating this milestone, however, developments in Chinese financial markets cast a harsh new light on the renminbi's attraction outside the nation's borders.

Share prices on the Shanghai and Shenzhen stock exchanges, which had risen vertiginously earlier in 2015, plunged in mid-summer amid signs of an economic slowdown, and on August 11, when central bank officials announced a 1.9 percent devaluation of the renminbi together with a technical change in the foreign exchange regime, markets turned panicky. Fearful that China was going back to its old ways of cheapening the renminbi to boost exports, investors rushed to pull money out of the country, taking advantage of newfound freedoms to do so. The authorities responded heavy-handedly as stocks sank further, prodding large financial institutions such as pension funds and insurance companies to buy shares, banning short selling under threat of imprisonment, and arresting scores of people – including a journalist at a highly regarded business magazine – for "spreading rumors."[32] In an effort to stanch the withdrawal of funds from China the central bank spent vast sums, around $100 billion a month, from its reserve hoard of foreign currencies to buy renminbi, and by the end of October 2016 reserves had shrunk to about $3.1 trillion, the lowest level in five years. When the renminbi-buying proved insufficient, regulators also clamped down hard on capital outflows in 2016 with a variety of procedural controls.[33] Although the official response showed that the initial panic was unjustified – the central bank was propping up the renminbi, not seeking a depreciation – the damage was done.

For all of China's glitzy financial infrastructure, the episode underscored how far the country's markets remained from true transparency with minimal government interference. And investors had new reason to worry that they might not be able to get their money out in periods of turmoil. In the aftermath, international use of the renminbi stalled and even went into reverse. The currency's share of cross-border payments peaked at 2.8 percent in August 2015 – an impressive figure, given that the program for renminbi use in trade settlement had started only in 2009 – but it declined to 1.8 percent in April 2016 and continued to hover around that level for some years thereafter.[34] Even in China's trade with regional neighbors such as Japan, South Korea, Thailand, and Indonesia, the renminbi was used in only a tiny fraction of exports and imports, ranging between 0.5 percent and 3.3 percent, in 2020.[35] The market for dim sum bonds shrank in 2016 and 2017, then ossified.

But the reasons for the renminbi's lack of international appeal go far beyond the 2015–2016 episode.

A much more important explanatory factor is the trend toward greater authoritarianism that has accelerated since Xi Jinping took China's helm in 2012 as general secretary of the Communist Party. More than at almost any time since the end of the Mao Zedong era, activists and dissidents are subject to intolerance and intimidation. Under Xi, state control over the economy has intensified, with far more ambitious goals and levers aimed at fostering national self-sufficiency in critical sectors such as new energy vehicles, biomedicine, and robotics.

Above all is an erosion of rule of law, which undercuts investors' confidence that property rights will be protected, contracts enforced, and impartial judgments rendered if their assets are subject to dispute.[36]

A decade or so prior to Xi's rise, during the years following entry into the WTO, China appeared to be reforming its legal order in ways that instilled rule of law, as it shed vestiges of Maoism and overhauled legal codes and regulations to conform with the obligations of the Geneva-based trade body. Regulators enforced rules under more transparent procedures, for example, and the judiciary – once full of retired military officers with no legal training – turned toward greater professionalism. But then came a "socialist rule of law" campaign emphasizing Communist Party doctrine and subordination of written law to the interest of social stability. Hopes for a significant judicial check on the party-state were further dashed in 2015 by a statement on the official website of the Supreme People's Court under the name of Chief Justice Zhou Qiang. "All courts shall use the spirit of Xi Jinping's series of major speeches to arm their minds, guide their practice, [and] foster their work," the statement said, adding that courts should "foster the creation of teams that are loyal to the Party, loyal to the State, loyal to the People, loyal to the Law." Even blunter was Zhou's 2018 statement, in a speech to jurists in Beijing, that "China's courts must firmly resist the Western idea of judicial independence and other ideologies that threaten the [Party's] leadership, including the separation of powers." Xi himself made similar comments in a 2018 speech.[37]

The tumultuous events of 2015–2016 came when China's fintech revolution was just getting underway, as was its establishment of the Cross-Border Interbank Payment System (CIPS), which is often depicted as a potential rival to CHIPS and SWIFT. These developments, cited in many recent discussions of the renminbi's potential, shall be examined in later chapters. But a book about the renminbi published in 2017, titled *Gaining Currency,* offers an assessment of its prospects that has held up well so far. The author, Eswar Prasad, former head of the IMF's China division, concludes: "Although it is likely to continue its ascent, the notion that the renminbi will become a dominant global reserve currency that rivals the dollar is far-fetched."[38]

To recap this chapter and the previous one: the economic history of the past half century is replete with events and developments that called the dollar's hegemony into serious question yet left its status essentially unaltered. These include the end of the Bretton Woods system, the inflation of the 1970s and '80s, the swelling of US trade deficits, the rise of Japan, the launch of the euro, the Global Financial Crisis, and the rise of China. At each juncture, forecasts of the greenback's demise turned out to be wrong, sometimes because of the weaknesses of challenger currencies, other times because of the dollar system's surprising resilience. Following the reversals that hit the renminbi in 2015–2016, the US currency appeared more indomitable than ever.

What good did this do for Americans? Economically, not much, as observed in a 2016 blog post by former Fed chairman Ben Bernanke, who was then a scholar at the Brookings Institution.[39] "The benefits of the dollar's status to the United States have been much reduced in recent decades," Bernanke wrote, drawing a contrast with the mid-1960s when French officials were complaining about exorbitant privilege. "In particular, the interest rates that the U.S. pays on safe assets, such as government debt, are generally no lower (and are currently higher) than those paid by other creditworthy industrial countries." As evidence, a chart on his post showed that inflation-adjusted interest rates paid by the governments of Canada, Germany, Japan, and Britain were all lower than that paid by the US Treasury.

Bernanke continued:

A great deal of U.S. currency is held abroad, which amounts to an interest-free loan to the United States. However, the interest savings are probably on the order of $20 billion a year, a small fraction of a percent of U.S. GDP, and that "seigniorage," as it is called, would probably still exist even if the dollar lost ground to other currencies in . . . international transactions. U.S. firms may face slightly less exchange-rate risk in international transactions, but that benefit should not be overstated since the dollar floats against the currencies of most of our largest trading partners. The safe haven aspect of the dollar is actually a negative for U.S. firms, since it implies that they become less competitive (the dollar is stronger) at precisely the times that global economic conditions are most difficult.

Overall, the fact that English is the common language of international business and politics is of considerably more benefit to the United States than is the global role of the dollar. The exorbitant privilege is not so exorbitant anymore.[40]

Bernanke was right in 2016, and his argument remains just as valid today. But in pooh-poohing the dollar's benefits, he was focusing to a narrow degree on his field of expertise, namely economics. In the realm of foreign policy, the dollar's status was conferring enormous advantages on Washington, and those advantages would be exploited to an even greater degree as new presidents came to power.

CHAPTER 5

WEAPONIZATION

For European leaders, the term that Donald Trump served as US president from 2017 to 2021 was a never-ending ordeal of bellicosity, insults, and maltreatment. But nothing Trump did infuriated the Europeans more than the intimidation that he subjected them to in mid-2018, using the dollar as a bludgeon.

At issue was Iran. Trump was determined to nullify a 2015 agreement between the Islamic Republic and the West under which Tehran promised to scale back its nuclear power program. Scornful of the Obama administration, which had taken the lead in negotiating the accord, Trump announced on May 8, 2018, that the United States would withdraw from what he called "a horrible one-sided deal." International sanctions aimed at crippling the Iranian economy would be reimposed, the White House said.[1]

The European Union declared its intention to part company with Washington on this matter. EU officials asserted that the 2015 pact, which they had helped negotiate, was working well, and that Iran was abiding by the terms, easing fears about its attainment of nuclear weapons. Therefore, they said, economic ties between Europe and Iran would remain intact, regardless of what the United States was doing.[2]

———

The Trump team responded, in effect: resistance is futile. Indeed it was, because resisters would risk being cut off from the dollar. To the humiliation of officials in European capitals, the continent's biggest multinational companies announced, one after another, that they were terminating business with Iran, in accord with Trump's demands. The Danish shipping giant Maersk, the French automaker Peugeot, the German conglomerate Siemens, and scores of others seeking to expand their Iranian operations stated grudgingly that they would sever those commercial links to avoid running afoul of US sanctions. Even though their own governments opposed Trump's approach and maintained laws supportive of continued trade with Iran, the European multinationals yielded to the threat of penalties too onerous to bear.[3]

The method Trump used to impose his will on Europe involved a form of dollar weaponization called secondary sanctions, which pack a punch far beyond the bounds of normal US legal jurisdiction. With secondary sanctions, foreigners are forced to make a choice — abide by Washington's sanctions, or say goodbye to the biggest and most lucrative market in the world. Whereas primary sanctions prohibit American firms and banks from doing business with a sanctions target, secondary sanctions require them to cease doing business with any financial institution or business that continues to transact with the target, no matter where in the world those transactions take place or what local laws apply. Thus any company outside the United States engaging in, say, purchases of Iranian oil or sales of machinery to North Korea may be subject to US sanctions — meaning it may be severed from the dollar-based financial system — and so may any bank providing it with loans or payment services. The dollar's centrality in international finance gives this measure great extraterritorial potency. As one Trump administration official explained in blunt terms at a September 2018 briefing for reporters about the Iran sanctions: "What we are saying is, if you decide to do business with an enemy of the United States of America, you will not be doing business with the United States. You will not have access to the US financial system. You will not be able to use the US dollar."[4] For good measure, Washington insisted that Iranian banks be disconnected from a central cog in the global payments infrastructure, the Belgium-based SWIFT, which succumbed to US pressure despite European objections.

Behold America's new, preferred way of waging war. The Pentagon directs the world's most formidable fighting force, bristling with stealth bombers, commando squads, laser-guided missiles, and aircraft carrier battle groups, but American leaders are increasingly loath to incur the sacrifice of blood and treasure entailed by military conflict. A much more politically palatable approach for achieving US foreign policy objectives is managed by the Treasury Department, which uses financial sanctions to punish, degrade, and coerce Washington's enemies — and, in some cases, to forcibly keep allies and neutral countries on its side. The cost and futility of "endless wars" in Iraq and Afghanistan spurred the White House and Congress to resort with dramatically greater frequency to financial sanctions in the second decade of the twenty-first century, as the data show: whereas the Treasury targeted only four foreign governments under sanctions programs at the start of the millennium, that number had risen to 22 by 2018.[5] Along with governments, sanctions targets include foreign individuals and companies, lists of which were growing by leaps and bounds at the time Trump took aim at Iran, with 600 additions in 2014, 500 in 2015, 600 in 2016, nearly 900 in 2017, and almost 1,200 in 2018.[6] In the years following the 2008 Global Financial Crisis, federal prosecutors helped turbo-charge the dollar's firepower by bringing numerous criminal cases against major foreign banks for violating US sanctions. Trump was a particularly pugnacious sanctions-wielder, but he merely accelerated and intensified an already-existing trend.

The difficulty of countering US financial sanctions was a source of immense frustration to the Europeans in 2018. EU officials tried all manner of maneuvers — some conciliatory toward the White House, others confrontational — to keep Trump's Iran policy from affecting their economic relations with the Islamic Republic. They requested that the US Treasury grant waivers from sanctions to European multinationals already doing business in Iran, on the grounds that such corporations should be allowed to continue operations under "grandfather clauses."[7] The Treasury showed scant inclination to approve such requests, so Brussels enacted a "blocking statute" prohibiting Europeans from complying with US sanctions and weighed a program providing monetary compensation to EU firms with Iran investments for the losses that sanctions would cost them.[8]

To no avail. Peugeot, which in 2017 had sold almost 440,000 vehicles in Iran – the company's second-largest market outside of France – said on June 4, 2018, that it would close down its joint ventures with Iranian carmakers.[9] Although Peugeot didn't sell cars in the United States (it stopped doing so in 1991), it raised considerable amounts of capital in US markets and wouldn't be able to do so if penalized by Trump administration sanctions. A similar explanation came from Total, the French oil super-major; it had a multibillion-dollar gas extraction deal with the Iranians which it would have to abandon because of the necessity of tapping US markets for funding.[10] Maersk said its tankers would stop taking assignments for Iranian oil shipments, Siemens followed by giving up on a locomotive order from Iran, and the same went for Airbus, British Petroleum, and Royal Dutch Shell, together with a host of medium-sized European banks with Iran links including Oberbank of Austria, Germany's DZ Bank, Italy's Banca Popolare di Sondrio, and France-based Wormser. Despite lacking direct exposure to the United States, those banks could not afford to lose access to dollars and pulled out from financing Iranian oil trades.[11]

Having failed to stop Trump's strong-arming on Iran, European politicians vowed to take more fundamental steps aimed at preventing repetitions in the future. In an op-ed published on August 21, 2018, in the daily *Handelsblatt*, German foreign minister Heiko Maas wrote: "It's essential that we strengthen European autonomy by establishing payment channels that are independent of the US,"[12] a view echoed a few days later by French finance minister Bruno Le Maire in a meeting with journalists. "With Germany, we are determined to work on an independent European or Franco-German financing tool which would allow us to avoid being the collateral victims of US extraterritorial sanctions," Le Maire said. "I want Europe to be a sovereign continent, not a vassal, and that means having totally independent financing instruments that do not today exist."[13] European Commission president Jean-Claude Juncker, addressing the European Parliament, bemoaned the fact that the dollar was so widely used for the continent's oil purchases and called for turning the euro into a global reserve currency that could rival the greenback, saying "the euro must become the active instrument of a new sovereign Europe."[14]

Understandable as the Europeans' teeth-gnashing may have been, it led to no substantive changes in international monetary arrangements. An institution dubbed the Instrument in Support of Trade Exchanges (INSTEX) was established in early 2019 with its own headquarters in Paris to facilitate the movement of non-dollar transactions between Europe and Iran. But to the chagrin of the officials who devised it, INSTEX didn't even complete its first transaction until March 2020 and was dismissed as useless by Iranians, who could clearly see that big European companies with US business interests wouldn't want to risk antagonizing Washington.[15]

How the dollar weapon developed, and how the United States honed it to the point that it could subdue even a huge economy like Europe, is chronicled in the next two chapters. It is a saga with some curious twists involving a handful of Treasury officials who, in the early 2000s, didn't fully comprehend the leverage they could exert over other countries until they actually exercised it, almost like youngsters experimenting with a chemistry set and exulting over the explosions they could ignite. Once they had a clear conception of the legal provisions and other tools at their disposal, they began deploying them to great effect, all the more so when Congress enacted legislation endowing them with additional powers and American prosecutors got into the act by using their authority to investigate and punish violators.

So potent an impact can it have, and so embittered a reaction does it evoke in targeted and threatened countries, that the weaponized dollar stirs unease about its potential excesses even among some US policymakers who have wielded it.

In 2016, his last year as Treasury secretary, Jacob Lew gave a speech expressing concern that America could come to rue the use of dollar-based sanctions "if alternatives to the United States as a center of financial activity, and to the U.S. dollar as the world's preeminent reserve currency, assume a larger role in the global financial system."[16] A couple of years later, in response to the Trump administration's hardline stance on Iran, Lew co-wrote an article in *Foreign Affairs* stating that the United States "largely gets its way because there is no alternative to the dollar. . . . But if Washington continues to force other nations to go along with policies that they consider both illegal and unwise, over the next 20 to 30 years, they are likely to shift away from the United States' economy and financial system."[17] John Kerry, who served with Lew in the cabinet as secretary of state, made the case more hyperbolically, warning that walking away from the Iran nuclear agreement would be "a recipe, very quickly . . . for the American dollar to cease to be the reserve currency of the world."[18]

Taking this line of reasoning to extremes, some observers envision a fate akin to karmic retribution befalling the United States. A book published in 2022 titled *Backfire: How Sanctions Reshape the World against U.S. Interests* warns that Washington had better temper its policies lest it get a taste of its own medicine when the euro or renminbi can be weaponized. "Such a shift will not happen, if it takes place at all, for several decades," writes author Agathe Demarais, a former French Treasury official, but "if American companies have to use currencies other than the U.S. dollar to conduct trade abroad, they will become exposed to the threat of extraterritorial or secondary sanctions from other major economic powers, such as the European Union or China. Given Europe and China's economic clout, such penalties would have a big, negative impact on American firms."[19]

Much more nuanced is the view taken by Daniel McDowell of Syracuse University in his book *Bucking the Buck,* which documents efforts by sanctions targets to de-dollarize. "If US reliance on sanctions continues to grow with the same level of intensity and frequency over the next twenty years, the number of anti-dollar states will continue to grow — especially if the United States employs financial sanctions unilaterally," McDowell writes. "While [the anti-dollar states] are unlikely to dislodge the dollar from pre-eminence, a less transformative outcome could still . . . chip away at the dollar's dominance in ways that limit the effectiveness of financial sanctions as a tool of statecraft."[20]

Indiscriminate use of dollar-based sanctions can undoubtedly redound against US interests for a host of reasons, including the one McDowell highlights. But predictions that it will lead to the US currency's downfall, or that the dollar weapon will be rendered totally impotent, or that similar weapons will be turned against US companies by countries using rival currencies, should be viewed with deep skepticism. To properly assess the weapon's firepower and durability, a detailed look at its history and inner workings is essential, starting with the operations of the global payments system — which brings us back to the subject of this book's first few pages, namely clearing and settlement in New York.

To recap a key point from those pages: CHIPS — the descendant of the New York Clearing House, founded in 1853 — clears and settles 95 percent of cross-border, dollar-denominated payments. As also explained in chapter 1, a very high percentage of the payments crossing borders are done in dollars. That makes CHIPS a "chokepoint" in the global economy, meaning that the government with legal jurisdiction over it can exercise power by limiting or excluding institutions that it wants to penalize.[21] (Some dollar payments from overseas get cleared on Fedwire, which is owned by the Federal Reserve System, but the majority go through CHIPS.) Not only does the US government hold legal jurisdiction over CHIPS, it also holds legal jurisdiction over the forty-plus megabanks that transact directly on CHIPS. Some of those banks are headquartered in the United States (such as Citibank, JPMorgan Chase, Bank of America, Bank of New York Mellon, and Wells Fargo), while others are headquartered abroad (for example, Banco do Brasil, Sumitomo Mitsui Banking Corp., Deutsche Bank, Standard Chartered Bank, State Bank of India, Bank of China, China Merchants Bank, and Société Générale) — but even the foreign CHIPS participants must be a US branch or subsidiary, with US banking licenses obliging them to comply with US law.[22] These banks are the main conduits for transnational money — or to be more precise, a subset of them are. Here's an eye-opening statistic cited in an authoritative book about payments, written by two former SWIFT executives, titled *The Pay Off*: "Payments are made to and from some 25,000 banks in over 200 countries, but almost every cross-border payment passes through one of just fifteen banks."[23]

For ordinary people, the system in which CHIPS operates is remote and arcane, every bit as much as earth-orbiting satellites that transmit signals and data around the globe. The payment infrastructure that most of us typically see consists of ATMs that dispense cash, point-of-sale terminals that record credit card numbers or scan account information from mobile phones, and monthly statements from banks and credit card companies. But that is merely the superficial, consumer-facing manifestation of a much vaster network of interbank connections. Internationally, this financial plumbing handles roughly a trillion dollars a day in cross-border transactions of various types. They include income payments (for example, businesses paying salaries to employees posted abroad), debt service (for instance, companies or governments paying interest or principal on borrowings from foreign lenders), and people-to-people remittances (the classic example being migrant workers sending money to families and friends in their native lands). By far the biggest amounts involve business-to-business payments, such as when a company in one country pays a supplier in another country for goods or services.

One of the most common misconceptions about this system is that money flows across international borders. It doesn't — unless we're talking about suitcases stuffed with cash. Appearances are deceiving; when you instruct your bank to wire a payment to a recipient overseas, the result can be seen from the decrease in your bank balance and the increase in the recipient's bank balance. But the money doesn't move, and that's more logical than it sounds — after all, it wouldn't do much good for someone in, say, South Africa to receive, say, Polish zloty. Rather, debits and credits reflecting the amount you're paying are recorded in the ledgers of your bank and your recipient's bank, and quite possibly a series of additional debits and credits at other banks will be required as well. If both you and your recipient have accounts at major global banks that deal with each other regularly in massive volumes, only a couple of debits and credits may be necessary, as the two banks can add or subtract the payment amount from their respective customers' balances and include that amount in calculations taken at a clearing house of how much each bank owes the other. But what if you and your recipient each use relatively small banks in your respective countries that don't interact directly? Then a longer series of steps will take place involving a system called correspondent banking. A correspondent bank holds deposits owned by other banks that it uses to provide payments on their behalf as well as other services required for international business such as foreign currency conversion. Most if not all of the CHIPS banks serve as correspondent banks.

Are intermediaries taking a cut of the action, in the form of fees, at each point along the way, including currency conversion? Sure they are; that's the main reason why cross-border payments are so widely reviled and why so many entrepreneurs are striving to create high-tech money transmission services that can better serve migrant workers and others who resent handing so much of their hard-earned cash to bankers. But it's important to bear in mind that many of the payments going through correspondent banking are of magnitudes far exceeding typical remittances by individuals — indeed, the amounts often total multiple millions of dollars per transaction — and one of the essential functions required for this system to work is liquidity, loads of it. The authors of *The Pay*

Off offer a homespun illustration involving a brother in the Netherlands who asks for a $100 payment to be made from his sibling's US bank account to someone in the United States; the brother promises to reimburse his sibling an equivalent amount in euros from a Dutch account. "I can easily accommodate my brother's $100 request, but if he were to ask me to pay $100,000 on his behalf, I'd tell him to take a hike; I wouldn't have nearly enough liquidity in my US account and, dear to me as he is, I am not going to store funds of that amount on the off-chance that he might want me to use them." The point, the authors continue, is that "large payments require significant liquidity from banks," and it's larger payments "that grease the wheels of international trade and finance."[24]

With all that as background, the role of CHIPS as a chokepoint – and the associated sanctioning power that Washington derives – can be readily comprehended. Any major bank, regardless of the country where it's based, needs to participate in the CHIPS-centered system or maintain a correspondent banking relationship with a participant bank; otherwise it can't process dollar transactions in any volume. For a bank, the possibility of being expelled or isolated from this system poses an existential threat. When US officials put a bank on a list of sanctions targets, they require other financial institutions to cease dealings with it, including correspondent banking, effectively destroying its capacity to conduct cross-border business and quite likely leading to its collapse. Therefore any company or individual targeted by sanctions will also encounter great difficulty conducting international transactions; few banks if any will dare serve such a customer.

To be clear, CHIPS doesn't screen transactions for prohibited activity. That's up to the banks themselves, the biggest of which spend billions of dollars annually on compliance departments staffed with thousands of people operating expensive hardware and software. The immense role played by the private sector, and the fact that it foots most of the bill, is one of the features of financial sanctions that makes the tool so appealing to Washington. It isn't just banks and other financial firms, either; a whole cottage industry has sprung up in the past few years that includes consultancies, law firms, software analyzers, and due-diligence investigators to provide advice on whether certain transactions might incite the wrath of US sanctions-enforcers.

"The private sector is the principal point of both the spear and shield – that is, it's the private sector's decisions that implement the government's financial regulations, and the private sector faces very harsh scrutiny when impermissible transactions are processed," Adam M. Smith, a partner at the law firm Gibson, Dunn & Crutcher and a Treasury official during the Obama administration, told me. "Most major companies will prefer to be over-compliant rather than risk being under-compliant."[25]

Another crucial point, Smith continued, is that the underlying statutes give the executive branch effectively unfettered power to impose restrictions or conditions on transactions and property under US jurisdiction. Take the International Emergency Economic Powers Act (IEEPA), enacted in 1977 and the principal statutory basis for US sanctions. To trigger IEEPA's immense authorities, which at the most extreme include freezing the assets of targets, "all the president has to do is to identify a 'national emergency,' " Smith said. "There's almost no jurisprudence (court rulings) on what a national emergency is, and certainly none that's particularly restrictive. All that exists in the case law so far is the opposite, frequently finding that the administration's power under IEEPA is uniquely broad."

The value of this uniquely American tool of foreign policy became evident only after a series of developments – notably a law-enforcement campaign against money laundering in the late twentieth century, and the response to the September 11, 2001, terrorist attacks. Examining how those events unfolded provides essential insight into the dollar weapon's effectiveness. The story begins with a look at how other forms of economic coercion were deployed during prior decades and centuries, with results that can charitably be described as mixed.

At a time when the dollar was just starting its rise to global supremacy, a US president with a temperament very different from Trump's envisioned the systematic use of national economic leverage in lieu of military force. Woodrow Wilson hoped not only that economic sanctions could spare the United States from sending troops abroad again as it had in 1917; he dreamt that such sanctions, applied multilaterally by the League of Nations, would enable all mankind to prevent war long into the future, an attractive proposition at a time when the world was still reeling from the Great War's carnage. The League's articles mandated that any country initiating aggressive war would be subject to an embargo – that is, a termination of trade and other commercial intercourse with foreign partners. Embargoes were the most common form of economic sanction that countries had wielded against adversaries throughout history – the first recorded user being Athens in 432 BC – and disasters often followed, as when Thomas Jefferson's Embargo Act of 1807 exacerbated tension with Great Britain while significantly damaging America's own economy. But the prospect of all League members joining in a collective embargo to totally isolate a target was such a "terrible remedy," as Wilson put it, that it would compel would-be invaders to try peaceful methods for resolving international disputes.[26]

Initial results were promising. Even though the United States rejected League membership, the League's sanctions threats in the 1920s helped deter small states – Yugoslavia and Greece – from sending their armies across their borders. But efforts to constrain big authoritarian powers in the following decade failed and ultimately backfired. The most disheartening example was a League embargo of Italy for its 1935 invasion of Ethiopia, which did not stop dictator Benito Mussolini from resorting to atrocities such as the use of mustard gas to defeat the Ethiopian resistance. The poor outcome of the Italian embargo is often attributed to the League's ineffectuality at enforcing its will, but in fact Italy suffered economic harm, including an estimated 61 percent decline in exports and 44 percent drop in imports, a 25 percent depreciation of the lira, and a shrinkage of 1.7 percent in Italian GDP. The embargo's shortcomings should be viewed from a broader perspective, as Cornell's Nicholas Mulder has shown in his magisterial history of this period, *The Economic Weapon*. Amid a Depression-era trend toward autarky – national self-sufficiency – countries that feared being the next sanctions targets, notably Germany and Japan, doubled down on efforts to insulate themselves from reliance on Western democracies, in part by seeking dominion over weaker neighboring countries, which only intensified the vicious circular forces propelling the world toward war. Thus arose the drive by resource-poor Japan, which was highly dependent on imports from the British Empire and the United States, toward establishment of a Greater East Asia Co-Prosperity Sphere that would ensure the supply of raw materials needed to fuel Japan's industrial and military machine. Angered by the viciousness of the Japanese military in China, President Franklin Roosevelt froze Japanese assets in the United States in late July 1941 and, together with

---

the British and Dutch, cut Japan off almost completely from foreign oil as well as other strategic necessities. Tokyo's response, driven in large part by desperation to secure control over the petroleum riches of the Dutch East Indies, was to attack Pearl Harbor along with Hong Kong, the Philippines, and Malaya.

The sanctions pattern that emerged in the 1930s — effectiveness at inflicting economic damage on target nations, but ineffectiveness at engendering desirable outcomes — was no anomaly. It would be repeated often during the second half of the twentieth century.

A total US embargo on Cuba following the 1959 revolution led by Fidel Castro deprived the island of a huge source of trade and tourism revenue but did not dislodge Castro from Havana. President Jimmy Carter froze Iranian assets in US banks after American diplomats were taken hostage in Tehran in 1979, and embargoed grain shipments to the Soviet Union in 1980 as punishment for Moscow's invasion of Afghanistan, but neither action achieved anything more than psychic satisfaction. The same was true in the late 1980s for Panama, whose leader, General Manuel Noriega, was indicted in US courts for drug smuggling. Panama was extraordinarily vulnerable because it used the dollar as legal tender, and when Washington prohibited all dollar transfers to Panamanian banks, the economy went into a tailspin as banks shut their doors and the authorities scrambled to devise a substitute currency. Yet Noriega clung to power and was overthrown only after President George H. W. Bush ordered US forces to invade in 1989.

Sanctions gained momentum in the 1990s nonetheless, for several reasons. First was a shining success — the dismantling of South Africa's apartheid regime after a decades-long embargo imposed by a broad coalition of countries. Whether sanctions deserved credit or not, the election of Nelson Mandela as South Africa's president in 1994 was hailed as illustrative of the good that could stem from concerted multilateral economic pressure.

Another key factor was the end of the Cold War and dawn of a unipolar era in geopolitics. With America's superpower unrivaled, and the problem of Soviet vetoes in the Security Council effectively eliminated, the UN — which had approved sanctions on only two targets in the previous four decades — voted a dozen times in the 1990s to slap comprehensive economic penalties on regimes that were challenging global norms. These included Iraq, for its invasion of

Kuwait; and Yugoslavia and Rwanda for human rights abuses. When Washington could not mobilize UN support to legitimize its measures, it took action unilaterally, much more often in the 1990s than previously. The most controversial by far was the 1996 Helms-Burton Act, named for the two Republican lawmakers who sponsored it, which authorized a form of secondary sanctions against foreign companies for doing business in Cuba. Outrage in Canada and Europe, where commerce and tourism with Cuba was viewed as normal, was defused only after the Clinton administration negotiated agreements that included promises by the White House to defer enforcement of the sanctions.

A backlash materialized. "Sanctioning Madness," the title of a 1997 *Foreign Affairs* article by Richard Haass, who was then director of foreign policy studies at the Brookings Institution, reflected a growing expert consensus.[27] In a series of influential books and articles, the economists Gary Hufbauer, Jeffrey Schott, and Kimberly Elliott highlighted the weaknesses of trade sanctions, including the likelihood that "black knights" could provide target countries with economic lifelines, as the Soviets did for Cuba.[28] By the late 1990s, sanctions were in considerable disrepute, accused of a host of sins. They often boomeranged by making targeted regimes, especially authoritarian ones, dig in even more fiercely and oppressively – the leading example being Saddam Hussein, who in the 1990s was entrenching himself in Baghdad notwithstanding a crushing UN embargo that was impoverishing millions of Iraqis.[29] Sanctions also inflicted collateral economic damage, sometimes on the United States itself, as in the case of Carter's grain embargo, which cost American farmers lots of money (and was shrugged off in Moscow). Overall, sanctions were seen as excessively blunt, spreading misery among ordinary civilians in the form of malnutrition and illness without altering the conduct of ruling elites or forcing regime change.

At the same time, the US government was ratcheting up financial pressure in more precise ways on one particular group of foreign enemies – drug traffickers and criminal syndicates. This would lead to more ambitious undertakings.

One of the most peculiar briefings I ever got as an economics reporter for the *Washington Post* came at a government building in a Virginia suburb where, in a setting a bit like a war room, I sat in front of a large screen and was asked by a

Treasury Department employee to name somebody I knew — a relative, a friend, any ordinary person — who lived in Florida. The Clinton administration, which was then in its final years, wanted to impress journalists like me with its rapidly growing capacity to crack down on money laundering, and this room was a showcase.

After struggling momentarily to think of Floridians I knew, I remembered my ex-mother-in-law, who had moved to a retirement community in Boca Raton. Her name soon popped up on the screen together with a remarkable set of her personal information — not only her address and phone number but the amount she had paid for her condo and the year she bought it, the amount of her mortgage and the bank where she obtained it, the model and year of her car and details about the loan she took out to buy it, her driver's license number, her date of birth, date of marriage, and many other tidbits. I was told that significantly more data about her could have been shown on the screen but that to protect her privacy it wouldn't be. The reason a Florida resident had been requested, the Treasury employee explained, was that the Sunshine State was ahead of most other states in compiling this kind of information, which was publicly available in various government offices, into centralized digital form. Other states were catching up, I was assured.

The building was the headquarters of the Financial Crimes Enforcement Network (FinCEN), a Treasury agency that collects and analyzes massive amounts of information about money flows in the United States in an effort to spot transactions by narcotics dealers and other malefactors. Whenever someone makes a purchase or bank deposit involving more than $10,000 in cash, for example, banks or other parties to the transaction are required to file a report with FinCEN and, if something fishy indicates that money laundering or tax evasion might be occurring, a "suspicious activity report" (SAR) gets filed. As my briefers explained, FinCEN checks its database for information about the individuals named in such reports to discern whether the transaction should be dismissed as presumably legitimate or whether it merits alerting federal, state, or local law enforcement that some further investigation might be worth pursuing. To my relief, my ex-mother-in-law had the sort of profile that, in FinCEN's eyes, would not raise any red flags, so any transactions involving her that were reported to FinCEN would almost certainly be discarded along with millions of others.

Spurring this high-level scrutiny was the expansion and intensification of the war on drugs. Dope kingpins need to give their riches the appearance of legitimacy, to avoid attracting attention from law enforcement and protect themselves against arrest for tax evasion. (Remember, it was a conviction for dodging taxes, not murdering rival gangsters, that brought down Al Capone.) A clever crook therefore launders dirty money to make it look clean – a classic example being taking bundles of cash to a casino, buying chips, and then cashing them in after pretending to strike it big at the roulette or blackjack tables, with the proceeds certified as gambling winnings before being deposited in a bank.

To combat such skullduggery, a formidable array of laws, regulations, agencies, and international organizations – each involving its own bureaucratese – was established in the latter decades of the twentieth century. Apologies to readers for the alphabet soup that follows; the acronyms will crop up, sometimes repeatedly, later in this book.[30]

The Bank Secrecy Act (BSA), signed into law by President Nixon in 1970, marked the first big step in Washington's battle against financial crime. The BSA, which was later amended and expanded, requires banks and other financial institutions to monitor their clients by maintaining records of their transactions as well as their identities and other personal information, and file SARs when circumstances warrant. Even then, it wasn't until 1986 that the United States outlawed money laundering, the first country to do so – and federal authorities soon saw that they had better prod other nations to follow suit lest their crackdown be for naught, given the opportunities for laundering funds overseas. Washington therefore persuaded the G-7 major industrial countries to establish the Financial Action Task Force (FATF), which set up shop in Paris in 1989 and promulgated dozens of recommendations regarding laws and regulations that governments ought to adopt. Although a "soft law" body, meaning that it is neither based on a binding treaty nor endowed with formal enforcement authority, the FATF has gained enormous influence over the way banks operate worldwide. Its standards, and monitoring of countries' compliance with those standards, oblige banks to implement strict "know your customer" (KYC) rules for the purposes both of anti–money laundering (AML) and, after the September 2001 attacks, counter-financing of terrorism (CFT). This means banks must obtain information about each customer's identity, business, source of funds, and country of origin—insisting, in the process, on verifying documents—as the basis for a risk profile, with greater scrutiny expected for higher-risk customers. If a country is deemed by the FATF to be falling short, it may be put on a FATF "noncomplier" list, which leads banks elsewhere to treat that country's banks much more cautiously—processing transactions slowly, charging more for services such as correspondent banking to compensate for the additional cost, or, in extreme cases, terminating business altogether.

Both governments and banks have learned the hard way that treating FATF standards cavalierly can lead to costly repercussions.[31] In the early 2000s, a FATF blacklisting of Nauru caused foreign banks to virtually blockade the tiny Pacific island, resulting in a collapse of its financial system. About a decade later, the global bank HSBC took a huge financial and reputational hit when it was caught allowing funds from two drug cartels, including one from Mexico, to flow largely unimpeded through its network. Instead of subjecting Mexican accounts to the rigorous scrutiny that the FATF mandates for countries with high risk of money laundering, HSBC put those accounts in its lowest-risk category—an act of negligence for which it had to cough up a $1.25 billion fine to the US government. Thanks to cases such as these, banks press their governments to adopt FATF-compliant laws, regulations, and enforcement regimes.

To show it meant business, the Clinton administration stepped up enforcement of anti–money laundering laws in 1995, with operations centered in the Treasury's Office of Foreign Assets Control (OFAC), which has often been described as "the most powerful government agency that nobody's ever heard of."

OFAC targeted numerous individuals and companies, mostly in Latin America, that were involved in the drug trade, by labeling them "Specially Designated Nationals" (SDNs). Anyone named an SDN on *la lista Clinton* instantly became a sort of untouchable for banks everywhere, because American entities of all kinds—citizens, businesses, financial institutions—were prohibited from conducting any sort of commercial transaction with them.[32] This meant that even banks in Colombia, where big drug syndicates operated, would want to ensure that neither their clients nor anyone dealing with their clients included anyone on *la lista*, for fear of being named an SDN too, which would be tantamount to doom for most banks.

How effective is this legal and bureaucratic apparatus in preventing drug lords from laundering their ill-gotten gains? The answer, unquantifiable as it may be, is "pretty useless." Any gangster with a smart lawyer or accountant can find ways to circumvent the rules, for example by reducing cash bundles to under $10,000 or putting seemingly legitimate confederates in charge of bank accounts. Charge an artificially low price, or pay an artificially high price, for the sale of some merchandise, and presto! — money can be moved from one place to another, with the appearance of an above-board transaction. When reporters like me pressed Treasury officials about such concerns, the response was invariably that money launderers were being "disrupted," even if they weren't being thwarted, and at least some criminals would abandon their pursuits because of the extra cost involved.

But with the ascension of George W. Bush to the presidency came a team with a new, skeptical approach to the issue. In mid-2001, Treasury Secretary Paul O'Neill, who held government bureaucracies in low esteem, ordered a sweeping review of anti–money laundering policies to see whether their effectiveness was commensurate with the burden imposed on banks.[33] O'Neill had a fervent ally in Lawrence Lindsey, the head of Bush's National Economic Council, who had written a book while at the conservative American Enterprise Institute think tank calling federal money-laundering rules "the kind of blanket search that the writers of the Constitution sought to prohibit." Washington's crackdown on money laundering appeared headed for a major retreat.

It didn't take long for the Bush administration to abandon any such plans. The war on money-laundering drug traffickers would soon expand into war on a whole new category of bad guys.

Ten days after the September 11 attacks, with Washington, DC, still under heavy military patrol, John Taylor, the undersecretary of the Treasury for international affairs, walked with a top aide through a tunnel near the White House to OFAC's offices, located across Pennsylvania Avenue from the main Treasury building. The time had come for OFAC to train its sights on terrorists and their financial backers.[34]

Although it was a Saturday morning, Taylor and the OFAC staff were working feverishly that weekend to complete an action plan by Monday for a coordinated international initiative to freeze funds in accounts held by individuals and groups suspected of terrorist connections. Easygoing and cerebral, with a stocky build and thick gray hair, Taylor was arguably ill-suited for this task, having spent most of his career as a highly regarded academic making the case for free-market policies and minimal government intrusion in monetary and financial affairs. As he later wrote: "I knew little about disrupting the flow of funds; my whole approach to international finance was to *encourage* the flow of funds."[35] But he had no difficulty grasping how the deadly assault on the twin towers in New York had changed the world.

Among the many shocking revelations that had emerged regarding the hijackers' assault was the ease with which they had gotten money from Al Qaeda abroad to pay for their activities in the United States as they trained and plotted. All 19 of them had opened accounts in their own names at financial institutions such as Sun Trust and Bank of America, where they received wire transfers from accounts in Dubai and withdrew cash as needed to pay for lodging, meals, and flight lessons. Since the whole operation cost only around $500,000, they were able to avoid triggering SARs by limiting the amounts of individual transactions.

Taylor and his Treasury colleagues were therefore deputized to root out and incapacitate terrorist bank accounts with the same fervor as the US military and intelligence agencies were ordered to hunt down the network of 9/11 perpetrators and bring them to justice.[36] First, they would draw up a list of Al Qaeda operatives and supporters, and then President Bush would issue an executive order that would be sent electronically to thousands of US banks requiring them to scan all their accounts for any sign that their customers included any of those listed, with any such accounts to be immediately frozen and barred from transactions with "US persons." At the same time, numerous foreign governments that Taylor and other Treasury officials had contacted would receive the same list and order their banks to take similar action. On September 24, Bush held a news conference in the Rose Garden to announce his order, which named 27 individuals and organizations including an Islamic charity. "This morning, a major thrust of our war on terrorism began with the stroke of a pen," Bush declared. "Money is the lifeblood of terrorist operations. Today, we're asking the world to stop payment."[37]

Within weeks, the list of sanctions targets grew significantly and Washington enlisted the support of multilateral organizations, notably the UN Security Council, which approved a resolution requiring all countries to criminalize terrorist financing; and FATF, which issued eight recommendations specifying strict standards for the anti-terrorist laws and regulations governments should adopt and implement.

Perhaps most significant of all, the USA PATRIOT Act, signed into law by Bush on October 26, 2021, raised to new heights the idea of forcing the world's bankers into the fight being waged by governments.[38] It gave the Treasury extraordinary flexibility to designate foreign jurisdictions, institutions, and whole classes of transactions as "primary money laundering concerns" — a designation that, like SDN, can translate into financial isolation with a high risk of financial death. Much greater stringency was required of US banks to exercise due diligence when they opened new accounts or executed transactions across borders, to make sure they were not handling funds for terrorists and other designated entities. Crucially, the act strongly pressured foreign banks to follow suit, by threatening banks from "high-risk" jurisdictions with loss of access to correspondent accounts at US banks. Even banks in countries with long traditions of financial secrecy, such as Switzerland, Luxembourg, and Liechtenstein, had to join banks elsewhere in exponentially increasing the number of auditors and investigators on their staffs as well as the volume of reports submitted to government authorities about suspicious activity. Excuses about legal prohibitions concerning their knowledge of clients' affairs would no longer pass muster.

The more that Treasury officials exercised the authority conferred on them by the USA PATRIOT Act, the more they marveled at their clout in far-flung parts of the globe. "We could prompt banks to make decisions to cut off banking relationships, isolating rogues from the international financial system — and we could rely on the business decision making of the banks themselves to do the heavy lifting," wrote Juan Zarate, one of the department's key policymakers, in his revelatory book *Treasury's War,* published in 2013.[39]

Of particular potency was Section 311 of the Patriot Act, which provided the legal basis for a project Zarate spearheaded, named the "Bad Bank Initiative," aimed at pulverizing banks that continued to serve as nodes of illicit activity. "With Section 311, we would be able to identify bad banks and label them as 'primary money laundering' concerns," Zarate wrote. "In all cases, the secretary of the treasury called for the closure of all correspondent accounts, thereby cutting off access to the US financial system. Although we could only directly affect bank activities in the United States, the intended effect would be global. Even though most bad banks had few or marginal dealings in the United States, Section 311 would immediately make them radioactive to [other] banks worldwide. . . . No bank wanted to run the risk of being cut off from the US banking system."[40]

One paradox of this development was that terrorist financing involves a kind of reverse money laundering. A criminal holding the proceeds from drug sales wants to cleanse that loot, whereas the flow goes in the opposite direction when a seemingly upstanding group — a religious or humanitarian institution, for example — funnels "clean" funds to the likes of Al Qaeda. That didn't stop Zarate and his colleagues from using their new powers whenever they were convinced money was being transmitted for nefarious purposes antithetical to US interests — in some cases drug trafficking and money laundering, in other cases terrorist financing. Over three years, starting in 2003, they targeted banks in Syria, Lebanon, Cyprus, Burma, Latvia, and Belarus as "primary money laundering concerns." In one indication of the fear they could generate, their invocation of Section 311 against Ukraine as a "high-risk" jurisdiction spurred a panicked Ukrainian parliament to approve tighter money laundering laws within a month. US banks were not immune, a stunning case being that of Riggs Bank, an institution dating from the 1840s that, as the biggest in Washington, DC, billed itself as "the most important bank in the most important city in the world." In May 2004, the Treasury slapped a $25 million fine on Riggs for laxity in its handling of transactions for foreign embassies, a scandal that led to the demise of the Riggs name and the bank's sale to PNC of Pittsburgh.[41]

The full force of the Treasury's new tool had yet to become manifest. Moreover, for help in detecting illicit activity amid the welter of cross-border money movements, the department was secretly obtaining information from a source with a unique trove.

Nestled on a lakeside near a nineteenth-century chateau in La Hulpe, Belgium, is the headquarters of SWIFT, an organization that might be called the switchboard of global finance. Notwithstanding the manicured lawn, tennis court, and surrounding forest where deer and pheasants roam, security is tight in this neo-classical building; most of the complex is off-limits to visitors and entry to some areas is accessible only through code-operated doors. Such safeguards protect both the physical and cyber integrity of a network through which more than 11,000 banks in more than 200 countries send and receive messages — about 45 million of them a day on average, in 2022 — almost every time they transmit international payments or engage in cross-border transactions involving securities, foreign exchange, letters of credit, and financing of imports and exports. Similar measures, including high fences and gates manned by security guards, keep prying eyes from SWIFT's main data centers, one of which is next to a Heineken plant in the Netherlands and the other of which is in Culpeper, Virginia.[42]

As anyone familiar with "SWIFT codes" may surmise, these strings of 8 to 11 characters identify sending and recipient banks when international payments are made. This doesn't mean that SWIFT holds or moves money itself; it is neither a bank nor a clearing and settlement institution. But the messages it transmits are essential to ensuring that international transactions can take place with everyone involved confident about the identity of the various counterparties and the validity of debit and credit instructions. In oversimplified terms, a typical message might say: "We hereby authorize you to pay 10,000 euros to the ABC Corporation and fund this transaction by debiting our bank's account at the XYZ Correspondent Bank while crediting an equal amount to your account." All this is conveyed using standardized codes and formats that minimize translation costs and confirm identities.

Until the mid-1970s when SWIFT was established, a bank wiring money overseas had to send several lines of instructions typed on telex machines to the recipient institution, a process prone to human error and mechanical snafus. Years of brainstorming among payment experts from major banks about how to create a private communications network led in 1973 to an accord among 239 banks from 15 countries for the formation of a cooperative society under Belgian law. After further development work, Prince (later King) Albert of Belgium sent the first SWIFT message on May 9, 1977.

The specificity of information in each SWIFT message — who the account holders are, their banks, the amounts transferred, dates and times of the transfer, and sometimes critical identifying data such as passport numbers — was alluring to US and international law enforcement as their campaign to foil money laundering gained momentum. In the early 1990s, top officials from the US Justice Department and FATF approached SWIFT with proposals for changes in its system that would facilitate investigations by enabling prosecutors to subpoena messages and obtain evidence about who was receiving money from where. The idea appalled SWIFT's CEO, Leonard "Lenny" Schrank, an American, who has recalled deeming it "unthinkable" that his institution, a private organization whose members were subject to a variety of privacy and data protection regulations, would hand over confidential material that banks had entrusted it with. The law enforcers went away empty-handed, having been told that SWIFT couldn't disclose the content of its messages; such information could only be extracted from individual banks.[43]

Then, a few weeks after the September 11 attacks, Treasury officials summoned Schrank to Washington. According to Zarate's recounting of the episode, General Counsel David Aufhauser "brazenly opened the meeting with a declaration: 'I want your data.' Without a pause, Schrank responded, 'What took you so long?' "[44]

By no means was Schrank giving US officials carte blanche to rifle through SWIFT traffic. He emphasized that SWIFT needed to maintain a neutral, apolitical stance lest its role as a crucial piece of the financial system's plumbing be threatened. Moreover, if the public learned about SWIFT's furnishing of confidential data, an uproar would ensue, especially in Europe where sensitivity about privacy is higher than elsewhere. Aufhauser retorted that the Treasury could issue subpoenas, and although SWIFT could challenge them in court, "I don't think this is a fight you can win. More importantly, it's a fight you don't want to win."[45]

After an initial SWIFT refusal, a compromise emerged, spelled out in a memorandum of understanding: SWIFT would respond to Treasury subpoenas, but only if they were aimed at specific data concerning transactions in which the Treasury had reason to believe a party was involved with terrorism. By the end of October 2001, information from SWIFT started to flow back to Washington, and it continued thereafter, with Aufhauser usually limiting subpoenas to one per month, each involving several data requests. Analysts at a CIA facility pored over the SWIFT material in pursuit of leads that might result in captures, with independent auditors overseeing the program to ensure the proper handling of data and restriction of queries to legitimate terrorism-related probes.[46]

Rising anxieties on the SWIFT board led the company to suspend the transmission of information in the spring of 2003. Jaap Kamp, a Dutch banker who chaired the board, flew to Washington along with Schrank to insist that the program had gone on too long. They heard pleas from top US officials including FBI director Robert Mueller that the financial data furnished by SWIFT was of great value in disrupting terrorists and saving lives,[47] and Aufhauser flew to Belgium armed with top-secret information about five such cases. "[Board] members sat there stunned and silent," according to Zarate, while "Schrank [and others] were clearly convinced — and relieved that their earlier decision to cooperate was justified."[48] The program resumed with an agreement that SWIFT employees, informally called "scrutineers," could sit next to the CIA analysts and object whenever they spotted some use of the data that went too far.[49]

The arrangement was kept under wraps for several years, despite a number of tense confrontations as more officials from Europe and elsewhere were briefed about the details and expressed consternation about what they had heard. Finally, the firestorm that Schrank had feared erupted in late June 2006 when the *New York Times* and other news organizations exposed the program, dismissing pleas from the White House that the revelation would only help terrorists and that the procedures agreed to with SWIFT protected the private data of ordinary citizens.[50]

Bush administration officials were furious over what they viewed as a breach of national security that deprived them of valuable intelligence. But the Treasury had not been relying entirely on SWIFT for information. Recognizing that it should no longer be a "passive consumer" of intelligence from the CIA and other spy agencies, the department got approval from Congress in 2004 to establish a new unit, the Office of Intelligence and Analysis, to be headed by an assistant secretary. This would make the Treasury unique among the world's finance ministries in having its own active intelligence-analyzing capability.[51]

Good intel would be all the more critical as US dollar weaponization was deployed against bigger and more sophisticated targets. An audacious escalation would come in 2005 — this time against not just a bank or coterie of evildoers, but a full-fledged governing regime.

CHAPTER 6

"OPEN AN ACCOUNT ON THE MOON—
WE CAN GO AFTER THAT"

"Supernotes" — counterfeit $100 bills of nearly flawless quality, printed with the same type of optically variable ink and high-tech presses used by the US Bureau of Engraving and Printing, on paper with almost identical fiber composition as genuine currency — were the topic of a classified briefing given in the spring of 2002 to a group of national security officials. The briefers were from the Secret Service, which has responsibility for protecting the dollar against counterfeiting. They didn't believe supernotes were being produced in anything close to sufficient quantities to threaten US economic welfare, but the jaw-dropping information conveyed at the briefing was evidence that the counterfeiters were no mere crooks but agents of the Democratic People's Republic of Korea (DPRK), as North Korea is officially known.

"We learned that since the late 1980s, North Korea had become the world's best counterfeiter of 100 dollar bills," David Asher, who was then a senior adviser for East Asian and Pacific affairs in the State Department, recalled some years later in a think-tank report. "We even saw surveillance photographs of members of the ruling elite passing the notes themselves in banks and casinos — a clear implication of their knowledgeable involvement."[1]

Counterfeiting was just one of many criminal activities that North Korea was engaging in, directly or indirectly through its proxies, according to research conducted by Asher and a handful of government colleagues charged with analyzing Pyongyang's methods of earning revenue from abroad. Evidence furnished by defectors from North Korea, supplemented by law enforcement and intelligence data, pointed to the regime's involvement in the dealing of illegal drugs — heroin, cocaine, methamphetamines — as well as weapons, counterfeit cigarettes, and even counterfeit Viagra. The money being reaped was far from adequate to boost the miserable living standards of ordinary North Koreans, but it evidently helped to finance the purchase of luxuries for elites who controlled the military and state security apparatus, thereby serving to entrench the rule of supreme leader Kim Jong Il.[2] Independent analysts were similarly concluding that North Korea had become a "Sopranos state," the term used by political scientist Sheena Chestnut in well-documented research.[3]

A Sopranos state would be the ideal testing ground for the Treasury's financial warriors to try out their new weaponry, especially since little else seemed to be working.

Ever since the 1953 armistice ending the Korean War, the United States had spared little in its efforts to squeeze the totalitarians in Pyongyang, a policy that continued as the Korean peninsula remained a post–Cold War flashpoint. For Americans, severe restrictions barred most dealings with North Korean companies and travel to the country, whose rulers took a mutually hostile stance toward interactions with most foreigners. Those measures had contributed to North Korea's overall destitution, especially during the 1990s after the collapse of the Soviet Union, but not sufficiently to keep the country from making alarming progress toward arming itself with nuclear weapons. Although the US military had the capacity to destroy North Korea's nuclear facilities, that option was all but ruled out because of the prospect that a retaliatory strike by the North would decimate Seoul, home to nearly ten million South Koreans. In the mid-1990s, the Clinton administration therefore resorted to negotiations by offering quid pro quos, defusing a tense confrontation with a deal: Pyongyang agreed to freeze the construction of nuclear reactors suspected of covert weapons development; in exchange, Washington agreed to provide the North Koreans with desperately needed energy generation supplies.

——

126

But crisis flared anew in late 2002 with revelations of intelligence showing that North Korea had embarked on clandestine efforts to produce highly enriched, weapons-grade uranium, in violation of previous international commitments. Even China, Pyongyang's longtime ally, was anxious enough about the prospect of a nuclear-armed North Korea to join in "Six Party Talks" starting in 2003 that along with North Korea included the United States, Russia, Japan, and South Korea. Slow progress in those talks exasperated the Bush administration, which had labeled North Korea part of the "axis of evil" along with Iraq and Iran.

How could Washington exert leverage over Pyongyang? Conventional trade sanctions and other forms of economic isolation appeared futile. US–North Korean trade was so negligible that there was nothing worth blocking, and the North Koreans could depend on their Chinese friends for enough commercial interaction to keep their economy afloat. But Treasury officials had ideas, based on their experience fighting "bad banks."[4] They had support from Asher, who had moved from the State Department to the National Security Council. Their problem was bringing others along.

"I was going to all these inter-agency meetings, and I can't tell you how many times I would say, 'We have this section 311 that we can use,' " Daniel Glaser, who was then Zarate's deputy at the Treasury, told me. "Practically every time I would show up, I would have to start over, because people would say, 'What's 311? Can you explain that again?' Nobody had heard of 311."[5]

After months of debate the Treasury finally got the go-ahead from the White House to unleash its new weapon — with galvanic results.

The direct target, a bank called Banco Delta Asia (BDA), was the epitome of financial obscurity. Most of its nine branches were located in Macao, a gambling enclave on China's southeast coast that was once a Portuguese colony. Family run, based in a building next to a centuries-old Jesuit mission, it had just 30,000 customers and less than $400 million in deposits.[6] But Treasury analysts had surmised based on months of scrutiny that it was one of several banks in the region that were in various ways facilitating North Korea's black-market enterprises, and its very smallness made it better for targeting than bigger banks with tighter links to the Chinese government, which if targeted might trigger diplomatic ructions.

In a press release issued on September 15, 2005, the Treasury said it was designating BDA as "a primary money laundering concern" under Section 311, declaring that the bank "has been a willing pawn for the North Korean government to engage in corrupt financial activities. . . . By invoking our USA PATRIOT Act authorities, we are working to protect U.S. financial institutions while warning the global community of the illicit financial threat posed by Banco Delta Asia."[7]

Within six days, panicked BDA customers withdrew $133 million in deposits — one-third of the total — and the Macao authorities took control of the bank, freezing $25 million in accounts related to North Korea. Much more stunning was the response of banks all over Asia, which moved swiftly to terminate all business with North Korean connections, legitimate or not, lest they become the next Treasury target. Even Chinese banks joined in shedding any remotely incriminating ties to Pyongyang; the Bank of China's branch in Macao, for example, froze all of its North Korean accounts. Whatever desire Beijing may have had to prop up the Kim Jong Il regime, it was overridden by the banks' fear of losing access to the dollar-based system in New York.[8]

The mere issuance of a notification tainting a small bank in Macao, in other words, resulted in pariah status for North Korea throughout the global financial system. "This was the moment of awakening to the power of the Treasury Department," Zarate wrote years later. "This was the coming-of-age of a new era of financial pressure and warfare."[9] Although Zarate maintains that he wasn't surprised, Glaser told me: "Nobody was more confident about our ability than I was, and even I was taken aback at how impactful it was."[10]

BDA officials denied that the bank was complicit in shady dealings, and the Treasury press release was studiously vague: "Sources show that senior officials in Banco Delta Asia are working with DPRK officials to accept large deposits of cash, including counterfeit U.S. currency, and agreeing to place that currency into circulation."[11] But the Treasury's evidentiary standard was not sky-high; at the time it first began implementing the money-laundering provisions of the Patriot Act, it operated according to an "80/20 rule," meaning it needed only 80 percent confidence of wrongdoing, based on an edict set by O'Neill when he was secretary.[12]

Turning up the pressure on Pyongyang, Christopher Hill, the assistant secretary of state for East Asian and Pacific affairs, told his North Korean counterpart: "We have the capacity to go after your activities all over the world. If you want to go open an account on the moon, we can go after that."[13] At another session, an inebriated North Korean negotiator blurted a confession to Victor Cha, the NSC Asian affairs director: "You Americans finally have found a way to hurt us."[14]

Painful as the BDA action may have been for North Korea, its effect on Pyongyang's policies is much more questionable. It came just at a time when the Six Party Talks were nearing fruition on a deal, and the North Koreans stormed out, refusing to continue until the financial damage they had suffered was reversed. The regime test-fired missiles in July 2006 and, three months later, conducted its first successful test of a nuclear device. An internal battle inside the Bush administration ensued, with Hill and his boss, Secretary of State Condoleezza Rice, denouncing the Treasury's move as impeding the ultimate goal of disarmament. Treasury officials vehemently resisted efforts to backtrack, arguing that doing so would be turning a blind eye to financial abuses. In the end, a messy compromise was struck after Hill offered to resolve the BDA issue if the North Koreans returned to the negotiating table. A complicated arrangement for releasing the $25 million in frozen funds took months to implement. Hawks decried what they saw as a "capitulation." North Korea ended up continuing on the path toward becoming a nuclear power.[15]

Still, the Treasury's weapon had also been tested — and its explosive potential against a nation-state demonstrated. The next major target would be bigger, and the outcome a more unqualified success.

When Treasury officials travel abroad, they usually meet their counterparts in economic policy agencies, for government-to-government negotiations or discussions about matters of mutual concern. Not so Stuart Levey, who was the first person to serve as undersecretary for terrorism and financial intelligence, a job he held from 2004 to 2011. Levey met with some foreign officials, but his trips were mostly for the purpose of meeting with executives of foreign banks. During his tenure he held over 100 meetings at financial institutions around the world, where he conveyed the message that some of the business they were doing was dangerous and should be terminated. Bankers paid close heed, keenly aware of the damage they could suffer at the hands of Levey's department.[16]

The topic of these meetings was almost invariably Iran, which like North Korea was a long-standing US antagonist with a vexing capacity for shrugging off conventional sanctions and other pressure tactics. Tehran had been added to Washington's terrorism list in the 1980s, placed under a full US embargo in the mid-1990s, labeled part of the "axis of evil" by George W. Bush, and subjected to multiple UN sanctions resolutions. The Islamic Revolutionary Guard Corps, the regime's ideological militia, had the dubious distinction of being the first section of a foreign military to be specifically targeted by US sanctions. Yet Iranian arms and aid continued to flow to organizations, groups, and paramilitary forces bent on undermining US-supported regimes throughout the Middle East. The country's highly productive oilfields generated abundant revenue from energy-hungry customers, especially in Asia. Most worrisome of all was the evident failure by the UN and International Atomic Energy Agency to keep Iran from approaching the capacity for manufacturing nuclear weapons–grade fuel. An Iranian nuclear arsenal, and the arms race it could trigger in a region seething with ethnic hatred, must be forestalled at all costs, in the view of US policymakers.

Having seen how the BDA designation had led banks to break off connections with North Korea, Levey reckoned that a similar strategy would work with Iran. In what would be dubbed a "whisper campaign," he embarked in 2006 on a series of journeys to Europe, the Middle East, and Asia, insisting on meeting with bank CEOs whom he warned that the Iranians were making illicit use of the global financial system just as the North Koreans had. Lest there be any doubt, the Treasury began to put Iranian banks on SDN lists. On September 8, 2006, OFAC blacklisted Bank Saderat, a large government-owned bank with 3,400 branches outside of Iran, which the Treasury accused of having been "a significant facilitator" of the activities of the militant Shiite group Hezbollah as well as "a conduit between the Government of Iran" and other radical Islamic organizations including Hamas, the Popular Front for the Liberation of Palestine–General Command, and the Palestinian Islamic Jihad. Like all Iranian banks, Bank Saderat was already barred from direct business with US banks, but now any transaction involving Bank Saderat — even ones that began and ended with foreign banks — could not pass through the US financial system. Next to be hit were other Iranian banks with significant international networks including Bank Sepah, Bank Melli, and Bank Mellat.

Levey's bank visits had an unmistakably intimidating quality, at least to some of his interlocutors, who couldn't help but feel that his message was: "Nice little bank you've got here — what a shame if something happens to it." A refusal to sever links with Iran, after all, would put a bank at risk of being given the BDA treatment. When I asked Levey about this in an interview, he replied: "Someone might say this was coercion, but we felt it was highlighting the way Iran was undermining the integrity of the international financial system by using it for illicit purposes — whether that is terrorism or pursuing weapons of mass destruction."[17]

I have seen no credible evidence that Levey issued explicit threats during these meetings with banks; it wasn't necessary, because he could base his case on the argument that the banks' reputations were at stake, knowing that they could draw their own conclusions about what the Treasury might do if they allowed their reputations to be sullied. In making his pitch, he typically presented briefing material showing how Tehran officials and the Revolutionary Guard used front companies and obfuscatory tactics to conduct international business for purposes such as acquiring nuclear equipment. As he explained in a televised interview during his Treasury days:

> At bottom here the financial industry does not want to be part of illicit conduct. Whatever the short-term gain for one transaction or one client, it's not worth it for them. . . . So if you go to them and you say "Listen, I have an intelligence community that helps me. I'm in a better position to acquire this information. Here's what we're seeing. We're seeing the following ways that [Iranians are] trying to work around your controls. We know you have good controls, but they are trying to penetrate your controls and get you to participate in transactions that if you knew the truth about them you never would participate in." If you share that information in that way, approach them as the allies that they really are, we get a very dramatically positive reaction. And they realize, look, that they can't differentiate when it comes to Iran or North Korea, they can't differentiate the legitimate from the illegitimate business. And so their best bet is to give it up altogether.[18]

Whether for reasons of safeguarding their reputations or protecting themselves from US sanctions, the banks responded in gratifying fashion. In April

---

2008, Levey told a Senate hearing that "the world's leading financial institutions have largely stopped dealing with Iran, and especially Iranian banks, in any currency."[19] By fall of that year, more than 80 banks had curtailed business with Tehran, according to a lengthy article by veteran journalist Robin Wright, who reported: "The momentum has surprised even Levey. . . . Even banks in Muslim countries, from Bahrain to Malaysia, have cut back their Iran business, bankers told me. Most surprising has been the shift by several Chinese banks."[20] Iranian officials angrily disputed Levey's claims about their banks' activities, but their fulminations — one of them denounced the Treasury for "assigning one of their Zionist deputies to halt the Iranian economy"[21] — only highlighted the toll he was taking. For Iranian companies, credit was becoming increasingly difficult to obtain, forcing some to resort to barter with foreign customers and suppliers.

In a tribute to Levey's effectiveness, the Obama administration kept him in his job. He was told to back off from pressuring Iran while the Obama team tried an initial round of diplomatic overtures, but his campaign resumed following revelations in September 2009 of a secret uranium-enrichment facility at Qom, which evoked international condemnation as anxiety soared anew over Tehran's nuclear ambitions.

Moreover, the brandishing of the dollar weapon was expanding to include a new group of American officials, striking even greater fear into the hearts of bank executives around the world.

Prosecutors, including the famed Manhattan district attorney Robert Morgenthau, trained their sights on foreign banks' dealings with Iran, adding an enforcement dimension to US financial sanctions that the Treasury alone could not exert.[22] By launching criminal proceedings against banks to determine whether they were transacting with blacklisted Iranians, prosecutors could use investigative techniques — wiretaps, searches, confidential informants — that financial regulators can only dream of. Morgenthau's office extracted a $350 million fine from UK-based Lloyds Bank in 2009 for conducting dollar transactions on behalf of Iranian front companies, and that was just the first major foray of a law enforcement campaign that, by 2016, would lead to the settlement of criminal charges and payment of billions of dollars in fines by nearly a dozen banking giants, mostly European, ranging from BNP Paribas to Credit Suisse to Commerzbank to Standard Chartered. A number of the banks were found to have "stripped" references to Iran from payment instructions in apparent efforts to evade US sanctions.

In some cases, the banks, aided by officials of their governments, fought the charges, arguing that the applicable US laws were confusing and that American prosecutors were unfairly targeting foreigners. But in the end, they settled, yielding to threats in several instances of losing their New York banking licenses, which would be catastrophic for their businesses. Not only did they have to pony up fines — almost $9 billion for BNP Paribas, a record criminal penalty at the time — but they also had to implement a variety of reforms in their operations, typically beefing up their staffs responsible for complying with anti–money laundering and sanctions laws (an expensive undertaking, costing hundreds of millions of dollars), and submitting to tight oversight by US regulators. HSBC, for example, increased the number of full-time employees on its compliance staff nearly sevenfold, to 8,300, in the five years following its 2012 settlement with the US government, and — to show its determination to mend its ways — hired Levey, who left the Treasury in 2011, as its chief legal officer.[23]

Hot on the prosecutors' heels was Congress, where antipathy toward Tehran led to the enactment of legislation arming the Treasury with unprecedented powers to impose secondary sanctions. Under the Comprehensive Iran Sanctions, Accountability, and Divestment Act (CISADA), the Treasury could bar US banks from maintaining correspondent accounts with any foreign bank that did "significant" business with sanctioned Iranian entities, regardless of whether such business was permitted under local law. This was a forerunner of the Trump administration's policy, and it drew resentment from US allies in Europe and elsewhere. But views in European capitals regarding Iran's behavior were increasingly aligning with those in Washington, and in 2011 the European Union itself ratcheted up economic pressure on Tehran including an oil embargo. Acting in concert, US and EU officials also forced SWIFT to kick major Iranian banks out of its messaging network.

Throughout this period of US-led financial constriction, Iran had remained defiant, rejecting demands that it curtail its nuclear program. Its agents, many of whom were placed strategically in parts of the world with lax governance, managed to procure essential imports the country needed and arrange revenue-generating petroleum sales. Although US sanctions were inflicting hardship on the Iranian populace, it was evidently insufficient to induce a policy change in Tehran, and a clamor was rising among hawkish elements in Washington that time was growing short to prevent a nuclear-armed Iran from becoming a reality.

The response was a cleverer — and harsher — application of the dollar weapon. To keep the Iranians from processing oil revenue through non-sanctioned parts of their financial system, the country's central bank, Bank Markazi, was designated a "primary money laundering concern" under Section 311 of the Patriot Act, along with the rest of the banking sector, in late 2011. Any foreign bank dealing with Bank Markazi would therefore risk being cut off from the US financial system under secondary sanctions, and Treasury officials visited banks in Europe, Asia, and the Middle East to ensure that this message was received loud and clear. But the new US rules had a strategically designed loophole aimed at severely restricting Iran's ability to sell oil. Foreign banks could be exempted from the secondary sanctions provided their home countries were "significantly" decreasing the amount of Iranian oil they were buying. This approach was practical enough to recognize that most countries importing Iranian oil couldn't stop immediately but could be induced to import substantially less.

By mid-2013, Iran's Asian customers were dutifully cutting their oil purchases — Japan by 45 percent, Taiwan by 57 percent, India by 30 percent, China by 21 percent. Combined with the EU embargo, the result was a plunge in Iran's oil exports, from 2.5 million barrels a day in 2011 to 1 million barrels a day in 2013, which contributed to a sharp recession in which GDP shrank by 6.6 percent, the exchange rate of the Iranian rial fell by almost 80 percent, and prices soared in Iranian markets for meat, grain, vegetables, and fruit.[24]

Iran returned to the negotiating table in mid-2012, and the following year the country's voters elected a new president, Hassan Rouhani, who ran on a pledge to revive the economy by resolving the nuclear issue and getting sanctions lifted. Momentum was now clearly on the side of a deal between Tehran and the six governments (the United States, Russia, China, Britain, France, and Germany) negotiating over its nuclear program. Two more years of brinkmanship were required to overcome resistance from supreme leader Ali Khamenei, who held ultimate decision-making power. But in mid-2015 a landmark agreement, the Joint Comprehensive Plan of Action (JCPOA), was signed, with the

---

aim of ensuring that Iran's nuclear facilities would be limited to non-military purposes.

The dollar weapon had proven its mettle, more conclusively than in the North Korean case because it led to policy concessions by the target country. What's more, the United States had coordinated the use of the weapon with other major powers, taking into consideration the potential impact on their economies. Levey's whisper campaign with banks raised hackles in allied capitals, as did US prosecutions, but the Obama administration consulted with foreign governments to ensure that the squeeze on Iran's oil production would not be so severe or precipitous as to cause economic damage globally.

The JCPOA would not survive the Trump administration, as previously noted. But even before Trump's arrival at the White House, the tool that Levey, Zarate, and their Treasury colleagues had devised was attracting notice abroad, much of it agitated, especially in countries on the outs with the United States. Far from standing still, governments of these countries began preparing defensive mechanisms and countermeasures in the hope of neutralizing Washington's new weapon, or at least buffering themselves against it. Initiatives taken by Russia, China, and North Korea merit special attention, each raising different sorts of questions about how much difference they might make.

Sergey Glazyev yielded to no one in his rancor over what he called America's "financial terrorism." An adviser to President Vladimir Putin with a PhD in economics from Moscow State University, Glazyev issued frequent broadsides on the subject. "We will encourage everybody to dump U.S. bonds, get rid of dollars as an unreliable currency, and leave the U.S. market," he declared on one occasion, and in an interview with the Russian news agency Tass he said: "The more aggressive the Americans are, the sooner they will see the final collapse of the dollar, and by getting rid of the dollar this would be the only way for victims of American aggression to stop this onslaught."[25]

Glazyev's rhetorical excesses aside, his view about the necessity of strong anti-dollar measures reflected the attitude that took hold in the Kremlin in 2014, when Russia was hit by financial sanctions in response to its invasion and annexation of Crimea. The Obama administration's initial sanctions on Moscow were engineered with restraint, based on consultation with European officials who were anxious to avoid disrupting flows of Russian energy exports. Only after Russian forces moved further into Ukraine were tougher steps taken by Washington and its allies that effectively blocked Russian firms from raising funds on international markets. Proposals to disconnect Russian banks from SWIFT were discussed but discarded as too extreme for such a major power. Still, the sanctions — combined with a decline in the price of oil, Russia's main export — pushed the economy into a deep slump. The reaction from Putin was to order an all-out effort to defend against whatever the West could throw at Moscow in the future.

Dubbed "Fortress Russia" as it unfolded, the strategy's main elements included the following: Debt owed to foreign creditors would be reduced, by both the public and private sectors. Fiscal policy would therefore be disciplined, and so would monetary policy, which would help enable the accumulation of foreign currency reserves that the Central Bank of Russia could use to defend the ruble and quell crises. Moreover, the dollar would play much less of a role in the nation's trade and finances, as would the system it dominates, including SWIFT.[26]

Wasting no time lest the threat of SWIFT disconnection become a reality, the central bank began establishing a SWIFT alternative in November 2014 called the System for the Transfer of Financial Messages (SPFS, for the romanized version of the Russian name), which became fully operational in 2017. Although having a SWIFT alternative didn't mean that foreign financial institutions would join — only a few joined SPFS, most from Belarus and other former Soviet republics — Russian banks could at least be assured of being able to communicate with each other. In a related move aimed at reducing reliance on Visa and Mastercard for processing consumer purchases, the central bank oversaw the creation of an independent network for credit card payments, and the Kremlin heavily promoted the use of a new homegrown card called Mir.

On a number of fronts, Fortress Russia policies worked surprisingly well in restoring economic and financial stability to Russia in the years following the 2014 imposition of Western sanctions. By 2019, the government's budget was solidly in surplus, and total public debt stood at about 15 percent of GDP, compared with an EU average of about 80 percent. Reserves had swelled by about half to $542 billion, a figure that would rise by tens of billions more before the February 2022 invasion of Ukraine. Although the austerity incorporated into

Fortress Russia policies caused economic growth and living standards to suffer—real disposable incomes declined every year from 2014 to 2017, and rose only marginally in the next couple of years—the pain was endurable, polls indicated, for a country that had undergone much worse during the period after the breakup of the Soviet Union.

But as for de-dollarization, Russia made limited headway.[27] To be fair, it had a long way to go; of the reserves held at the central bank in 2013, the dollar accounted for more than 40 percent, and more than 80 percent of Russian exports were invoiced in the US currency. The central bank began trimming its dollar-denominated holdings, which declined to 24 percent of the total in 2020 and 16 percent in early 2022, with the euro overtaking the greenback as the biggest single currency in the central bank's portfolio. That, however, was the easy step. The central bank could control the composition of its reserves by buying and selling as it pleased, but that didn't mean that Russian companies, which must deal with foreign suppliers and customers, would be able to export and import in non-dollar currencies.

Thanks in part to official exhortations to conduct more trade in euros, rubles, and renminbi, Russian firms reduced the amount of exports they invoiced in dollars by more than 20 percentage points between 2013 and 2020. But the greenback was still the invoiced currency for nearly 60 percent of the country's exports.

Among the trading partners with whom Russia significantly cut dollar-invoiced exports were India and the European Union, as Daniel McDowell notes in his meticulously researched analysis of de-dollarization initiatives taken by countries threatened by US sanctions. But the data marshalled by McDowell are striking in showing how far short Moscow's efforts fell. In 2020, the dollar's share of Russian exports to the European Union was still 40 percent, about the same as Europe's own currency, the euro. Moreover, Russia's imports overall continued to be heavily dollar-dependent. Perhaps the most telling example McDowell cites is that of trade between Russia and Turkey, where the dollar remained the dominant currency used in 2020, similar to its level in 2013. "The dollar's significant and stable role in Russian-Turkish trade during this period is notable," McDowell observes, "given that Washington targeted both countries and Putin and [Turkey's President Recep Tayyip] Erdoğan have both pledged to push for trade settlement in local currencies. Despite their mutual interest in achieving this outcome, de-dollarization remained elusive."[28]

The biggest successes for Putin's campaign came in Sino-Russian trade, where the euro surpassed the dollar as the main vehicle currency for Russian exports to China. In Beijing, after all, the authorities were sympathetic to the goal of a less dollar-dominated monetary system, and had their own ideas about how it might be pursued.

Coincidence or not, the timing is noteworthy: in April 2012, just one month after Iranian banks were disconnected from SWIFT, the People's Bank of China announced plans to establish a network of its own for the international transmission of funds. Launched in 2015, at a ceremony in Shanghai, the network's name was the Cross-Border Interbank Payment System (CIPS).[29]

CIPS was a step up from Russia's SPFS because it was not only a messaging system like SWIFT; it combined messaging functionality with clearing and settlement. It therefore poses a potential threat to the role of CHIPS as a chokepoint in the worldwide flow of funds. If a substantial portion of the trillions of dollars that now go through CHIPS were to go through CIPS instead, Washington's ability to impose financial sanctions would be degraded. The degradation would be all the more severe if a substantial portion of the messages that are currently transmitted via SWIFT were to be switched to CIPS.

The immensity of those "ifs" is evident from data showing that the average daily value of transactions cleared and settled by CIPS — about 650 billion yuan, or $90 billion, in the first four months of 2024 — is dwarfed by the comparable figure for CHIPS of $1.8 *trillion*. Moreover, the number of banks using CIPS is only one-seventh of the number using SWIFT, and the vast majority of transactions going over CIPS involve SWIFT messaging, because banks evidently find SWIFT more convenient. The relative puniness of CIPS hasn't stopped speculation that the tables may turn eventually, however.

"CIPS . . . is not yet ready to serve as an alternative messaging system for cross-border payments outside of China. Even so, that day will come," writes Rush Doshi in his book *The Long Game: China's Grand Strategy to Displace American Order.*[30] (Doshi served as China director at the National Security Council from 2021 to 2024.) Gal Luft and Anne Korin, the authors of

De-Dollarization, put it this way: "CIPS and SPFS are nowhere near becoming as widely used as SWIFT. . . . But today is today and tomorrow is tomorrow."[31]

Boosting optimism about the long-term prospects of CIPS is the rapid growth of the system's use.[32] The value of transactions over CIPS more than doubled from early 2020 to early 2023, and more than 500 banks joined as indirect participants during that period. As of early 2024, a little over 1,500 financial institutions had connected to CIPS, including some of the world's biggest banks, for instance Citibank, Standard Chartered, and BNP Paribas, along with others from Asia, Europe, Africa, North America, Oceania, and South America.

But the likelihood that CIPS will ever come close to outstripping CHIPS can be discounted for one simple reason: CIPS clears and settles transactions in renminbi, whereas CHIPS does so in US dollars. As seen in chapter 4, the factors limiting the renminbi's use outside of China are deeply rooted in the fundamental nature of the nation's financial and political system. Yes, Beijing has taken countless steps to enhance the renminbi's internationalization, including with agreements between the People's Bank of China and foreign central banks to swap currencies — almost 40 at last count[33] — and further liberalization of its financial markets; it has also moved much more quickly than other major powers to launch a digital version of its currency (a subject which will be covered in a later chapter). Together with CIPS, these moves may facilitate transactions that evade Washington's detection, making China itself less vulnerable to US sanctions. But anyone holding renminbi-denominated assets is bearing the risk of being unable to move those assets in and out of China, because the authorities have shown themselves capable of arbitrarily reimposing capital controls. Perhaps more important for renminbi asset holders is the question of how they think they would fare in the event of a legal dispute — could a Chinese court, which must ultimately answer to the Chinese Communist Party, be relied upon to rule fairly, in the way American courts would? As long as such concerns persist, the renminbi's internationalization will remain stunted relative to the dollar, and the same goes for CIPS relative to CHIPS.

CIPS is not China's only ploy for countering US financial sanctions. Another is "burner banks" — that is, banks specially created or designed to avoid transacting in US dollars, rendering them impervious to the Treasury's SDN designations. As the term suggests, there's an analogy with "burner phones" bought by drug dealers to evade detection by law enforcement before being thrown away. (These banks are also sometimes called "expendable," "sacrificial," or "single purpose," but the term "burner banks," coined by Tom Keatinge of the Royal United Services Institute, a British think tank, is the most memorable.) One prominent example is the Bank of Kunlun, a financial institution based in the western province of Xinjiang which was bought by the oil giant China National Petroleum Corp. in 2009 and used mainly to buy oil from Iran. Although the Treasury sanctioned the Bank of Kunlun in 2012 for helping Iranian banks move millions of dollars, the bank was able to continue operating since it conducted no business that involved clearing and settling in New York. Russia has employed similar techniques, using small banks for arms trading so that larger banks don't become sanctions targets.[34]

Couldn't burner banks be widely used to circumvent the US dollar–dominated financial system and subvert America's financial sanctions power? In theory, it might seem so; a network of such banks could maintain links exclusively among themselves, clearing and settling payments without having to go through big correspondent banks. But remember: the US Treasury has an office devoted to gathering and analyzing intelligence, and it would easily detect such a burner-bank network. The Treasury could threaten to impose secondary sanctions on any bank or company dealing with the burner banks – a threat that few banks could afford to ignore, since most of them need the ability to clear and settle in US dollars via CHIPS and its correspondent banking network in order to conduct international business. That may explain why burner banks have been limited in number and duration; the Bank of Kunlun stopped handling payments from Iran in 2018.[35]

For evasion methods that are more redolent of cloak-and-dagger escapades, another sanctions target is unsurpassed.

In waters off the coast of Taiwan, a tanker named the *Diamond 8* sidled up to another vessel in May 2020 and received a transfer of oil before sailing to its destination, the North Korean port of Nampo, where the oil was offloaded. That transfer and delivery, caught in a series of satellite images, was one of several voyages the *Diamond 8* took to North Korea in 2019 and 2020, sometimes turning off its required tracking signal and at other times transmitting a signal that falsely identified it as a different tanker. Although on paper its management was the responsibility of an Indonesian company registered in the Seychelles, the *Diamond 8* — and two ships that transferred oil to it — was connected through murky corporate linkages to an oil trading business with operations throughout East Asia headed by Tony Tung, a native of Fujian province in China who had been investigated in China and Taiwan for smuggling and bribery. (His only conviction was overturned.)[36]

The voyages of the *Diamond 8* were part of an elaborate network that kept North Korea well supplied with oil despite a drastic tightening of sanctions after the regime's test in January 2016 of a nuclear device that it proudly proclaimed to be a hydrogen bomb. North Korea has no domestic petroleum reserves, so the UN approved measures limiting its oil imports as part of a prohibition on the transfer of "any item," except food or medicine, that "could directly contribute" to its military capabilities. But in the years since the US Treasury issued its shock designation of BDA that made North Korean entities toxic in international banking circles, officials in Pyongyang had become adept at finding partners abroad that were willing — for a price — to help the regime surmount economic and financial isolation. The oil sector was just one example.

North Korea conducts much of its international commerce — both legal and otherwise — through state trading companies (STCs), whose rapidly rising sophistication was documented in illuminating research published in 2016 by two scholars, John Park of Harvard and Jim Walsh of MIT.[37] Their conclusions were based on interviews with STC managers — not people currently employed by North Korea, of course, but rather former STC managers who had fled the country and could be found among the 30,000 North Korean defectors residing in South Korea. In a nutshell, Park and Walsh found that sanctions had had perverse and unanticipated effects by significantly improving North Korea's sanctions-busting proficiency.

According to Park and Walsh, "The BDA episode demonstrated to the North Koreans that their illegal activities were vulnerable to U.S. sanctions against international banks, especially those using dollars. The DPRK would have to find new partners and new instruments of finance that would allow them to operate outside the reach of the U.S. Treasury Department." After a visit to Pyongyang in 2009 by Chinese premier Wen Jiabao signaled Beijing's willingness to accept a deepening of bilateral ties, "the DPRK regime expanded its use of private Chinese middlemen. It also contracted with more capable private firms than it had in the past. New sanctions raised the risk of doing business with North Korea, as the U.S. and others had hoped, but Pyongyang responded by paying higher fees to compensate for the increased risk. Higher fees, in turn, drew larger and more sophisticated Chinese partners."

Instead of taking short trips to China as they had in the past, North Korean STC managers began moving to major Chinese cities for extended periods and enrolling their children in local schools, enabling them to enjoy treatment similar to that accorded other foreign businesspeople, the interviewees explained. To obtain goods that North Korea couldn't legally acquire, they used third parties; as Park and Walsh wrote: "The STCs, acting in their own name or through a shell company, contracted with private firms in China. The Chinese brokers, in turn, signed contracts with Chinese suppliers. The suppliers assume they are doing business with a Chinese firm, not a North Korean one. Once the brokers acquired the targeted goods from the unsuspecting supplier, they were transferred to the intended endpoint, the DPRK." It helped, Park and Walsh added, that the Chinese–North Korean border is nearly 900 miles long: "Gone are the days of having to rely exclusively on North Korean ships secretly ferrying parts from a port in the Middle East. Chinese partners instead hide North Korea's relatively small consignments amid the massive volume of regular commercial activity within China's domestic market. Once in this flow, defectors noted that the consignment would essentially be 'hiding in the open.' "

North Korea may be an outlier—it is "the paradigmatic hard target," as two other experts, Marcus Noland and Stephan Haggard, put it in a 2017 book.[38] But it clearly illustrates that dollar weaponization, for all its potency, has limitations. That didn't stop the Trump administration from using it to a fare-thee-well.

"As I have stated strongly before, and just to reiterate, if Turkey does anything that I, in my great and unmatched wisdom, consider to be off limits, I will totally destroy and obliterate the economy of Turkey. (I've done it before!)."[39]

So tweeted the President of the United States on October 8, 2019, in response to Turkey's dispatch of troops into northern Syria. The bluster typified

Trump's approach to the wielding of sanctions. He enjoyed signing executive orders, which he brandished for photographers with his trademark glower, and his aides confided to the media that he got special gratification from the ones enacting sanctions because he saw it as a near-costless way of smacking down foreign antagonists.[40] It might seem logical to conclude that his administration was exceptionally adroit at weaponizing the dollar to achieve foreign policy goals, based on the events recounted at the beginning of chapter 5 concerning the abject submission of European companies in 2018 to US secondary sanctions threats. The facts indicate otherwise.

The reimposition of sanctions on Iran sent the country's economic recovery into reverse, with oil exports cut in half, GDP contracting by 12 percent between 2018 and 2021, inflation skyrocketing, and the currency in free fall. Living standards were squeezed to the point that the share of Iranians who could be considered middle class shrank from 45 percent of the population in 2017 to 30 percent by 2020.[41] But Tehran refused to accede to the much more extreme demands set by US negotiators, and although the prospect of regime change appeared to rise when anti-austerity protests erupted in Iranian cities, the leadership remained entrenched with no progress toward ending its nuclear program.[42] If anything, the sanctions proved counterproductive by making Iran more disposed toward anti-American policies and actions; hardliners in Tehran could claim that there was little purpose to making concessions with a superpower that would renege on its agreement, while at the same time moderate forces were undercut, as shown in a book by four US-based scholars with deep knowledge of the country. "The past two presidential elections [2013 and 2017] we told people, 'Go vote so we don't get sanctioned anymore and we can solve our issues with the West,'" a former student activist named Shadee is quoted as telling the authors. "But after everything we've been through because of Trump pulling out of the deal and reimposing sanctions . . . I cannot go back out on the streets and try to convince people to vote. What am I going to say? We have no arguments left. We've been rendered speechless."[43]

A similar outcome materialized in Venezuela. Despite Trump's efforts to topple President Nicolás Maduro by tightening measures against the nation's oil sales, Maduro clung to power. These sanctions too are blamed for unintended consequences, notably a flood of Venezuelan immigrants to other Latin

American countries and, later, the United States as Venezuela's economy crumbled. Defenders of the sanctions counter that Venezuela's impoverishment was due to Maduro's gross economic management, and that the influx of Venezuelans across the US border, which spiked after 2021, occurred on the Biden administration's watch. But the decision to sanction Caracas was made over strenuous objections from some officials, who warned that the move could come back to haunt Washington. "I said the sanctions were going to grind the Venezuelan economy into dust and have huge human consequences, one of which would be out-migration," Thomas Shannon, who served as undersecretary for political affairs at the State Department from 2016 to 2018, told the *Washington Post*. "The sanctions clearly helped generate faster out-migration. And you knew it was only going to be a matter of time before these people decided to migrate north."[44]

As for Russia, a US attempt to inflict financial pain in 2018 resulted in a costly debacle. The Treasury targeted Oleg Deripaska, a billionaire close to Russian president Vladimir Putin, following congressional enactment of a sanctions package against Russian oligarchs.[45] Among Deripaska-controlled companies that were put on the SDN list was Rusal, the world's second-largest aluminum company. The designation rendered Rusal an international pariah, unable to obtain dollar payments for its aluminum, and unable to get banks to handle its debt payments, because its erstwhile business partners were terrified of being labeled SDNs too. To the dismay of America's European allies, who were not consulted beforehand, aluminum prices surged by 20 percent amid fears of a global shortage as Rusal's operations in Ireland and Sweden ground to a halt. German automakers sounded the alarm that their factories might too have to stop production for lack of aluminum, endangering hundreds of thousands of jobs. To salvage as much as he could from his empire, Deripaska negotiated a deal with OFAC wherein he reduced his stake in Rusal, taking a multibillion-dollar hit to his wealth. In return, Washington beat an embarrassing retreat, easing sanctions that it had slapped on without due appreciation for the ripple effects. The episode was a textbook example of the collateral economic damage that can result from the dollar weapon's punishing impact.

Notwithstanding the dearth of policy changes by US adversaries, the Trump team remained enamored of dollar weaponization, using it without regard for (or perhaps in gleeful anticipation of) the hostility it might arouse in foreign capitals. In September 2020, Secretary of State Mike Pompeo announced that Fatou Bensouda, chief prosecutor of the International Criminal Court (ICC), would be targeted because of an investigation she was pursuing into war crimes in Afghanistan including allegations against US troops. The Hague-based ICC, which was established to adjudicate accusations of war crimes and other atrocities such as genocide, didn't have authority to pursue charges against Americans because the United States is not an ICC member, according to the Trump administration (a position disputed by the court). As if she were a financial miscreant, Bensouda's bank account at the United Nations Federal Credit Union was frozen, and US companies and individuals were barred from transacting with her.[46] She vowed to press on with her investigation, and got relief in the spring of 2021 when a new US administration came to Washington. Pompeo's successor, Anthony Blinken, said the United States continued to "disagree strongly" with the ICC's stance but would seek to resolve the dispute by other means.[47]

Dollar weaponization had come far since the September 11 attacks when the Bush administration, realizing that anti-money laundering laws might be useful against targets other than drug traffickers, put OFAC to work in the war on terror. The tool's expanded use by the Obama and Trump administrations had hit target countries hard. Although the results often fell short from Washington's standpoint — targets staunchly resisted changing their policies and behavior in a number of instances — there was no gainsaying the US currency's globe-girdling dominion.

But as the 2010s were ending and the 2020s dawned, another phenomenon was fueling downbeat conjecture about the dollar's future — the rapid development of digitized currency, the subject to which this book turns next.

CHAPTER 7

NEWFANGLEDNESS

A glorious stretch of beach beckoned in Nassau, capital of the Bahamas, as I set off on a four-mile walk one sunny morning in November 2022. The heat and humidity rose to uncomfortable levels as midday approached, but I was determined to achieve my mission — using a newfangled type of money that few Americans have encountered.[1]

After nearly an hour and a half I arrived, dripping with sweat, at my destination, a health food restaurant called NRG, where I ordered a superfood salad and an "Ocean Bliss" smoothie. Then it was time for the newfangled part: I paid the bill — 25 Bahamian dollars, including tip — by opening an app on my iPhone, pointing the camera at a QR code, entering the amount, and tapping "confirm."

Newfangled?! My salad-and-smoothie purchase must sound downright oldfangled to anyone familiar with Apple Pay, Google Pay, Alipay, WeChat Pay or the many other forms of mobile services that involve pointing smartphones at QR codes. But I was using the world's first central bank digital currency (CBDC), which the Bahamian authorities charmingly named the "Sand Dollar." Often mistaken for cryptocurrency, CBDCs are different in a crucial respect — they are backed by a government entity. The Sand Dollar, which was launched in October 2020, is a liability of the Central Bank of the Bahamas, the same as Bahamian dollar bills and coins. Paying with Sand Dollars is legally equivalent to paying with cash in Bahamian dollars; although the transaction is in cyber-space, payment goes directly into the digital wallet of the recipient, who holds an asset backed by the central bank rather than an obligation of a bank or credit card or other private intermediary.

Along with the fact that I paid with the world's first CBDC, my exertions en route to that salad-and-smoothie meal are also noteworthy. The length of my walk showed how challenging paying with Sand Dollars can be, because hardly any Bahamians use them and very few merchants accept them. I took the long stroll to NRG only because it was on a list, sent to me by the central bank, of a handful of places in Nassau where Sand Dollars could be used for payment. In just about every other place where I needed to pay for something – restaurants, shops, hotels – Sand Dollars were refused, and some people knew little or nothing about the digital currency even though it had been issued two years previ-ously. "Isn't that like crypto?" scoffed the feisty taxi driver who picked me up at the airport. After I explained the government's role, she became even more dismissive. "Thieves and crooks!"

My experience was borne out by statistics showing that at the time of my visit, Sand Dollars accounted for less than one-tenth of 1 percent of the money in circulation in the Bahamas.[2] The situation was similar in other countries that had issued CBDCs. In Nigeria, for example, the eNaira marked its one-year anniversary in October 2022 with the authorities so desperate to encourage its use that they were offering drivers of three-wheeler taxis a 5 percent bonus for taking it.[3]

The limited uptake of the Sand Dollar should be kept in mind as the story of monetary digitization unfolds in the next two chapters. A heated debate is un-derway in Washington and other world capitals about whether governments ought to issue CBDCs or leave the issuance of digital money to private firms and other non-state innovators. In the United States, advocates for a US CBDC warn that since the People's Bank of China has issued an official digital currency, known as the e-CNY, the Fed had better match it. Their fear is that the e-CNY will become so widely used around the world as to dethrone the greenback and, worse yet, facilitate the transmission of sensitive personal, corporate, and gov-ernment data back to the Chinese Communist Party. On the other side of the debate are critics condemning CBDCs as tools of repression that will enhance the ability of all governments — not just China's — to spy on and coerce their citizenry into submission. CBDCs could be manipulated by the powers-that-be to achieve political goals, for example freezing the holdings of disfavored groups or blocking donations to them. Or the software could be programmed to encourage and discourage certain behavior, perhaps by limiting alcohol purchases by heavy drinkers or denying junk-food orders by overweight consumers.

My Bahamian beach trek suggests that those conjuring up such dystopian scenarios are going overboard. There are many good reasons for issuing a CBDC, and many good reasons against. But both proponents and opponents of CBDCs would be well advised to consider the apathetic attitude in the Bahamas, where a CBDC has existed the longest. To paraphrase a hippie-era antiwar slogan: suppose they gave a CBDC and nobody came?

We will return to CBDCs later in this chapter. They are only part of the revolutionary transformation taking place in the world of money, with potentially profound ramifications for the dollar. In some countries, government-backed fast payment systems with innovative features have made phenomenal progress in recent years, two shining examples being India's Unified Payments Interface (UPI) and Brazil's Pix.[4] Introduced in 2016, UPI gives Indians simple and free account-to-account transfers using QR codes and a variety of mobile phone apps. Pix, boasting a similarly easy-to-use mobile app, signed up two-thirds of Brazilian adults within a year after its launch in November 2020 and overtook credit cards as the country's leading payment method.

Speed and convenience of payments are just the start of what's coming, according to seers of the new age. They proclaim that the "internet of information" — email, messages, photos, etc. — is giving way to an "internet of value" enabling massive transfers, free of intermediaries such as banks or credit card companies, of all sorts of items ranging from stocks and bonds to real estate and works of artistic creativity. Technology is already reducing the cost of switching among different currencies, which could lead to the "unbundling" of the three functions of money; even if one currency offers advantages as a means of exchange, others might work better as a unit of account or store of value, with a few taps of a smartphone app making the switch cheap and easy.

The "programmability" of digital money — combining instruments of payment with software conveying instructions for some activity to occur — holds promise for all manner of life-enhancing conveniences. Goods ordered online may be paid for automatically upon delivery; self-driving cars may maneuver through heavy traffic by paying others to change lanes; homeowners in urban downtowns may rent their driveways for people seeking parking spaces; electricity and gas meters may read themselves and send payment to utility companies. "Micropayments" involving amounts of well under one cent automatically sent each time you use a search engine or social media platform could lead to the displacement of giant companies like Google and Facebook that depend on ad revenue and the exploitation of user data, the ultimate result being a more decentralized and democratic web.

Among the more persuasive proselytizers for using technology to reengineer money is Neha Narula, director of MIT's Digital Currency Initiative. "Just like the internet changed the way we communicate, programmable money will change the way we pay, allocate, and determine value," Narula told a wide-eyed audience in a 2016 TED Talk. "Imagine a world where I rent out my health data for large-scale data analysis to a pharmaceutical company. They provide me with a cryptographic proof that they are only using my data in a way we agreed, and they pay me for what they find out. . . . Interestingly, this changes the way security works in our world. When we are better able to allocate value, people will use their energy for more productive things. What if it cost a fraction of a cent to send email? Would we still have spam?"[5]

Another monetary futurist, David Birch, envisions a time when "there are hundreds, thousands or even millions of kinds of money," with mobile technology allowing smooth conversion to take advantage of their different features and benefits. "While one kind of money might be best for Starbucks, another kind might be better for your pension," Birch writes in a 2020 book, *The Currency Cold War*. "Your phone will show you the price of your latte in London loots, but you will transfer money in California cabbages, Apple apples, and San Francisco parking permits."[6] Communities of people linked by common interests and values — geographical, political, cultural, even religious — will create and use currencies that reflect those interests and values, he argues: "I might choose to save Islamic e-Dinars that are backed by gold. You might choose to save kWh$$$ that are backed by renewable electricity. We will still be able to do business together, because exchanges on our AI smartphones shall make it so."

Fantastical as such speculation may be, it highlights the expanding dimensions of the challenges facing the dollar in the twenty-first century. Will the dollar's global dominance decline, and US sanctions power erode, as technological advances enable new forms of payment transmission around the world? Conversely, might the dollar's hegemonic status be enhanced by American adoption of digital currency innovations? Should the state's role in digital monetary issuance be more interventionist, or less? As we saw in chapter 1, public confidence in the dollar depends crucially on state power exercised by various arms of the federal government, but when it comes to digital greenbacks, can the state be trusted to refrain from snooping or exerting control over private behavior? And in this new era, can US interests in maintaining sanctions power be reconciled with American support for individual liberty?

A tour d'horizon of monetary digitization helps lay the groundwork for answering such questions, starting with developments long before the creation of the Sand Dollar.

The first gold and silver coins were minted around 600 BC in the Anatolian kingdom of Lydia, replacing ingots and lumps of precious metal that had to be weighed for their value to be verified. Paper money first came into widespread use during China's Song Dynasty (AD 960–1279), relieving people of carrying heavy strings of bronze coins. Then, during the Renaissance, financiers in Italian city-states refined the use of ledgers to record transmissions of value, debiting the accounts of payers and crediting the accounts of payees so that parties separated by vast geographical distances could transact with one another using trusted intermediaries. Centuries later, advances in electronics enabled speedier processing, a turning point being the launching of Western Union's business of sending instructions for financial transactions over telegraph lines in 1871. These are all examples of how technology plays a disruptive role in the monetary realm, a process that has accelerated enormously in recent decades as banks and other financial service providers have gone from recording debits and credits by hand and keypunch to relying on computerized automation.

At each step of the way, laws had to be enacted and revised to instill trust in the value of items being exchanged. When checks came along, the law was updated to make clear that checks are orders to pay from the check-writer's bank account. Debit cards necessitated more legal fixes so that the insertion of a debit card in a card reader and the pressing of "OK" would be legally just as valid as the writing of a check. Problems of theft and fraud led to the enactment of still more laws — when a debit card is stolen, for example, the card's legitimate owner generally isn't liable for purchases made by the thief. Laws such as these are essential for the proper functioning of a modern economy; people and businesses need assurance of the legal enforceability behind items of value that they receive.

Among the most consequential inventions, widely adopted by credit card companies in the late 1970s, was the "magstripe" embedding the holder's card number, name, and other identifying information on the back of a card, enabling payments to be validated with a simple swipe. (Before then, as readers of a certain age will remember, customers had to endure frustrating waits for merchants to obtain authorization from credit card companies by phone.) Soon thereafter, with the advent of the internet age, came Amazon and other online retailers, and then PayPal, which gave individuals the ability to send money digitally not only to businesses but to each other.

For all the convenience afforded by these new payment methods, beneath the facade they are ultimately linked to accounts at financial institutions. Paying the bill at a restaurant with a Visa card, or ordering a toaster on Amazon, or using PayPal to buy a vintage baseball card from a collector on eBay, all involve the input of personal data to authenticate the payer's identity and assure the seller that sufficient funds are available for the agreed-upon payment. Senders' accounts are debited, and receivers' accounts credited, in a manner analogous to Renaissance-era ledgers although clearing and settlement take place via computerized systems.

As those systems advanced in the 1980s and 1990s, worries spread among groups of computer scientists with radical, anti-government leanings — "a mob of ponytailed coders," as one sympathetic history describes them[7] — who called themselves "cypherpunks." They saw clear risks that privacy and free-speech rights might be trampled if so much of individuals' hard-earned wealth and spending activity was stored on digital ledgers easily trackable by government authorities. As one of the gurus of the movement, David Chaum, wrote in a seminal article, "Some of our basic liberties may be threatened by computerization under the current approach."[8]

To see why, consider the properties of cash, use of which has steadily dwin-
dled in recent decades. Cash is a bearer instrument, transacted peer to peer; that
is, bills and coins are presumed to be owned by the person holding them, and
only the giver and receiver are involved. Nobody has to authorize the spending
of cash, so it's "permissionless." Although the privacy that results has a big
downside—the facilitation of criminal activity—the upside is the assurance of
censorship resistance. Individuals can feel secure handing over cash to support
any political, social, or religious cause, no matter how unpopular. They can also
feel safe from exposure by using cash to pay for something legally permissible
that society might hold in disdain (pornography or sex toys, for example) or
to pay for treatment of health or medical conditions that they want to keep
confidential.

By contrast, money linked to financial institutions—checks, credit cards,
bank transfers, Apple Pay, etc.—entails involvement by third parties that record
the details on ledgers showing who the payer and payee are as well as the amount
paid. Rather than peer to peer it is intermediated, and rather than permissionless it requires permission from banks, which are obliged to enforce KYC rules.
Benefits abound, to be sure, and they go well beyond the convenience of pulling
a card or mobile device out of one's pocket at the point of sale instead of a wad of
bills. Suppose the toaster you ordered from Amazon is defective—don't you
want irrefutable proof that you paid for it, so you can get a refund? Suppose you
need to borrow money—don't you want banks and credit card companies to see
what a creditworthy person you are? (Even if you aren't creditworthy, isn't it
reasonable for financial institutions to have the best data possible for extending
credit?) Furthermore, don't we all favor giving law enforcement better tools for
catching, say, child pornographers? Yes, but all that data stored on financial institutions' servers presents obvious potential for abuse, whether by private firms
or governments with Big Brother proclivities.

Efforts to develop payment systems with cash-like anonymity protection—
Chaum's, launched in the mid-1990s, was called "DigiCash"—flopped com-
mercially. But that didn't go far enough anyway for most of the cypherpunks,
who were wracking their brains trying to devise a form of money that eliminated the need for banks, corporations, central banks, and other intermediaries
altogether. A solution finally came at the end of October 2008, coincidentally a

month and a half after the Lehman bankruptcy, just as public revulsion with financial institutions was reaching all-time highs.[9]

This, as is known by all members of the crypto faithful, was the moment when a paper titled "Bitcoin: A Peer-to-Peer Electronic Cash System" materialized online. Its mystique is all the greater thanks to the insistence of its author, Satoshi Nakamoto, to refrain from revealing anything about his (her? their?) identity even to the cypherpunks, and to vanish in December 2010 without sending the cypherpunks any further messages. But Satoshi (as the author is universally known) clearly shared the cypherpunks' yearning for a top-to-bottom disruption of the financial status quo. "The root problem with conventional currency is all the trust that's required to make it work," Satoshi wrote in a 2009 message board post that is viewed as something akin to Holy Writ in crypto circles. "The central bank must be trusted not to debase the currency, but the history of fiat currencies is full of breaches of that trust. Banks must be trusted to hold our money and transfer it electronically, but they lend it out in waves of credit bubbles with barely a fraction in reserve. We have to trust them with our privacy, trust them not to let identity thieves drain our accounts."

Because of banks' untrustworthy behavior, Satoshi made this new currency peer to peer. Because of central banks' untrustworthy behavior, he ensured that the currency's supply would be strictly capped. And to keep control of the currency from all big institutions, governmental or corporate, he made the system decentralized, with users themselves running the code that makes it all work. Applying his skill at cryptography and software programming, he achieved all those goals while simultaneously instilling the network with trust about the validity of transactions — ensuring, in particular, that if someone paid for something with bitcoins, they were using bitcoins they really owned and not bitcoins they had already spent. No new statutes were required, since (to use a cherished crypto catchphrase) "code is law."

Computer geeks raved at the ingenuity. Economists ranted at the daftness. Whichever camp you are in, a grasp of the basic mechanics is essential for understanding the arguments about other forms of monetary digitization, including CBDCs.

Anyone with a laptop or smartphone can download the software to use Bitcoin, for free and without asking permission, since no permission-giver

---

exists. Instead of inputting your real name or phone number or email address, you create a "wallet" identified by a jumble of 34 characters called a public key, which is visible to everybody else, and you also get a 64-character private key that's sort of like a password except only you have it rather than any central authority. The two keys are related by complex cryptography, so use of the private key proves your legitimate ownership of whatever Bitcoin is in the wallet held by the public key. There are many ways to start filling your Bitcoin wallet; the most common and convenient is to open an account at a crypto exchange such as Coinbase and, by linking your bank account, convert fiat to Bitcoin, although some people prefer to use "self-hosted" wallets on the theory that they will be more private and less vulnerable to hackers.

Sending or receiving Bitcoin is, in essence, the transmission of a message ("Address X is sending 5 bitcoins to Address Y") that leads to the updating of a ledger—not so dissimilar to the way transactions occur in the banking system via the crediting and debiting of accounts. Unlike bank ledgers, though, Bitcoin's ledger isn't maintained in a central place; this is where decentralization comes in. The ledger is "distributed," that is, spread among myriad "nodes" on the laptops and mobile devices of Bitcoin users, any one of whom can look to see who owns what and which bitcoins have been transferred when—with the important caveat that everyone's identity remains concealed behind those public keys.

Just as a purchase by Amex or Mastercard requires some assurance that the transaction is legitimate, making a Bitcoin payment also entails a validation process, except it's also decentralized. Groups of Bitcoiners called "miners," who could be people or organizations anywhere in the world, use powerful computers to certify that every transfer of bitcoins comes from a wallet that genuinely owns said bitcoins. (Efforts by malefactors to spend bitcoins they don't legitimately hold will almost surely get rejected.) Every ten minutes or so, after about 2,500 transactions have been validated, a "block" showing those transactions is appended to the "blockchain"—that is, a chain of all the previous blocks containing an immutable record of all transactions.

This process is notorious for wasting electricity equivalent to the gigawattage used by medium-sized countries such as Finland or Chile. That's because miners use their computers—actually, industrial park–sized aggregations of supercomputers equipped with ultra-sophisticated, energy-guzzling chips—to do something else during the process of validating Bitcoin transactions. They also race, using pure brute computing force, to guess an extremely long number generated by the Bitcoin algorithm. The first to guess correctly appends the new block of validated transactions to the blockchain, and also gets rewarded with a few new bitcoins, which have metaphorically been "mined" just as if they were newly extracted gold. There's method to this madness; the huge investment that miners make in their equipment incentivizes them to sustain Bitcoin's value, which in turn incentivizes them to help keep the whole network honest. "Proof of work," this is called in crypto lingo, although a more apt term might be "proof of waste."

The reasons for economists' derision start with the obvious point that Bitcoin is merely lines of software code. Harkening back to the explanation in chapter 1 of what lies behind fiat currency, there's no scaffolding of state support imparting value to Bitcoin. "Creating money out of thin air" is an accusation that crypto enthusiasts often level at the fiat-currency system, but the air that Bitcoin is created from is much thinner. Bitcoin can't be used to pay the IRS, and even in countries where political leaders have decreed it to be legal tender — the only ones at this writing being El Salvador and the Central African Republic — most ordinary people shun it.

One of the supposed merits of Bitcoin — the finite amount that can ever be created — is not the least bit meritorious to anyone familiar with elementary macroeconomics. Satoshi wrote the code to ensure that the maximum amount mined would be 21 million bitcoins, the idea being to provide an ironclad guarantee against inflationary printing of the sort that has plagued many a fiat currency. That makes Bitcoin's "monetary policy" even more rigid than the gold standard, which had disadvantages galore, as will be recalled from chapter 2. An economy's money supply should ideally expand, in an "elastic" manner, along with the capacity to produce goods and services; if it doesn't — as the supply of gold didn't in much of the late nineteenth century — deflation is the result. Deflation is nice for creditors and investors, who get their repayments and investment returns in money that buys more than it did before, but it's typically injurious for most everyone else.

Furthermore, imitators began materializing as Bitcoin's novelty gained public notice, flooding cyberspace with dozens, hundreds, and eventually thousands of new cryptocurrencies running on blockchains and based to varying degrees on Satoshi's open-source software. Many of these "altcoins," such as Dogecoin (named for an internet meme featuring a Shiba Inu dog), weren't designed to have limited supplies, and no matter how furiously Bitcoin boosters denounced them as ersatz "shitcoins," their proliferation corroded Bitcoin's anti-inflation sheen. After all, in a world where anyone with a little coding expertise could post a jargony white paper on the web and sell digital tokens purporting to be money, where was the advantage over Weimar Germany with its wheelbarrows of cash?

Above all, Bitcoin and its copycats fell miserably short of fulfilling the key functions of money as their values soared and plunged. In a 2010 episode fabled in crypto lore as the first instance of Bitcoin being used to buy something, a software architect in Jacksonville, Florida, named Laszlo Hanyecz paid 10,000 bitcoins for two pizzas, which translated into a value of roughly one-third of a cent per bitcoin. Within a couple of years bitcoin was changing hands at more than $120 before spiking to $1,238 in 2013, falling below $100 a few months later, and then climbing to just over $20,000 in December 2017 – gyrating all the while from day to day and week to week. This is nobody's idea of a proper medium of exchange; indeed, even in the case of the pizza purchase, the bitcoins went not to a pizzeria but to someone in California who called the local Papa John's in Hanyecz's neighborhood and paid by credit card.

Just wait until the market and the technology mature, crypto enthusiasts insisted – and indeed, developers inspired by Satoshi's creation engineered all sorts of advancements. Among the most significant, Ethereum was proposed in a 2013 white paper by a 19-year-old self-taught software whiz named Vitalik Buterin, whose idea was to use blockchains not only for exchanging money but for conducting all manner of transactions. On the Ethereum blockchain, which was launched in 2015 and has its own currency called Ether, people can create "smart contracts" in which payment is made only if certain conditions are met. Instead of written contracts drafted by lawyers that can be taken to court, smart contracts are self-executing, meaning that they depend on code and the blockchain for enforcement – again, peer to peer with no intermediaries. Moreover, transactions can be executed in "atomic swaps," which refers to the inseparability of each provision. Either all parties fulfill the agreed conditions, in which case full execution takes place all at one time, or execution does not occur at all.

This is the programmable money of which MIT's Narula spoke, the drug company paying her for her health data being a good example of how it might work. Another example might be a crop insurance policy for a farmer needing protection against crop-ruining drought, by which the farmer would automatically receive, say, 50 Ether (worth about $130,000 at this writing) if rainfall failed to exceed a pre-agreed level.

But for all their talk of "democratizing finance," "economic empowerment," and other gauzy ideals, enthusiasts have struggled to identify real-world purposes for crypto. It has been shown to work reasonably well for illicit transactions, famously on a web-based exchange called Silk Road, operated by the pseudonymous "Dread Pirate Roberts," where buyers and sellers of drugs used Bitcoin to avoid detection by law enforcement until October 2013, when the FBI caught Roberts (real name: Ross Ulbricht, who was sentenced to life in prison). Perhaps the most convincing use case that crypto defenders have advanced is censorship resistance for people in countries such as Venezuela, Turkmenistan, or Equatorial Guinea who need some means of protecting their property from oppressive regimes. But mostly, crypto has served as a tool for speculation based on hopes that coin prices will rise in fiat terms, with prices depending solely on what others will pay. Crypto is unlike other assets whose value is based on real-world fundamentals, such as stocks, which represent claims on companies' profits; or bonds, which pay predictable streams of interest; or houses, which can be lived in or rented. "Investors" euphoric over surging gains on their crypto holdings tend to be dismissive of warnings that they are participating in a pyramid scheme that is sure to collapse when the supply of greater fools runs out. The establishment of well-funded exchanges such as Coinbase has helped ease traders' fears about the countless hacks and scams that have afflicted crypto. Never mind that such huge intermediaries are inimical to the idea of decentralization that animated the cypherpunks in the first place.

During most of crypto's first decade, bemused detachment prevailed among the world's financial authorities, especially after an unprecedented boom in 2017 gave way to "Crypto Winter" in 2018, with Bitcoin's price falling by nearly two-thirds in the first few weeks of the year. But soon thereafter came a development that jolted economic officialdom from indifference.

———

Cloistered in a room full of whiteboards on Facebook's corporate campus in Menlo Park, California, a small team kept their project hush-hush for over a year, with only their highest-ranking superiors apprised of their top-secret mission. Finally, in mid-June 2019, came the big reveal at a press launch that, even by Silicon Valley standards, stood out for the grandiosity of its verbiage. Facebook executive David Marcus, a veteran of startups and digital payment ventures, unveiled plans for a global currency called Libra,[10] the avowed purpose of which was to "empower billions of people, reinvent money and transform the global economy so that people everywhere can live better lives."[11]

Libra would be permissionless – that is, open to anybody – and would run on a blockchain. In those respects it was similar to Bitcoin and other cryptocurrencies. But rather than fluctuating it would be a stablecoin, maintaining a steady value in fiat terms based on backing from a reserve of low-risk assets denominated in major international currencies including the dollar, euro, and yen. From digital wallets downloaded to mobile devices, users could convert their local currency into Libra and then send it "to almost anyone with a smartphone, as easily and instantly as you might send a text message and at low to no cost," Facebook proclaimed in its announcement.[12]

Keenly aware of the many scandals that had engulfed Facebook, in particular those involving abuse of users' data, Marcus and his team designed Libra to be governed by an association of more than two dozen companies and nonprofits, with Facebook included along with the likes of Visa, Mastercard, Vodafone, eBay, and Spotify. But it was clear that Facebook was in the lead, and that the 2.5 billion people with accounts on the social media site would give Libra a potential user base unlike any other currency in the world.

Stablecoins had been part of the crypto universe since 2014, when the one that is currently the biggest was created by a company called Tether. Most of them promise to hold their value against the US dollar, and they are important for the functioning of crypto trading because they run on blockchains and can therefore be used for buying or selling other blockchain-based assets.

Libra was proposing to be entirely different from garden-variety stablecoins (about which more later). For starters, Libra would be used by consumers for payments rather than by crypto traders. Moreover, because it would be pegged to a basket of currencies rather than just one, it would be a supranational form of money somewhat like the SDR. People could fly from New York to Paris or São Paulo or Jakarta and pay their expenses in Libra, or place orders with e-commerce companies abroad for goods priced in Libra, all of which would involve transactions running through Facebook's digital ecosystem. This was digital money with serious pretensions of being a medium of exchange and unit of account.

To the chagrin of Marcus and Facebook CEO Mark Zuckerberg, governments and financial regulators responded with hostility to the idea of upending the global monetary system, especially since the upender was to be Facebook. Central bankers bristled over the prospect that Libra might undermine their authority over the supply of money. "No private entity can claim monetary power, which is inherent to the sovereignty of nations," declared French and German officials in a joint statement vowing to stop the project from advancing.[13] Although Facebook and its partners tried to assuage such concerns with assurances that Libra would have a neutral impact on monetary policy, plenty of other criticisms were raised. If Libra were successful, its reserve might total a trillion dollars or more, which could pose a risk of destabilizing the whole global economy should the currency be subject to some sort of shock. And since Libra's big selling point was making cross-border payments easy and seamless, it would probably facilitate money laundering and sanctions evasion too, government authorities figured.

The most formidable obstacle Libra faced was its provenance. "Do you really think people should trust Facebook with their hard-earned money?" Sherrod Brown, the top Democrat on the Senate Banking Committee, asked Marcus at a hearing.[14] Before long, the Libra Association was losing member firms fearful of being tarred with the anti-Facebook brush, leading the *Wall Street Journal* to report in October 2019 that the project was "on life support" a mere five months after its launch.[15] When Zuckerberg himself appeared at a US House hearing, lawmakers subjected him to a six-hour grilling that inflicted further damage on Libra's odds of survival. One of the least persuasive arguments that Zuckerberg and Marcus made was that Libra would "bank the unbanked" by providing financial services to the billions of people around the world who lack bank accounts. This line of reasoning (also advanced by Bitcoin's champions) is based on the faulty assumption that technical problems are chiefly responsible for keeping poor people from gaining access to money, rather than social and economic barriers. Equally futile were semi-patriotic appeals by Facebook executives that the alternative to Libra would be a Chinese-led network with obvious perils to personal privacy. When Marcus warned of an "internet of surveillance" if Beijing's digital renminbi triumphed over Libra, he was savaged thusly by Jemima Kelly in the *Financial Times:* "That's right, Facebook — literally the poster-child for 'surveillance capitalism'; a company whose business model has centred around surveilling its users and selling the data to other companies — is going to save the world from the internet of surveillance."[16]

Bowing to reality, Facebook and its partners scaled back Libra's ambitions and rolled out a new proposed version in April 2020. Instead of a multicurrency coin that had seemed to challenge the US dollar, the focus would be on creating a number of single-currency digital coins — Libra dollars, Libra euros, Libra yen, etc. — each backed by reserves of the respective currencies. Moreover, the network would no longer be permissionless; users would have to be vetted, with tight scrutiny to minimize the possibilities for money laundering and other illicit transactions. And the following month, the Libra Association took a further dramatic step in addressing concerns about its compliance with law enforcement: the new CEO was none other than Stuart Levey, the former Treasury undersecretary whose role in pressing sanctions on Iran (and remedying HSBC's compliance shortcomings) was chronicled in chapter 6. Under his leadership, Libra was also rebranded — the currency would henceforth be called "Diem" — to underscore its departure from the original Facebook vision.

"The reason I was willing to get involved was that I wanted to create a safe variation of crypto — safe for consumers, safe from illicit finance, with safe reserves and customer money completely segregated," Levey told me. "And we would make sure you couldn't transact anonymously. We would KYC everybody who would use this stablecoin. When I talked to people in the government, it was clear we had done everything they wanted us to do from an illicit finance perspective, certainly more than anyone in the space had dreamed of doing."[17]

The green light to go ahead was denied nevertheless, the crucial moment coming at a breakfast meeting attended by Fed chairman Jerome Powell and Treasury Secretary Janet Yellen on June 24, 2021. Although Powell said he was willing to allow trials for Diem, given all the measures that Levey and his team had taken, he added that as a technocratic institution, the Fed would need administration support. Yellen, who had deep reservations about Diem, wouldn't give it.[18]

That was the project's death knell. In early 2022, its remaining assets were sold to a California bank. Its legacy would be significant nonetheless. What if other Facebooks were out there, cooking up major initiatives in the field of monetary digitization? Minds were now focused, at high levels.

Basel, a town of stereotypical Swiss orderliness near the French and German borders, is home to the Bank for International Settlements (BIS), which is often described as "the central bank for central banks."[19] Founded in 1930 mainly to help central bankers administer Germany's World War I reparations payments, the BIS remained in operation even after Adolf Hitler came to power and repudiated reparations, because the leading central bankers of the day found it a congenial place to get together. Central bankers view themselves as conducting policy on an ethereal, apolitical level, and the BIS offered a refuge where they could interact with their peers at a comfortable distance from the pressures exerted by their governments and parliaments. On the second Sunday of nearly every month, the heads of major central banks (or their alternates) would gather over a sumptuous dinner, followed by meetings the next day—a routine they carried on throughout the 1930s, even as Europe girded for war. One friendship formed there—between Montagu Norman, governor of the Bank of England, and Hjalmar Schacht, president of the German Reichsbank—was so warm that in January 1939, with the outbreak of World War II less than a year away, Norman traveled to Berlin for the christening of Schacht's grandchild, who was named Norman in the Englishman's honor.

The current BIS headquarters, built in the late 1970s, is a cylindrical building, sometimes likened to a nuclear-plant cooling tower or the flat-topped mountain where aliens land in the movie *Close Encounters*. Spotless, retro-style white-leather sofas and chairs line the lobby and corridors, matching the architecture. About 600 staff members work in this building and another building nearby on the various services—chiefly economic research and management of foreign exchange reserves—that the BIS performs for the 63 central banks that own it. Gatherings of central bank officials and various international financial bodies continue to take place often there, in brightly lit conference rooms and a dining room on the 18th floor that affords a panoramic view of the Rhine rolling past Basel's quaint spires.

The BIS closet is hardly skeleton-free — it accepted looted Nazi gold during the war — and unsurprisingly, it remains subject to dark conjecture about goings-on within its securely guarded interior. A classic of the genre is *The Tower of Basel: The Shadowy History of the Secret Bank That Runs the World,* a book that casts a suspicious eye on BIS meetings attended by powerful central bank chieftains who maintain strict confidentiality about their discussions.[20] But for those of a less conspiratorial bent, the BIS can be perceived as providing a valuable global service by fostering interaction among policymakers who often need to coordinate with each other. Reports prepared by BIS staff and speeches by its high-ranking officials emanate frequently, both reflecting and helping to inform thinking in central banks around the world.

On the subject of monetary digitization, the BIS has become the world's foremost advocate for the creation of CBDCs, with technical support from multidisciplinary teams in Hong Kong, Singapore, London, and other cities as well as Basel. But it came to this position reluctantly. At first, BIS officials took a dim view of proposals for central banks to get into the digital currency act.

In a March 2019 speech, BIS general manager Agustín Carstens, a former governor of the Bank of Mexico, derided CBDCs as neither necessary nor desirable. He began by pointing out that money is heavily digitized already: "The important part of the acronym CBDC is not the 'D' for 'digital,' " Carstens said. "Nowadays, nearly everyone has access to digital payments. Whenever you or I pay using a bank debit card or use a banking app on our mobile phone, the payment is made digitally and often instantly. Instead, the important part of CBDC is the 'CB' for 'central bank.' A CBDC would allow ordinary people and businesses to make payments electronically using money issued by the central bank."[21]

For now, Carstens noted, only commercial banks have access to central bank digital money. (As will be recalled from chapter 1, these are reserves — accounts that banks hold at central banks, which get credited and debited electronically as banks transfer funds among themselves.) Should ordinary people and businesses also be allowed to deposit money directly with central banks? The logical outcome, Carstens warned, would oblige central banks — bureaucratic government institutions — to get into the sort of lending business that banks are much better suited to conduct. "The central bank would need to meet business owners, interview them about why they need a loan, and decide on how much each should receive," he said. "We can ask ourselves whether this is the kind of financial system that we would like to have as the ultimate set-up."

There are obvious ways around that problem, Carstens acknowledged. Central banks could avoid getting into the lending business if they sent customer deposits to commercial banks, which would maintain their role as lenders. Or a two-tier structure could be used for CBDC — similar to the way cash works — with ordinary customers getting CBDC only from commercial banks, which would in turn get them from central banks. But that might lead to other dangers for the stability of the whole financial system. In times of stress, "money moves away from banks that are perceived as risky towards banks that are perceived as safer," Carstens said, and "if depositors also have the choice of putting their money in a digital currency of the central bank," a "flight to safety" could be exacerbated.

For good reason, Carstens concluded, very few central banks surveyed by the BIS expected to issue a CBDC. "Research and experimentation have so far failed to put forward a convincing case," he said. "In sum, central banks are not seeing today the value of venturing into uncharted territory."

Three months later, Carstens was changing his tune. "It might be that it is sooner than we think that there is a market and we need to be able to provide central bank digital currencies," he told the *Financial Times* on June 30, 2019.[22] Moreover, the BIS announced that day that it was establishing an "Innovation Hub," whose first head would be Benoît Cœuré, a highly regarded French economist, to "foster international collaboration on innovative financial technology within the central banking community."[23]

Note the timing: during the period between Carstens's negative speech on CBDCs and his shift to a more favorable position came the announcement by Facebook and its partners in mid-June 2019 of the plan to create Libra. BIS officials insisted that Libra wasn't the sole factor; the Innovation Hub had been in the works prior to Libra's unveiling. But as Carstens admitted a few months later, Libra had been "a wake-up call. . . . We central bankers were in a comfort zone, but [Libra] showed we needed to change."[24] Cecilia Skingsley, who currently heads the Innovation Hub, recalls seeing "a lot of surprised faces" about Libra among central bankers who gathered at the BIS annual meeting in mid-2019. "There was a revelation. We are actually in a competitive business," she told me.[25]

The number of central banks that anticipated issuing CBDCs was indeed small in the first few months of 2019, as Carstens had said. Sweden's Riksbank was planning to launch pilot versions of an "e-krona" because the use of cash was dwindling to the point that Swedish merchants were refusing to accept it anymore. Work on the Sand Dollar was well underway at the Central Bank of the Bahamas, whose governor, John Rolle, championed the idea partly for financial inclusion reasons; the country is an archipelago with many remote islands where banks are reluctant to open branches.

The CBDC project of a much bigger country's central bank was also making progress that was drawing rapt attention in many corners of the globe.

CHAPTER 8

TO CBDC OR NOT TO CBDC

In mid-April 2020, a grainy screenshot leaked by an unknown person circulated on Chinese social media showing the image of a one-yuan note adorned with the face of Mao Zedong. This was the public's first glimpse of China's CBDC — specifically, a test version of the interface that customers of a large state-owned bank would see on their mobile phones when they used the DC/EP, or "digital currency/electronic payment," as it was then called. (The name e-CNY came later.) The screenshot showed that when users opened their wallet apps, various functions would be accessible, allowing them to track transactions, manage accounts, and link the wallet to their existing bank accounts.[1]

Pilots were soon underway in large Chinese cities including Shenzhen, Suzhou, and Chengdu. Civil servants in one Suzhou district were to start receiving half their transport subsidies in the new digital currency in May. Five months later, the phone screens of 50,000 Shenzhen residents lit up with messages informing the owners that they had won a lottery for "red envelopes" of DC/EP worth 200 yuan (about $30), which they could spend by pointing their phones at merchants' QR codes. This digital freebie resulted in more than 62,000 transactions, giving confidence to the People's Bank of China, which had started researching the idea of a digital currency in 2014, that its experiment would work.[2]

Here is a sampling of the apprehension that these developments evoked:

The pilot project . . . is a clear sign that China is years ahead of the United States in the development of what is likely to become a central component of a digital world economy.

U.S. policymakers are unprepared for the consequences. The advent of digital currencies will degrade the efficacy of U.S. sanctions. . . . And China, meanwhile, will use the combination of its digital yuan and strong electronic-payment platforms (such as Alipay and WeChat) to expand its influence and reinforce its capacity for economic coercion in Africa, the Middle East, and Southeast Asia.

—Aditi Kumar and Eric Rosenbach, "Could China's Digital Currency Unseat the Dollar?" *Foreign Affairs,* May 20, 2020

If [the United States] fails to acknowledge the transformative potential of a digital yuan in the absence of a US digital dollar, it may risk its hard-earned, historical economic superiority.

—Michael Greenwald, "Digitizing the Dollar in the Age of COVID-19," *New Atlanticist* (The Atlantic Council), April 22, 2020

The goal of DCEP is to extend the international reach of the renminbi and replace the U.S. dollar as the de facto global currency.

There are only three certainties in life: death, taxes and buying things from China. China can require that any trading partners of Chinese companies complete transactions in DCEP. If you want goods from China, you buy them with DCEP. . . . With control of that infrastructure, China would have . . . an unprecedented tool for monitoring individuals' activities wherever they are.

—Morgan Beller, "China Is Winning the Digital Currency War with the U.S.," *The Information,* February 11, 2021

[The] world's financial hegemon [is] vulnerable to a potentially fatal challenge. This new Chinese system not only defends the [Chinese Communist Party] against the twin threats of crypto and big tech, while ensuring that all Chinese

citizens' transactions are under surveillance; it also includes an offensive
capability to challenge the U.S. dollar's dominance in cross-border payments.
— Niall Ferguson, "Don't Let China Mint the Digital
Currency of the Future," Bloomberg, April 4, 2021

The rapid digitalisation of the renminbi . . . could be the key that accelerates
the decline of the dollar's dominance as the world's leading reserve currency. It
could also hasten the acceptance of the renminbi as the main rival to the US
currency.
— Michael Hasenstab, "China's Digital Currency Is a
Threat to Dollar Dominance," *Financial Times*, April 13, 2021

One major reason for such hand-wringing was that by 2020, the technological sophistication of retail payments in China had far surpassed that of the United States, Europe, Japan, and other advanced economies. Foreigners who visited China or lived there recounted wondrous yet unnerving tales about the methods Chinese used to conduct their financial affairs. Understandably, Westerners found it disconcerting that modes of payment common in their countries, such as credit cards, were scorned as out-of-date by Chinese merchants, who had become accustomed to mobile phone apps for all manner of transactions. In China, even beggars displayed QR codes to minimize the hassle of bestowing alms. One of my Canadian colleagues living in China spun an entertaining yarn about a street-stall maker of Shandong-style savory pancakes (a popular breakfast snack) who, thanks to mobile payment apps, served lines of commuters near a subway station without having to take off her gloves to count change. Indeed, her customers could scan her QR code even before arriving at the stall to let her know how they wanted their pancakes prepared—with hot sauce, spring onions, or lettuce.[3]

All the more stupefying was the short span of time in which this advancement had occurred. Until around 2013, China's financial system could fairly be described as antiquated, with most consumers using cash for daily purchases and savers confined to storing their money at banks staffed by insouciant clerks offering meager interest rates capped below inflation by government edict. Only about one in six people had credit cards, and many merchants refused them anyway.[4]

The lack of an entrenched modern financial infrastructure provided an ideal market environment for entrepreneurs Jack Ma of Alibaba and Pony Ma (no relation) of Tencent to devise technologies that could leapfrog the West. And leapfrog they did, taking advantage of the ubiquity of mobile phones among China's 1.4 billion people. At first, during the early 2000s, they stumbled into payments innovation because they needed a way for merchants to receive funds for goods sold online. In China, where consumers didn't trust merchants and vice versa, there was no reliable way of clicking "pay" on a site such as Amazon that retained customers' credit card numbers. Once the popularity of their early payment methods became apparent, the two companies added an array of other features in their "super apps," Alipay and WeChat. Among the most important disruptions came in mid-2013 from Alibaba, whose e-commerce site Taobao (search for treasure) was supplemented with Yuebao (leftover treasure), a money market fund that enabled Alipay users to earn more than 6 percent interest on their idle funds—forcing banks to start offering decent rates on regular deposits. Soon thereafter the fintech giants were providing consumer and small-business credit (aided by their access to their users' data, by which they could assess people's creditworthiness), insurance, ride hailing, ride payment, utility bill payment, parking, and everything needed for a restaurant meal—making the reservation, viewing the menu, ordering food, ordering delivery, and paying the bill. By 2017 China was ranked number one in the world for fintech adoption.

But government officials, who had cleverly allowed the disruption of the old banking-centric financial system, grew increasingly wary of the control the tech duopoly held over so much of the country's wealth and data. Together, the two firms accounted for 94 percent of online payments in 2020, with Ant (Alibaba's affiliate) having 900 million users and WeChat having 800 million. Worried about the implications for financial stability, regulators imposed tough new restrictions on Ant's lending, and when Jack Ma gave a speech in October 2020 criticizing Beijing's overzealous intervention in markets, his company's planned offering of new shares was canceled, reportedly on orders from President Xi Jinping. Although the episode was seen abroad as a crackdown on Jack Ma for daring to defy the Communist hierarchy, Pony Ma's empire was hit with similar regulations.

It was in this context that the DC/EP rollout occurred. The chief motivation for China to launch its CBDC was to rein in Alipay and WeChat, create an alternative payment method, and thereby prevent the loss of control over payments and credit allocation. Another spur was Libra; Chinese officials were if anything even more agitated than their Western counterparts about the Facebook-engendered global digital currency, which they saw as potentially undermining their grip on money within their own national borders. These essentially domestic concerns, rather than ambitions for world monetary domination, were the primary drivers of China's CBDC project, according to virtually every assessment I've seen by experts with deep knowledge of Chinese finance, including, notably, by Martin Chorzempa of the Peterson Institute for International Economics, whose book *The Cashless Revolution* is the most authoritative history of Chinese fintech.

It is important to be clear-eyed, though, about the fact that Chinese citizens' financial information is far from safe against surveillance by a party-state that is increasingly intolerant of the slightest dissent. As Chorzempa writes in his book, the e-CNY presents "a privacy nightmare . . . and the consequences to civil liberties could be dire."[5] He is rightly unimpressed by Chinese central bankers' promises that monitoring of e-CNY transactions will be limited – "controllable anonymity," they call it, with small accounts requiring only a phone number to open and phone companies prohibited by law from providing government agencies with identifying information about the account holders. Such legal hurdles would not stop determined government officials from freezing the e-CNY wallets of people deemed insufficiently loyal to the Communist Party, such as human rights lawyers.

This is a regime, after all, that exploits myriad technologies – closed-circuit video cameras, facial recognition, and geolocation data, among others – to catch people for offenses as minor as jaywalking. Government censors constantly sift through traffic on WeChat, which most Chinese use for exchanging messages, posting photos, paying bills, and coordinating with work colleagues.[6] Rule-breakers have found themselves unable to board trains or planes because law enforcement officials have suspended their payment methods. In fact, Beijing exercises so much surveillance and coercive power already that the additional snooping capacity provided by the e-CNY may therefore be limited.[7]

The biggest worry about the e-CNY is that authoritarian governments around the world could adopt the technology for their own CBDCs and use it to surveil their own citizens. But that doesn't mean Americans or other people in advanced democracies should be quaking in fear that they will soon be at the mercy of privacy-compromising Chinese monetary instruments.

Although merchants almost everywhere in the world accept Alipay and WeChat Pay—they want business from Chinese tourists, of course—that's not the same as market penetration or takeover by Chinese-controlled entities in the financial sector. Efforts by Alibaba and Tencent to expand and obtain users abroad have mostly flopped, which is no coincidence. The firms enjoyed spectacular growth in their home market because China's primitive financial system needed such massive improvement; as Chorzempa shows, the Chinese super-app model had much less to offer in the markets of advanced countries.

As for the e-CNY's international prospects, the impact will be marginal at best in the competition between the renminbi and the dollar. Digitization changes nothing about the fundamental factors—Beijing's weak rule of law prime among them—that limit the renminbi's appeal to international investors. (Whether the e-CNY might help boost evasion of US sanctions is a separate question, which will be addressed later.) Furthermore, lurid claims that millions of Westerners' mobile phones will become loaded with e-CNY are based on misconceptions about how CBDC works. Being digital and under more direct control of official entities than paper currency, CBDC isn't analogous to rolls of bills that can circulate black-market-style around the world. Even if the People's Bank of China permitted nonresidents to use e-CNY outside of Chinese national borders (which it appears loath to do), the monetary authorities of the United States and other nations would have a big say as well over whether foreign CBDCs could be widely accepted for payment within their jurisdictions. Central banks will almost certainly strike multilateral CBDC agreements among themselves to protect their own national currencies from encroachment.

Now for the kicker about the e-CNY:

In March 2023, two reporters from the *South China Morning Post* went to the largest and most popular shopping mall in Suzhou, where pilot trials for the new currency had commenced almost three years earlier. Their findings were

---

similar to mine in the Bahamas regarding the limited uptake of the Sand Dollar. Not that it was difficult to use e-CNY, but hardly anybody did. As the article observed, "Alipay and WeChat Pay . . . offer a myriad of services, from retailing and catering to medical services, that ensure convenience in their respective ecosystems to keep subscribers from looking to engage with other platforms. The e-CNY . . . offered consumers neither additional convenience nor any compelling reason to be regular users."[8]

A drink shop employee at the mall told the reporters that in the time the store had enabled e-CNY payment, she had not encountered a single person who wanted to use it. "You're the first one to propose to use e-CNY," the reporters quoted her as saying. The story was much the same at another shop, where an employee said customers used e-CNY only about once a month. Michelle Feng, a government employee interviewed by the reporters, said that at the request of the authorities she opened an e-CNY wallet, where her salary and bonuses have been deposited—but she transfers the whole amount to her bank account and uses it via Alipay and WeChat Pay. "Why should I bother to download another app and use e-CNY when I'm already so used to Alipay and WeChat Pay for many years?" she asked.

The mall was no anomaly. Data for the third quarter of 2022 showed that transactions involving the e-CNY by Chinese consumers were valued at barely more than 0.1 percent of the comparable figure for private digital systems.[9]

The Chinese themselves, in other words, show little sign of using their CBDC. Why, then, should the United States issue one? Some US policymakers have been asking similar questions for some time.

Gravity and earnestness, rather than humorous turns of phrase, are hallmarks of speeches by Fed officials. An exception was the address delivered in late June 2021 by Randal Quarles, who was then the Fed's vice chair for supervision. Beneath his conservative, Republican, Mormon exterior, Quarles has a dry wit, which he used to good effect in what has come to be known as the "parachute pants speech."[10]

Americans have a penchant for getting carried away by novelty, which can lead to "occasionally impetuous, deluded crazes or fads," Quarles told the audience, a convention of Utah bankers. "Sometimes the consequences are in hindsight merely puzzling or embarrassing, like that year in the 1980s when millions of Americans suddenly started wearing parachute pants."

"But the consequences can also be more serious," he added — and the same sort of misguided enthusiasm, driven by a "fear of missing out," appeared to be driving a "fever pitch" of calls for the Fed to issue a CBDC. To set up his argument, he posed a basic question that must be addressed in any deliberate consideration of CBDC: "What problem would a CBDC solve?"

Like Carstens, Quarles started with the observation that there is nothing new about transacting digitally; "the dollar is already highly digitized," and even though many Americans still use paper checks, the process of interbank check collection is almost entirely electronic. The US system "is not perfect — some types of payments should move more quickly and efficiently," Quarles acknowledged, citing the high costs of cross-border payments as a particularly troublesome example, but "work is already underway to improve it." Large-value payments already move almost instantaneously on Fedwire and CHIPS, and as for lower-sized amounts, a network for bank customers called the automated clearinghouse (ACH), once notorious for slow processing, has started enabling same-day settlement of many payments. Moreover, development was proceeding apace on a service called FedNow, which "will soon provide recipients of small-value payments with immediate access to their funds in commercial bank accounts," Quarles said. (With participation by some, but not all, US banks, FedNow went live in mid-2023.)

Quarles then considered — and dismissed — some of the main arguments for a US CBDC, starting with the alleged threat to the dollar: "The dollar's role in the global economy rests on a number of foundations," he said, citing the same factors that have been chronicled in this book. "None of these are likely to be threatened by a foreign currency, and certainly not because that foreign currency is a CBDC." Turning to the issue of Americans who lack bank accounts, he noted that the percentage of unbanked households dropped from 8.2 percent in 2011 to an estimated 5.4 percent in 2019, and although it would be "a worthwhile goal" to reach everyone, "I am far from convinced that a CBDC is the best, or even an effective, method to increase financial inclusion."

Whatever the benefits of CBDC, they were surely outweighed by the risks, Quarles contended, citing cyberattacks as one worrisome threat because, "compared to the Federal Reserve's existing payment systems, there could be far more entry points to a CBDC network." Then he turned to the knottiest CBDC problem of all — the Big Brother implications. The Fed would have to ensure that a CBDC doesn't facilitate illicit activity, but that would entail an extremely difficult tradeoff against excessive government intrusion in citizens' personal lives. "At one extreme, we could design a CBDC that would require CBDC holders to provide the Federal Reserve detailed information about themselves and their transactions; this approach would minimize money-laundering risks but would raise significant privacy concerns," he said. "At the other extreme, we could design a CBDC that would allow parties to transact on a fully anonymized basis; this approach would address privacy concerns but would raise significant money-laundering risks."

The parachute pants speech was an entertaining and insightful piece of repartee in an international dialogue that has taken place, often at a high level of wonkiness, about whether CBDC is desirable and, if so, how it should be designed. Among the issues addressed by economists, technologists, and policymakers in fora such as conferences, academic papers, and books are the following: Should CBDC be "retail" (available for use by the general public) or "wholesale" (meaning that only banks and other financial intermediaries could use it)? If retail, mightn't that risk exacerbating financial crises, in the event that holders of bank deposits pull their money out of banks to seek the 100 percent government-backed safety of CBDC? Or might that risk be mitigated by limiting the amounts of CBDC that individuals can hold at one time? Should CBDC offer a modest interest yield that could be turned negative under certain circumstances, giving central banks a new tool for combating recession by incentivizing people and businesses to spend and invest their money sooner rather than later? Should CBDC run on blockchains or some other type of database?

What about governance, such as restrictions on the things CBDC could be used to pay for? It may seem obvious that payment for illegal activities should be prohibited, but as the savvy Canadian money expert John Paul Koning has observed, defining what's lawful and what isn't can be "much trickier than it sounds," one example being determining whether porn sites have taken sufficient care to prevent display of video involving children. With tongue only partly in cheek, Koning speculated that CBDC issuance would oblige the Fed to

---

appoint a "porn expert . . . to regularly check up on clip sites for compliance."[11] Although solutions may be devised for extracting central banks from such duties, the possibilities for becoming embroiled in political controversy are endless.

A desire to avoid these and other pitfalls explains why Fed chairman Jerome Powell adopted the following mantra about CBDC: "It is more important to get it right than to be first,"[12] by which he meant that long and hard deliberations will be required before any decisions are made. When the Federal Reserve Bank of Boston, together with MIT's Digital Currency Initiative, launched a technical research program on CBDC called Project Hamilton in August 2020, Fed officials stressed that the work would be "hypothetical" and that no consensus existed within the Fed system about which direction to take.[13] Although some Fed governors, notably Vice Chair Lael Brainard, were favorably disposed toward issuing CBDC in some form, others echoed Quarles's view. Even in 2023 and 2024, divisions within the Fed persisted, and in any event Powell and his colleagues acknowledged that they can't act without approval from Congress.[14]

The Biden administration, too, struck an ambivalent stance. An executive order on digital assets issued in September 2022 instructed the Treasury to "lead an inter-agency working group to consider the potential implications of a U.S. CBDC" and spelled out broad guidelines that should be followed. But the White House stopped short of endorsing the idea, saying "further research and development . . . is needed."[15]

The administration's caution proved wise, at least on political grounds. The battle over CBDC in the United States has degenerated from the wonky to the wacky.

Cudgels have been taken up by prominent figures who are much less thoughtful than Quarles — a combination of hard-core conservatives and conspiracy-theorizing leftists who talk about CBDC as if it were a Deep State plot aimed at totalitarian mastery over every American.[16] Just look at what happened in Ottawa in early 2022, they say, when Canadian authorities froze the assets of "Freedom Convoy" truckers who protested Covid vaccine mandates by blockading traffic at the US-Canada border.

Florida governor Ron DeSantis won approval from his state legislature for a bill to block acceptance of a federally sponsored CBDC in the Sunshine

State, declaring in a March 2023 press release: "The Biden administration's efforts to inject a Centralized Bank Digital Currency is about surveillance and control. . . . We will not adopt policies that threaten personal economic freedom and security." Several other states are considering following Florida's lead as these words are being written, and after launching his failed candidacy for the 2024 Republican presidential nomination, DeSantis whipped up the crowd in a televised interview, telling commentator Tucker Carlson that CBDC "will allow them to prohibit 'undesirable' purchases like fuel and ammunition. So, the minute you give them the power to do this, they're going to impose a social credit system on this country. CBDC is a massive threat to American liberty. On January 20, 2025, it goes to the ash heap of history in this country."

Senator Bill Hagerty, a Tennessee Republican, has tweeted similar sentiments about CBDC ("would give the federal gov. unprecedented insight into your life"), and Michael Flynn, the retired Army general who served briefly as Trump's national security adviser, thunders against CBDC in rallies he holds around the country. Trump himself swore in early 2024 that if he won the November election, he would "protect Americans from government tyranny" by "never allow[ing] the creation" of a CBDC. On the left, CBDC foes include Robert F. Kennedy Jr., the anti-vaxxer who challenged Biden for the Democratic nomination; he denounced CBDCs as "instruments of control and oppression [that] are certain to be abused."

The peculiar thing about much of this rhetoric is that it's based on exaggerated ideas about the extent of financial privacy that US citizens currently have. Any transaction Americans make that is linked to their bank accounts — payments with credit cards, debit cards, PayPal, Venmo, Apple Pay, etc. — can be traced and subject to scrutiny by law enforcement agents, provided, of course, that the agents have obtained a warrant from a judge. Under the Constitution's Fourth Amendment protections against "unreasonable searches and seizures," judges aren't supposed to issue such warrants absent "probable cause, supported by oath or affirmation" that criminal activity is occurring. Judicial decisions and congressional legislation have added a few extra elements to the rules governing personal financial records, but the broad constitutional principle applies, just as it does to other forms of police surveillance such as wiretaps.[17]

In any healthy democracy, a retail CBDC would be subject to similar principles, obliging law enforcement to go through appropriate legal channels before gaining access to data on a user's device or wallet provider. The Bank of England's Jon Cunliffe has drawn a useful distinction in explaining how the digital pound (a.k.a. "Britcoin") will work: it won't be anonymous, but it will be private. Full anonymity, after all, would give anyone using CBDC the opportunity to engage in all manner of nefarious acts, with the convenience of digital transmission; privacy would assure users that their data and transactions couldn't be surveilled without the same kind of protections against abuse that currently apply to bank-linked accounts. "For a CBDC, we would completely respect that balance," Cunliffe has said.[18]

That leaves the question of how to manage the balance. Various proposals have been advanced and put into practice. In the Bahamas, for example, a threshold system is in effect, allowing citizens to use Sand Dollars anonymously up to a certain amount, above which KYC rules apply.[19] A person can hold up to $500 at a time in a digital wallet, and transact up to $1,500 per month, without providing identification or linking the wallet to a bank account. (One way to do so is to buy Sand Dollars at kiosks, using cash.) People wishing to hold larger amounts in their wallets must present government-issued identification or link their wallets to bank accounts. Other, higher-tech solutions include cutting-edge cryptographic techniques, among them zero-knowledge proofs, which (to greatly oversimplify) allow a party to verify a statement without revealing additional data. Touters of zero-knowledge proofs contend that they can ensure individual users' privacy on digital ledgers without compromising law enforcement agencies' ability to fight crime. But zero-knowledge proofs are too slow and clunky to handle the huge number of transactions that must be processed every second in modern payment systems; developers may or may not overcome this obstacle.

In any event, issuance of a CBDC wouldn't mean everyone has to use it (unless you believe conspiracy theorists who claim that this is the Deep State's secret plan). The forms of payment that Americans like now — cash, checks, credit or debit cards, etc. — would still be widely used, as they should be depending on circumstances. Churchgoers would continue to put mostly bills and coins in collection plates, in part to avoid inconveniencing their places of worship with credit card fees. Shoppers looking to make an expensive purchase — a laptop computer, say, or a refrigerator—will presumably use their credit cards, which not only provide protection against defective goods but enable the buyer to borrow the cost.

To CBDC or not to CBDC—that is one question. To have totalitarianism or not to have totalitarianism—that is an entirely separate question. By this I mean that whatever form our currency takes, our government's respect (or lack thereof) for individual rights is far more important. If a country's government falls into the hands of authoritarians who are inclined to maintain power via all manner of undemocratic means, it will hardly matter whether a CBDC has been issued. The freezing of Freedom Convoy members' assets, whether justified or not, was undertaken without Canada having issued a CBDC. As long as government is prevented by Fourth Amendment–type rules from unreasonable searches and seizures of individual people's data, and as long as the authorities abide by the rule of law regarding such searches and seizures, a CBDC should not result in violations of privacy. DeSantis and his ilk are stooping to what historian Richard Hofstadter has called "the paranoid style in American politics."

Still, the central point that Quarles made in his parachute pants speech must be confronted. Before embracing CBDC as a solution, it is essential to identify what problem(s) it addresses. It is also essential to consider whether alternatives might solve those problems better.

In a casino with any pretension of classiness, one of the first things gamblers do is buy chips. Throwing cash on the blackjack or roulette tables is a big no-no as far as the croupiers and bouncers are concerned, not least because of the inconvenience involved; dollar bills are time-consuming to count and are often crumpled. Tuxedos and evening gowns may not be *de rigueur* on a casino floor, but chips are, thanks to the ease with which they can be stacked and kept track of.

With good reason, casino chips are an oft-cited metaphor for stablecoins, which derive their name from their promise to hold their value against a fiat currency or other reference asset. That's because stablecoins are pretty much essential for placing bets in the high-stakes crypto universe. Whereas fiat currencies can't be used directly on blockchains, stablecoins are designed to exist only "on chain." Hence their principal use—trading and speculating in blockchain-based crypto assets and DeFi (decentralized finance).

But stablecoin-minters harbor ambitions to serve much larger markets, on the theory that blockchains will one day become the main platforms for all kinds of transactions.[20] In 2021, those ambitions swelled as the total value of stablecoins in circulation quadrupled, to over $175 billion.[21] That meteoric growth — indeed, the mere fact of stablecoins' existence — gave the companies that issue them a key advantage in their campaign to convince US policymakers that the future of the digital dollar rests with stablecoins rather than CBDC.

As noted above, Tether has been around since 2014; its coin, known as USDT, is by far the biggest in the market, with almost a 75 percent share, more than three times that of its nearest competitor, USD Coin (USDC). (PayPal entered the market in August 2023 with its own PYUSD, the success of which remains unclear.) Each of them is linked to the US dollar, with a promise of a $1-per-coin value, which the issuers vow is backed by ample reserves of dollar-denominated assets. And since nearly all other stablecoins are also dollar-linked, that means Americans shouldn't view their country as lagging behind in the digital currency race, according to officials of stablecoin-issuing firms. On the contrary, "the US is leading the world in a critically important industry," wrote Dante Disparte, chief strategy officer and head of global policy for Circle, the company that issues USDC, in a July 2021 essay.[22]

Such arguments resonate on Capitol Hill, where the crypto industry has deployed battalions of lobbyists skilled in the arts of persuasion along with copious amounts of campaign donations. Members of the House and Senate tend to be anxious about the dollar's vulnerability to potential rivals, and stablecoin boosters are clever at exploiting that sentiment.

"To strengthen the dollar's dominance as the global reserve currency, our main priority should be to spread dollars far and wide — to make them available to anyone and everyone around the world," Jake Chervinsky, chief policy officer for an industry group called the Blockchain Association, told a House subcommittee in April 2023. "Stablecoins represent a categorical improvement on legacy payment infrastructure, allowing users to transfer any amount of value to any person anywhere in the world nearly instantly and at nearly zero cost."[23]

Lest America's ascendancy in this market segment cause my fellow US citizens to indulge in an orgy of chest-puffing, however, some less-than-savory aspects of the industry's operations merit consideration. One serious rap against stablecoins is that they're unreliable chips, not truly worth $1 per coin as they claim.

A notorious illustration of stablecoins' fragility was the implosion in May 2022 of TerraUSD, created by a Stanford-educated South Korean named Do Kwon whose brashness was encapsulated in his taunt to critics: "I don't debate the poor on Twitter."[24] Having grown during 2021–2022 to a market capitalization of $18.7 billion, TerraUSD attained a No. 3 ranking among stablecoins, all the more remarkably because it was an "algorithmic" version, basing its one-for-one valuation against the dollar not on reserves of real-world assets but rather an automated arbitrage strategy involving a related cryptocurrency. TerraUSD's lack of intrinsic value became apparent to all when an initial trickle of selling on May 8, 2022, led to a cascade in following days, rendering the coin worthless and resulting in tens of billions of dollars in losses.[25]

Tarring all stablecoins with the Do Kwon brush would be grossly unfair, particularly to USDC and its issuer Circle, which has gone far in providing well-documented evidence about the adequacy and high quality of its reserves, which are mostly US Treasury securities and cash. Tether is another story, however.[26] Managed from offshore entities, it is replete with red flags, starting with its long-standing failure to submit to a thorough audit of its books and the explanation by a spokesman that the company doesn't want to reveal the "secret sauce" behind the popularity of its tokens on crypto platforms. Regulators and assorted law enforcement agencies have hit the company with fines to settle allegations over falsehoods and misrepresentations regarding its financial soundness. Several people in its top ownership and executive ranks have histories of involvement with enterprises accused of various malefactions, and their simultaneous control over Bitfinex, a major crypto exchange, arguably constitutes a flagrant conflict of interest that would never be permitted in properly regulated financial markets. None of this has kept Tether from remaining atop the stablecoin world; information that it has grudgingly provided about the tens of billions of dollars' worth of Treasury bills, commercial paper, cash equivalents, and other safe assets that it holds has evidently sufficed to satisfy a critical mass of market players.

If only Congress would enact legislation establishing a sound regulatory framework for stablecoins, they could evolve successfully from casino chips into

---

179

the mainstream payments realm, the industry's champions contend.[27] Suppose, for example, issuers were required to hold HQLA (high-quality liquid asset) reserves—short-term Treasuries, bank deposits, etc.—equal to at least 100 percent of all outstanding coins. Suppose further that transparency rules obliged them to publish monthly disclosures or audits of their financial condition, and only firms complying with such requirements would be entitled to use the term "stablecoin" for their product, just as the name "bank" is restricted to institutions obtaining legal authorization.

A hypothetically well-regulated stablecoin, after all, would be similar to other financial products that Americans use all the time. People put their idle cash into bank deposits, with the expectation that they can get it back in full with a smidgen of interest, or if they want something yielding a bit more they choose money market funds that guarantee a stable price of $1 per share. What distinguishes stablecoins is that they're on blockchains. In addition to running 24 hours a day including weekends and holidays, blockchains hold out the prospect of innovative payment functionalities using smart contracts. As noted above, these could include insurance payouts in the event disasters occur. Micropayments could become a common method for supporting artists, musicians, or other creative individuals; freelance journalists could receive a fraction of a cent for every "like" their articles get, as Circle's Disparte has suggested.[28]

But a more apt parallel for stablecoins, even less flattering than casino chips, is the profusion of notes issued by individual banks that Americans used as money during the Free Banking Era.[29] Just like the bills engraved with portraits of Daniel Boone or images of farmers harvesting wheat chronicled in chapter 2, stablecoins are obligations of purely private entities, whose ability to make good on their promises is regarded with full confidence in some cases but not all the time. This analogy rankles industry representatives, who reasonably argue that well-crafted regulation could protect stablecoins from the ills that plagued the US monetary system in the mid-nineteenth century. But stablecoins used for payments would raise new problems stemming from the fragmentation of money issuance.

Stablecoins are bearer instruments; possession is ownership, and represents a claim on the issuer (Tether, say, or Circle). When you transfer a stablecoin to someone else, the new owner acquires that claim, without any involvement by the issuer such as identity verification to ensure compliance with AML/KYC/CFT laws. Crypto evangelists have trumpeted this feature of stablecoins — the "transactional freedom" that they provide, as bearer instruments that can be transmitted permissionlessly, with reduced susceptibility to government surveillance — as a selling point.[30] From the user's standpoint, the appeal is obvious; not so from the standpoint of those trying to police the international financial system for illicit activity. The scenario of stablecoins making it possible to "spread dollars far and wide," in the previously mentioned words of the Blockchain Association's Jake Chervinsky, may sound like an American geopolitical dream come true. It could well be the opposite.

Let's say you're a Russian dealer in shady commodities looking to buy a few hundred thousand barrels of Venezuelan oil, but it's too risky to pay for it by transmitting US dollars using conventional methods because the Venezuelan state oil company is sanctioned. Luckily for you, Tether affords a workaround. You send millions of dollars' worth of the USDT stablecoin to a broker in Caracas who can convert it into cash — $100 bills, lots of them, which are widely used in inflation-plagued Venezuela and perfectly acceptable to the state oil company.

"No worries, no stress," you tell your Venezuelan oil contact. "USDT works quick. . . . That's why everyone does it now. It's convenient, it's quick."

That is exactly what Yury Orekhov did — and those were the exact words he used, according to an indictment unsealed on October 19, 2022, by federal prosecutors in Brooklyn. Because Orekhov and his confederates used USDT to buy Venezuelan oil in ways that technically didn't touch the US financial system, they neatly dodged American sanctions; the crimes of which they were accused involved a bevy of other malefactions, including smuggling advanced microprocessors with military applications into Russia.[31]

Tether again! Like the proverbial bad penny, it increasingly pops up in investigations involving money laundering, fraud, the funding of North Korea's nuclear program, and other such illicit capers — because it's both stable in value and often difficult to track. In his exposé of crypto titled *Number Go Up*, Bloomberg News investigative reporter Zeke Faux describes how Chinese gangs operating in Cambodia use USDT as their preferred currency for "pig butchering," in which victims are duped into transferring assets to scammers posing as romantic suitors. Likewise, Tether's US dollar stablecoins are the main vehicle used by Garantex, a Moscow-based crypto exchange, that enables Russians — many evidently connected with criminal entities — to move billions of dollars to countries such as the United Arab Emirates where the funds can be withdrawn as spendable fiat from local partner operations.[32]

Here is another case where the sins and abuses of one cryptocurrency should not be generalized to the whole asset class. Crypto has come a long way from its early years when it was simple for crooks to exploit. Nowadays, customers of reputable crypto exchanges must undergo KYC verification when they open accounts; in the United States and other major industrialized democracies these companies are obliged to obey the same laws as standard money service businesses and maintain robust AML compliance programs. Coinbase, for example, has more than 400 employees who work on tasks including filing SARs and blocking the transmission of funds to or from blockchain addresses that are blacklisted.[33]

Furthermore, because blockchain transfers take place on public ledgers, with anyone able to see how funds move from one address to another, law enforcement agencies can trace transactions even more easily than they can in the "tradFi" (traditional finance) system. For officials at agencies such as FinCEN, this feature enables unprecedented capacity for tracking flows — as many illicit actors have learned, to their sorrow, after being nabbed. Not only that, but "freeze and seize" functions can be programmed into digital assets, so when government gumshoes identify an address as suspicious or illicit, exchanges and stablecoin-minters can aid the crackdown by interdicting and impounding funds associated with that address pending an investigation. Tether itself has dutifully executed "freeze and seize" orders; in late 2023, for example, it froze stablecoins in 41 wallets controlled by people on OFAC's SDN list, including one involved with a North Korean hacking group, and in 32 other wallets linked to terrorism and warfare in Ukraine and Israel.[34]

But loopholes and evasion techniques abound for circumventing restrictions.[35] Perhaps most important is the lack of controls over many "on-ramps" and "off-ramps" — the junctures where customers convert fiat into crypto and vice versa. When on-ramps and off-ramps are closely regulated and monitored, as they are for transactions on exchanges such as Coinbase, lawbreakers are usually hamstrung from turning their ill-gotten gains into freely usable money; not so in cases where scrutiny is lax or absent. Among the most malicious manifestations of successful off-ramping is ransomware, in which cybercriminals hack the computers of, say, a US hospital or school system and threaten to destroy the files or publicly disseminate sensitive data about patients or students unless payment in some form of crypto is received. Most ransomware gangs are Russian, and use exchanges in Russia to off-ramp their crypto into rubles without any interference from governmental authorities — provided, of course, that the gangs refrain from attacking Russian companies.[36]

On top of that are "mixers" (also known as "tumblers"), which obscure the clarity of blockchains by pooling all sorts of cryptocurrencies together and swapping them in long series of complicated transactions, finally spitting them out to the intended destinations in a manner designed to make the coins untraceable. Further obfuscation comes in the form of "self-hosted" crypto wallets for people who don't want to transact on exchanges. With a couple of mouse clicks, anyone can set up a self-hosted wallet and begin transmitting funds without KYC verification — the result being another blind spot in the government's surveillance capacity.

Together with the Justice Department and other law enforcers, the Treasury scrambled during the Biden administration to plug the loopholes and foil the evaders. In 2022 and 2023 OFAC sanctioned a number of mixers — Tornado Cash, Blender.io, Sinbad, and others — much to the fury of libertarians who argued that mixers serve legitimate privacy needs of people and companies.[37] Also sanctioned have been Garantex and other exchanges that the Treasury views as noncompliant, although this hasn't stopped many of these exchanges from flourishing. And in a move that drew worldwide headlines, in November 2023 a host of federal agencies lowered the hammer on Binance, the biggest crypto exchange, extracting a guilty plea for sanctions violations from the company and on criminal money laundering charges from its billionaire founder Changpeng Zhao (a.k.a. "CZ"). Shocking lapses in Binance's vetting of its customers came to light in an indictment showing that from 2017 to 2021 most clients could sign up for accounts with nothing more than an email address;

although thousands of its users were in US-sanctioned Iran, the firm didn't bother filing SARs and failed to collect full KYC information until 2022. The fines levied on CZ ($50 million) and Binance ($4.3 billion) were relatively modest, but much more painfully for the firm, its settlement included an agreement to drastically upgrade its AML/KYC compliance operation, with monitors from the government directly overseeing the staff for up to five years. Upon seeing the details, prominent crypto critic John Reed Stark exulted that the settlement will "expos[e] the company—and its customers—to a 24/7, 365-days-a-year financial colonoscopy."[38]

Tether also came squarely into the Treasury's gunsights. In late 2023, Deputy Secretary Wally Adeycmo warned Congress that certain dollar stablecoin transactions abroad "involve no U.S. touchpoints," and he pressed for legislation that "could explicitly authorize OFAC to exercise extraterritorial jurisdiction over transactions in stablecoins pegged to the USD," even if the stablecoin issuer is based offshore as Tether is. Foreign stablecoin issuers shouldn't be able to take advantage of the US dollar's global status without "procedures to prevent terrorists from abusing their platform," Adeyemo contended.[39]

Conceivably, Tether and other stablecoins will advance technologically to the point where their software can detect involvement by illicit actors and prevent transactions from proceeding. If so, that would eliminate one major impediment to their suitability in the world of legitimate payments. But stablecoins have other big shortcomings.

Look what has happened to stablecoins during recent periods of financial turmoil.[40] In May 2022, when a series of crypto firms crashed and burned, Tether's coins traded for as low as 95 cents on the dollar before recovering, and the following autumn, amid the spectacular downfall of the crypto exchange FTX, one unit of Tether dipped to about 97.7 cents thanks to large-scale redemptions. As for Circle's USDC, it dropped briefly below 87 cents in March 2023 owing to reports that it kept some of its reserves at Silicon Valley Bank, which was suffering from a run on its deposits. Those sharp declines highlighted the fact that stablecoins are tradeable, at prices that regularly fluctuate around the promised $1 level. The deviation from par is usually very small, as little as a few hundredths of a percent, but it is a deviation nonetheless.

A bombshell report by Moody's Analytics in late 2023 showed that "depegging" of stablecoins is neither a rare nor a minor occurrence. Depeggings happened more than 700 times in 2022 and more than 600 times in the first nine months of 2023 among the largest, fiat-backed coins such as USDT and USDC, according to the report, which defined a depegging as a fluctuation against the fiat peg of more than 3 percent during a single day.[41]

Therein may lie an important part of the answer to the question posed in the parachute pants speech — what purpose would a CBDC serve?

It is time to return to a concept introduced in this book's first chapter: the "singleness of money." In terms of US currency, a dollar is worth exactly $1.00, and a hundred dollars is worth exactly $100.00, whether you're paying with public money (bills from your wallet) or private money (say, a check or debit card drawn directly on your bank account, or a credit card or phone app or other payment method ultimately linked to your bank account).

The singleness of money gives us confidence as we transact — paying for small-ticket items (say, a coffee), or big-ticket items (say, a major appliance), or receiving wages, salaries, and other income. It affords similar confidence to businesses and large institutions as they dispense and receive much greater sums. The dollars I transmit to you have exactly the same monetary worth as the dollars you transmit to me, whichever bank we have our accounts at, whichever payment method we use. Underlying our comfort level about that is our awareness that those dollars could be converted into bills with the words "legal tender" on them, anytime we want, even if neither of us actually bothers to go to an ATM or bank teller window to make a withdrawal.

Recall too the role played by another form of money — central bank reserves, held at the Fed — that is essential to sustaining singleness in a system involving the electronic transfer of enormous amounts of dollars. Instead of bags of specie moving from one bank to another as in mid-nineteenth-century New York City, settlement action takes place on the Fed's balance sheet. The Fed debits or credits the reserve accounts of banks as their customers make or receive payments, for which the customers' own accounts are debited or credited. This process is only one part of the legal and regulatory framework underpinning the dollar, but it is crucial. All of the dollars involved are fully fungible with each other, valued at par, and the absence of concern about that—the widely shared trust in its verity—is a significant boon to Americans' material well-being.

These closely linked principles—the singleness of money, and the *sine qua non* of a well-functioning central bank—are at the heart of a forceful argument by the BIS in favor of CBDC. In June 2022, as part of its annual report, the Basel-based institution released a publication titled "The Future Monetary System" envisioning a world of far-reaching technological advancements in money based upon digital instruments issued by central banks or ultimately backed by them.[42]

The timing could hardly have been better from the BIS standpoint. It came in the aftermath of TerraUSD's collapse and a slew of losses, layoffs, bankruptcies, and freezes of customer funds at crypto hedge funds, lenders, brokerages, and exchanges. "Recent events have revealed a vast gulf between the crypto vision and its reality," the report observed, with more than a hint of schadenfreude. But regardless of whether prices of Bitcoin, Dogecoin, and others were soaring or plunging, crypto could not serve as proper money because of its "fundamental flaws," according to the report, which proposed an "alternative vision . . . rooted in the trust provided by central bank money."

Hyun Song Shin, the BIS economic adviser and head of research who served as the report's chief intellectual author, pushed the case further in news conferences, interviews, and presentations. A native of South Korea with three degrees from Oxford including a doctorate in economics conferred in 1988, Shin speaks with a sober locution befitting his academic background (he was a Princeton professor before moving to the BIS in 2014). But in spreading the CBDC gospel, he sometimes employs rhetoric redolent of the pitches that tech bros make to Silicon Valley venture capitalists. "The potential is huge. We're on the cusp of a major development," he said on *Fintech Beat,* a podcast hosted by Georgetown University law professor Chris Brummer. "And it's not science fiction."[43]

Shin's self-proclaimed "motto," repeated at every opportunity: "Anything crypto can do, CBDC can do better."[44] (A couple of exceptions for which crypto is superior, he caustically observed, are money laundering and ransomware attacks.) He conceded that crypto has given "a glimpse of all these exciting things" that could be done with digital tokens, such as programmability and smart contracts. But a CBDC could enable similar functionality, for example by running on a permissioned blockchain (not a Bitcoin-style permissionless one, with all the associated problems including electricity wastage), and could thus be programmable, with transactions executed atomically when agreed conditions are met. And because it would rest on the "secure foundation of central bank money," a CBDC could do those things without sacrificing the singleness of money and other benefits that come with the existing monetary system, Shin asserted.

The BIS vision is intended for all countries rather than any one in particular. But it provides a much-needed dose of cogency to the CBDC debate in the United States. "China has a CBDC, so we'd better have one too" is a lame argument for issuance of a US CBDC, as are others that Quarles considered and wrote off in the parachute pants speech. In their 2022 report, and in subsequent reports and papers, Shin and his BIS colleagues put the pro-CBDC case on much sounder footing.

Under a scheme that the BIS is promoting, the whizzy instruments that the general public would use are "tokenized deposits."[45] These aren't CBDCs — and that's important, because it may help defuse the political firestorm in the United States over CBDCs potentially infringing on personal liberty. Although one type of CBDC would be part of this arrangement — the wholesale kind, used only by banks and other financial institutions — retail CBDC (the kind individuals use) wouldn't necessarily be included.

As their name implies, tokenized deposits are a form of bank deposit; they represent claims by depositors on their commercial banks, just as regular deposits do. But instead of being mere entries on a normal ledger that go up or down along with inflows and outflows, tokenized deposits are digital representations of deposits that can be transmitted on programmable ledgers, making them amenable to the sort of "if-then or else" conditionality afforded by smart contracts and atomic settlement.

Tokenization is a term that is increasingly used in a variety of ways, so to be clear about the meaning here, let's put it in the context of more familiar things. Take checks again: they are paper representations of orders to pay, and stock certificates are paper representations of ownership in corporations; those instruments can also be represented digitally in the form of electronic data entries at banks and brokerage firms, with statutes specifying the legal rights of payers and payees and buyers and sellers. Tokenization takes digitalization of an asset or liability one big step further, by including the rules governing transfers so that conveyance can involve contingent performance of action. At its simplest, this could be the example noted above of payment for something—a toaster, or shares of Apple stock—taking place only after delivery, and delivery taking place only after receipt of payment.

Tokenized deposits already exist, albeit in highly restricted form. The first was JPM Coin, issued by a unit of the megabank JPMorgan Chase, whose CEO Jamie Dimon scorned Bitcoin as a "fraud" but acknowledged that blockchain had intriguing potential.[46] It is available only to the bank's corporate clients for transacting with each other on a business-to-business basis, using a private blockchain, mostly involving financial securities.[47] A number of other major financial firms have developed their own iterations.

At some point, Shin and his colleagues imagine, tokenized deposits will go retail—that is, into the market for the general public. If and when that happens, customers would be able to go to their banks and convert deposits into tokenized versions, which could be used to buy goods, services, or other assets for which a programmable form of money is advantageous. The singleness of money would be preserved because tokenized deposits could also be converted back into regular deposits, or into cash, at par. They would even be covered by deposit insurance (on the same terms as regular deposits, presumably) and other protections of banking regulation and supervision that give people confidence to park money in the banking system. Further ensuring singleness, transactions would settle behind the scenes, as they do in the current system, in central bank money. Specifically, they would settle in wholesale CBDC, which would serve a similar role as reserves do currently, being decreased at a sender's bank and increased at a receiver's bank, although with added features enabled by programmability.

To show the potential applications of such a system, the BIS cites global supply chains, where goods made by firms spread around the world are shipped from one to another before final assembly. Difficulties often arise, and deals may fall through, because of payment problems, which tokenized money could help overcome. Suppose, for example, an Italian luggage maker wants to buy fabric from India, but both the luggage and fabric makers are wary of each other; the

---

luggage company wants to defer payment until the fabric is delivered, while the fabric maker — who has workers to pay and bills coming due for materials — insists on up-front payment. A tokenized deposit could be programmed, using GPS, to guarantee payment once a ship transporting the fabric has passed a certain geographical landmark. Or it could be programmed so that payment reverts back to the luggage maker if the fabric fails to arrive within 30 days.

Going further into tech-bro mode, Shin touted real estate as a "really interesting and exciting use case" in a talk at the University of California, Berkeley. Buying or selling a house or apartment, he noted, is probably the biggest transaction most people make in their lifetimes, and the buyer wants to ensure proper transfer of ownership while the seller wants to ensure receipt of payment. Even after the price is agreed on, a number of procedures involving weeks of expensive work by intermediaries are typically necessary: land registries and property titles must be checked, often in files at municipal government offices, and the absence of unpaid taxes and prior liens or other possible obstacles such as cultural landmark designations must be confirmed. But suppose land registries and all those other pieces of information were put online in tokenized form. "If we can do that," Shin said, "there's nothing in principle that would stop us from putting tokenized real estate on the same platform as we put tokenized deposits," which would mean a house sale could take place atomically. Payment would be transmitted in tokenized deposits provided that the necessary conditions were met, and property ownership would also be conveyed in tokenized form at the exact moment that payment was received.[48]

Crypto enthusiasts have also claimed home sales as a future use case. But the assets that change hands in the crypto-verse aren't real, like stocks, bonds, buildings, or land; instead, they largely consist of non-fungible tokens (NFTs) such as digital images of cartoon simians from the "Bored Ape Yacht Club" collection, which enjoyed a surge of popularity among celebrities, as well as bubbly prices, in early 2021. That is no coincidence, Shin argues. "It goes back to the decentralized nature of crypto itself," he said when I interviewed him on a visit to the BIS, and he elaborated in comments that are worth quoting at length:

> In the old days, when you sold something like a corporate bond, you had a paper certificate. You actually handed over the certificate, and the other person handed

over, say, gold coins. Now these things are accounted for in book entries at centralized securities depositories. You don't need paper certificates; brokers notify the depository, and everything is done with book entry. Of course there's a whole legal framework behind that, to certify ownership and so forth.

What would it take for there to be a securities registry in Ethereum? That's the venue where you have these bored apes. It's completely decentralized. What legal framework would allow you to transfer real assets? And these are borderless platforms — which country is going to allow their securities to be recorded on Ethereum? Who's going to oversee it? Where's the regulator?

Tokenization isn't simply digital representation of something; it's digital representation that assures the buyer that when you acquire the token you have also acquired the underlying asset. In the case of houses, it's necessary for the land registry to cooperate, to alter its records to show that a particular house has been tokenized so it can only be bought and sold in tokenized form and not in the conventional way. You need a lot of steps for that to happen.

That's why I've said crypto has given us a glimpse of what's possible. There's trading of bored apes and NFTs, but in the real world, as soon as we take a step inside, there's a whole legal infrastructure and regulation and institutional backing that underlies it. It's easy to take our institutions for granted, but they exist for a good reason.[49]

Not all countries have good institutions. In some, such as Argentina, Zimbabwe, and Lebanon, the term "trusted central bank money" could be ridiculed as an oxymoron. For the citizens of those countries, it may be desirable, even a matter of life or death, to have access to Bitcoin or stablecoins linked to sound fiat currencies. Allowing such instruments to exist makes sense for that reason.

But this is a book about the US dollar. The central bank that issues it has shown that trust in its governance is well deserved. The Fed's chair and governors are appointed by the president, confirmed by the Senate, and regularly summoned for interrogation by congressional committees. Although they err sometimes, particularly in optimizing the tricky balance between inflation and recession, they take their mandate to serve the public interest seriously.

That doesn't mean Fed officials or other US policymakers will opt for an approach like the one the BIS advocates. On a webinar in which Shin presented his case, this stinging rejoinder came from Fed governor Christopher Waller, a leading CBDC skeptic: "Too often I see research papers on CBDC that look like infomercials. . . . 'It slices! It dices! It minces! It mashes!' And the whole idea is to keep you from asking, do I really need this thing?"[50]

Shin's response: advancements in the realm of money, finance, and payments will go in a variety of novel directions that can't currently be foreseen, much as mobile phone apps did after the 2007 introduction of the iPhone. "When we think about the monetary system and think about policy for the next five to ten years," he said, "we should be trying to anticipate what the system will look like, what the technology might enable you to do, five to ten years from now, rather than looking backward and saying, do we need it right now."

Speaking of what the system will do five to ten years from now, might CBDC and other new monetary technologies lead to a weakening – or even an evisceration – of America's ability to use the dollar as a key instrument of its national security policy?

Sitting in a conference room at the BIS headquarters in Basel, I watched a demonstration, via a video feed from Hong Kong, of an experimental project involving CBDC that has triggered both excitement and unease in the currency world.

After an exchange of polite introductions, an economist with the BIS Innovation Hub's Hong Kong center shared her computer screen, on which lines of white code zipped and blipped across a black background in the lower left corner. She then explained what she was about to show – the sending of a CBDC version of the Thai baht called the "e-THB" from Hong Kong to Thailand, for the purpose of settling an international trade deal between a Hong Kong company and a Thai company. The amount sent would be 4 million baht.

The economist clicked on drop-down menus, selected options, and filled in fields to set the transaction terms. She entered the 4 million baht amount, chose the relevant pair of currencies used by sender and receiver – the e-HKD (a CBDC version of the Hong Kong dollar) and the e-THB – and entered an exchange rate; then, when prompted to select a settlement time, she chose "immediately." Once her request was initiated, it went to a commercial bank for an automated screening process that included a series of checks for limits set by participating central banks.

Seconds later, the transaction was confirmed and settled. Shazam! — or, depending on your perspective, yikes!

The project that the economist demonstrated is called mBridge (the "m" stands for "multiple CBDC"), a joint initiative of the BIS and four central banks in Thailand, Hong Kong, the United Arab Emirates, and China.[51] It uses a custom-designed private blockchain called the mBridge ledger, which transmits wholesale CBDC. No actual money changed hands in the demo that I watched, but during a pilot that took place over six weeks in August and September 2022, more than $22 million worth of real transactions were completed among 20 commercial banks on behalf of corporate clients in the four participating jurisdictions. Of course, even in the pilot, the CBDCs were just prototypes; of the four participating central banks, only China's has actually issued a CBDC.

"Sandbox" is the term technologists use for this type of project, because it takes place in a sequestered environment for testing purposes. In addition to mBridge, central banks around the world have undertaken other sandbox projects in recent years, often with the encouragement or active involvement of the BIS.[52] They include Jasper-Ubin (involving the Bank of Canada and Monetary Authority of Singapore), Stella (the ECB and Bank of Japan), Aber (Saudi and UAE central banks), Jura (the Bank of France and the Swiss National Bank), and Dunbar (Reserve Bank of Australia, Central Bank of Malaysia, Monetary Authority of Singapore, and South African Reserve Bank). The overall aim is to overcome drawbacks in the traditional correspondent banking model for making cross-border payments, which is plagued by high costs and low speed, and may involve multiple banks spread over different time zones and operating hours. In some small developing countries, banks with correspondent networks have pared back their operations to the point where affordable access to cross-border payments is difficult.

The "yikes" factor with mBridge arises because the People's Bank of China is one of the participating central banks — it was responsible for much of the software and coding for the ledger — and the US dollar plays no role in the project's cross-border payments. For those reasons, mBridge has drawn attention as a possible turning point in the currency competition between Washington and Beijing. It is, by some accounts, the vehicle by which China will fully exploit its first-mover advantage in CBDC. The sandbox project of today, the mBridge ledger, or something like it, may in the not-too-distant future provide the means for China to transact in e-CNY with as many countries as it likes. As an alternate infrastructure outside the dollar system, it would create a channel for international money flows with no visibility for Washington, the perfect foil for Chinese policymakers against the US-led sanctions regime.[53]

"Yikes"-shrieking is not wholly unwarranted. US sanctions have created enormous incentives for many governments to seek ways of dodging the dollar. Although doubts abound about the scalability of mBridge (that is, its capacity for handling large volumes of transactions), it could conceivably develop with Beijing's support into a high-tech, high-functioning corridor for the settlement of non-dollar payments using CBDCs. Indeed, at a late October 2024 summit in Kazan, Russia, of BRICS (named for its founding coalition of emerging market economies – Brazil, Russia, India, China, and South Africa), Putin proposed developing just such a thing, a modified version of m-Bridge that would be called "BRICS bridge." Given the know-how that Chinese central bankers have gained from their involvement in mBridge, who would dare to rule out the possibility of technologically novel forms of monetary transmission that cut the dollar out as middleman in some substantial amount of international trade?

But depicting these transmission systems as "killer apps" for sanctions-busting is overdone. Agreement would be required on complex rules concerning how exchanges of one CBDC for another are handled – the main issues including financial crime monitoring, foreign exchange dealing, payment settlement, and provision of the huge amounts of liquidity needed to facilitate large-scale cross-border payments. If large numbers of countries are involved, which would presumably be the objective, reaching such an accord would take many years, assuming it could be achieved at all. Perhaps because of those practical obstacles, or perhaps because of fears that the US Treasury would be able to sabotage any such system by targeting participating governments and banks, Putin's proposal got a tepid reception at the Kazan summit.[54]

Moreover, some of the shrieking – not all, but some – appears to be based on faulty notions about how financial sanctions work. It might seem as if everything depends on agents sitting in the basement of the US Treasury or far-flung CIA outposts who monitor flows of money all over the world, so the instant that someone enters "USD" as the currency for a payment, the agents can pounce and block the transaction if an SDN is involved. Some of that cloak-and-dagger activity undoubtedly occurs, but it's not nearly as consequential as the Treasury's power to order large banks to cease doing business with an SDN, or with all the banks the SDN does business with. As noted in earlier chapters, banks pretty much everywhere need access to New York–based dollar clearing and settlement if they want to provide financial services for firms of significant size. As a result, Washington's powers of intimidation will still be formidable – the e-CNY, mBridge, and BRICS Bridge notwithstanding – given the dollar's international status.

Our focus now shifts from the futuristic topic of monetary digitization back to lower-tech issues. The events chronicled in this chapter – the rollout of the e-CNY, the US debate over CBDC, the stablecoin boom, the publication of the BIS vision, the testing of the mBridge ledger – all transpired in the early years of the 2020s. During that same period, major developments outside the digital realm were entrenching the dollar's primacy, and providing new justification for its use in sanctions.

CHAPTER 9

ROARING IN THE TWENTIES

"Clueless." "Boneheads." "Going loco." Those were a few of the epithets that Donald Trump hurled in 2018 and 2019 at the Fed, in particular Chair Jerome "Jay" Powell.[1] Fixated on the Dow Jones Industrial Average as a metric that he hoped would boost his chances for reelection, the president blew his stack over a Fed interest rate hike in the fall of 2018 that caused stocks to dip. The news media was full of reports about Trump's inquiries to aides about whether he could fire Powell, whose appointment in 2017 he lamented as the worst decision of his presidency. Advisers reportedly persuaded Trump to drop the idea in late 2018; they explained that Fed governors, who are appointed to 14-year terms, could only be removed for serious dereliction of duty, not a policy dispute, although the law was less clear about the president's authority to revoke the four-year term of the chair.[2] That didn't stop Trump from repeatedly expressing his displeasure in following months, especially during downdrafts in the Dow, over what he viewed as the Fed's overly tight policy. Refusing to acknowledge that his trade war with China was at least partly responsible for falling stocks, Trump tweeted: "My only question is, who is our bigger enemy, Jay Powel [sic] or Chairman Xi?"[3]

This was quite a departure from presidential civility toward the Fed that had prevailed since the consecration of the central bank's independence during the

Volcker era. Under an informal rule laid down in the early days of the Clinton administration by Robert Rubin, who then chaired the National Economic Council, the Fed was off-limits for criticism by the White House or other parts of the executive branch—and the rule was scrupulously followed during Clinton's two terms and the two administrations that followed. The reasoning was simple: pressuring the Fed, especially in public and especially for monetary easing, would only sow doubt about its commitment to maintaining price stability. Counterproductive consequences would likely ensue, including market jitters, and Fed officials might well dig in their heels to avoid any appearance of political servility.

Fed independence was not the only pillar of dollar dominance that Trump battered. Another was rule of law, for example when he used threats of government crackdowns to strong-arm individual companies into keeping factories open, and most infamously when he tried to reverse the outcome of the 2020 election. But as this chapter will show, the dollar's primacy would not only survive Trump's 2017–2021 term in office but end up strengthened by the time he left the White House, a trend that would continue when Joe Biden took over. The fortification of the dollar's status would be attributable in large part to actions taken by the very institution that so irked Trump—the Powell-led Fed.

Powell is not an economist like the three economics PhDs (Alan Greenspan, Ben Bernanke, and Janet Yellen) who preceded him as Fed chair.[4] Growing up in Chevy Chase, Maryland, the second of six children, he attended Georgetown Prep, an all-boys Jesuit high school, and from there went to Princeton and Georgetown Law School, from which he graduated in 1979. But he had ample experience in the intersection between financial markets and government, having moved from law to investment banking in 1983 and following his boss to the Treasury, where he rose to undersecretary for domestic finance in the early 1990s. More valuable than any formal training or professional background, perhaps, were his natural people skills. Upon being appointed to the Fed as a governor in 2012, he devoted himself to gaining economic expertise by reading extensively—books, articles, blogs, anything he could find—and asking staffers for briefings, which enhanced his reputation for modesty. As chair, his disarming congeniality served him well in harnessing the talents of others in the Fed's top policy echelons who boasted sterling economic credentials, including Vice

Chair Lael Brainard, Vice Chair Richard Clarida, and New York Fed president John Williams.

Throughout the barrage of invective from Trump, Powell maintained an imperturbable stance in public, refraining from firing back and sticking to economic issues. When asked point-blank about whether Trump's comments were influencing Fed decisions, he had a stock reply: the central bank would neither allow itself to be swayed by politics nor feel compelled to prove its manhood; monetary policy would be dictated solely by economic considerations. He did his utmost to quell any doubt about his resolve, telling Nick Timiraos of the *Wall Street Journal* in an off-the-record conversation: "I'd rather go in the books as a terrible Fed chair than somebody who knuckled under."[5]

But the presidential assault complicated his job, by adding a new and crucial priority — ensuring that the Fed's institutional integrity would endure. Awkwardly, Powell and his colleagues were coming around to the view in early 2019 that they had gone too far in raising rates in 2018; inflationary pressures were much more subdued than they had expected. Accordingly, they decided to make a course correction toward an easier policy — a step fraught with humiliating potential because it carried the implicit admission that Trump's complaints had been well founded. Extremely nuanced communication would therefore be necessary to show the economic justification for every policy move.[6]

Three times the Fed lowered rates in 2019, enabling the economy to barrel along in the longest expansion on record, with the unemployment rate at 3.5 percent, the lowest since 1969. Those easing measures didn't go fast or far enough for Trump, who continued blasting away, accusing Powell of having "no guts" and a "horrendous lack of vision." Asked by a reporter in August 2019 whether he wanted the Fed chief to resign, the president replied, "Let me put it this way: If he did, I wouldn't stop him."

Trump's intimidation of the Fed reached its zenith — or nadir, depending on your perspective — on March 14, 2020, at a press conference with his recently formed Coronavirus Task Force. The virus had then killed 50 Americans, the president said, far lower than the death toll in other countries, which he cited as proof of how effectively and energetically his team and every part of the US government was responding — except the Fed; it "should be much more proactive," he griped. A reporter then asked, given Trump's constant carping over the Fed, "why don't you dismiss the chairman? Or do you think you're powerless to do so?" In reply, Trump strongly hinted that he might order Powell's demotion: "No, I think I have the right to do that or the right to remove him as chairman. He has, so far, made a lot of bad decisions in my opinion. . . . I have the right to remove, I'm not doing that . . . I have the right to also take him and put him in a regular position and put somebody else in charge and I haven't made any decisions on that."[7]

It will never be known how much further Trump might have gone in bending the Fed to his will, or what that might have done to the standing of the central bank and the currency it issues. Fast-moving events were confronting Powell with bigger worries than Trump, and vice versa.

By the dawn of the 2020s, the market for US Treasury securities had evolved in ways that would have been unfathomable to the government bond traders of the mid-1970s — the hotshots riding limousines out of Wall Street saloons, whom we met in chapter 3. First there was the market's sheer size, with $18 trillion in Treasury obligations outstanding, of which about 40 percent were held overseas, and trading running at an average of nearly $600 billion a day.[8] (By comparison, $30 billion of daily trading in Treasuries was viewed as a staggering volume in the mid-1970s.)[9] Another feature of the 2020s market that was undreamt-of in the mid-'70s was the prevalence of "high-frequency trading" involving the holding of positions for fractions of a second based on algorithmic formulas.

Trillions of dollars! High frequencies! Algorithms! What could go wrong?

The liquidity of this market is crucial for the dollar's global standing, as we have seen. To restate the point: confidence that there are so many buyers and sellers of Treasuries, and that even in a crisis a purchase or sale will amount to little more than a drop in a big bucket, makes the dollar attractive to multinational banks, Asian pension schemes, Middle Eastern sovereign wealth funds, and a myriad of other institutions and businesses. Treasury securities don't yield a high return compared with other, riskier investments, but they do provide assurance that, when obligations are coming due under emergency conditions, the necessary cash can be obtained immediately.

Beyond that, proper functioning of the Treasury market can fairly be described as important for economic well-being in virtually every corner of the globe, because the daily churn of hundreds of billions in Treasuries sets the yield for the closest thing in the world to a risk-free asset. That yield in turn serves as a benchmark against which investors and lenders assess all sorts of debts, such as bonds issued by other governments, short-term commercial paper issued by companies, business borrowings from banks, home mortgages, auto loans—the list goes on. The yield on Treasury bills due to mature in three months or six months is the risk-free standard that enables investors and lenders to determine what interest rate will induce them to extend credit for a few months; the yield on two-year Treasury notes or ten-year Treasury bonds provides similar information for the extension of credit for longer terms.

Now suppose the assumptions in the previous two paragraphs about the workings of the Treasury market were to prove misplaced. What if the world's safest asset couldn't be readily sold, or if sales of sizable amounts could only be consummated at sharp or unpredictable discounts from the latest prices? Since Treasuries could no longer be deemed safe under such circumstances, how high would their yields have to rise to compensate investors for the heightened risk, how badly would all other markets be discombobulated as a result, and how much more costly would it become for anyone, anywhere, to obtain credit?

The outbreak of the Covid-19 pandemic gave the financial world a brief but terrifying encounter with the chaos that could ensue from a Treasury market breakdown.[10] In the second week of March 2020, as minds reeled from the virus's proliferation, wild swings in Treasury yields began materializing on bond traders' screens, along with a sudden blowout of gaps between bids and offers—that is, the prices buyers were willing to pay and sellers were willing to accept. A couple of similar episodes had occurred in previous years, but none were comparable to this one.

"There's a fundamental problem in the Treasury market. It's just not functioning," Gregory Peters, a senior portfolio manager at PGIM Fixed Income, told the *Financial Times* after a day of particularly glitchy and distorted trading conditions on March 11. "It is freaking people out." Traders at another firm, TwentyFour Asset Management, tried to sell a "modest" holding of 30-year Treasuries that week, but when they asked three major banks for prices, two refused even to bid, according to a message to clients from the CEO, Mark Holman, who wrote: "This was extraordinary, and unprecedented in our experience."

A report issued on March 12 by Mark Cabana, a strategist at Bank of America, said the market had become "overwhelmed by liquidity concerns" and warned that "if the US Treasury market experiences large-scale illiquidity it will be difficult for other markets to price effectively and could lead to large-scale position liquidations elsewhere." Echoing that view in a *New York Times* article, Rick Rieder, chief investment officer of global fixed income at BlackRock, said: "If you don't know where the safest asset in the world is, it becomes next to impossible to figure out where everything else is." The stress was exacerbated by the disarrangement of working from newly rigged home offices; as another fund manager told the *Financial Times,* traders "can't communicate with colleagues properly" because they are "isolated at home in their sweatpants."[11]

Grounds for economic pessimism would only intensify in March as America began to shut down in response to evidence of the virus's infectiousness and lethality. During the second week of that month, Seattle became the first major US city to close its public schools, the US government banned incoming travel from Europe, the World Health Organization officially declared a global pandemic, and Dr. Anthony Fauci, the federal government's top infectious disease expert, told Congress that Covid was ten times as deadly as seasonal influenza. In following days Disneyland closed, Broadway went dark, the National Basketball Association suspended its season, New York City ordered thousands of bars and restaurants to stop serving customers, Detroit's Big Three automakers ceased production at their plants, and Washington closed US borders with Canada and Mexico to all but essential traffic.

Stocks fell so steeply during the first three weeks of March that temporary trading halts, called circuit breakers, were triggered several times on US stock exchanges. A decline in share prices was a rational response to the certain loss of corporate income from widespread cessation of business operations, and by itself did not signal anything systemically amiss. Much more troubling was a simultaneous drop in Treasury prices, the result of a worldwide "dash for cash," as the media aptly called it. Everyone wanted dollars; against a basket of major currencies, the greenback surged over 8 percent between March 8 and 20.[12] But a desperate scramble for liquid resources needed to pay bills meant that equally intense efforts were underway to sell Treasuries, which the market couldn't accommodate nearly as efficiently as participants had come to expect.

—

Just as it had during the Global Financial Crisis, the Fed would fulfill the lender-of-last-resort responsibilities that central banks bear in such situations. What about *international* lender of last resort, though — would the Fed reprise that role? Acute demand for dollars overseas was increasingly manifest during the first couple of weeks of March, and calls were mounting for the Fed to arrange swaps of currencies — dollars for euros, dollars for yen, dollars for Swiss francs, etc. — of the sort it had implemented with foreign central banks a dozen years earlier. Whether it would be able to do so was far from clear, given Trump's penchant for conducting diplomatic relations like New York real estate deals. *Financial Times* columnist Gillian Tett quoted a former central banker who was involved in the 2008 swap lines as wondering: "Is the White House going to demand a quid pro quo from places like Europe or Japan?"[13]

In early March, the Fed responded to the contractionary impact of the pandemic with emergency cuts in interest rates, but the ructions in the Treasury markets showed unmistakably that the crisis was of a different category than an economic downturn. In part, the problem with Treasuries reflected the abnormal degree of selling pressure — mutual funds, for example, were experiencing massive investor withdrawals, and they sold Treasuries to generate the cash needed to satisfy demands for redemptions. But another factor was the volatility engendered by the aforementioned algorithms.

Orderly trading in Treasuries, as in many other types of securities, depends on market makers who buy and sell throughout the trading day — a thin-margin, high-volume business, as noted in chapter 3. For Treasuries, this function has traditionally been played by an elite group of financial institutions, many with household names (such as Citi, JP Morgan, Goldman Sachs, and Morgan Stanley), that hold special status with the Fed as "primary dealers." Among their most important roles is to transact directly with the New York Fed's trading desk as it buys and sells Treasuries in its efforts to influence interest rates. In exchange for that privilege, these financial institutions are expected to make markets in Treasuries, maintaining a narrow spread between bids and offers, whether overall prices are rising or falling. Of course, they are allowed to protect themselves against injurious losses that might result from selling bonds for less than they have paid; if prices slide, they can adjust their bids and offers.

But after the Global Financial Crisis, these big dealers pulled back somewhat from the Treasury market, mostly because of new regulations aimed at bolstering the financial soundness of major banks. It is not necessary to go into the details here other than to say that algorithmic trading, some of which was conducted by hedge funds, filled much of the void. These computerized systems facilitate vast numbers of transactions each day, matching buyers and sellers with bid and offer quotes in a blink of an eye, and they perform especially well in calm markets. But in March 2020, with prices oscillating violently from minute to minute, the algorithms—which are programmed to widen bid-asked spreads as risk increases—caused already illiquid market conditions to become even more so.[14] In automatic obeisance to their models' recognition of greatly heightened money-losing dangers, market makers retreated from trading large amounts and in some cases stopped quoting prices altogether, which exacerbated the panicky atmosphere. To make matters worse, losses that the hedge funds were suffering on their Treasury-market bets caused their lenders to hit them with margin calls, and to satisfy those obligations the hedge funds themselves had to unload tens of billions of dollars' worth of Treasuries at a time when buying had all but evaporated.

To keep the US economy afloat, the Fed's response included many of the measures taken in 2008—cutting interest rates to zero, which Powell announced at a Sunday press conference on March 15; deploying an alphabet soup of facilities to incentivize the funneling of credit throughout the private sector; and creating special entities to purchase risky assets. In 2020 Powell and his colleagues would go many steps further, both quantitatively and qualitatively, crossing red lines that the Bernanke Fed had only tiptoed up to.[15] The 2020 initiatives included purchasing newly issued bonds from large US corporations, in effect lending directly to them; buying municipal bonds and exchange-traded funds (ETFs) that invest in "junk" (low-rated) bonds; and establishing a "Main Street Lending Program" to buy bank loans to small and medium-sized businesses. "Quantitative easing" (QE) also took place at an unheard-of scale and speed—the Fed purchased about $2 trillion worth of Treasuries and related securities, all within the first two months after the start of the Covid outbreak. By hoovering up so many Treasuries, the Fed played the role of dealer of last resort, serving as buyer to pretty much anyone who wanted to sell, restoring normality to the market and giving market makers the confidence to intermediate transactions as they had before. On March 23, 2020, the Fed issued what was essentially a "whatever it takes" statement, vowing to buy Treasuries "in the amounts needed to support smooth market functioning."[16]

Some of these measures generated controversy over the degree to which the Fed was inserting itself into the functions of private markets. But the overall rationale was straightforward and unassailable — averting a collapse of the US economy and the financial system on which it depended. Unlike in 2008, fundamental blame for the crisis lay with a microscopic pathogen, not reckless behavior by Wall Street. Therefore it would have been illogical for the Fed to be much bothered by concerns about moral hazard (rescuing people from the consequences of their own actions); it was bailing out firms and institutions facing financial devastation for reasons completely beyond their control. Easily defensible too were the actions taken to stabilize trading in Treasuries. Taking a hands-off stance to the snarling of such an important market would have constituted the financial policy equivalent of criminal negligence.

On the global front as well, the Powell Fed surpassed the crisis-fighting actions of its predecessor. Trump turned out to be no obstacle; at a time when he was battling criticism over his administration's handling of the pandemic he had little time to focus on the fine points of international financial policy. Powell and his colleagues were therefore able (with support from Treasury Secretary Steven Mnuchin) to address the problems caused by foreigners' frantic efforts to obtain dollars in the spring of 2020, which included large-scale selling of Treasuries similar to that occurring in US markets. On March 15, the Fed expanded and eased the terms of swap lines with the ECB and central banks of Japan, Britain, Switzerland, and Canada. Four days later swap lines were extended to nine other central banks, resulting in total swaps of over $440 billion by the end of April. And this time the Fed took the novel step of offering to help central banks that had been excluded from swaps during the Global Financial Crisis, which included the central banks of India, China, Taiwan, and Thailand. Under the "FIMA repo facility" (formal name: Temporary Foreign and International Monetary Authorities Repo Facility), central banks holding US Treasuries could exchange them with the Fed for dollars; the foreign central bank would be obligated to repurchase (repo) the Treasuries at maturity.[17]

For the second time in a dozen years, the Fed was acting as backstop for the entire global economy. "One may argue whether the US is still the indispensable nation. What is clear is that, in a crisis, the Federal Reserve is the indispensable central bank," wrote Robert Dohner, a former Treasury economist, in a commentary published on April 2, 2020.[18] The Fed's readiness to ensure the supply of dollars worldwide — and the urgency of the demand to which it was responding — drove home the lessons of 2008 about the US currency's international status. The dollar's peerlessness was further beyond question than ever.

All was forgiven as far as Trump was concerned. On March 23, the president called Powell to congratulate him on the raft of measures announced that day, and told reporters: "He's really stepped up over the last week. I called him today and I said, 'Jerome, good job.' "[19] There was even more for Trump to cheer in the months that followed, as the economy recovered from the Covid shock at a faster clip than forecasters had expected, and the stock market recouped its losses by August. Credit belonged to the Fed for its boldness as well as a fiscal package bigger than any previously enacted, the Coronavirus Aid, Relief, and Economic Security Act, also known as the CARES Act, which provided $2.7 trillion in support for American households and businesses, including direct payments of up to $1,200 for adults and $500 for children under 17.

But unseeing what had happened was both impossible and inadvisable. Looking back in an October 2020 speech, Fed vice chair Randy Quarles observed that, "for a while in the spring the outcome was — as the Duke of Wellington said of Waterloo — 'a damn, close-run thing.' "[20]

For the dollar, that point was worth brooding over. "Damn, close-run things" shouldn't be possible in the Treasury market, which is supposedly the financial world's safest haven. The dollar's dominance may have been freshly reaffirmed, thanks to the Fed's reassertion of its role as international lender of last resort. But the vulnerabilities exposed in the trading of US government debt during the March madness of 2020 would need addressing.

Moreover, the Fed's interventions in the Treasury market, while undoubtedly helping in the short run, may have created longer-run concerns about moral hazard that were not so easy to dismiss. By pouring its bottomless supply of liquidity into the parched market, the Fed saved hedge funds that had bet heavily on tiny differentials between prices for Treasuries and related Treasury futures (instruments for buying or selling bonds at a set price on a future date). Having seen that Fed officials will do everything in their power to prevent such illiquidity from reaching a critical stage, traders might be emboldened to take ever-riskier positions, increasing the likelihood of another burst of turmoil in the future, some market veterans warned.[21]

Broader issues for the dollar loomed in 2021 as the Biden administration took over in Washington — notably a bout of inflation that would raise the first significant doubt in 40 years about the dollar's purchasing power. But events would show again that, for better or worse, it's a dollar world; we all just live in it.

Ever since its inclusion in a 1955 speech by William McChesney Martin, who chaired the Fed at the time, the "punch bowl" quip has served as a guiding principle for how Fed officials, and central bankers in many other countries, think about their jobs. As Martin put it, the Fed must be prepared to act like "the chaperone who has ordered the punch bowl removed just when the party was really warming up."[22] The central bank's mandate for price stability cannot possibly be fulfilled, in other words, without a willingness to restrain the economy from growing too robustly lest businesses and workers embark on a self-reinforcing cycle of rising wages and prices. For all the debates that have raged over macroeconomic policy in subsequent decades, punch-bowl removal has remained a Fed imperative.

In August 2020, as America's pandemic struggles continued, Powell served notice of a subtle but significant modification in the Fed's approach, in a speech laced with jargon — "flattening of the Phillips Curve," for example, along with "natural rate of unemployment," "proximity of interest rates to the effective lower bound," and "equilibrium real interest rate."[23] If the Fed chief had boiled it all down to layman's terms, he might have put his message this way: we're going to leave the punch bowl out longer than we have in the past.

This was no sudden whim. It went back to a review that Powell had initiated in 2018 of the Fed's basic framework for setting policy, to determine whether an updating was needed to reflect changes in the way the US economy worked.[24] Time after time in the years since the Global Financial Crisis, worries about inflation had proven almost comically exaggerated. When the Fed, aiming to promote recovery from the Great Recession, held interest rates at or near zero and embarked on successive rounds of QE that pumped up the central bank's asset holdings from $900 billion before the crisis to $4.5 trillion in 2014, conservatives howled that the dollar was being ruinously debased. Yet the overall price level remained stable — so stable, in fact, that the Fed's annual inflation target of 2 percent, established in 2012, was repeatedly undershot. Desirable as that was in many respects, it carried seeds of danger. Public expectations of negligible inflation would mean interest rates would remain stuck at rock-bottom levels too, so if the economy fell into recession the Fed would be almost powerless to use one of its most potent recession-fighting tools — cuts in the cost of borrowing.

Furthermore, economic data aplenty indicated that the Fed's conventional models weren't reflecting more recent realities. Among the most surprising bits of evidence was the quiescence of inflation in 2018 and 2019 even though the unemployment rate had dropped well below levels once thought certain to ignite wage-price pressure.

What really cinched it for Powell and other top Fed officials was a series of events around the country, called "Fed Listens," at which members of the public — small business owners, union leaders, and representatives of community organizations — were invited to tell how monetary policy affected their livelihoods. "Just riveting" was how Powell described one such event in Chicago in June 2019, where he heard speakers from low-income communities talk about the benefits that a strong labor market could provide by creating employment opportunities for people at the margins of society.[25]

While carefully emphasizing determination to maintain price stability, therefore, the Fed's new approach gave higher priority than before to full employment. Under "Flexible Average Inflation Targeting" (FAIT), the central bank would maintain its 2 percent target but treat it as less sacrosanct. If inflation exceeded the target, that would be fine, even welcome, if it was making up for periods below target. Most important — and here's where the punch bowl came in — the Fed wouldn't act preemptively to tighten as it had before when demand for labor was strong. Instead, it would wait for unmistakable evidence that inflation was materializing at an unacceptably high pace, and react only then.

Well-intentioned as it was when Powell unveiled it in August 2020, FAIT would be put to the test — and fare poorly — under classic conditions of too much money chasing too few goods.[26]

The too-much-money part came mainly from a huge slug of government spending, including another round of "economic impact payments" for individuals. The American Rescue Plan, initiated by Biden in the early days of his presidency, added $1.9 trillion in outlays atop the CARES Act and a $900 billion bill approved in the closing days of the Trump administration. Having gained control of both houses of Congress, Democrats were dismissive of lectures about fiscal prudence from Republicans, who had shown little concern about a 2017 tax cut that had helped swell federal debt to nearly 100 percent of US GDP by the end of the Trump years. Nor were Democrats deterred by reservations expressed by those within their own camp, the most outspoken being former Treasury secretary Larry Summers, who argued that the stimulative effect would be excessive. It was best to "go big," according to proponents of the spending, given the uncertainty about whether the recovery might be subpar like the one that had followed the Great Recession; and in any case, the Treasury could borrow the money cheaply.

The too-few-goods part came mainly from pandemic-related supply-side problems. Autos were the canonical case. Hertz, Avis, Enterprise, and other car-rental companies had sold much of their fleets during lockdowns, so when newly vaccinated Americans began traveling again, a shortage of available vehicles caused rental prices to skyrocket. Automakers eager to crank up assembly lines were hamstrung by supply-chain disruptions in the production of semiconductor chips, the result of factory closures in the Far East. Container ships were stuck in ports, and the average wait time for goods manufactured in China increased by nearly a month. Chemicals, electronics, shoes, almost any manufactured item – if just one of the many components necessary for production was unavailable or held up in transit, producers had to shut down or inform customers that delivery would be delayed. As such bottlenecks multiplied throughout the economy, scarcity was rationed with higher prices.

"Transitory" was thus the word widely applied by Fed and Biden administration officials – along with many private sector economists – when inflation began ticking up in the spring of 2021, with the consumer price index (CPI) reported at 4.2 percent higher and 5 percent higher, respectively, than the year-earlier figures for April and May. Once shortages eased, bottlenecks loosened, and other supply constraints were resolved, then inflation would subside on its own, according to this soothing forecast. But the conviction of "Team Transitory" weakened as more data in the fall showed that rents and housing prices were jumping — much harder to explain away — along with the cost of other items in the basket of goods and services used to measure ordinary Americans' living expenses. "Team Permanent" gained the upper hand, and rumblings of discontent over the decline in the dollar's purchasing power turned into a roar. Asked on November 30 whether inflation was transitory, Powell said, "I think it's probably a good time to retire that word."[27] That month the Fed began phasing out monthly purchases of Treasury and mortgage-backed securities — in effect taking its foot off the monetary accelerator.

Even so, it wasn't until March 2022 — when the CPI leaped by 8.5 percent on a year-over-year basis, the fastest rise since 1981 — that the Fed stepped on the brake, by raising the federal funds rate from its near-zero level. Having adopted FAIT, and vowed to stick by it, Powell and his colleagues feared that they would lose credibility were they to act sooner. For failing to tighten the previous fall, the Fed was lambasted as fumbling its most important mission.[28] But once the central bank began lifting interest rates, it did so unhesitatingly, 11 times in 2022 and 2023 including four consecutive increases of three-quarters of a percentage point. The model he would follow, Powell averred, was that set by Volcker, whom he described at a March 2022 congressional hearing as "the greatest economic public servant of the era." Was he prepared to do whatever it took to tame inflation, even if it meant dampening growth? "I hope that history will record that the answer to that question is yes," Powell replied.[29] In keeping with that statement the Fed resisted calls for rate cuts in the first half of 2024, to the point that critics were accusing it of allowing the economy to weaken dangerously in the late summer.[30]

But as the effects of the Fed's anti-inflation policies took hold, the world got a reminder of another memorable phrase in monetary history, uttered half a century earlier by then Treasury secretary John Connally: "The dollar is our currency, but it's your problem."

For millions of people in countries such as Ghana, Egypt, and Pakistan, it wasn't just the inflationary pressure driving up the price of bread, fuel, and medical supplies that was squeezing their livelihoods in 2022. It was also the rapidly rising exchange rate of the currency in which those items are often priced on world markets.

The dollar was on a tear. Having already strengthened on foreign exchange markets in the second half of 2021, the greenback zoomed further upward in 2022, reaching multidecade highs in the fall of that year. Higher US interest rates, combined with evidence of the Fed's resolve to maintain price stability, rendered the dollar far more attractive to investors than other currencies. By the end of September, the yen had depreciated 20 percent against the dollar; the euro — worth more than a dollar for two decades, as much as $1.57 at one point — was trading at $0.96, down 16 percent since the start of 2022; and sterling was also perilously close to dollar "parity" at an exchange rate of $1.03 per pound, a level not seen since 1985. Emerging market currencies had also fallen sharply against the dollar, the biggest swooners including the Egyptian pound, Hungarian forint, and South African rand.[31]

A global economy already battered by the pandemic and the Russian invasion of Ukraine looked even wobblier as a result of the dollar's might. Currency depreciation can be a blessing in disguise for a country, by making its exports more competitive. But that isn't nearly so valid when the dollar is surging, because so many exports are invoiced in dollars. For that reason IMF economists, who had dug deeply into trade statistics, warned in a 2020 study that a strong dollar could dampen the recovery from the Covid shock in many parts of the world, especially emerging and developing countries.[32]

On the import side as well, the arithmetic was unpleasant. Past spikes in world food prices, in 2007–2008 and 2010–2012, had coincided with declines in the dollar's exchange rate, which dampened the effect on food import bills for many developing countries. But in 2021–2022, those countries were being hit with a double whammy in the form of higher food prices and depreciation of their currencies against the dollar, making it harder to keep their citizens from going hungry. World wheat prices, for example, were up 89 percent in October 2022 compared with the average in 2020, but thanks to the strong dollar the cost of imported wheat in local currency was 106 percent higher in Peru, 112 percent higher in Egypt, 132 percent higher in Pakistan, and 176 percent higher in Ethiopia, according to a study by the United Nations Conference on Trade and Development.[33]

—

The bleakest situations faced countries and companies that had borrowed in dollars; their debts would have to be repaid in a currency that was worth considerably more than when the obligation was incurred. Memories were invoked of the early 1980s, when debt burdens crushed economies in Latin America and sub-Saharan Africa; and of the late 1990s, when financial panics ravaged Thailand, Indonesia, South Korea, Russia, and Brazil. "Dollar's Rise Spells Trouble for Global Economies," stated a headline in the *Wall Street Journal* on September 18, and a *New York Times* headline put it even more gravely a few days later: "A Strong Dollar Is Wreaking Havoc on Emerging Markets. A Debt Crisis Could Be Next." A prime example, the *Times* reported, was Ghana, where a 40 percent plunge in the Ghanaian cedi against the dollar meant that each barrel of oil the country imported—which is priced in dollars—cost nearly twice as much in cedi terms.[34]

The dollar's wrecking-ball effect was not a new phenomenon. It had been observed often in the past, and one of the most striking facts about it is its heads-you-lose, tails-you-lose quality. The global economy may be destabilized when a tight Fed policy leads to dollar strength; it may also be destabilized, albeit in a different way, when an easy Fed policy leads to dollar weakness. In the "global financial cycle" (a term coined by the economist Hélène Rey of the London Business School, who has carefully documented it), a Fed easing and the associated lowering of US interest rates causes a rise in investors' appetite for risky assets, resulting in a rush of capital into emerging markets, and the whole process reverses when the US central bank tightens. Either way, an unholy ruckus may erupt in foreign capitals.[35]

One such ruckus came in 2010, during the Bernanke-led Fed's QE program aimed at imparting more vitality to the anemic US recovery. Much to the displeasure of officials abroad, the dollar fell and American capital flooded into emerging markets, which raised fears there about overheating and inflation. The Brazilian real had risen about 25 percent against the dollar, and with the country's exporters suffering from an erosion of international competitiveness, Finance Minister Guido Mantega lobbed an unsubtle verbal grenade at the Fed, depicting Brazil as caught "in the midst of an international currency war." His German counterpart, Wolfgang Schäuble, chimed in with an accusation that Fed officials were "steer[ing] the dollar exchange rate artificially lower with the help of their printing press." At the November 2010 summit of Group of Twenty (G-20) leaders in Seoul, members of the US delegation took plenty of heat for the Fed's allegedly irresponsible actions. A mere three years later, the opposite problem arose. When Bernanke hinted in 2013 that the Fed would raise interest rates, emerging markets were hit with a slowdown resulting from a sudden outflow of capital. Amid much anxiety about the "fragile five" (Brazil, India, Indonesia, South Africa, and Turkey), critics again spoke out against Washington's imperviousness to the international implications of its monetary policies.[36]

There has been no shortage of proposed remedies. Many are inspired by the international currency dreams of Keynes and Triffin. In 2019, Mark Carney, then the governor of the Bank of England, gave a speech suggesting that a Libra-like digital instrument, combining several currencies, managed by the world's central banks – Carney called it a "synthetic hegemonic currency" – would help "dampen the domineering influence of the US dollar on global trade."[37] A book by Columbia University's José Antonio Ocampo, a former finance minister of Colombia, likewise urges creation of an internationally issued global reserve asset to protect the world against the boom-bust cycles of the dollar-dominated system.[38]

Someday – decades in the future? centuries? millennia? – the human species may evolve to the point where nationalistic sentiment is sufficiently subdued for multilateral cooperation of the sort Carney and Ocampo propose. For now, there is no viable alternative besides resignation to the fact that the Fed is a "monetary superpower," as the economists David Beckworth and Christopher Crowe have put it[39] – and foreign economic policymakers would be well advised to adapt accordingly. The Fed has to keep its eye squarely on domestic conditions in the United States; that's its legal mandate, and it isn't about to modify its monetary policies to take account of circumstances abroad. Imagine what would have happened in early 2022 if Powell and his colleagues had waited even longer before taking anti-inflation tightening measures, out of concern that a rise in the dollar would damage economies in Europe, Latin America, Asia, and Africa. Quite apart from the political tantrum that Congress would have thrown, such a decision would have been lousy policy-wise. Inflation would surely have risen higher and faster than it did, which would have meant putting the economy through even more of a wringer to restore price stability. Risking a deep recession in the United States does no favors for economies around the globe.

Fortunately, speculation about a major debt crisis in 2022–2023 turned out to be a false alarm, a few scattered defaults notwithstanding. Many governments had learned lessons from the crises of the late twentieth century and fortified themselves against a spike in the dollar. Most importantly, large emerging economies – Brazil, India, South Africa, and others – were borrowing mainly in their own currencies rather than in dollars, even though the interest cost they had to pay was a little higher. That was a major shift. In 2019, roughly four-fifths of the bonds outstanding outside of the United States, Europe, and Japan were in the borrowers' own currency, compared with less than one-fifth around the turn of the millennium.[40]

As impactful as the dollar was in currency markets in 2022, its deployment for geopolitical purposes that year was of far greater import in world affairs.

CHAPTER 10

PUNCHES LANDED, PUNCHES PULLED

"Good to see all of you again, but this is a briefing I never wanted to give," Daleep Singh, the deputy national security adviser for international economics, told the White House press corps on February 24, 2022, the day that Russia invaded Ukraine.[1]

Singh was one of the key architects of the sanctions that were being imposed on Russia, and the fact that he was conducting the briefing – rather than a military commander, or secretary of defense – meant that "kinetic war" involving US troops would not be part of Washington's response to Putin.

But sanctions can be kinetic in their own way, and in the week that followed, Singh was sending urgent messages to the Federal Reserve Bank of New York, where he had previously served as an executive vice president. *Was anything untoward happening with the hundreds of billions of dollars in reserves held in accounts at the New York Fed by foreign central banks and other government agencies?* There was no way to be certain what sort of reaction might be triggered by a surprise that the United States and its allies had sprung on Moscow – the freezing of $300 billion-plus in reserves held by the Russian central bank. Might other countries be so spooked that they would pull their reserves from the New York Fed?

"I wanted to be on speed dial with them," Singh told me. "I wanted to be on top of those developments in real time." To Singh's relief, the word back from his

—

former New York Fed colleagues was that "there was no visible shift" in the foreign accounts.[2]

The trepidation that Singh felt encapsulates the audacity of the Russia sanctions program. The events of February 2022 showed that Washington would go to extraordinary lengths in using its dollar weapon against adversaries that egregiously violated international norms, and it would make sure to have plenty of allied support. As we know now, the damage inflicted on the Russian economy, although substantial, fell far short of the economic Armageddon that was widely predicted. But that was not for lack of willingness to exert daring, bolt-from-the-blue forms of financial leverage.

Ironically, the Biden administration came to office intending to take a restrained approach to sanctions, a pivot from the Trump years when a record number of people, companies, and other entities were blacklisted. A review of sanctions policy concluded in October 2021 that the tool had been overused and that, to more effectively serve national security interests, a recalibration was in order. Sanctions subjected to rigorous scrutiny before they were levied had a greater likelihood of achieving their goals, the review found, so henceforth the interagency vetting process would more heavily weigh the risk of unintended harm to innocent civilians, opposition from allies, and other economic and geopolitical fallout. Securing international cooperation instead of going it alone would be a critical component of the strategy.[3]

The new policy had barely taken effect before the commencement of a menacing buildup of Russian troops on the Ukrainian border. To game out the US response to a variety of scenarios — a limited incursion into the parts of Ukraine dominated by ethnic Russians, for example, versus an all-out attack on Kyiv — the White House assembled a "Tiger Team" in November 2021 that conducted tabletop exercises, including one with cabinet officials, and assembled a playbook of options. Treasury Secretary Yellen began contacting her European counterparts to consider possible economic responses, as did Singh, who was coordinating with a top aide to European Commission president Ursula von der Leyen.[4]

The Europeans were reluctant to go too far in sanctioning Moscow, since their economies were more deeply integrated with Russia's — the world's 11th largest, with a GDP of $1.5 trillion — than America's was. Not only did Europe depend heavily on Russia, the world's No. 2 oil exporter, for its energy needs; European companies shipped about $100 billion annually to the Russian market, roughly ten times as much as US firms. For their part, Biden administration officials were leery of disrupting Russia's oil industry lest that cause world petroleum prices to soar at a time when the rising cost of gasoline was a major driver of US inflation. While keeping their cards close to their chests, the Group of Seven (G-7) major economies issued frequent warnings that they were prepared to go much further sanctions-wise against Moscow than they had previously, in the hope of deterring Putin.

Russian columns blitzed into Ukraine nonetheless on February 24, with rockets exploding in downtown Kharkiv, the nation's second-largest city, and phalanxes of helicopters dropping paratroopers to occupy an airport near Kyiv. The sanctions levied immediately in response by the G-7 included some of the tougher penalties that US officials had said were under consideration — restrictions blocking four major Russian banks from the global financial system as well as cutoffs of high-tech exports to the Russian market. Still, this initial package was widely deemed underwhelming, mainly because — due to European objections — it didn't expel Russian banks from SWIFT.[5] Political pressure for a bolder counterpunch swelled as people across the world watched scenes of the Russian bombardment together with President Volodymyr Zelensky exhorting his people to repel the invaders, followed by news reports of his statement in a video call with EU leaders that "this might be the last time you see me alive." De-SWIFTing was the main rallying cry of demonstrators in Western capitals who presumably had only dim notions of what SWIFT was.

An option so beyond the pale that it hadn't even come up in media reporting about sanctions possibilities thus shot to the top of G-7 policymakers' agendas. This was the idea of targeting Russia's reserves, which had a forceful advocate in Chrystia Freeland, the Canadian finance minister and deputy prime minister.[6] Freeland's maternal grandparents were Ukrainian, and her mother helped draft Ukraine's constitution; she is also deeply versed in the region's dynamics, with degrees in Russian history and Slavonic studies from Harvard and Oxford as well as a background as Moscow bureau chief for the *Financial Times*, and as the author of a book about the corruption that plagued Russia in the 1990s.

The proposal to target reserves championed by Freeland was undoubtedly harsher than de-SWIFTing. As symbolically important as SWIFT was, kicking Russian banks out was unlikely to impair Russia's ability to function economically; the banks could use other methods, such as email or even phone or fax, to send the messages required for international fund transfers. A big reserve hoard, on the other hand, was a key element of "Fortress Russia," the suite of policies Putin had initiated over the previous eight years to bulletproof his country's economy against coercion from Washington. Russia's central bank had amassed more than $640 billion in gold and foreign assets, which could ensure that the country had plenty of hard currency to continue buying goods and services from abroad and protect the ruble from a catastrophic depreciation. In accord with Moscow's de-dollarization goals, the central bank held only about 16 percent of its reserves in US Treasuries and other dollar-denominated securities, and it had loaded up on gold and Chinese renminbi, which together accounted for about 35 percent; much of the rest was denominated in euros. But by prohibiting anyone from transacting with the central bank or on its behalf, the United States and its allies could effectively render useless much of the amounts held in dollars and euros.

Central bank reserves are not to be trifled with. The principle of sovereign immunity applies to them when they're held in accounts abroad as most are. Not that sanctioning a central bank was unheard of; as noted in chapter 6, OFAC had designated Iran's Bank Markazi as a primary money laundering concern in 2011. But Iran had been declared responsible for state-sponsored terrorism. If Russia's reserves could be frozen by simple edict, what might that indicate about the regard for the sanctity of property rights in Washington and the capitals of its allies? Isn't the lack of freedom to move money in and out of renminbi one of the main reasons often cited for the low international status of China's currency?

Those considerations were overridden, as Zelensky's impassioned pleas and popular revulsion over Russia's brutality transformed the G-7 discussions.[7] Even Germany, which had long maintained fraternal relations with Russia as a cornerstone of its foreign policy, swung in favor of aggressively confronting Putin. By the first weekend after the invasion, transatlantic talks about the reserve-freezing idea reached a frenzied pitch amid concerns that Moscow might be getting wind of the plan and would move reserves to venues beyond the West's control.

At her Toronto home on Saturday, February 26, Freeland was on hold in a teleconference session with EU officials when a call came through on her iPhone from Ukrainian prime minister Denys Shmyhal, who was in a bunker in Kyiv, where night was falling. Freeland held the iPhone to her video screen so Shmyhal could join, and they got the word they were desperately hoping to hear—EU approval of the reserve freeze.[8] Although Yellen still needed convincing, agreement came in the evening, Washington time, after Mario Draghi, the Italian prime minister and former ECB president, helped bring the Treasury secretary around. A joint US-Europe-Canada statement was issued at 5 p.m. Washington time, approved the next day by Japan (where the time difference had prevented officials from joining all the discussions): "Restrictive measures" would "prevent the Russian Central Bank from deploying its international reserves in ways that undermine the impact of our sanctions." For good measure, "selected Russian banks [would be] removed from the SWIFT messaging system." On Monday, February 28, the Treasury formally announced that OFAC "prohibited United States persons from engaging in transactions with the Central Bank of the Russian Federation," adding: "This action effectively immobilizes any assets of the Central Bank of the Russian Federation held in the United States or by U.S. persons, wherever located."[9]

The bottom fell out of the ruble exchange rate on that Monday—the Russian currency lost about one-quarter of its value against other currencies—and the authorities closed the stock market. Long queues formed at ATMs in Moscow, St. Petersburg, and other major cities; supermarket shelves were stripped bare amid panic buying over rising prices and fears of food shortages; riders on the Moscow Metro reported being unable to get past faregates because the Apple Pay and Google Pay apps they ordinarily used for swiping had evidently been disconnected; seats on flights out of the country on international airlines quickly sold out as Aeroflot, the national carrier, was banned from using European air space.[10]

"In the space of a single day, February 28, Vladimir Putin's 'Fortress Russia' collapsed," wrote Anders Aslund, a prominent Swedish economist who specializes in Eastern Europe. "A fair guess is that the annual inflation rate will reach at

least 50%, and that Russian GDP will likely fall by at least 10% this year."
Similar projections of a deep recession, with Russia's economic output estimated
to shrink between 8.5 percent and 15 percent, came from the IMF, the World
Bank, the European Bank for Reconstruction and Development, the Institute of
International Finance, and many Russian forecasters as well. "This will be a gi-
gantic, transformational downturn," Ruben Enikolopov, rector of the New
Economic School in Moscow, was quoted as saying in the *New York Times*. Oleg
Deripaska, the billionaire Russian industrialist, likened the impact to the
wrenching crisis Russia suffered in 1998 following a debt default, but added
that it would be "three times worse and will last three years." Reflecting the
sense of jubilation among Western officials, French economy minister Bruno Le
Maire crowed: "We will cause the collapse of the Russian economy."[11]

The reserve freeze had clearly caught Moscow off guard. "Nobody who was
predicting what sanctions the West would pass could have pictured that," Sergei
Lavrov, the Russian foreign minister, told an audience at a Moscow institute on
March 23. "It's just thievery."[12] The shock value was one reason its potency was
widely hailed. "This maneuver has always been possible in theory, but few had
imagined using it," wrote Sebastian Mallaby, a senior fellow for international
economics at the Council on Foreign Relations, in his *Washington Post* column.
"Now, its power has been laid bare. Overnight, it can turn a financially sound
economy into a basket case."[13]

On the battlefield, Russia's supposedly invincible military was suffering one
setback after another at the hands of roused Ukrainian warriors. But for those
who thought that Putin's regime was also about to get the crippling economic
punishment that it deserved — I count myself among them — a big letdown was
coming.

On winding passes in the Caucasus mountains near the Russian border with
Georgia, miles-long caravans of trucks packed with cargo snaked across the
frontier. Along Indian Ocean sea lanes, tankers laden with Urals oil, the flagship
Russian brand, steamed to refineries that had never bought Russian crude before. In Armenia, opportunistic merchants bought smartphones from abroad
for transshipping to the Russian market. In Moscow's auto showrooms, an SUV
called the Haval, produced by China's Great Wall Motors, became a hot seller.[14]

—

Those are a few anecdotal snippets that help account for Russia's success at weathering sanctions. Instead of a double-digit GDP contraction, the nation's economy underwent negative real growth of a mere 2 percent in 2022. Restaurants and bars in Moscow and St. Petersburg were bustling, and the GUM department store near Red Square, although devoid of Western-branded luxury goods, was full of shoppers.[15]

Sanctions-imposed costs were burdening the Russian economy in ways that would impair Putin's capacity to pursue military adventures like the one in Ukraine – but it would take a long time, as Biden administration officials and other sanctions boosters were forced to admit. In articles published around the invasion's one-year anniversary, the catchphrases used by many Western experts were that sanctions should be regarded as "a marathon, not a sprint" and that since Russia's economy was "stagnant, not crippled," an "economic war of attrition" should continue but could not substitute for other, more important policies, in particular the provision of aid and military weapons to Kyiv.[16]

Part of the explanation lay with the preparations that had been laid under the direction of Elvira Nabiullina, the economist who headed Russia's central bank, for insuring that the domestic payments system would continue to function with relatively minor disruption and the nation's banks could transact with each other (see chapter 6). Although Visa and Mastercard withdrew from the Russian market, that stopped Russians only from using those cards for purchases from abroad; there was no problem paying for things within the country. The domestic card network that had been established several years earlier was proving to have been a brilliant stroke of foresight, as was the Kremlin-boosted Mir card, of which more than 100 million cards had been issued since its launch in 2015.[17]

But more important in accounting for the muted effect of the sanctions were major holes that existed from the outset in the measures taken against the Kremlin, and Moscow's adeptness at finding ways to circumvent some of the restrictions that blocked its normal access to global markets.

Washington pulled a big punch that it might have used – secondary sanctions. European officials, who were still smarting from Trump's threats that had stopped their companies from transacting with Iran, flatly opposed the use of similar extraterritorial policies to force other countries into line on Russia. The

Biden administration, being much less inclined to unilateralism than its predecessor, accepted the need for restraint, on the theory that secondary sanctions would achieve only a "Pyrrhic victory" if used against large nonaligned nations such as India, Indonesia, South Africa, Turkey, Brazil, and Saudi Arabia, according to Singh. "Our judgment was over time, it will be far more effective to positively induce and attract these countries to our coalition than to coerce them at the barrel of an economic weapon," Singh told me.[18]

Other huge punches were pulled when the sanctions were designed to accommodate Russia's importance as a commodity exporter—of not just oil, gas, and coal but also fertilizer, wheat, and other grains.[19] Depriving international markets of those goods would have led to shortages in a world already reeling from price shocks, so Western policymakers permitted Russian exports to continue and also allowed the retention of SWIFT membership for Russian banks that processed payments for oil and gas. Even though Europe went far toward weaning itself from Russian energy supplies in 2022 and 2023, Moscow shifted its oil shipments to India, China, and other countries that were not part of the sanctioning alliance; Indian refineries lapped up Urals crude to the tune of two million barrels a day. In this way, Russia was able to generate substantial amounts of hard currency each month, compensating for the loss of access to the central bank's reserves. A variety of Russian banks and corporations acquired an estimated $147 billion in new assets in 2022 which, though not formally held by the government, gave Moscow increased fiscal and monetary breathing room. "Shadow reserves," one study called them, noting that "little is known about their physical locations or currencies of transaction." Hong Kong and the United Arab Emirates were likely repositories.[20]

That didn't mean Russia could use its earnings to buy everything it needed from abroad. The country's imports fell by more than half in the first three months after the invasion as shipments from European firms dried up and bans took effect on exports to Russia of strategically important items such as advanced semiconductors. By that measure, it looked as if sanctions were working brilliantly at disconnecting Russia from the global economy.[21] But friendlier foreign suppliers, notably Chinese manufacturers, soon filled the gaps. By mid-2023, imports had recovered and goods from China—which had accounted for less than a quarter of Russia's imports before the invasion—swelled to nearly half the total. Six of the top ten motor vehicle brands in Russia were Chinese, for example, compared with none three years earlier.[22] Although established Chinese firms were evidently taking care to avoid exporting prohibited items that would run afoul of OFAC, an investigation by the Japanese newspaper the *Nikkei* revealed that US-made semiconductors were flowing into Russia via circuitous routes, mostly involving small traders in Hong Kong and mainland China that are difficult to monitor.[23]

Moreover, a group of former Soviet republics—Armenia, Georgia, Kyrgyzstan, Uzbekistan, and Kazakhstan—became transshipment hubs, importing chips and other goods with possible military uses from the West and exporting them to Russia. The sums involved appear to have been only a small fraction of the previous flow of goods into Russia, according to a study of the data called "The Eurasian Roundabout," published by the European Bank for Reconstruction and Development. But for certain products such as computers the amounts were greater, and new supply routes took only about two to four months to set up, the study found.[24]

Determined to tighten the screws on Moscow, Washington and its allies imposed a "price cap" of $60 a barrel on Russian oil in late 2022 and Europe adopted an embargo, halting its purchases from Russia in favor of other sources. The idea was to keep world petroleum markets stable by allowing Russian crude to continue flowing but minimize the profits and thus the tax revenue that the country's finance ministry could reap. The price cap took advantage of the fact that oil tankers need insurance coverage for potential spills and other disasters; under threat of OFAC sanctions, insurance companies and shippers were banned from handling Russian crude unless it was sold below the cap.

Results in the early months of 2023 were promising, with the Urals grade of crude selling at much wider gaps to international benchmark prices than before, and Russian oil revenue down by about 50 percent in the January–May 2023 period compared with a year earlier.[25] Dismayed by the threat to his government's budget—oil revenues are the single largest contributor—Putin demanded that his underlings find ways to shrink the *diskont*. They did.[26]

To counter the price cap, Moscow amassed a "shadow fleet" of tankers—estimated at somewhere between 180 and several hundred—by using a network of front companies to buy aging vessels that might normally be retired from

———

service and sold for scrap. Then, by stripping these tankers of ownership or in-surance ties that might have made them subject to sanctions, Russian operatives enabled the ships to transport oil without regard for the cap. Although this pro-gram was costly — used tanker prices soared, cutting into the Russian oil indus-try's overall profitability — it proved effective. Moreover, even when "mainstream" tankers transported oil from Russia's Pacific coast ports, duplici-tous traders evidently falsified records attesting to price-cap compliance in many cases.[27]

In the closing months of 2023, the sanctions program appeared on the surface to be more toothless than ever. Urals crude was fetching around $74 a barrel, with almost no Russian oil sold below the price cap. Russia's economic growth, which outpaced that of the United States in 2023, was projected at 2.6 percent in 2024, according to the IMF, compared with US projected growth of 2.1 percent.[28]

But America's financial warriors weren't done yet.

One tanker belonging to Russia's state-owned shipping company was drifting, its engines idled, around the Laccadive Sea near Sri Lanka in November 2023 instead of delivering its $50 million cargo of crude from Sakhalin Island to an Indian port. Half a dozen other tankers in Russia's shadow fleet were idling in ports for unusually lengthy periods, and the following month several more tankers inexplicably halted, one by one, in mid-voyage from Sakhalin to India.[29]

Around the same time, banks in Turkey, the United Arab Emirates, and China began curbing dealings with Russian clients and companies, a notable example being Emirates NBD, a giant Dubai-based bank, which shut down ac-counts held by Russian oligarchs and firms involved in the trading of commodi-ties and weapons for Moscow. Russia's imports from key trading partners including Turkey, China, and Kazakhstan declined — sharply, in some cases — in the first quarter of 2024.[30]

The precise reasons for these disparate developments were impossible to confirm. But they almost certainly reflected the long arm of the US Treasury. In the final quarter of 2023, OFAC had put eight shadow-fleet tankers on the SDN list, having found legal grounds for doing so, and this was evidently ren-dering those vessels off-limits for oil deliveries, or at least causing Russia's cus-

———

tomers to have second thoughts and insist on steep price discounts.[31] Moreover, President Biden had signed an executive order shortly before Christmas that finally deployed secondary sanctions against Putin's regime, by authorizing the Treasury to blacklist banks anywhere in the world that helped Moscow buy military technology and equipment. Treasury and State Department officials traveled to the United Arab Emirates and Turkey to back up the executive order with pointed calls for compliance.[32]

Encouraged by the impact of the late-2023 executive order, the Biden team rolled out a major expansion of its secondary sanctions program in mid-June 2024 (objections from European governments having evidently been overcome). A new order gave OFAC the authority to target foreign financial institutions dealing with more than 4,500 Russian entities, including most of the country's biggest banks. In other words, the risk of being severed from the dollar-based clearing system would now confront any bank in, say, China or India that interacted with a Russian bank.[33]

This was a significant screw-tightening — although once again, it included exemptions for transactions involving oil and agricultural products for fear of the inflation that could result from squeezing Russian suppliers out of those markets. The measures therefore stopped well short of more sweeping steps urged by some that would have choked off a greater amount of Moscow's revenue from oil exports. Behind closed doors Treasury officials were reportedly clamoring for much more aggressive sanctions against the shadow tanker fleet, but were overruled by White House aides who warned that doing so could lead to a supply-demand imbalance in global petroleum markets, causing prices to spike anew. Whether or not this was a good decision, here's the crucial point: had US officials dared risk the consequences, they surely could have dealt a much more injurious blow to Putin; this was evidence of the dollar weapon's circumspect use rather than its impotence.

Meanwhile, the freezing of Russian reserves in February 2022 turned out to be financially consequential after all — not the knockout smash that some had initially thought, but a useful means by which to help Ukraine and administer an extra dollop of punishment to Moscow.

At a mid-2024 meeting in Italy, the G-7 struck a deal about how to put the immobilized reserves to work. The accord capped a contentious debate: At one extreme were calls for the G-7 and EU countries to confiscate the roughly $300 billion in funds, the bulk of which consisted of €190 billion held in Euroclear, a Belgian securities custodian, where Russia had deposited them. Advocates of confiscation argued that the money should be handed to Ukraine as a form of reparations that, in a just world, Russia should be obliged to pay. At the other extreme were warnings that expropriation was, at best, questionable under international law and would damage the credibility of Western governments as defenders of the global rules-based system.

The pact that emerged was an ingenious compromise that would use the interest income and other returns generated by the reserves as the backing for $50 billion in loans that G-7 countries would provide to Ukraine. The word "loans" might sound as if Kyiv would have to deplete its own resources to repay the money, but there would be no such obligation, since repayment would come over a series of years from the interest flows. Nor would G-7 taxpayers be burdened; again, those interest flows would ensure that the loans were repaid. At the same time, the principal amount of Russia's reserves was being left untouched, in deference to the international legal niceties. Details remained to be thrashed out, and nobody was claiming that Russia had much at stake financially — the holdings were already beyond Moscow's reach and were not going to be returned unless Putin offered an almost-inconceivable capitulation. But using the money to help bankroll Ukraine's defense had obvious appeal, especially at a time when Congress was reluctant to do so.[34]

Many years may pass after this book is published before the impact of the sanctions on Russia can be comprehensively assessed. Russia's military and industry have surely had to resort to costly, inefficient, and shoddy suppliers to some extent, and the country's long-term trajectory will undoubtedly suffer from the loss of foreign investment, withdrawal of hundreds of Western firms, and exodus of hundreds of thousands of highly educated people. By going all-out with the freezing of Russia's reserves, implementing an array of other painful measures, and mobilizing a formidable supporting coalition of advanced economies, the United States sent a thunderous message of intolerance for — and readiness to strike hard against — Putinesque aggression toward peaceful neighboring countries. That message will hopefully intimidate, deter, or at least give serious pause to would-be Putins in the future.

———

But Russia's resilience in 2022 and 2023 taught dollar weaponizers a humbling lesson about the limitations of the tool when it comes to large economies, especially those that make lots of products that the world needs. The bigger the target, the harder it is to make it fall.

To hear some tell it, the United States not only overestimated the potency of its sanctions on Russia but shot itself in the foot, creating perfect conditions for the dollar to get its comeuppance at long last. Moscow was cozying up to Beijing to an extent previously unseen, with the media full of images showing Putin and Xi posing chummily at summits clasping hands while declaring their nations' "no-limits" friendship and mutual determination to combat American hegemony in all forms. An oft-drawn conclusion was that by going to such extremes in its efforts to isolate Russia economically, Washington had set itself up for its own monetary undoing.

"The Anti-Dollar Axis," the title of a *Foreign Affairs* article published shortly after the invasion, stated the thesis baldly: "Biden's flexing of American economic muscle will only embolden Russia and other U.S. rivals, including China, to deprive the United States of the very power that makes sanctions so devastating," wrote the authors, Zongyuan Zoe Liu of the Council on Foreign Relations and Mihaela Papa of Tufts University's Fletcher School of Global Affairs. "Russia and China will expedite initiatives to 'de-dollarize' their economies, building alternative financial institutions and structures that both protect themselves from sanctions and threaten the U.S. dollar's status as the world's dominant currency."[35]

This line of reasoning, and variations on it, attracted a number of adherents, making 2022 and 2023 exceptionally fecund for doomsday predictions about the US currency's place in the global monetary system. Several possible dollar alternatives were mooted, including a currency jointly issued by the BRICS, one version of which would be gold-backed. More commonly mentioned was the renminbi, being the well-established currency of a country accounting for 18 percent of world GDP.

Among the headlines on articles published in mainstream media outlets were the following: "China, Russia and the Race to a Post-Dollar World," "Russia and China Are Threatening the Power of the Dollar," "China Takes the

Yuan Global in Bid to Repel a Weaponized Dollar," "BRICS Currency Could End Dollar Dominance," "China Capitalises on US Sanctions in Fight to Dethrone Dollar," "Move Over, U.S. Dollar. China Wants to Make the Yuan the Global Currency," and "The Yuan's the New Dollar as Russia Rides to the Redback."[36]

Plenty of fodder for such articles was generated in the months after the invasion of Ukraine, much of it concerning the boom in Sino-Russian trade, a rapidly growing portion of which was conducted in renminbi. Whereas the renminbi accounted for almost none of the revenue that Russia earned on the oil, gas, and other commodities it exported to China before February 2022, Russian firms were accepting the Chinese currency for about 14 percent of their sales to the Chinese market by early 2023. For their part, Chinese manufacturers of autos, electronics, and equipment were being paid in renminbi for about 23 percent of their sales to Russia in 2022, up from just a few percent in prior years.[37]

Greater excitement followed reports that the renminbi was making inroads into world petroleum markets, long the dollar's sole preserve. On March 15, 2022, the *Wall Street Journal* broke the news that Saudi Arabia was in "active talks" with China to price some of its oil sales in renminbi, and a French firm, TotalEnergies, accepted renminbi for a China-bound shipment of liquefied natural gas.[38] Hardly a month seemed to go by without one country or another announcing joint plans with China to conduct more of their trade in their own currencies instead of dollars – Brazil, Argentina, Pakistan, Iraq, and Bolivia were among those doing so. And in 2024, the amount of cross-border transactions conducted in renminbi by Chinese importers and exporters rose to the highest level ever, comprising about 36 percent of the total.[39]

How much more evidence could possibly be required for the dollar's imperilment, and the renminbi's prospects for eventually supplanting it? Tons, actually; upon close scrutiny, the data reported as this book neared completion in summer 2024 showed nothing to suggest that the international roles of the US and Chinese currencies are starting to converge.[40]

The increasing use of the renminbi in international commerce has been almost exclusively confined to bilateral trade between China and other countries (China-Russia trade or China-Bolivia trade, for example). If the renminbi were being used a lot in "third country trade," as the dollar is – that is, between pairs of countries other than the currency's issuer (between Colombia and South Korea, for example, or Singapore and Jordan) – that would signify real internationalization. But instances of that are rare, if not totally absent.[41]

The renminbi's share of overall international payments has thus remained stuck in low single digits, at about 4.5 percent, and the Chinese currency's share of international reserves was similarly paltry, at a little above 2 percent (seventh in the world, behind the Canadian and Australian dollars), according to data released in mid-2024. As for the dollar, there is no indication that its huge lead over other currencies in every conceivable metric of internationalization, as cited in chapter 1, has significantly changed.[42]

By one measure, China's recent de-dollarization efforts have made progress. Now that the renminbi is being used more in China's bilateral trade with other countries, Beijing has insulated itself to some degree from the threat of US sanctions. Having seen what Washington did to Moscow, Beijing has greater incentive than ever to "de-risk" its economy from US coercion in the event of conflict, a likely flashpoint being Taiwan. (More about that in the next chapter.) CIPS and mBridge may afford China an extra level of assurance that, in a crisis scenario, it could maintain access to global markets for commodities and other essential goods. But that's a far cry from dollar dethronement. Indeed, it's an insult to the intelligence of the Chinese leadership to think that they harbor fantasies of dethronement in the foreseeable future.

To illuminate the difficulty of effecting major change in the world currency hierarchy, consider the much-ballyhooed discussions between Saudi Arabian and Chinese officials over the renminbi's use in global petroleum markets. In a visit to Riyadh in December 2022, Xi told Arab leaders that China would aim to pay for oil and gas in renminbi, and the warm welcome he received aroused speculation of a seismic shift in the dollar's status.[43] But strong financial reasons militate against such an outcome.

The Saudis *could* sell their crude for renminbi; although oil has been priced in dollars for decades, two countries can agree to settle their obligations in any mutually acceptable currency they choose. "They can use Dr. Pepper bottle caps if they want," wrote Patrick Chovanec, an economist and investment strategist, in an insightful Twitter thread. "The question is whether that's convenient and useful to both countries."[44]

If the Saudis took renminbi instead of dollars for oil, they would have to figure out what to do with it. They could use it to pay for Chinese goods, but they export considerably more oil to China than they import in goods from China, so they would still be left with a substantial renminbi hoard. Although they could invest it in Chinese securities, "Chinese capital markets are not nearly as large or liquid" as US markets, Chovanec pointed out. "Permission is required to move large sums of money in and out. The range of investments is comparatively limited, and arguably riskier."

China, meanwhile, would be confronted with a different but parallel dilemma. As the world's leading exporter, it is already sitting on a vast stockpile of dollars in its foreign exchange reserves, and its export machine is reaping more dollars every month. The monetary authorities in Beijing can — and do — invest those dollars in US Treasuries, but they have had "a hard time over the years deploying them all in anything more productive" than that, as Chovanec observed. So why would they *want* to use renminbi to pay for Saudi oil when they could spend some of their dollar hoard instead and keep it from getting even more bloated? "The point is not that purchasing oil with [renminbi] is impossible, but that it's eminently possible, and you have to ask why they aren't already doing it, and whether those reasons are likely to change," Chovanec concluded.

Similarly instructive is another phenomenon that materialized after the imposition of sanctions on Russia, called the "rupee trap."

As noted above, Russia was allowed to continue exporting its oil, and one of the main markets for Urals crude was India. Some Indian customers wanted to pay in rupees, which Russian exporters accepted until Moscow realized that it had accumulated billions of rupees that it couldn't use. Here's why: Russia's $41.5 billion in exports of oil to India vastly exceeded its $2.8 billion in imports from India. Thus, although Russia could use some of its rupee earnings to buy Indian goods, it was stuck with the rest.

"This is a problem," Russian foreign minister Lavrov acknowledged to reporters at a May 2023 meeting in the western Indian state of Goa. "We need to use this money. But for this, these rupees must be transferred in another currency, and this is being discussed now."[45]

In sum, it isn't easy for the Anti-Dollar Axis to get its act together. Even if it shows signs of doing so — if, say, China persuades Saudi Arabia to accept renminbi in payment for oil, as it may well do — that will not vitiate the underlying fundamentals. The Axis is up against a currency that is readily usable not only to buy or sell goods on international markets but also to invest in safe, liquid assets, in ways that set it far apart from the rest of the currency pack. The declaration by the BRICS of their intention to issue their own currency was rightly derided by economists as the monetary version of sound and fury signifying nothing; how could a coalition of countries so disparate in economic policy, state of development, culture, and even geography manage such an endeavor?

But the Anti-Dollar Axis is a thing, fueled by resentment over America's penchant for hegemonic overreach that is held in countries with a substantial portion of the world's population. Imagine a US administration, full of smugness about the greenback's indomitability, using it against a sanctions target for much less morally justifiable reasons than in the case of Russia in 2022, or against another large country with little regard for the economic blowback. Such scenarios merit reflection on the importance of keeping the dollar's great power from being used irresponsibly.

CHAPTER 11

. . . COMES GREAT RESPONSIBILITY

It is up to you, the reader, to decide whether the US dollar's international dominance is a good thing or a bad thing. If you're sympathetic to regimes such as the ones ruling Russia and Iran, or if you believe for other reasons that the United States is an irredeemably malign force in the world, then you presumably wish the dollar were just another currency, no more important in global commerce than, say, the Vietnamese dong. The same may go if you're a radical libertarian, or belong to the cults of hard (gold-backed) money or crypto, or if you're an adherent of theories that the Fed is manipulated by exploitative "globalist" bankers.

Most of us who don't hold those sorts of views have ample reason for deeming the dollar's global status to be desirable, whatever our nationality. First, it means that the world has a convenient and widely used means for intermediating transactions across borders, continents, and oceans; without it there would be less trade, less investment, and less economic growth.[1] However fiercely opinions may differ on the rules governing globalization, everyone should agree on the benefits of an efficient monetary system for facilitating international economic activity.

Second, for all of America's faults, its ability to use the dollar weapon is welcome, especially at times when deploying military force would be worse.

However gross the liberties that the Trump administration took in using the US currency for coercive purposes, the United States has historically been the closest thing to a benevolent hegemon that the world has, and the added leverage it gains by dint of the dollar's primacy has been broadly salutary. The clearest justification for this argument was Russia's invasion of Ukraine; a feeble sanctions package in February 2022 would have sent a profoundly disheartening message of passivity. The successful use of economic pressure on Iran that led to the JCPOA in 2015 is another case in point. To be sure, it is anybody's guess what the future will bring under a second Trump term and beyond.

But whether you approve of dollar dominance or not, doubts about its durability should be put to rest. This is not just because of all the embarrassingly off-target claims about the dollar's prospects from decades past; it is because of the factors documented at length in previous chapters regarding the solidness of the dollar's foundations and the alternatives' lack of credibility. The clamor for the greenback's downfall from prominent figures like Brazil's Lula, and the commentary egging them on, is akin to howling at the moon, or spitting into the wind, or whatever other metaphor you can think of for an exercise in futility. (The caveat mentioned in chapter 1 – "barring catastrophic missteps by the US government" – still applies. More on this caveat later.)

The freezing of Russia's reserves – and proposals for their outright confiscation, to pay for Ukraine's reconstruction – is no doubt sending shivers through finance ministries and central banks in certain capitals around the world, where officials may be brainstorming about how to move away from dollar dependence. Even without being privy to those discussions, one can easily imagine the quandary the brainstormers face when conversation turns to the greenback's putative competitors, in particular the renminbi. Memories may be dredged up of the ways in which China has flexed its economic muscle for foreign policy purposes in the not-too-distant past. In 2010, for example, China's imports of salmon from Norway mysteriously collapsed following the awarding in Oslo of the Nobel Peace Prize to a Chinese dissident. In 2017, South Korean businesses dependent on Chinese customers underwent a battering – notably, when dozens of Lotte department stores in Chinese cities were closed for "fire hazards" – amid friction between Beijing and Seoul over the placement of US missiles in South Korea. Then, in 2020, triggered by the Australian government's call for an independent inquiry into the origins of Covid-19, China erected barriers to imports of Australian wine, barley, beef, and seafood in apparent retaliation for Canberra's alignment with Washington on a range of issues. In short, the idea that a renminbi sanctions bludgeon would be wielded with greater benevolence than dollar-based sanctions is difficult to square with Beijing's past actions.[2]

Even thornier, for any country or private investor considering a shift into renminbi, are concerns about the impartiality and caprice of the Chinese legal system. For that reason as well as others previously mentioned, it is safe to assume that there is no serious rival to the dollar's reign as top global currency. That in turn means that America's financial sanctions will continue to pack a wallop for a long time to come.

Yes, nations targeted by US sanctions can find ways to dodge them, parry them, blunt them, deflect them, bypass them, and wriggle around them. As we have seen, some of these evasion methods are "analog" — turning off ship transponders, falsifying oil sales records, dispatching agents to friendly countries or parts of the world with lax governance to arrange importation of goods, buying high-tech devices from small merchants who are difficult to monitor, and so on. "Digital" methods may well become effective in the future, as the technology for cross-border transmission of CBDCs improves sufficiently that financial transactions of significant scale can take place beyond Washington's surveillance capacity. Independent financial networks such as the one Russia established for domestic credit card payments and its Mir card can shield countries from the harshest impact of sanctions; likewise, CIPS and mBridge may help China continue to conduct international commerce if it is targeted.

But as long as the dollar remains the most-used currency in international trade and finance — as it appears all but certain to do — banks all over the world will need to clear and settle large payments in New York as they do now. As a result, OFAC's ability to designate SDNs will retain considerable potency.

Does that mean the United States should feel empowered to impose sanctions with impunity? That brings us back to the Spider-Man adage.

The more we use it, the more likely we are to lose it. So goes an oft-expressed admonition, well worth heeding, about the pitfalls of excessive dollar weaponization. It doesn't necessarily imply that the dollar's supremacy is at risk; only ill-informed critics of US sanctions take the argument that far. But if the United States wantonly severs targets from the dollar-based system, it will unquestionably increase incentives for foreign governments to develop mechanisms for conducting their international commerce without dollar involvement, in ways that Washington can neither detect nor block.

The most cogent presentation of this argument, as noted in chapters 5 and 6, can be found in *Bucking the Buck*, by Daniel McDowell of Syracuse University. Backed by reams of data, the book shows that countries threatened by US sanctions are trying their utmost to de-dollarize, and even though they haven't gotten very far, Washington should recognize the potential for its sanctioning power to diminish over time and exercise discernment accordingly, McDowell asserts. "Dollar dominance is a critical and unrivaled power resource for the United States that is worth protecting," he writes. "Employing [financial sanctions] too often could jeopardize the future effectiveness of US sanctions capabilities. . . . There may come a day when an American president will need to call upon the full legal authority of the US Treasury to inflict severe financial costs on an adversary that poses an existential threat to the United States and its allies. In the meantime, Washington would be wise to limit its use of financial sanctions for the sake of preserving the tool for such a moment."[3]

Paradoxically, McDowell's careful research could be used to support a quite different conclusion from the one he arrives at. If US sanctions potency is in danger of eroding a few years from now as he suggests, mightn't that militate in favor of imposing sanctions sooner rather than later, while their effectiveness is at or near its height? To the extent that sanctions power is a "wasting asset," isn't that a reason to err *less* on the side of caution?

To be clear, McDowell's analysis is valuable and his bottom line is 100 percent correct, namely that the United States should refrain from the indiscriminate levying of dollar sanctions of the sort that became common during the latter years of the 2010–2020 decade. Only in cases where US "core interests" (or those of America's allies) are truly at stake, and the desired result is both aligned with US foreign policy goals and reasonably possible to accomplish, should the weapon be deployed. As McDowell also writes, "Washington should coordinate financial sanctions with its major allies in Europe and Asia wherever possible."

But there are much more compelling reasons to adopt a discerning policy concerning dollar-based sanctions than the goal of preserving the tool's future effectiveness. Again, the pithiest insight can be gleaned from that character in Marvel comics and films who conscientiously utilizes his superhuman strength, agility, and web-spinning prowess. The dollar's power as a sanctions weapon should be exercised with commensurate responsibility. This principle should apply whether or not the power is in danger of erosion.

The very purpose of sanctions is to inflict economic pain, and as demonstrated in work published in 2023 by Francisco Rodríguez, a professor at the University of Denver, the consequences on vulnerable segments of the population in target countries are often severe. Determining precisely whether sanctions or other factors in target countries are to blame is extremely difficult. But in surveying a wide range of studies Rodríguez found "consistently statistically significant adverse effects" of sanctions on indicators including poverty rates, inequality, child mortality, undernourishment, and life expectancy.[4]

The US government often tries to aim sanctions as much as possible at target country elites — the impounding of Russian oligarchs' yachts was a well-publicized example — while sparing the innocent with provisions such as humanitarian exceptions allowing the importation of medicine and other essential items. But evidence from Iran indicates how achievement of those goals often falls short. Data cited by Rodríguez show that during the most intense periods of sanctions imposed by the Obama administration, Iranian households belonging to low- and middle-income groups, or those headed by the old and unemployed, were more likely to fall into poverty than other, better-off groups. Moreover, significant shortages of drugs affected the health of Iranians even though OFAC ostensibly allowed medicine shipments. Rodríguez cited the case of an order for a drug necessary for liver transplants that "failed to reach Iran, despite having all the required OFAC licenses, because no bank would perform the transaction" — a classic example of private sector overcompliance.

In addition to humanitarian considerations are diplomatic ones. Anger over US bullying may damage Washington's ability to maintain alliances, even in countries that aren't targeted by dollar weaponization. Europe's reaction to Trump's Iran sanctions, and Lula's indignation about the greenback's dominance, illustrate this point. Other foreign leaders have echoed Lula's sentiments, one example being Kenya's relatively pro-Western president William Ruto, who fumed in a June 2023 address to the Djibouti parliament: "How is US dollars part of the trade between Djibouti and Kenya? Why?" Although Ruto may be helpless to alter the main currency used in Djibouti-Kenya commerce, US officials who want the cooperation of such leaders on climate change, or international peacekeeping, or freedom of ocean navigation, or any number of other issues, would do well to avoid using financial sanctions in a cavalier manner.[5]

Finally, and most important, is the danger of collateral damage, which is heightened in cases where the target country can hit back in some way. When the target is really, really big, then the responsibility that comes with the wielding of the dollar's great power is all the greater.

With Taiwan under threat of imminent attack by the People's Liberation Army, the US government announced that it would "stand with our friends in Taiwan," not only by dispatching US forces to strike Chinese targets but by preparing "to impose maximum economic pressure in the event of an invasion, including sanctions against most major Chinese banks, including kicking China off the SWIFT system." Undeterred, Beijing launched massive air strikes on Taiwan along with an amphibious assault, and retaliated against US sanctions by, among other things, banning the export of electronic goods. Chinese authorities conveyed their belligerence thusly: "We are going after companies like Apple, Dell, HP. You want a new iPhone? Guess what. You are not going to get it."

The good news is, this was just a game, complete with tabletop maps and blue and red counters, played on Capitol Hill on April 19, 2023, to simulate a fictional confrontation over Taiwan in 2027.[6] On the Blue Team, playing the United States, were members of the House Select Committee on the Chinese Communist Party; on the Red Team, playing China, were staffers from the Center for New American Security (CNAS). The vow to exert "maximum economic pressure" on Beijing came from committee chair Michael Gallagher, a Wisconsin Republican, and the "Chinese" bombast regarding iPhones came from Stacie Pettyjohn, director of the CNAS Defense Program.

The bad news is, the scenario was all too plausible. Ever since Communist forces gained control of the Chinese mainland in 1949 and their Nationalist foes fled to Taiwan, the government in Beijing has sworn to reunify the country, by force if necessary, in the event that the authorities in Taipei declare formal independence. US leaders of both major parties, meanwhile, have grown increasingly hostile toward Xi's oppressive rule and resolute in declaring America's solidarity with Taiwan's self-governing democracy. Their conviction that Washington would hold a strong hand in a conflict over the island swelled after the imposition of sanctions on Russia.

Slapping Beijing with a package of measures similar to those used against Moscow — as Gallagher vowed in his capacity as head of the Blue Team — would no doubt deal a paralyzing blow to the Chinese economy. The impact on China would be especially disruptive if the coalition that stood up to Russia joined in imposing sanctions along with the United States; that would leave Chinese officials with few, if any, options for shielding their central bank reserves from being frozen. The problem is that the shock waves would pound the economies of virtually every nation on earth, including America's, and Beijing's retaliatory measures would augment the damage in ways that Putin can only dream about.

China's GDP is ten times that of Russia's. Its four major banks rank among the world's 30 "systemically important" financial institutions, the crippling of which could drag down other giant banks around the globe. And its manufacturing sector is deeply intertwined with that of all advanced economies. Of 120-odd global manufacturing sectors, one-third of them are dominated by Chinese exporters, meaning they hold more than a 50 percent market share, according to estimates by *The Economist*. In the lithium-ion cells used in electric vehicle batteries, for example, China accounts for about two-thirds of world production, as well as four-fifths of solar panels, and 86 percent of rare-earth minerals used in a variety of high-tech products. China's share of global exports of computers is an estimated 80 percent; for smartphones, it's 67 percent. Pharmaceutical ingredients needed to make drugs, purified neon required for semiconductor fabrication, dyes used in medical imaging — Chinese firms are key suppliers of these and a long list of other products.[7]

Global supply chains, in other words, give China control over chokepoints that US leaders would ignore at their peril in a showdown over Taiwan. American politicians may shrug at the potential loss of the huge assets that foreign multinationals hold in China, which include an estimated $3.6 trillion in direct investments, including factories; even if Chinese seizure of those assets sent stock markets plummeting (would it ever!), that might seem an endurable price for defending a democratic ally. But smoothly functioning global supply chains, nearly all of which involve some Chinese parts or components, are critical to untold numbers of American jobs. An example came during the pandemic, when lockdowns in China in 2022 led to shortages of wire connectors—a low-tech input, but important enough in aircraft that it caused delays in the production of Boeing jets. Beyond job losses, how about the prospect of shelves at Walmart, Target, and Best Buy being stripped of merchandise?

The term "massive global costs" was thus aptly used in a June 2023 study of Taiwan crisis scenarios regarding the impact of "maximalist" sanctions on China. "Approximately $3 trillion in trade and financial flows"—a sum nearly equivalent to the GDP of the United Kingdom—"could be put at risk, primarily from disruptions to trade settlement," wrote the authors, who hailed from the Atlantic Council, a Washington think tank, and the Rhodium Group, a research firm with extensive China experience. "This is only a rough estimate and is likely an undercount, but it illustrates the scale of economic activity at risk from full-scale sanctions on China's largest banks. . . . The economic impact of such moves would be dramatic, both for China and for the world."[8]

Surely the oft-reported US-China "decoupling" will significantly reduce dependence on Chinese industry, tilting the scales in America's favor? Maybe in my grandchildren's lifetimes, not mine. (At this writing, I'm 72 and in excellent health.) Talk to people in the foreign business community in China, as I have, and they'll tell you: no country comes close as a producer of manufactured goods at scale. This is not because Chinese labor costs are low—wages for Chinese workers are actually higher than in many Asian countries—but because China boasts far superior roads, rail lines, skilled engineers, logistics, and networks of vendors for all manner of parts and services that need to be sourced locally. Many firms with large plants in China have moved some facilities to India and Southeast Asia, as a way of de-risking against geopolitical tension. But even these relocated operations depend heavily on Chinese suppliers and sub-suppliers. Samsung, for instance, shifted much of its mobile phone production to Vietnam, where it makes millions of phones for export to the West, but those phones contain a large number of made-in-China components.[9] A slew of economic analyses based on deep dives into trade statistics demonstrates conclusively how pervasive this phenomenon is, and how Chinese manufacturers remain crucial even for many imported goods that are labeled as produced elsewhere.[10]

Hopefully, the grim determination to back Taiwan expressed by US politicians like Gallagher will have a sobering effect on Xi and others in the Politburo. As colleagues of mine at the Center for Strategic and International Studies have written: "There is deterrence value in the United States and its allies and partners making clear to Beijing that any use of force against Taiwan would on its own impose enormous costs as well as trigger massive sanctions."[11]

Hopefully, too, US policymakers will become better educated about the folly of cocksureness when it comes to sanctioning China. Perhaps more tabletop exercises in America's halls of power will help. If the world is truly lucky, Washington and Beijing will start dialing down tensions rather than constantly ratcheting them up, and eventually reach some accommodation that preserves both Taiwanese democracy and peace in East Asia. The economic costs mentioned above don't even include the ones that would result from a shooting war in the Taiwan Strait, which would be orders of magnitude greater in financial terms, not to mention horrific with respect to loss of life.

Circumspection in weaponizing the dollar is probably the most important way in which US policymakers should take the Spider-Man adage into account. There are others.

Here is a plea, for everyone involved in policy discussions about the digitization of money. Henceforth, please omit references to the international dominance of the dollar, or at least keep the issue in proportion. The dollar's salvation doesn't depend on a US CBDC or dollar stablecoins. All too often, advocates for these various types of digital currencies use the dollar's status as a key talking point in pitching their preferred approaches for how the future of money should evolve. It's possible that technological advancements in the digital transmission of value will enable more sanctions-busting at some point down the road. But payment technology is very low on the list of factors determining the international currency hierarchy.

Promulgators of hysteria over China's CBDC, in particular, should cease and desist. The e-CNY is not going to become a medium of exchange in places like Kansas and Idaho, much less turn the mobile phones of people living there into instruments of Chinese spy craft. That said, there are legitimate grounds for concern that many countries, especially those run by leaders with autocratic tendencies, will issue CBDCs with Chinese characteristics – that is, with features enabling their governments to exert greater surveillance and control over their citizenry.

An alternative will likely be needed, with solid free-speech and privacy protections. The nation best suited by far to provide it is the United States, which should accept this responsibility with Spider-Man-like dutifulness. The European Central Bank is working on a CBDC, as is the Bank of England, and although the Fed doesn't have to follow them down that path, US officials need to be in a position to influence international debates about principles and standards governing digital assets. The United States can count on having a "seat at the table" in such discussions, but for its voice to carry maximum weight, the American financial and payments system will have to be at the technological cutting edge, or at least clearly headed in that direction. Moreover, the dollar's well-recognized global status will accord it uniquely potent attraction as a model for other countries' digital currency policies.

For these reasons and others, the most promising way forward is for the United States to embrace the BIS vision for tokenized deposits, introduced in chapter 8. If Hyun Song Shin is right, as I believe he is, tokenized deposits will afford the greatest opportunities for fintech innovators to revolutionize payments and finance while maintaining central bank money firmly at the foundation of the monetary system. For America to keep pace with the next big thing in digital money, this is the ideal way to go.

Whatever form it takes, the digital money that Americans use in the future should be protected against government intrusion in ways that are at least as strong as they are now – that is, with the overarching principle being the constitutional prohibition against unreasonable search and seizure. Libertarians have argued that existing protections aren't sufficient, that financial privacy is too vulnerable to state snooping and interference because of the powers granted to federal agencies under laws and regulations such as the Bank Secrecy Act, and that AML/KYC rules are ineffective anyway in catching the vast majority of financial crimes.[12] Debate about strengthening privacy protections may be in order, but America made a fundamental choice after the September 11 attacks that the government must be empowered to prevent abuse of the financial system for illicit purposes. As we have seen, those powers have helped make it possible for Washington to impose and enforce dollar-based sanctions.

Tokenized deposits tick all the right boxes. They would presumably be accorded the same privacy protections as regular bank deposits, and would also be subject to AML/KYC rules. If successful, moreover, they would fortify the role that banks play in payments, which would help in bolstering US sanctions power. The reason sanctions work is that banks and other financial intermediaries employ thousands of people to scrutinize the trillions of dollars in transactions that they process, under the threat of severe penalties for laxity. It is in US national security interests to preserve that arrangement as much as possible.

With properly stringent regulation, dollar-based stablecoins can and should be encouraged to play a meaningful part in the payments system. Competition is healthy; stablecoins may offer innovative features that stimulate other payment providers, including banks offering tokenized deposits, to up their game. Stablecoins, Bitcoin, and other cryptocurrencies also offer financial lifelines for people in countries with oppressive rulers and dysfunctional monetary regimes, as noted in chapter 8.

But remember that the original inspiration for crypto was to disrupt, bypass, and degrade the established network of banks and financial intermediaries. As unlovable as banks and fee-grubbing intermediaries may be, getting rid of them or ruining their financial health would be bad for US sanctions power. If Washington cares (as it should) about maintaining its ability to levy financial sanctions, it should design a legal and regulatory framework that prioritizes tokenized deposits over stablecoins and crypto.

Sadly, prospects for an enlightened US digital currency policy are bleak. The crypto industry is flush with cash, and dispensing it for political advantage in pernicious ways.

On July 27, 2024, Donald Trump strode to the podium at the Bitcoin 2024 conference in Nashville, Tennessee, amid boisterous cheers. The attendees knew that Trump had a history of disparaging their favored digital instruments; in 2019 he tweeted: "I am not a fan of Bitcoin and other Cryptocurrencies, which are not money . . . and based on thin air," and in 2021 he said in television interviews that bitcoin "seems like a scam . . . the currency of the world should be the dollar. . . . [Crypto is] potentially a disaster waiting to happen."[13] But the crowd was also keenly aware that Trump was viewing the issue in a whole new light now that he was running to return to the White House, and the decibel level of the pumped-up audience rose as he unveiled specifics of his plan to make the United States "the crypto capital of the planet and the Bitcoin superpower of the world."[14]

If elected, Trump said, his administration would amass a "strategic national bitcoin stockpile," starting with the 210,000 bitcoins (then worth about $14 billion) that the federal government had seized from criminals and which would be held rather than sold to avoid depressing prices. To the maximum extent possible, he continued, bitcoin mining would take place on American soil, under eased government regulations. The loudest roars of approval came when he promised to fire Gary Gensler, the chair of the Securities and Exchange Commission (SEC), who had become the crypto community's bête noir because of his agency's enforcement actions against some of the industry's biggest firms. No longer would crypto exchanges and coin issuers be "persecuted" by the likes of Gensler, who saw crypto markets as rife with fraud. "From now on, the rules will be written [by those] who love your industry, not hate your industry," Trump said. "Bitcoin and crypto will skyrocket like never before."

Nobody was under the illusion that Trump had educated himself on crypto technology or had undergone some sort of road-to-Damascus conversion. He was "pretty clearly pandering," one attendee was quoted as saying,[15] as witnessed by Trump's closing words: "Have a good time with your bitcoin and your crypto and everything else that you're playing with." Rather, Trump's change of heart was attributable to millions of dollars in contributions heaped on his campaign by crypto tycoons, and his recognition of the industry's growing clout.

In the two years since a series of scandals and implosions befouled crypto's image, prices of many crypto assets had rebounded—at about $68,000 on the day of Trump's speech, bitcoin was up more than fourfold from its November 2022 low—and Big Crypto was marshaling a war chest with the single-minded aim of obtaining more compliant policy from Washington. Crypto-focused political action committees (PACs) had raised $194 million by the fall of 2024, more than any other industry group, according to FollowTheCrypto.org, a data-compiling project. The largest single spending operation in the 2024 election cycle was a PAC called Fairshake, funded largely by billionaires who had made fortunes in crypto. Fairshake was targeting politicians who favored regulatory crackdowns on the sector, while pouring money into campaigns of pro-crypto candidates, regardless of party affiliation or general ideology. Fairshake's $10 million helped defeat Rep. Katie Porter in the California Democratic Senate primary, and the chair of the Senate Banking Committee, Sherrod Brown of Ohio — who together with fellow Democrats on the panel has blocked crypto-friendly legislation from passage — was girding for a deluge of Fairshake spending against him in his tight reelection race. Fearful of ceding Big Crypto campaign cash entirely to the GOP and alienating pro-crypto voters, some Democratic politicians scrambled to appease the industry with calls for their party to adopt a "forward looking approach" regarding digital assets, including the replacement of Gensler.[16]

Potentially more consequential was Trump's choice of his vice-presidential running mate, Senator JD Vance of Ohio, who is no Johnny-come-lately to crypto. When Vance won his Senate race in 2022 his financial disclosure showed that he held bitcoin valued at between $100,000 and $250,000, and as a senator he supported measures to ease regulation of the sector. His most influential mentor is Peter Thiel, a billionaire entrepreneur and bitcoin enthusiast who helped Vance become wealthy in Silicon Valley. Thiel contributed $15 million in support of Vance's Senate campaign and played a key role in mobilizing fellow tech titans to boost Vance's prospects for joining Trump on the GOP ticket. Thiel's monetary theories are rooted in his fervently espoused libertarianism; his perception of the Fed as a money-printing, currency-debasing tool of oppressive government was manifest in a keynote address he gave to the Bitcoin 2022 conference, where he declared that "central banks are bankrupt . . . we are at the end of the fiat money regime." Similar views are shared by several other tech billionaires who are close to Vance and Thiel.[17]

Yet another motive for Trump's embrace of crypto emerged shortly after his Nashville speech, when he joined his sons in promoting a venture called World Liberty Financial (WLF), aimed at facilitating the use of digital assets in borrowing and lending, with financing provided by the sale of tokens to investors. Having been "orange-pilled" (crypto lingo for indoctrinated), Trump sons Donald Jr., Eric, and Barron teamed up with WLF's co-founders, Chase Herro and Zachary Folkman, whose pasts were strewn with so many failures and disreputable activities that even crypto supremos cringed over the potential for fresh blots on the industry's image. "These guys are total losers with very questionable business track records," Nic Carter, an investor in blockchain startups, told the *Financial Times*. Nevertheless, Trump appeared on a livestream to tout investment in WLF with his sons, along with Herro and Folkman. "Crypto is one of those things we have to do," he said. "Whether we like it or not, I have to do it."[18]

Not that Trump was intending for crypto to thrive at the dollar's expense. He frequently warned about the greenback's status during the Biden administration, declaring that "if we lost the dollar as the world's currency . . . that would be the equivalent of losing a war."[19] To prevent such an outcome, he vowed to use his favorite tool — tariffs. "Many countries are leaving the dollar," he told supporters at a Wisconsin rally. "I'll say, `You leave the dollar, you're not doing business with the United States, because we're going to put 100 percent tariffs on your goods'"[20] — as if dollar dominance were a function of foreign government decisions rather than the preferences of multinational firms, investors, financial institutions, and other private actors. But his family's involvement in WLF means that he has a personal financial stake in crypto, which makes it all the more certain that he will exercise his powers over regulatory policy in the industry's favor, blatant though the conflict of interest may be.

Without getting into the details of crypto regulation — a subject worthy of a whole other book — I can easily imagine that the upshot of all this will be a major increase in the number of unsuspecting Americans losing their savings in crypto schemes and getting ripped off by fintech charlatans. The nation's financial stability will be endangered as risks rise of contagion spreading from failures in the crypto sector to the wider economy. And if something like Trump's "strategic national Bitcoin stockpile" is established, taxpayer money will go to prop up the value of an asset supposedly inspired by libertarian ideals. (Paging Satoshi, whoever and wherever you are: Surely you find this as sickening as I do?)

Still, the dollar's dominance is unlikely to be affected. Even if all of the promises Trump made at the Bitcoin conference were to become official US policy, that by itself would not alter the greenback's international status. America would become a shoddier place. But the reasons for its currency supremacy would remain fully intact.

America doesn't force other countries to use the dollar (Trump's tariff threat being an exception that proves the rule). Nor does Washington exercise leverage

---

to keep other currencies down in the global monetary pecking order. As will be recalled from chapter 4, US officials actively pressured Japan to internationalize the yen, and as for the euro, Washington welcomed its creation, taking the position that if it was good for Europe it would be good for the United States too.

That's how it should be. American interests would be helped, not hurt, if other major economic powers overcame the hindrances that keep their currencies from rivaling the dollar. Suppose the nations of the eurozone banded together more closely, enhancing the harmonization of their fiscal and banking policies so as to minimize the risk of another crisis like the one that struck in 2010. Suppose Japan successfully tackled its demographic problems and became an economic dynamo again. Suppose China allowed money to move in and out of the country with total freedom and adopted rule of law that everyone, foreign investors included, could fully trust. The euro, the yen, or the renminbi, or perhaps all three, would presumably rise many notches in global league tables, leading to an equivalent fall in the dollar's standing. And the world would be a better place in important respects.

The world might be more financially stable, too, because a multipolar currency regime would create more safe havens to flee to during crises. A number of economists have warned that excessive reliance on a single dominant currency is unhealthy in the long run; America's share of the global economy is destined to shrink further over the next few decades as emerging markets continue to grow, so the US Treasury may generate an insufficient amount of safe assets to satisfy international demand, especially when financial strains arise. Among the scholars making this argument are Pierre-Olivier Gourinchas, the IMF's chief economist, and the London Business School's Hélène Rey, who perceive the risk of a "new Triffin dilemma," drawing a parallel with the Belgian economist's prophecies about America's inability to back the dollars in circulation during the Bretton Woods era.[21] Berkeley's Barry Eichengreen has added his intellectual heft to this school of thought with research showing that historically it is normal, and preferable, to have more than one major international currency. As Eichengreen puts it: "Just like biodiversity makes for a more robust global ecology, a multipolar system will be more robust."[22]

But assuming there will be no happy confluence of events resulting in currency multipolarity, the United States will continue to bear outsized responsibility for disaster prevention in the global financial system. (As is hopefully evident by now, this is yet another invocation of the Spider-Man adage.) Most obviously, this will entail the Fed's preparedness to ease dollar shortages overseas using swap lines and similar facilities as it did in 2008 and 2020. The political cost may be steep; members of Congress – and possibly even presidents – may object to extending this form of aid to foreign countries. But to recall the words (cited in chapter 3) of Timothy Geithner, then the New York Fed president, at the Fed meeting in late October 2008: "The privilege of being the reserve currency of the world comes with some burdens." This is one of them. In cases where the Fed can't provide swap lines to a country for one reason or another during a crisis, it will behoove Washington to be supportive of speedy IMF assistance.

Another urgent task in this regard is fixing the market for US Treasuries. In mid-2023, evidence mounted of high-risk bet-taking by hedge funds of the sort that fueled the near-breakdown in March 2020. This was distressingly similar to what some experts had predicted at the time of the pandemic turmoil, namely that the Fed's rescue of the Treasury market would lead to moral hazard by encouraging dangerous speculation on the assumption that the central bank would step in to stave off catastrophe. How vulnerable the market is to unanticipated shocks is impossible to say, but reports issued by regulators provided grounds for a heightened degree of anxiety.[23]

New safeguards approved by the SEC include tighter oversight of big players and establishing a centralized clearing system for trades tied to Treasuries – but these rules may not hold up. Hedge funds struck back with a lawsuit in early 2024 calling the SEC's measures "arbitrary and capricious" as well as economically misconceived. Other proposals involve modifying bank regulations to induce more holding of Treasuries by big banks. The details are technical; assessing which of the proposals would be best is beyond the scope of this book (as well as beyond the expertise of its author). But as should be clear from the account of events in chapter 9, the stakes are too high for Washington to ignore.

Furthermore, the Treasury market is set for an explosion in volume in coming years, for reasons that any casual reader of US news will have heard about – the soaring deficits and debt of the federal government. This is yet another issue where it is incumbent on the United States to avoid abusing the powers that come with dollar dominance.

Two arguments, diametrically at odds with each other and both wrong, are often made about the relationship between the dollar and US budgetary policy. The first might be called the General Jack D. Ripper theory, after the character in the movie *Dr. Strangelove* who obsesses about America being sapped of "precious bodily fluids." It goes like this: If dollar dominance is lost – due to, say, China's CBDC, or the launching of a BRICS currency, or some other cause – superpower status will become unaffordable for the United States. The federal government will be unable to borrow, or at least the cost of doing so will skyrocket. Washington won't be able to fund its budget deficit at reasonable interest rates, nor will Americans be able to enjoy an abundance of cheap imports, because foreigners will no longer lend the money to enable us to do so. Once our currency is no longer top dog, we'll forfeit not only our financial sanctions power but the comfortable living standards that exorbitant privilege provides.

A quick googling of data readily available on the internet is all that's required to show the fallacious assumptions underlying this line of thinking. The dollar's status doesn't give the US government the ability to borrow at lower rates than other countries; indeed, the yield on the benchmark ten-year Treasury bond in September 2023 was substantially higher than the comparable bonds for Japan, France, Germany, Canada, Australia, and – believe it or not – Greece. (This is an updated version of the 2016 observation Ben Bernanke made, cited in chapter 4, when he wrote, "The exorbitant privilege is not so exorbitant anymore.") Nor is the United States uniquely able to live beyond its means by importing more than it exports; during the decade 2010–2019, Australia, Canada, and Great Britain all ran bigger current account deficits, as a percentage of their GDPs, as Paul Krugman has pointed out.[24]

Doesn't America gain some economic and fiscal benefit from dollar dominance? Of course it does; the worldwide demand for Treasuries surely helps to keep interest rates in the United States lower than they would be otherwise. But there are disadvantages too, mainly because the dollar's global role results in an exchange rate that is higher against other currencies than it would be otherwise, and this adversely affects the competitiveness of American manufacturers. The US currency's strength on foreign exchange markets in recent years has drawn frequent denunciations from Trump, who contends it gives foreign-made goods an unfair advantage, and Vance has gone so far as to question whether the dollar's reserve currency status constitutes "a massive tax on American producers."[25] If, as some expect, this issue becomes a bone of international contention, it will be important to avoid conflating the dollar's role in global commerce with its exchange rate. Although there is some relationship, the effect of the former on the latter is modest, as indicated by the fact that the greenback has both risen and fallen steeply on currency markets for a wide variety of reasons during its many decades of international primacy.[26]

To sum up the defects of the General Jack D. Ripper theory: Maybe the economic pluses of the dollar's global role outweigh the minuses, or maybe it's vice versa. Even if the net effect is positive, the magnitudes involved are not crucial for our nation's economic vitality, much less our precious bodily fluids.

The second argument goes like this: The US Treasury issues debt in the world's safest asset, and in the indisputably dominant global currency, so it's all but inconceivable that foreigners would stop lending to the federal government at affordable interest rates. Therefore, Washington can go on spending with abandon while dispensing with the unpleasant duty of extracting high enough taxes to bring outlays and revenue into closer balance.

I was cutting my teeth as an economics reporter when the "deficits don't matter" theory was first generating controversy in the late 1970s and early 1980s. I was unfavorably impressed. It went against everything I'd learned in economics courses – that big deficits are fine during recessions but not when the economy is growing rapidly. I was therefore sympathetic to the prevailing orthodoxy that the deficits the federal government was running, which were about 5 percent of GDP, merited indictment of the Reagan administration and Congress for gross fiscal improvidence. If someone had told me then that the deficit would widen to between 8 and 10 percent of GDP for three consecutive years, as happened in 2009–2011, and to the 12 to 15 percent of GDP range in 2020–2021, I would have wondered how the republic could possibly survive.

It's now abundantly evident that the US government (and other governments too) can afford to run much wider deficits than had been previously imagined, and that doing so is desirable – essential, even – under certain circumstances. When the economy is struggling to recover from the biggest downturn since the Great Depression, or when a pandemic poses an economic threat

---

tantamount to war, the government should spend whatever is necessary to restore normal growth and stave off collapse, waiting until later to figure out how to pay for it. Austerity is especially dumb, almost masochistically so, if interest rates are low and the government's cost of borrowing is minimal. Deficit scolds have been rightly mocked for bemoaning the rise in the national debt, which has reached 100 percent of GDP, a level once thought certain to result in an economic death spiral. America is not Greece. The Greek government doesn't print the money that it borrows in; a debt crisis of the sort that Greece fell into is virtually impossible for the United States.

My deficit scolding instincts have been quelled in recent years, but they're twitching anew as I look ahead to the coming decade and beyond, because the US fiscal outlook is dismal. According to projections by the nonpartisan Congressional Budget Office, the gap between federal outlays and revenue will average 6.3 percent of GDP during 2025 to 2034,[27] and that's surely too optimistic an estimate for a number of reasons. (The agency is required to make its projections based on unrealistic assumptions about current laws and policies remaining in effect.) A more reality-grounded projection would be for deficits in the 6.5 percent to 10 percent of GDP range.[28]

Moreover, super-low interest rates are almost certainly a thing of the past, now that the Fed is back in inflation-fighting mode. When the central bank had the luxury of ignoring inflation and worried instead about stagnant growth, it could buy government bonds in massive quantities, helping to keep interest rates near zero. With the Fed obliged to shed its bond holdings as it shifts from QE to QT (quantitative tightening), yields on Treasuries have risen above 5 percent in early 2024, and even though rates may decline somewhat nobody anticipates a return in the foreseeable future to ultracheap levels.

Under those circumstances, deficits can have a corrosive impact. The huge amount of borrowing that the Treasury must do is likely to push interest rates higher for everybody. Companies will be less inclined to pour capital into plant and equipment or other long-term investments, so the productivity of the labor force will be stunted, hurting the nation's long-term prospects.

It would be hubristic, to say the least, for Washington to stay on its current fiscal path based on confidence in the world's readiness to provide finance on generous terms, *ad infinitum,* for American profligacy. Even with dollar dominance, US prosperity would be at risk; you don't have to be an adherent of the General Jack D. Ripper theory to feel duly alarmed.

The political system appears utterly incapable of providing a remedy. Republicans cut taxes when their party holds the White House, and use their power in Congress to block Democratic presidents from raising significant amounts of new tax revenue. Democrats, fed up with GOP hypocrisy on the fiscal issue, are increasingly inclined to throw caution to the wind on government spending programs. Each party can use legislative tactics almost unique to the US system — filibusters, government shutdowns, debt-limit standoffs, and the fiendishly complex budget and appropriations process — to protect their priorities from measures that would meaningfully shrink the gap between outlays and revenue. I don't mean to suggest an equivalency of blame; the Republicans, in my view, are far more culpable. But it is hard to argue with the ratings agency Fitch for its downgrade of US Treasury debt in August 2023, which cited as one of the main reasons "a steady deterioration in standards of governance."[29] That is an understated way of referring to the dysfunctionality that heightens the danger of the aforementioned catastrophic policy missteps.

By the time you hold this book in your hands, the second Trump administration will have commenced, and a Republican-controlled Congress will have convened with many pro-crypto lawmakers whose elections Big Crypto lavishly underwrote. Dollar supremacy survived Trump 1.0, and I believe it will survive version 2.0 as well. Yes, that's how strong my faith in it is, and it certainly won't depend on a big "strategic bitcoin reserve," which crypto zealots tout — for arrantly self-serving reasons — as a dollar fortifier.[30] Nor will it depend on fist-shaking against countries that try to de-dollarize, as Trump did after his election when he threatened the BRICS with tariffs if they pursue their flaky plan for a common currency.[31] Whatever approach Trump 2.0 takes on the dollar, I hope that the historical facts presented in previous chapters — and the insights I have drawn from them — will prove useful in informing the public debate.

One order of business in 2025 will involve a test of America's fitness, or lack thereof, to issue the world's dominant currency. The compromise agreed in May 2023 raising the ceiling on federal government debt is due to expire, so new legislation will be required for the Treasury to continue borrowing. Many eloquent pleas have been lodged urging Congress to end, once and for all, the need for such legislation, because it often leads to confrontations in which a budget deal of some sort is struck just in time to avert a US government default.[32]

Presumably a debt-limit deal will be easy to achieve in 2025, given the election result. But it's possible to foresee a stalemate sometime in the future in which far-right lawmakers refuse to provide the necessary votes and the Treasury, unable to raise new cash, is forced to default on some of its obligations. Even though investors could take comfort from the expectation that the Treasury would make good on its debt eventually, a prolonged default would surely prove calamitous to the market for Treasury securities.

Other wounds that America might inflict on itself could also affect the dollar's status. Presidential attacks on Fed independence may go even further than those that Trump leveled in 2018–2020, or the rule of law may be shredded to the point where international investors see little difference between the impartiality of US and Chinese courts. Another possibility is that tensions between the United States and China reach such a boiling point that the world splits into two economic blocs that are nearly isolated from each other, one dominated by the dollar and the other by the renminbi. Still another is that the White House could be occupied by a person who, like JD Vance, is heavily influenced by the likes of Peter Thiel, and decides to upend the fiat money system. Or Trump could do something similar, swayed perhaps by his orange-pilled sons, despite his avowals of support for the greenback's global role.

If US policy goes in those directions, dollar dominance will be lost or diminished. That will be the least of our worries, because so many other malign consequences will ensue. The point is, the benefits that come with a hegemonic currency are America's to squander.

It is pleasant to imagine that none of those things will come to pass, and the dollar's dominance will endure. It is pleasanter still to sink into reverie about a world in which nations get along so beautifully that a truly global currency becomes viable and sanctions can be dispensed with. Until then, the big question is whether the United States will act as a responsible steward of the great power that the dollar confers. If it doesn't, then curses against King Dollar may be justified. Let us hope that, instead, the future brings ample grounds for raising a toast to the king's reign: Long may it abide!

———

AUTHOR'S NOTE AND ACKNOWLEDGMENTS

On March 3, 2020, came the news that this book was a "go," in the form of an email notifying me that the Smith Richardson Foundation would provide a generous grant to support my work. Allan Song, the foundation's senior program officer who handled my grant proposal, added a humorous admonition for me to observe as I set about my research: "Make sure to wash your hands religiously!" — a reference to the virus that was then just starting to spread from the Chinese city of Wuhan to the rest of the world.

At that time, the book was envisioned to be similar to the journalistic investigations I've done in the past about behind-the-scenes activities of the world's top economic policymakers. I would travel to destinations including China, Russia, Iran, and several European nations, where I would dig deeply into efforts to circumvent sanctions that the US government had imposed using the dollar as a weapon. The main question I would attempt to answer was whether excessive exploitation of the power conferred by the dollar's global status might diminish its utility. Were governments at odds with the United States succeeding at creating alternative financial channels outside the dollar-based system, and if not, were they likely to do so in the foreseeable future? In addition to interviewing officials in capitals such as Beijing, Moscow, and Tehran and looking into sanctions-evasion activities by private businesses in those countries, I would

---

251

travel from my home in Japan to Washington for research into how US authorities were planning to ensure that dollar weaponization would retain its potency.

Events intervened, first and foremost being the necessity of taking considerably greater precautions against Covid than hand-washing. For me, getting "fully vaccinated" (remember that term?) took until June 2021 because of the methodical approach taken by the Japanese government. As a result I put off the travel I had initially anticipated, and even after I was finally able to leave Japan in the summer of 2021 my time and energy were diverted by sad family responsibilities as both my mother and stepfather reached the ends of their lives. Although the disruption owing to my family situation seemed quite manageable at the time — I firmly resolved to pick up where I left off and start traveling again in late 2021 — the Omicron variant and "breakthrough infections" materialized, so I waited for a booster shot, which I got in February 2022. Then, just days before I flew off on a trip to Washington, came the Russian invasion of Ukraine, which added a huge new dimension to my project's scope; the book would obviously have to be expanded to incorporate substantial material and analysis about the sanctions imposed on Moscow. In months thereafter it became increasingly clear that quite aside from Covid, I would be foolhardy to travel to Russia and China for the purpose of asking sensitive questions that might well strike the local authorities as grounds for my detainment.

Unwelcome as these developments were, I believe this book turned out much the better by differing from the sort in which I have specialized. It reflects insights I gleaned from many interviews and some travel, as well as reporting that I've done in the past, but it is based heavily on work produced by others — countless books, articles, expert analyses, online discussions (conference panels, podcasts, etc.), congressional hearings, and news reports that, as I pored over them, led me to the realization that I should write a broader book about the dollar than one that focused mainly on the sanctions issue. Books on the dollar have been published before, of course, by giants in the field of monetary economics and history; they include Barry Eichengreen's *Exorbitant Privilege* and *Globalizing Capital*, Eswar Prasad's *The Dollar Trap*, and Benjamin Cohen's *Currency Power* and *Currency Statecraft*. But as superb as those books are — I have relied extensively on their lessons — they have been overtaken by recent events, and I concluded that there was an urgent need for the dollar's role to be re-analyzed in a more up-to-date context.

——

AUTHOR'S NOTE AND ACKNOWLEDGMENTS

I am profoundly grateful to Smith Richardson for providing the financial resources that made the book possible, and to Allan for providing wise guidance that proved invaluable as the project took shape. I also appreciate the foundation's forbearance concerning the longer-than-expected time it took to complete. The Center for Strategic and International Studies helped make the arrangement work by giving me a position as a senior associate (nonresident) in the Economics Program, for which I thank Matthew Goodman, the former senior vice president for economics, and other CSIS colleagues who handled the administrative tasks involved.

Yale University Press and its editorial director, Seth Ditchik, came highly recommended by several author friends, so I was thrilled when Seth responded positively to my email querying about his possible interest in a publishing contract. I was even more pleased when the experience of working with Seth proved just as rewarding as my friends had suggested. Seth's editorial assistant, Chelsea Connelly, was the soul of both efficiency and congeniality; copy editor Erica Hanson devoted meticulous care to improving the manuscript; and production editor Jeff Schier skillfully saw the project through its final stages to publication. I also thank others involved with the editorial process at Yale Press including an anonymous reviewer who read the manuscript and had very nice things to say about it.

Among people I interviewed, only a handful are quoted in the book—Danny Glaser, Stuart Levey, Hyun Song Shin, Daleep Singh, Cecilia Skingsley, Adam Smith, and Olaf Unteroberdoerster. But in addition to them I owe thanks to many more people who took time to help me grasp the complexities of myriad economic, geopolitical, legal, financial, and technological events and issues. The list is too long to include everybody, but I must give special mention to Thomas Cowan, JP Koning, Gerard DiPippo, Mark Sobel, Steven Kamin, Gottfried Leibbrandt, Natasha De Terán, Hilary Allen, David Lewis, Tom Keatinge, Daniel Neilson, and Stephen Cecchetti (the last of whom will probably take strong issue with my conclusions about digital currency policy but I thank him anyway for stimulating discussions). I also appreciate the time taken by officials at the Fed, CHIPS, IMF, and BIS who helped with specific questions, mostly on deep background for my enlightenment. A few of the interviewees read portions of the manuscript and provided helpful suggestions—for that I am also grateful, with the usual caveat about remaining errors of omission and commission being solely my responsibility.

AUTHOR'S NOTE AND ACKNOWLEDGMENTS

Full disclosure: If this book is run through a plagiarism-detection program, a number of passages may raise red flags. The reason is that I have cribbed liberally from my own writing, mostly from books and articles that I wrote for the Centre for International Governance Innovation (CIGI), where I was a senior fellow from 2010 to 2023. Of course, I never, *ever* crib other peoples' writing, but in cases involving my own work where I slaved over the original wording, I felt entitled to recycle that creative energy, so to speak, for the sake of saving time. I am obliged to acknowledge CIGI for granting me permission to reproduce this material, for which CIGI holds the copyright, and I have diligently credited CIGI in each instance. A couple of other passages draw on pieces I wrote while a reporter, and they are also cited appropriately.

As with my previous six books, I am indebted to my wife Yoshie, albeit for a different reason. Whereas she endured my long absences for research trips during my work on previous books, this time she had to endure my constant presence at home during pandemic lockdown, much of which I spent doing the aforementioned poring over reading material. For me, being cooped up to minimize risk of infection was much less of an ordeal than it might have been, thanks to the pleasure of her company; the experience provided fresh evidence — if any were needed — of my good fortune in being married to her.

A note about the snarky reference to crypto in the book's dedication: It may provoke accusations that I'm manifestly a tool of the financial establishment. But anyone temped to draw such conclusions might want to consider the book I wrote 20 years ago about the Argentine financial crisis of 2001–2002, which heaped a hefty portion of blame on investment banks and institutional money managers, and was dedicated as follows: "To my children: Nina, Nathan, Dan, and Jack, whom I will always love unconditionally, even if they go to work on Wall Street."

As for the people (currently ages six and three) to whom this book is dedicated, their merriment when I visited the Bethesda, Maryland, home of my daughter and son-in-law added a huge measure of joy to my Washington research trips. The younger of the two entered the world shortly before my parents left it, so just as her big brother had done before her, she provided a reminder of what is important in my life, with even more exquisite timing.

Kamakura, Japan
August 9, 2024

———

254

NOTES

CHAPTER 1

1. "Historical Note" in New York Clearing House Association records, 1853–2006, Columbia University Libraries Archival Collections, https://findingaids.library.columbia.edu /ead/nnc-rb/ldpd_7094252/dsc. See also James Sloan Gibbons, *The Banks of New-York: Their Dealers, the Clearing House, and the Panic of 1857* (New York: D. Appleton & Co., 1858); William Jay Gilpin and Henry E. Wallace, *The New York Clearing House* (New York: Moses King, 1904); and Martin Campbell-Kelley, "Victorian Data Processing: Reflections on the First Payment Systems," *Communications of the ACM* 53, no. 10 (October 10, 2010), https://www.umsl.edu/~sauterv/analysis/p19-campbell-kelly.pdf.

2. Gibbons, *The Banks of New-York*, chapter 18.

3. "CHIPS, Annual Statistics from 1970 to 2024," https://media.theclearinghouse. org/-/media/New/TCH/Documents/Payment-Systems/CHIPS-Volume-and-Value_May. pdf?rev=2393796a8ff642a3848758b204914cd3.

4. The Clearing House, "CHIPS Public Disclosure of Legal, Governance, Risk Management, and Operating Framework," June 2022, https://mc-e3a82812-8e7a-44d9-956f-8910-cdn-endpoint.azureedge.net/-/media/New/TCH/Documents/Payment-Systems/CHIPS_Public_ Disclosure_June_2022_v2.pdf?rev=b254e7fb55614372934b4eef76dca8fd.

5. Joe Leahy and Hudson Lockett, "Brazil's Lula Calls for End to Dollar Trade Dominance," *Financial Times*, April 13, 2023.

6. Carol Bertaut, Bastian von Beschwitz, and Stephanie Curcuru, " 'The International Role of the U.S. Dollar' Post-COVID Edition," FEDS Notes, Federal Reserve Board, June 23, 2023, https://www.federalreserve.gov/econres/notes/feds-notes/the-international-role-of -the-us-dollar-post-covid-edition-20230623.html.

---

7. Figures on use of the dollar in invoicing, borrowing, and foreign exchange trading come from " 'The International Role of the U.S. Dollar' Post-COVID Edition." Figures on South Korean and Australian exporters' invoicing in dollars come from Shang-Jin Wei, "A Reality Check for the Renminbi," Project Syndicate, April 6, 2023, https://www.project-syndicate.org/commentary/renminbi-still-no-match-for-us-dollar-by-shang-jin-wei-2023-04; and Australian Bureau of Statistics, "Export and Import Invoice Currencies, 2020–21," https://www.abs.gov.au/articles/export-and-import-invoice-currencies-2020-21#:~:text=Back%20to%20top-,Key%20Statistics,and%2032.2%25%20in%20the%20AUD.

8. The graph in figure 2, and the overall point about the significance of foreign exchange swaps, is drawn from Hyun Song Shin, "The Dollar-Based Financial System through the Window of the FX Swaps Market," speech at the Peterson Institute for International Economics conference on "Floating Exchange Rates at Fifty," Washington, DC, March 24, 2023, https://www.bis.org/speeches/sp230324a.pdf.

9. Jon Cunliffe, "Do We Need 'Public Money'?" speech at the Official Monetary and Financial Institutions Forum (OMFIF) Digital Money Institute, London, May 13, 2021, https://www.bankofengland.co.uk/speech/2021/may/jon-cunliffe-omfif-digital-monetary-institute-meeting.

10. The quoted excerpts in this paragraph come from the following: Ruchir Sharma, "A Post-Dollar World Is Coming," *Financial Times,* August 28, 2022; Zoltan Pozsar, "Great Power Conflict Puts the Dollar's Exorbitant Privilege under Threat," *Financial Times,* January 19, 2023; and Niall Ferguson, "America's Power Is on a Financial Knife Edge," *Sunday Times,* September 15, 2019.

11. The quoted excerpts in this paragraph can be found in the following: Jeff Cox, "Stanley Druckenmiller Says the Fed Is Endangering the Dollar's Global Reserve Status," CNBC, May 11, 2021, https://www.cnbc.com/2021/05/11/stanley-druckenmiller-says-the-fed-is-endangering-the-dollars-global-reserve-status.html; Gal Luft and Anne Korin, *De-Dollarization: The Revolt against the Dollar and the Rise of a New Financial World Order* (independently published, 2019); and *Fox and Friends,* March 25, 2023, https://twitter.com/BitcoinNewsCom/status/1640302421762007044?s=20.

12. See .ifunny.co/picture/when-cbdcs-become-reality-card-declined-please-delete-all-tweets-IPVq4h3YA.

CHAPTER 2

1. Nellie Bly (born Elizabeth Jane Cochran), *Around the World in Seventy-Two Days,* chapter 1, in *The Complete Works of Nellie Bly* (Shrine of Knowledge, 2020).

2. Bly, *Around the World in Seventy-Two Days,* chapter 9.

3. See Barry Eichengreen, *Exorbitant Privilege: The Rise and Fall of the Dollar and the Future of the International Monetary System* (New York: Oxford University Press, 2011), for much of the history on which this chapter and the next is based. Also invaluable is Neil Irwin, *The Alchemists: Three Central Bankers and a World on Fire* (New York: Penguin Books, 2013), chapters 2, 3, and 4; Barry Eichengreen, Arnaud Mehl, and Livia Chitu, *How Global Curren-*

cies Work: Past, Present, and Future (Princeton, NJ: Princeton University Press, 2018), chapter 3; and Barry Eichengreen, "International Currencies in the Lens of History," in *Handbook of the History of Money and Currency,* ed. Stefano Battilossi, Youssef Cassis, and Kazuhiko Yago (Singapore: Springer, 2020).

4. See Helen Fessenden, "When Banking Was 'Free,' " *Econ Focus,* Federal Reserve Bank of Richmond, First Quarter 2018, https://www.richmondfed.org/publications/research/econ_focus/2018/q1/economic_history; and Joshua R. Greenberg, *Bank Notes and Shinplasters: The Rage for Paper Money in the Early Republic* (Philadelphia: University of Pennsylvania Press, 2020). The economist George Selgin has provided invaluable insight by challenging interpretations of this period that he views as distorted, Greenberg's in particular. See Selgin, "The Fable of the Cats," *Cato at Liberty* (blog), July 6, 2021, https://www.cato.org/blog/fable-cats; and "Joshua Greenberg on Antebellum Paper Money," *Cato at Liberty* (blog), March 31, 2021, https://www.cato.org/blog/joshua-greenberg-antebellum-paper-money.

5. See Roger Lowenstein, *Ways and Means: Lincoln and His Cabinet and the Financing of the Civil War* (New York: Penguin Press, 2022) for an authoritative account.

6. On the gold standard, see Liaquat Ahamed, introduction to *Lords of Finance: The Bankers Who Broke the World* (New York: Penguin Press, 2009); Barry Eichengreen, *Globalizing Capital: A History of the International Monetary System, Third Edition* (Princeton, NJ: Princeton University Press, 2019), chapter 2; and Jacob Goldstein, *Money: The True Story of a Made-Up Thing* (New York: Hachette, 2020), chapter 10.

7. On the Overend Gurney incident recounted in the paragraph that follows, see Rhiannon Sowerbutts, Marco Schneebalg, and Florence Hubert, "The Demise of Overend Gurney," *Bank of England Quarterly Bulletin* 2016 Q2, https://www.bankofengland.co.uk/-/media/boe/files/quarterly-bulletin/2016/the-demise-of-overend-gurney.pdf; Felix Martin, *Money: The Unauthorized Biography—From Coinage to Cryptocurrencies* (New York: Alfred A. Knopf, 2014), chapter 12; and Irwin, *The Alchemists,* chapter 2.

8. Walter Bagehot, *Lombard Street: A Description of the Money Market* (New York: Charles Scribner's Sons), 51.

9. See, e.g., Abigail Tucker, "J. P. Morgan as Cutthroat Capitalist," *Smithsonian Magazine,* January 2011.

10. See Roger Lowenstein, *America's Bank: The Epic Struggle to Create the Federal Reserve* (New York: Penguin Books, 2015), chapter 4; and Irwin, *The Alchemists,* chapter 3.

11. See Lowenstein, *America's Bank,* for a detailed account.

12. For the rise of the dollar and US financial industry in the wake of World War I, see Eichengreen, *Exorbitant Privilege,* chapter 2, and Eichengreen, Mehl, and Chitu, *How Global Currencies Work,* chapter 3.

13. For the Fed mistakes and gold standard strictures that contributed to the Great Depression, see Ahamed, *Lords of Finance,* chapter 20, and Barry Eichengreen, *Golden Fetters: The Gold Standard and the Great Depression, 1919–1939* (New York: Oxford University Press, 1992).

14. Ben S. Bernanke, introduction to *21st Century Monetary Policy: The Federal Reserve from the Great Inflation to COVID-19* (New York: W. W. Norton).

———

15. Ahamed, *Lords of Finance,* chapter 21; Eichengreen, *Golden Fetters.*

16. Much of this section is drawn from my book *Off Balance: The Travails of Institutions That Govern the Global Financial System* (Waterloo, ON: Centre for International Governance Innovation, 2013), 16–18. But for much more detailed accounts of the Bretton Woods conference and its historical context, from which key details are included here, see Benn Steil, *The Battle of Bretton Woods: John Maynard Keynes, Harry Dexter White, and the Making of a New World Order,* A Council on Foreign Relations Book (Princeton, NJ: Princeton University Press, 2013); and James M. Boughton, *Harry White and the American Creed: How a Federal Bureaucrat Created the Modern Global Economy (and Failed to Get the Credit)* (New Haven, CT: Yale University Press, 2021). See also Ahamed, *Lords of Finance,* chapter 22; Eichengreen, *Exorbitant Privilege,* chapter 3; and Gianni Toniolo, *Central Bank Cooperation at the Bank for International Settlements, 1930–1973* (New York: Cambridge University Press, 2005), chapter 8.

17. See Ivo Maes with Ilaria Pasotti, *Robert Triffin: A Life* (New York: Oxford University Press, 2021); Triffin, *Gold and the Dollar Crisis* (New Haven, CT: Yale University Press, 1960); and "Statement of Robert Triffin to the Joint Economic Committee of Congress," Washington, DC, December 8, 1960.

18. See Jeffry A. Frieden, *Global Capitalism: Its Fall and Rise in the Twentieth Century* (New York: W. W. Norton, 2006), chapters 11 and 12. The figure on US gold holdings is cited in Sandra Kollen Ghizoni, "Nixon Ends Convertibility of U.S. Dollars to Gold and Announces Wage/Price Controls," Federal Reserve History, written November 22, 2013, https://www.federalreservehistory.org/essays/gold-convertibility-ends.

19. See Eichengreen, *Exorbitant Privilege,* chapter 3, and for a rigorous analysis, see Benjamin Cohen, *Currency Power: Understanding Monetary Rivalry* (Princeton, NJ: Princeton University Press, 2015), chapter 3.

20. Quoted in Eichengreen, *Exorbitant Privilege,* chapter 3.

21. Charles de Gaulle, press conference, February 4, 1965, English translation available at https://collections.library.yale.edu/catalog/11787140.

22. Cohen, *Currency Power,* chapter 7.

23. See Ghizoni, "Nixon Ends Convertibility"; William L. Silber, *Volcker: The Triumph of Persistence* (New York: Bloomsbury Press, 2012), chapter 2; Eichengreen, *Exorbitant Privilege,* chapter 3.

24. Silber, *Volcker,* chapter 3.

25. Paul A. Volcker with Christine Harper, *Keeping At It: The Quest for Sound Money and Good Government* (New York: PublicAffairs, 2018), chapter 5. Volcker's reference to foreign dollar liabilities meant holdings of Treasury securities and other dollar-denominated securities by central banks, as well as dollars held in commercial banks abroad.

26. See William Safire, *Before the Fall: An Inside View of the Pre-Watergate White House* (New York: Doubleday, 1975), for a reasonably close-to-verbatim account of the proceedings at this meeting. All the quotes from participants in this section come from Safire's book. But a thorough account, putting the episode in historical perspective, is Jeffrey E. Garten, *Three Days at Camp David: How a Secret Meeting in 1971 Transformed the Global Economy*

(New York: Harper, 2021). Also invaluable is Roger Lowenstein, "The Nixon Shock," *Bloomberg Business Week,* August 5, 2011, https://www.bloomberg.com/news/articles/2011-08-04/the-nixon-shock?embedded-checkout=true.

27. The transcripts of tapes from the system that Nixon had secretly installed at the White House are replete with evidence that politics were uppermost in Nixon's mind in his considerations about international economic policy. See James L. Butkiewicz and Scott Ohlmacher, "Ending Bretton Woods: Evidence from the Nixon Tapes," *Economic History Review* 74, no. 4 (November 2021): 922–945.

28. Quoted in Irwin, *The Alchemists,* chapter 5. See Robert H. Ferrell, ed., *Inside the Nixon Administration: The Secret Diary of Arthur Burns, 1969–1974* (Lawrence: University Press of Kansas, 2010), 49.

29. Richard Nixon, "Address to the Nation Outlining a New Economic Policy: 'The Challenge of Peace,' " August 15, 1971, https://www.presidency.ucsb.edu/documents/address-the-nation-outlining-new-economic-policy-the-challenge-peace.

30. Quoted in Volcker, *Keeping At It,* chapter 6.

31. Leonard Silk, "The Dollar's Tribulations," *New York Times,* July 4, 1973.

32. Quoted in Perry Mehrling, *Money and Empire: Charles P. Kindleberger and the Dollar System* (New York: Cambridge University Press, 2022), chapter 6.

CHAPTER 3

1. David Mulford, *Packing for India: A Life of Action in Global Finance and Diplomacy* (Lincoln, NE: Potomac Books, 2014), chapter 6.

2. David E. Spiro, *The Hidden Hand of American Hegemony: Petrodollar Recycling and International Markets* (Ithaca, NY: Cornell University Press, 1999). The memo, signed by then Treasury undersecretary Jack F. Bennett, is on pages 111–112.

3. A great deal of scholarship and journalism has shed light on the interactions between the United States and Saudi Arabia during this period, with Spiro's *Hidden Hand of American Hegemony* among the most revelatory. It is clear that the Saudi regime sought and got American support for its security, while undertaking to take steps that would be helpful to US economic interests, including pricing oil in dollars and investing much of the revenue from oil sales in Treasury securities. But the evidence also strongly suggests that the Saudis recognized the close alignment of their economic interests with those of the United States and that using the dollar made the most financial sense for them. In addition to Spiro's book, see Rachel Bronson, *Thicker Than Oil: America's Uneasy Partnership with Saudi Arabia* (New York: Oxford University Press, 2006), chapter 6; Bessma Momani, "GCC Oil Exporters and the Future of the Dollar," *New Political Economy* 13, no. 3 (2008): 293–314, https://uwaterloo.ca/scholar/sites/ca.scholar/files/bmomani/files/gcc_oil_exporters_and_the_future_of_the_dollar_forthcoming_in_new_political_economy.pdf; Robert G. Kaiser and David Ottaway, "Oil for Security Fueled Close Ties," *Washington Post,* February 11, 2002. Also invaluable, although account must be taken of the bias of its authors (present and former SAMA employees) is Ahmed Banafe and Rory Macleod, *The Saudi Arabian Monetary Agency, 1951–2016: Central Bank of Oil* (London: Palgrave Macmillan, 2017), chapter 4.

4. Mulford, *Packing for India,* chapter 6.

5. Mulford, *Packing for India,* chapter 6.

6. Banafe and Macleod, *The Saudi Arabian Monetary Agency,* chapter 4.

7. Paul Blustein, "Look Who Made It in Wall Street!" *Forbes,* February 1, 1977. The first part of this section, recounting how the Treasury markets worked in the mid-1970s, is heavily drawn from my article.

8. John F. Lyons, "Can the Bond Market Survive?" *Institutional Investor,* May 1969.

9. In the provocative formulation of David Spiro, the United States was extracting a "double loan" from the rest of the world. Spiro, *The Hidden Hand of American Hegemony,* chapter 5.

10. Quoted in Jonathan Kirshner, "Dollar Diminution and the Consequences for American Power," in *The Future of the Dollar,* ed. Eric Helleiner and Jonathan Kirshner, chapter 9. See Susan Strange, "The Persistent Myth of Lost Hegemony," *International Organization* 41, no. 4 (1987): 551–574.

11. Arthur F. Burns, "The Anguish of Central Banking," The 1979 Per Jacobsson Lecture, Belgrade, September 30, 1979, http://www.perjacobsson.org/lectures/1979.pdf.

12. See Irwin, *The Alchemists,* chapter 5, for an excellent summary of the Fed's travails during this period.

13. See Spiro, *The Hidden Hand of American Hegemony,* chapter 5; and Joel Harris, "The Last Great Dollar Crisis," *Wall Street Journal,* December 1, 2009.

14. Mulford, *Packing for India,* chapter 6.

15. See Steven Solomon, *The Confidence Game: How Unelected Central Bankers Are Governing the Changed World Economy* (New York: Simon & Schuster, 1995), chapter 10.

16. Paul Blustein, "Monetary Zeal: How Federal Reserve under Volcker Finally Slowed Down Inflation," *Wall Street Journal,* December 7, 1984. This section draws heavily on my article, except where noted.

17. Volcker, *Keeping At It,* chapter 8.

18. See Silber, *Volcker: The Triumph of Persistence,* chapter 11. Volcker told his biographer: "It was among the most difficult things I've done in my professional life. Jimmy Carter had appointed me, and I voted for him in 1976, and would do so again in the upcoming election. But no matter what I thought or felt, there was no choice other than to increase the discount rate. I had a job to do." For his part, Carter noted in his published diary that his advisers had been very concerned about appointing Volcker to the Fed chair, adding that "our trepidation about Volcker's appointment was later justified" when the Fed "raised interest rates to very high levels . . . a negative factor in my 1980 reelection campaign." See Jimmy Carter, *White House Diary* (New York: Farrar, Straus and Giroux, 2010), 348.

19. Quoted in Silber, *Volcker: The Triumph of Persistence,* chapter 13, citing the transcript of the Federal Open Market Committee Meeting, October 5, 1982, p. 19.

20. Clyde H. Farnsworth, "A View That's as Rosy as Red Ink," *New York Times,* November 3, 1987.

21. Stephen Marris, *Deficits and the Dollar: The World Economy at Risk* (Washington, DC: Institute for International Economics, 1985), "Summary," xxi.

22. Much of this section is drawn from my book *Off Balance*, pp. 26–31. For more detail on the Plaza Accord and the history of this period, see Yoichi Funabashi, *Managing the Dollar: From the Plaza to the Louvre* (Washington, DC: Institute for International Economics, 1988); and David M. Andrews, ed., *International Monetary Power* (Ithaca, NY: Cornell University Press, 2006).

23. Mulford, *Packing for India*, chapter 7.

24. "Announcement of the Ministers of Finance and Central Bank Governors of France, Germany, Japan, the United Kingdom, and the United States," September 22, 1985, http://www.g8.utoronto.ca/finance/fm850922.htm.

25. Diane B. Kunz, "The Fall of the Dollar Order: The World the United States Is Losing," *Foreign Affairs*, July/August 1995.

26. "After Half a Century at the Top, the Dollar's Dominance is Waning," *The Economist*, February 25, 1995.

27. This episode is recounted in John B. Taylor, *Global Financial Warriors: The Untold Story of International Finance in the Post-9/11 World* (New York: W. W. Norton, 2007), chapter 10.

28. Much of the material in this section is drawn from my book *Off Balance*, pp. 45–49. For more historical background and detail on the global imbalances of the early 2000s, see Martin Wolf, *Fixing Global Finance* (Baltimore: Johns Hopkins University Press, 2010); Stephen S. Cohen and J. Bradford DeLong, *The End of Influence: What Happens When Other Countries Have the Money* (New York: Basic Books, 2010); and Steven Dunaway, "Global Imbalances and the Financial Crisis," Council on Foreign Relations Special Report No. 44, March 2009.

29. Foreigners owned 11 percent of US equities (corporate stocks), 24 percent of US corporate bonds, and 57 percent of marketable US Treasuries as of June 2007, according to calculations by Kristin Forbes of MIT. See Kristin J. Forbes, "Underlying Determinants of Global Currency Status," in *The Euro at Ten: The Next Global Currency?*, ed. Jean Pisani-Ferry and Adam S. Posen (Washington, DC: Peterson Institute for International Economics and Bruegel, June 2009), 42–43.

30. Quoted in "Shrink-Proof," *The Economist*, September 20, 2003.

31. Paul Blustein, "U.S. Trade Deficit Hangs in a Delicate Imbalance," *Washington Post*, November 19, 2005. For another example of my worries about the dangers to the dollar stemming from mounting US trade deficits, see Blustein, *And the Money Kept Rolling In (And Out): Wall Street, the IMF, and the Bankrupting of Argentina* (New York: PublicAffairs, 2005), 234.

32. Nouriel Roubini and Brad Setser, "Will the Bretton Woods 2 Regime Unravel Soon? The Risk of a Hard Landing in 2005–2006," paper written for the symposium "Revived Bretton Woods System," organized by the Federal Reserve Bank of San Francisco and the University of California, Berkeley, February 4, 2005, https://pages.stern.nyu.edu/~nroubini/papers/BW2-Unraveling-Roubini-Setser.pdf.

33. See Adam Tooze, *Crashed: How a Decade of Financial Crises Changed the World* (New York: Penguin Books, 2018), chapter 3.

34. Bo Nielsen and Adriana Brasileiro, "Wise Heads Desert Falling US Dollar," Bloomberg News, November 5, 2007 (published in *Sydney Morning Herald,* November 10, 2007); Nelson D. Schwartz, "Dollar Gets a Snub from the Catwalk," *New York Times,* November 11, 2007.

35. See Tooze, *Crashed,* chapter 8, Irwin, *The Alchemists,* chapter 11, and Daniel McDowell, *Brother, Can You Spare a Billion? The United States, the IMF, and the International Lender of Last Resort* (New York: Oxford University Press, 2017), chapter 7, for authoritative accounts of the Fed's role as international lender of last resort during this period.

36. Tooze, *Crashed,* chapter 8, citing Patrick McGuire and Goetz von Peter, "The US Dollar Shortage in Global Banking and the International Policy Response," Bank for International Settlements Working Paper 291, October 2009.

37. In *The Alchemists,* chapter 11, Neil Irwin reports: "During the panic, this information was so closely held – and had it been known publically, so potentially explosive – that only two people at each of the dozen reserve banks were allowed access to it."

38. Federal Reserve Board, transcript of "Meeting of the Federal Open Market Committee on October 28–29, 2008," p. 35, https://www.federalreserve.gov/monetarypolicy/files/FOMC20081029meeting.pdf. This quote and others from the meeting are cited in McDowell, *Brother, Can You Spare a Billion?,* chapter 7, which provides a rigorous analysis of the implications.

39. The names of the rejected countries were redacted from the transcript, but information later emerged that Chile, Peru, the Dominican Republic, and Indonesia sought swap lines, in some cases in early 2009. See Eswar S. Prasad, *The Dollar Trap: How the U.S. Dollar Tightened Its Grip on Global Finance* (Princeton, NJ: Princeton University Press, 2014), chapter 11.

40. Transcript of October 28–29, 2008, meeting, p. 36.

41. Transcript of October 28–29, 2008, meeting, pp. 36–37.

42. Transcript of October 28–29, 2008, meeting, p. 21.

43. Zhou Xiaochuan, "Reform the International Monetary System," March 23, 2009, https://www.bis.org/review/r090402c.pdf.

44. United Nations, "Report of the Commission of Experts of the President of the United Nations General Assembly on Reforms of the International Monetary and Financial System," New York, 2009.

45. For Steinbrück's quote, see Noah Barkin, "U.S. Will 'Lose Financial Superpower Status,'" Reuters, September 25, 2008, https://www.reuters.com/article/financial-germany-steinbrueck-idUKLNE48O02G20080925. Sarkozy is quoted in Tooze, *Crashed,* chapter 8; also at http://www.g20.utoronto.ca/g20plans/g20leaders081114.pdf.

46. Jonathan Kirshner, "After the (Relative) Fall: Dollar Diminution and the Consequences for American Power," in *The Future of the Dollar,* ed. Helleiner and Kirshner, chapter 9.

47. Antonio Mosconi, "The World Supremacy of the Dollar at the Rendering," *New Federalist,* October 2, 2009, https://www.thenewfederalist.eu/The-World-Supremacy-of-the-Dollar-at-the-Rendering-1917-2008?lang=fr.

---

48. Matthew C. Klein and Michael Pettis, *Trade Wars Are Class Wars* (New Haven, CT: Yale University Press, 2020), chapter 6.

49. Eichengreen, *Exorbitant Privilege,* chapter 5, cites three studies, using various metrics to calculate the reduction in interest rates that American borrowers enjoyed: Roger Craine and Vance Martin, "Interest Rate Conundrum," *B.E. Journal of Macroeconomics* 9, no. 1 (2009): 1–27; Harm Bandholz, Jorg Clostermann, and Franz Seitz, "Explaining the US Bond Yield Conundrum," *Applied Financial Economics* 19 (2009): 539–550; and Frank Warnock and Virginia Warnock, "International Capital Flows and U.S. Interest Rates," *Journal of International Money and Finance* 28 (2009): 903–919.

CHAPTER 4

1. Paul Blustein, "Capitalizing on the Euro," *Washington Post,* July 4, 2002. This section on the euro draws heavily from my book *Laid Low: Inside the Crisis That Overwhelmed Europe and the IMF* (Waterloo, ON: Centre for International Governance Innovation, 2016).

2. C. Fred Bergsten, "The Dollar and the Euro," *Foreign Affairs,* July/August 1997.

3. Quoted in Cohen, *Currency Power,* chapter 8. See Robert A. Mundell, "The Euro and the Stability of the International Monetary System," in *The Euro as a Stabilizer in the International Economic System,* ed. Robert A. Mundell and Armand Cleese (Boston: Kluwer Academic), 57–84. Mundell's assertion can be found in the abstract of his chapter at https://link.springer.com/chapter/10.1007/978-1-4615-4457-9_5.

4. Slovakia would become the 16th country in the eurozone on January 1, 2009; Estonia, Latvia, Lithuania, and Croatia joined in later years.

5. Quotes in this paragraph come from Lucas Papademos, "Opening Address," in *The Euro at Ten: Lessons and Challenges,* European Central Bank, Fifth ECB Central Banking Conference, November 13–14, 2008, p. 16, https://www.ecb.europa.eu/pub/pdf/other/euroattenen2009en.pdf; "The Euro Decade and Its Lessons," *Wall Street Journal,* January 2, 2009; and Jacob Comenetz, "At Ten, the Euro Is Looking Strong," *Die Welt,* January 2, 2009, https://www.welt.de/english-news/article2961100/At-ten-the-euro-is-looking-strong.html.

6. Quotes in this paragraph come from Elias Papaioannou and Richard Portes, "The Intentional Role of the Euro: A Status Report," European Commission, Economic Papers 317, April 2008, https://ec.europa.eu/economy_finance/publications/pages/publication_summary12411_en.htm; and Menzie Chinn and Jeffrey Frankel, "Why the Euro Will Rival the Dollar," *International Finance* 11, no. 1 (2008): 49–73.

7. Parag Khanna, "Waving Goodbye to Hegemony," *New York Times,* March 6, 2008.

8. See Blustein, *Laid Low,* chapters 4–16, from which the remaining material in this section was drawn.

9. See Mulford, *Packing for India,* chapter 7, for a description of the convivial atmosphere at these evening gatherings as well as the formal negotiating sessions.

10. Mulford recounts this anecdote in his memoir, *Packing for India,* chapter 7, and it rings true – Sprinkel, whom I covered as a reporter, often peppered his economic arguments with folksy references to his Missouri upbringing. But Mulford names the animals in question as puppies, not piglets, which I believe is based on a faulty recollection. "Tail docking" is a common practice among hog farmers to reduce tail biting among pigs; there is no reason for inflicting any similar cruelty on puppies. Sprinkel died in 2009.

11. For detailed analyses of Japan's policies during this period and the results for the yen, see Cohen, *Currency Power,* chapter 5, and *Currency Statecraft: Monetary Rivalry and Geopolitical Ambition* (Chicago: University of Chicago Press, 2019), chapter 6; Eichengreen, Mehl, and Chitu, *How Global Currencies Work,* chapter 9; and Saori N. Katada, "Can China Internationalize the RMB? Lessons from Japan," *Foreign Affairs,* January 1, 2018.

12. Eichengreen, Mehl, and Chitu, *How Global Currencies Work,* chapter 9.

13. Bill Powell and Peter McKillop, "Sayonara, America," *Newsweek,* August 19, 1991.

14. Cohen, *Currency Power,* chapter 5.

15. Kunz, "The Fall of the Dollar Order."

16. Mark Z. Taylor, "Dominance through Technology: Is Japan Creating a Yen Bloc in Southeast Asia?" *Foreign Affairs,* November/December 1995.

17. Katada, "Can China Internationalize the RMB? Lessons from Japan."

18. Interview with the author.

19. For more detailed accounts, see Eichengreen, *Exorbitant Privilege,* chapter 3; and John Williamson, "Understanding Special Drawing Rights," Policy Brief 09-11, Peterson Institute for International Economics, June 2009, https://www.piie.com/publications/policy-briefs/understanding-special-drawing-rights-sdrs.

20. To be more precise, SDRs are doled out to countries in proportion to their IMF quotas, which are based on a formula that reflects a variety of factors including GDP, openness to the global economy, economic variability, and international reserves. Also, when countries exchange SDRs into hard currencies such as dollars, they pay a nominal interest rate.

21. Zhou, "Reform the International Monetary System."

22. See, for example, Eric Helleiner, "The IMF and the SDR: What to Make of China's Proposals?" in "The Future of the International Monetary Fund: A Canadian Perspective," ed. Bessma Momani and Eric Santor, CIGI/CIC Special Report, pp. 18–22, https://www.cigionline.org/static/documents/the_future_of_the_imf_0.pdf.

23. Barry Eichengreen, "Out of the Box Thoughts about the International Financial Architecture," IMF Working Paper, WP/09/116 (May 2009), pp. 9–11, https://www.imf.org/external/pubs/ft/wp/2009/wp09116.pdf.

24. My account of China's economic policies during the period of the 1990s and early 2000s, leading up to the Global Financial Crisis, is drawn from my book *Schism: China, America and the Fracturing of the Global Trading System* (Waterloo, ON: Centre for International Governance Innovation, 2019), chapters 2 and 6.

25. For a detailed explanation of Central Huijin, see Mark Wu, "The China Inc. Challenge to Global Trade Governance," *Harvard International Law Journal* 57 (2016): 261–324.

26. "Law of the People's Republic of China on Commercial Banks," http://www.npc.gov.cn/zgrdw/englishnpc/Law/2007-12/12/content_1383716.htm.

27. A comprehensive and lucid account of China's efforts to internationalize the renminbi is Eswar S. Prasad, *Gaining Currency: The Rise of the Renminbi* (New York: Oxford University

Press, 2017). Also invaluable are Paola Subacchi, *The People's Money: How China Is Building a Global Currency* (New York: Columbia University Press, 2017); Eichengreen, *Globalizing Capital,* chapter 7; and Cohen, *Currency Power,* chapter 9, and *Currency Statecraft,* chapter 7.

28. Qu Hongbin, "Renminbi Will Be World's Reserve Currency," *Financial Times,* November 11, 2010, https://www.ft.com/content/392e077e-ecdb-11df-88eb-00144 feab49a.

29. Arvind Subramanian, introduction to *Eclipse: Living in the Shadow of China's Economic Dominance* (Washington, DC: Peterson Institute for International Economics, September 2011).

30. See Prasad, *Gaining Currency,* chapter 6, for an authoritative account of this series of events. Prasad is the former head of the IMF's China division.

31. "IMF Executive Board Completes the 2015 Review of SDR Valuation," December 1, 2015, https://www.imf.org/en/News/Articles/2015/09/14/01/49/pr15543.

32. Edward Wong, Neil Gough, and Alexandra Stevenson, "China's Response to Stock Plunge Rattles Traders," *New York Times,* September 9, 2015, https://www.nytimes.com/2015/09/10/world/asia/in-china-a-forceful-crackdown-in-response-to-stock-market-crisis.html; Amie Tsang, "Caijing Journalist's Shaming Signals China's Growing Control over News Media," *New York Times,* September 6, 2015, https://www.nytimes.com/2015/09/07/business/media/caijing-journalists-shaming-signals-chinas-growing-control-over-news-media.html.

33. Don Weinland, "China's Capital Controls Dent Inbound Investment," *Financial Times,* April 19, 2017, https://www.ft.com/content/07392a72-241b-11e7-a34a-538b4cb30025; Charles Clover, "Foreign Companies in China Hit by New Exchange Controls," *Financial Times,* December 7, 2016, https://www.ft.com/content/a6d0552a-bbc4-11e6-8b45-b8b81dd5d080.

34. Prasad, *Gaining Currency,* chapter 5.

35. Hiro Ito and Masahiro Kawai, "The Global Monetary System and Use of Regional Currencies in ASEAN+3," in *Redefining Strategic Routes to Financial Resilience in ASEAN+3,* ed. Diwa Guinigundo, Masahiro Kawai, Cyn-Young Park, and Ramkishen S. Rajan (Mandaluyong City, Philippines: Asian Development Bank, December 2021), 124–125, https://www.adb.org/sites/default/files/publication/757221/strategic-routes-financial-resilience-asean3.pdf.

36. Material on the erosion of rule of law in this section is drawn from my book *Schism,* chapters 4 and 8.

37. See Carl Minzner, "China's Turn against Law," *American Journal of Comparative Law* 59 (2011), http://ir.lawnet.fordham.edu/faculty_scholarship/4; Rebecca Liao, "Judicial Reform in China," *Foreign Affairs,* February 2, 2017; Zhou Qiang, "Fostering Courts That Are Loyal to the Party, Loyal to the State, Loyal to the People and Loyal to the Law," 2015, www.court.gov.cn/zixun-xiangqing-13285.html (in Chinese), cited in European Commission, "On Significant Distortions in the Economy of the People's Republic of China for the Purpose of Trade Defence Investigations," Commission Staff Working Document, December 20, 2017, chapter 3; Reuters, "China's Top Judge Warns Courts on Judicial Independence,"

January 15, 2017, https://www.reuters.com/article/us-china-policy-law-idUSK-BN14Z07B; and Charlotte Gao, "Xi: China Must Never Adopt Constitutionalism, Separation of Powers, or Judicial Independence," *The Diplomat,* February 19, 2019.

38. Prasad, conclusion to *Gaining Currency.*

39. Ben S. Bernanke, "The Dollar's International Role: An 'Exorbitant Privilege'?" Brookings Commentary, January 7, 2016, https://www.brookings.edu/articles/the-dollars-international-role-an-exorbitant-privilege-2/.

40. Based on a comprehensive survey and analysis of the scholarly literature, Eric Helleiner of the University of Waterloo made a similar argument: "Not only are many of the benefits more modest than often suggested, but there are also considerable economic and political costs associated with [key currency] status." See Helleiner, "Downsizing the Dollar in the Age of Trump? The Ambiguities of Key Currency Status," *Brown Journal of World Affairs* 23, no. 2 (Spring/Summer 2017), https://bjwa.brown.edu/23-2/downsizing-the-dollar-in-the-age-of-trump-the-ambiguities-of-key-currency-status/.

CHAPTER 5

1. Mark Landler, "Trump Abandons Iran Nuclear Deal He Long Scorned," *New York Times,* May 8, 2018; The White House, "President Donald J. Trump Is Ending United States Participation in an Unacceptable Iran Deal," Fact Sheet, May 8, 2018, https://trumpwhitehouse.archives.gov/briefings-statements/president-donald-j-trump-ending-united-states-participation-unacceptable-iran-deal/.

2. Laurence Norman, "Europe Pulls Together in Bid to Preserve Iran Deal," *Wall Street Journal,* May 9, 2018.

3. Ellen Wald, "10 Companies Leaving Iran as Trump's Sanctions Close In," *Forbes,* June 6, 2018.

4. Michael Peel, "US Warns European Companies Not to Defy Iran Sanctions," *Financial Times,* September 6, 2018.

5. Daniel McDowell, "OFAC Sanctions and the New Dollar Diplomacy," *World Politics Review,* December 17, 2019; and McDowell, "New Era of Financial Sanctions," chapter 4 in "The US, EU, and UK Need a Shared Approach to Economic Statecraft. Here's Where to Start," The Atlantic Council, September 28, 2023, https://www.atlanticcouncil.org/in-depth-research-reports/report/us-eu-uk-need-shared-approach-to-economic-statecraft/#adapting-to-de-dollarization.

6. Peter E. Harrell and Elizabeth Rosenberg, "Economic Dominance, Financial Technology, and the Future of U.S. Economic Coercion," Center for New American Security, April 29, 2019, p. 7, https://s3.us-east-1.amazonaws.com/files.cnas.org/hero/documents/CNAS-Report-Economic_Dominance-final.pdf?mtime=20190423154936&focal=none.

7. Jack Ewing and Stanley Reed, "European Companies Rushed to Invest in Iran. What Now?" *New York Times,* May 9, 2018.

8. European Commission, "Updated Blocking Statute in Support of Iran Nuclear Deal Enters into Force," press release, August 6, 2018, https://ec.europa.eu/commission/presscorner/detail/en/IP_18_4805.

9. Matthew Dalton, "Peugeot to Halt Iran Investments as U.S. Reinstates Sanctions," *Wall Street Journal,* June 4, 2018.

10. David Keohane and Najmeh Bozorgmehr, "Threat of US Sanctions Pushes France's Total out of Iran," *Financial Times,* August 20, 2018.

11. Wald, "10 Companies Leaving Iran"; Benoit Faucon and Sarah McFarlane, "King Dollar Tightens Noose on Iranian Economy," *Wall Street Journal,* June 25, 2018; Clifford Krauss, "Trump Hit Iran With Oil Sanctions. So Far, They're Working," *New York Times,* September 19, 2018.

12. Guy Chazan, "Germany Calls for Global Payments System Free of US," *Financial Times,* August 22, 2018.

13. William Horobin and Birgit Jennen, "EU Looking to Sidestep U.S. Sanctions with Payments System Plan," Bloomberg News, August 27, 2018, https://www.bloomberg.com/news/articles/2018-08-27/eu-looking-to-sidestep-u-s-sanctions-with-payments-system-plan?embedded-checkout=true.

14. Mehreen Khan and Jim Brunsden, "Juncker Vows to Turn Euro into Reserve Currency to Rival US Dollar," *Financial Times,* September 12, 2018.

15. See Daniel McDowell, *Bucking the Buck: US Financial Sanctions and the International Backlash against the Dollar* (New York: Oxford University Press, 2023), chapter 7; Adnan Mazarei, "Can Europe Circumvent the Iran Sanctions and Save the Nuclear Deal?" *Realtime Economics* (blog), Peterson Institute for International Economics, July 8, 2019, https://www.piie.com/blogs/realtime-economic-issues-watch/can-europe-circumvent-iran-sanctions-and-save-nuclear-deal; and Michael Peel, Andrew England, and Najmeh Bozorgmehr, "European Trade Channel with Iran Facilitates First Deal," *Financial Times,* April 1, 2020.

16. US Department of the Treasury, "Excerpts of Secretary Lew's Remarks on Sanctions at the Carnegie Endowment for International Peace," press release, March 30, 2016, https://home.treasury.gov/news/press-releases/jl0397.

17. Jacob J. Lew and Richard Nephew, "The Use and Misuse of Economic Statecraft," *Foreign Affairs,* November/December 2018.

18. Warren Strobel, "Dollar Could Suffer If U.S. Walks Away from Iran Deal: John Kerry," Reuters, August 12, 2015, https://www.reuters.com/article/us-iran-nuclear-kerry-idUSKCN0QG1V020150812.

19. Agathe Demarais, *Backfire: How Sanctions Reshape the World against U.S. Interests* (New York: Columbia University Press, 2022), chapter 9.

20. McDowell, introduction to *Bucking the Buck.*

21. The importance of CHIPS for US sanctions has been recognized by a number of scholars, including McDowell in *Bucking the Buck,* chapter 2, and Pierre-Hugues Verdier in *Global Banks on Trial: U.S. Prosecutions and the Remaking of International Finance* (New York: Oxford University Press, 2020), chapter 1.

"Chokepoints" are a key facet of the perspective on international relations advanced by Henry Farrell and Abraham L. Newman in their seminal article "Weaponized Interdependence: How Global Economic Networks Shape State Coercion," *International Security* 44, no. 1 (2019): 42–79, and in their subsequent work. The term refers to the capacity of states that control key financial and technological hubs in the global economy to exercise coercive power by denying access to adversaries. In Farrell and Newman's words, the chokepoint effect "involves privileged states' capacity to limit or penalize use of hubs by third parties (e.g., other states or private actors). Because hubs offer extraordinary efficiency benefits, and because it is extremely difficult to circumvent them, states that can control hubs have considerable coercive power, and states or other actors that are denied access to hubs can suffer substantial consequences."

22. A list of CHIPS participants can be found on the CHIPS website at https://media.the clearinghouse.org/-/media/New/TCH/Documents/Payment-Systems/CHIPS_Participants_ Revised_05-26-2023_v2.pdf?rev=b10a8db587344f7fad70612dccaa55f9.

23. Gottfried Leibbrandt and Natasha De Terán, introduction to *The Pay Off: How Changing the Way We Pay Changes Everything* (London: Elliott & Thompson, 2021).

24. Leibbrandt and De Terán, *The Pay Off*, chapter 17.

25. Interview with the author.

26. This section draws on a number of historical studies of sanctions, with the main ones including Nicholas Mulder, *The Economic Weapon: The Rise of Sanctions as a Tool of Modern War* (New Haven, CT: Yale University press, 2022); Bruce W. Jentleson, *Sanctions: What Everyone Needs to Know* (New York: Oxford University Press, 2022); Daniel Drezner, "The United States of Sanctions," *Foreign Affairs,* September/October 2021; Benjamin Coates, "A Century of Sanctions," *Origins,* December 2019, https://origins.osu.edu/article/economic-sanctions-history-trump-global?language_content_entity=en; and Cohen, *Currency Statecraft,* chapter 5.

27. Richard N. Haass, "Sanctioning Madness," *Foreign Affairs,* November/December 1997.

28. The latest version of these scholars' collaborative effort is Gary Clyde Hufbauer, Jeffrey J. Schott, Kimberly Ann Elliott, and Barbara Oegg, *Economic Sanctions Reconsidered,* 3rd ed. (Washington, DC: Peterson Institute for International Economics, 2009).

29. Richard Nephew, *The Art of Sanctions: A View from the Field* (New York: Columbia University Press, 2018), chapter 2.

30. For detailed accounts of how AML/KYC/CFT laws and regulations evolved and work, see Julia C. Morse, *The Bankers' Blacklist: Unofficial Market Enforcement and the Global Fight against Illicit Financing* (Ithaca, NY: Cornell University Press, 2022); and Benn Steil and Robert E. Litan, *Financial Statecraft: The Role of Financial Markets in American Foreign Policy* (New Haven, CT: Yale University Press, 2006), chapter 3.

31. See Morse, *The Bankers' Blacklist,* chapter 3, for detailed accounts including the Nauru and HSBC cases cited here.

32. Regarding *la lista Clinton,* see Juan Zarate, introduction to *Treasury's War: The Unleashing of a New Era of Financial Warfare* (New York: PublicAffairs, 2013).

33. David S. Cloud and Jacob M. Schlesinger, "U.S. Treasury Hopes to Ease Burden of Anti-Laundering Efforts on Banks," *Wall Street Journal,* July 7, 2001.

34. John B. Taylor, *Global Financial Warriors: The Untold Story of International Finance in the Post-9/11 World* (New York: W. W. Norton, 2007), chapter 1.

35. Taylor, *Global Financial Warriors,* chapter 1.

36. Taylor, *Global Financial Warriors,* chapter 1.

37. US Department of State, "President Freezes Terrorists' Assets," Remarks on Executive Order, September 24, 2001, https://2001-2009.state.gov/s/ct/rls/rm/2001/5041.htm.

38. See Steil and Litan, *Financial Statecraft,* chapter 3.

39. Zarate, *Treasury's War,* chapter 6.

40. Zarate, *Treasury's War,* chapter 6.

41. Zarate, *Treasury's War,* chapter 6.

42. Information about SWIFT, including its history, purpose, operation, and physical plant, can be found in Michael Peel and Jim Brunsden, "Swift Shows Impact of Iran Dispute on International Business," *Financial Times,* June 6, 2018; and Susan V. Scott and Markos Zachariadis, *The Society for Worldwide Interbank Financial Communication (SWIFT): Cooperative Governance for Network Innovation, Standards and Community* (Routledge, 2014); and from the SWIFT website, swift.com.

43. Eric Lichtblau, *Bush's Law: The Remaking of American Justice* (New York: Pantheon Books, 2008), chapter 8; Scott and Zachariadis, *The Society for Worldwide Interbank Financial Communication,* chapter 5.

44. Lichtblau, *Bush's Law,* chapter 8; Zarate, *Treasury's War,* chapter 2.

45. Zarate, *Treasury's War,* chapter 2.

46. Zarate, *Treasury's War,* chapter 2; Lichtblau, *Bush's Law,* chapter 8; Scott and Zachariadis, *The Society for Worldwide Interbank Financial Communication,* chapter 5.

47. Lichtblau, *Bush's Law,* chapter 8; Zarate, *Treasury's War,* chapter 2.

48. Zarate, *Treasury's War,* chapter 2.

49. Lichtblau, *Bush's Law,* chapter 8; Zarate, *Treasury's War,* chapter 2.

50. Eric Lichtblau and James Risen, "Bank Data Is Sifted by U.S. in Secret to Block Terror," *New York Times,* June 23, 2006.

51. Zarate, *Treasury's War,* chapter 8.

CHAPTER 6

1. David L. Asher, "Pressuring Kim Jong Il: The North Korean Illicit Activities Initiative, 2001–2006," in David L. Asher, Patrick M. Cronin, and Victor D. Comras, "Pressure: Coercive Economic Statecraft and U.S. National Security," Center for a New American Security, January 2011, chapter 3, p. 31, https://www.cnas.org/publications/reports/pressure-coercive-economic-statecraft-and-u-s-national-security.

2. Asher, "Pressuring Kim Jong Il."

3. Sheena E. Chestnut, "The 'Sopranos State'?" North Korean Involvement in Criminal Activity and Implications for International Security" (honors thesis, Stanford University, 2005), https://nautilus.org/wp-content/uploads/2012/09/0605Chestnut1.pdf, and "Illicit Activity and Proliferation: North Korean Smuggling Networks," *International Security* 32, no. 1 (2007): 80–111. See also Raphael Perl, "Drug Trafficking and North Korea: Issues for U.S. Policy," Congressional Research Service, December 5, 2003, https://digital.library.unt.edu/ark:/67531/metacrs4345/; report updated January 25, 2007, available at https://sgp.fas.org/crs/row/RL32167.pdf.

North Korea denied involvement, and even if hard proof had been forthcoming the scale of the revenue reaped is obviously difficult to assess. Stephan Haggard and Marcus Noland, longtime scholars of the opaque North Korean economy, are skeptical of claims that the amounts involved have been vast; in a 2017 book, they wrote: "We estimate that at the end of the Kim Jong-il era in 2011, the illicit share of exports was in the range of 5–20 percent, with our best guess at roughly 10 percent." But they agree that "North Korea did have its Soprano state moment" during the first decade of the 2000s. Stephan Haggard and Marcus Noland, *Hard Target: Sanctions, Inducements, and the Case of North Korea* (Stanford, CA: Stanford University Press, 2017).

4. Zarate, *Treasury's War,* chapter 9.

5. Interview with the author.

6. Tom Mitchell and Robin Kwong, "BDA Revives Memories of Macao's Past," *Financial Times,* March 19, 2007.

7. US Treasury, "Treasury Designates Banco Delta Asia as Primary Money Laundering Concern under USA PATRIOT Act," press release, September 15, 2005, https://home.treasury .gov/news/press-releases/js2720#:~:text=Banco%20Delta%20Asia%20has%20 been,and%20Financial%20Intelligence%20(TFI).

8. David Lague and Donald Greenlees, "Squeeze on Banco Delta Asia Hit North Korea Where It Hurt," *New York Times,* January 18, 2007; Jay Solomon and Neil King Jr., "How U.S. Used a Bank to Punish North Korea," *Wall Street Journal,* April 12, 2007.

9. Zarate, *Treasury's War,* chapter 10.

10. Interview with the author.

11. US Treasury, "Treasury Designates Banco Delta Asia as Primary Money Laundering Concern."

12. Zarate, *Treasury's War,* chapter 1.

13. Solomon and King, "How U.S. Used a Bank to Punish North Korea."

14. Quoted in Zarate, *Treasury's War,* chapter 10.

15. Zarate, *Treasury's War,* chapter 11; Asher, "Pressuring Kim Jong Il"; Steven R. Weisman, "The Ripples of Punishing One Bank," *New York Times,* July 3, 2007; Haggard and Noland, *Hard Target,* chapter 6.

16. This section draws heavily on books by two former US officials who were deeply involved in the sanctions campaign against Iran, Juan Zarate and Richard Nephew. See Zarate, *Treasury's War,* chapters 13–14, and Nephew, *The Art of Sanctions,* chapters 5 and 7. Also invaluable is Robin Wright, "Stuart Levey's War," *New York Times Magazine,* October 31, 2008; Pierre-Hugues Verdier, *Global Banks on Trial: U.S. Prosecutions and the Remaking of International Finance* (New York: Oxford University Press, 2020), chapter 4; Giri Rajendran, "Financial Blockades: Reserve Currencies as Instruments of Coercion," in *The Power of Currencies and Currencies of Power,* ed. Alan Wheatley (New York: Routledge, 2013); and Suzanne Katzenstein, "Dollar Unilateralism: The New Frontline of National Security," *Indiana Law Journal* 90, no. 1 (2015), https://www.repository.law.indiana.edu/ilj/vol90/iss1/8.

17. Interview with the author.

18. *The Charlie Rose Show,* October 6, 2010, https://charlierose.com/videos/15683.

19. Quoted in Nephew, *The Art of Sanctions,* chapter 5.

———

20. Wright, "Stuart Levey's War."

21. Wright, "Stuart Levey's War."

22. An illuminating and detailed account of these prosecutions, from which this paragraph and the next are drawn, is Verdier, *Global Banks on Trial,* chapter 4.

23. See Peter Lee, "How Gulliver Fixed HSBC for the Future," *Euromoney*, July 6, 2017. For helping to enlighten me on the HSBC case and related episodes, I am grateful to Stephen J. Fallon, who shared his dissertation for a master's degree in international relations at Cambridge University, "US Leveraging of Foreign Banks for National Security Objectives from 2005 to 2020" (September 2023).

24. See Rajendran, "Financial Blockades," for these figures and other details about the impact of the ratcheting up of sanctions in late 2011.

25. The quotes from Glazyev in this paragraph can be found in Daniel Gross, "Did Russia Just Dump a Huge Amount of U.S. Government Bonds?" *Daily Beast,* July 12, 2017, https://www.thedailybeast.com/did-russia-just-dump-a-huge-amount-of-us-government-bonds; and "Kremlin Advisor Reveals 'Cure for US Aggression,' " Tass, April 22, 2017, https://tass.com/politics/942643.

26. Information about the "Fortress Russia" strategy and the economic outcome can be found in "The Kremlin Has Isolated Russia's Economy," *The Economist,* April 23, 2021; Henry Foy, "Russia: Adapting to Sanctions Leaves Economy in Robust Health," *Financial Times,* January 30, 2020; Henry Foy and Max Seddon, "Rising Poverty and Falling Incomes Fuel Russia's Navalny Protests," *Financial Times,* February 7, 2021; McDowell, *Bucking the Buck,* chapter 5; and "Russia's Mir Payment Cards to Give Visa and MasterCard a Run for Their Money," Tass, May 2, 2017, https://tass.com/economy/944174.

27. The information and data about Russia's de-dollarization efforts in this section come from McDowell, *Bucking the Buck,* chapters 3 and 5.

28. McDowell, *Bucking the Buck,* chapter 5.

29. For information about CIPS, see Barry Eichengreen, "Sanctions, SWIFT, and China's Cross-Border Interbank Payments System," The Marshall Papers (essay series), Center for Strategic and International Studies, May 20, 2022, https://www.csis.org/analysis/sanctions-swift-and-chinas-cross-border-interbank-payments-system; Emily Jin, "Why CIPS Matters (and Not for the Reasons You Think), *Lawfare,* April 5, 2022, https://www.lawfaremedia.org/article/why-chinas-cips-matters-and-not-reasons-you-think; Cissy Zhou, "China Scrambles for Cover from West's Financial Weapons," *Nikkei Asia,* April 13, 2022; and McDowell, *Bucking the Buck,* chapter 8. Data concerning daily transactions of CHIPS can be found at "CHIPS: Annual Statistics from 1970 to 2024," https://media.theclearinghouse.org/-/media/New/TCH/Documents/Payment-Systems/CHIPS-Volume-and-Value_May.pdf?rev=2393796a8ff642a3848758b204914cd3, and for CIPS at https://www.cips.com.cn/en/index/index.html.

30. Rush Doshi, *The Long Game: China's Grand Strategy to Displace American Order* (New York: Oxford University Press, 2021), chapter 10.

31. Luft and Korin, *De-Dollarization,* chapter 1.

32. See McDowell, "New Era of Financial Sanctions," and "Cross-Border Interbank Payment System," Wikipedia, https://en.wikipedia.org/wiki/Cross-Border_Interbank_Payment_System.

---

33. See Benn Steil, Elisabeth Harding, and Samuel Zucker, "Central Bank Currency Swaps Tracker," Council on Foreign Relations, October 2, 2024, https://www.cfr.org/tracker/central-bank-currency-swaps-tracker.

34. See Jing Yang, "Why China's Banks Won't Come to Russia's Rescue," *Wall Street Journal,* March 4, 2022; Alexandra Stevenson and Keith Bradsher, "China Has Tools to Help Russia's Economy. None Are Big Enough to Save It," *New York Times,* March 11, 2022; "America's Aggressive Use of Sanctions Endangers the Dollar's Reign," *The Economist,* January 18, 2020.

35. Chen Aizhu and Shu Zhang, "As U.S. Sanctions Loom, China's Bank of Kunlun to Stop Receiving Iran Payments—Sources," Reuters, October 23, 2018, https://jp. reuters.com/article/us-china-iran-banking-kunlun-exclusive-idUSKCN1MX1KA; Maziar Motamedi, "Policy Change at China's Bank of Kunlun Cuts Iran Sanctions Lifeline," *Bourse & Bazaar,* January 2, 2019, https://www.bourseandbazaar.com/articles/2019/1/2/policy-change-at-chinas-bank-of-kunlun-cuts-sanctions-lifeline-for-iranian-industry.

36. Christoph Koettl, Muyi Xiao, Stella Cooper, Aaron Byrd, Natalie Reneau, and Amy Chang Chien, "A Tanker and a Maze of Companies: One Way Illicit Oil Reaches North Korea," *New York Times* (visual investigations), March 22, 2021, https://www.nytimes.com/video/world/asia/100000007422226/north-korea-winson-oil-tanker.html.

37. John Park and Jim Walsh, "Stopping North Korea, Inc.: Sanctions Effectiveness and Unintended Consequences," MIT Security Studies Program, August 2016, https://www.belfercenter.org/sites/default/files/legacy/files/Stopping%20North%20Korea%20Inc%20Park%20and%20Walsh%20.pdf.

38. Haggard and Noland, conclusion to *Hard Target.*

39. @realDonaldTrump on X, October 19, 2017, https://x.com/realDonaldTrump/status/1181232249821388801.

40. Alan Rappeport and Katie Rogers, "Trump's Embrace of Sanctions Irks Allies and Prompts Efforts to Evade Measures," *New York Times,* November 15, 2019.

41. Hadi Kahalzadeh, " 'Maximum Pressure' Hardened Iran against Compromise," *Foreign Affairs,* March 11, 2021.

42. See Jentleson, *Sanctions,* chapter 5, for a harsh but fair verdict on Trump's Iran sanctions. For an eye-opening investigation into how Iran has weathered and evaded sanctions in recent years, see Ian Talley, "Clandestine Finance System Helped Iran Withstand Sanctions Crush," *Wall Street Journal,* March 18, 2022.

43. Narges Bajoghli, Vali Nasr, Djavad Salehi-Isfahani, and Ali Vaez, *How Sanctions Work: Iran and the Impact of Economic Warfare* (Stanford, CA: Stanford University Press, 2024), chapter 2.

44. Jeff Stein, Ellen Nakashima, and Samantha Schmidt, "Trump White House Was Warned Sanctions on Venezuela Could Fuel Migration," *Washington Post,* July 26, 2024.

45. For an excellent account of this episode, see Demarais, *Backfire,* chapter 6. Also invaluable is McDowell, *Bucking the Buck,* chapter 5; and Joshua Kirschenbaum, "Deripaska, EN+, and Rusal: A Split Decision with Implications for U.S. Sanctions," German Marshall

Fund, https://www.gmfus.org/news/deripaska-en-and-rusal-split-decision-implications-us-sanctions.

46. Pranshu Verma, "Trump's Sanctions on International Court May Do Little Beyond Alienating Allies," *New York Times,* October 18, 2020.

47. Anthony J. Blinken, "Ending Sanctions and Visa Restrictions against Personnel of the International Criminal Court," press statement, US Department of State, April 2, 2021, https://www.state.gov/ending-sanctions-and-visa-restrictions-against-personnel-of-the-international-criminal-court/.

CHAPTER 7

1. This account of my use of the Sand Dollar draws heavily on my article "Can a Central Bank Digital Currency Work? The Bahamas Offers Lessons," Centre for International Governance Innovation, December 14, 2022, https://www.cigionline.org/articles/can-a-central-bank-digital-currency-work-the-bahamas-offers-lessons/.

2. IMF, "The Bahamas: 2022 Article IV Consultation—Press Release; Staff Report; and Statement by the Executive Director for the Bahamas," May 9, 2022. https://www.imf.org/en/Publications/CR/Issues/2022/05/06/The-Bahamas-2022-Article-IV-Consultation-Press-Release-Staff-Report-and-Statement-by-the-517631.

3. Anthony Osae-Brown, Mureji Fatunde, and Ruth Olurounbi, "Digital-Currency Plan Falters as Nigerians Defiant on Crypto," Bloomberg News, October 25, 2022, https://www.bloomberg.com/news/articles/2022-10-25/shunned-digital-currency-looks-for-street-credibility-in-nigeria?leadSource=uverify%20wall#xj4y7vzkg.

4. See "A Digital Payments Revolution in India: How Emerging Economies from India to Brazil Built Alternative Payments Models," *The Economist,* May 15, 2023.

5. Neha Narula, "The Future of Money," https://www.ted.com/talks/neha_narula_the_future_of_money.

6. David G. W. Birch, *The Currency Cold War: Cash and Cryptography, Hash Rates and Hegemony* (London: London Publishing Partnership, 2020), chapter 9.

7. Paul Vigna and Michael J. Casey, *The Age of Cryptocurrency: How Bitcoin and Digital Money Are Challenging the Global Economic Order* (New York: St. Martin's Press, 2015), chapter 2.

8. David Chaum, "Security without Identification: Transaction Systems to Make Big Brother Obsolete," *Communications of the ACM* 28, no. 10 (1985): 1044.

9. The literature on cryptocurrency and related digital assets is too voluminous to cite in full here, but the following is a list of work that I found most invaluable: Vigna and Casey, *The Age of Cryptocurrency;* Eswar S. Prasad, *The Future of Money: How the Digital Revolution Is Transforming Currencies and Finance* (Cambridge, MA: Harvard University Press, 2021); Nathaniel Popper, *Digital Gold: Bitcoin and the Inside Story of the Misfits and Millionaires Trying to Reinvent Money* (New York: Harper, 2016); Nik Bhatia, *Layered Money: From Gold and Dollars to Bitcoin and Central Bank Digital Currencies* (self-pub., 2021); Erik Townsend, *Beyond Blockchain: The Death of the Dollar and the Rise of Digital Currency* (independently published, 2018); J. Christopher Giancarlo, *CryptoDad: The Fight for the Future of Money*

(Hoboken, NJ: John Wiley & Sons, 2022); Matt Levine, "The Only Crypto Story You Need," *Bloomberg Businessweek,* October 31, 2022, https://www.bloomberg.com/features/2022-the-crypto-story/#xj4y7vzkg; Siddharth Venkataramakrishnan and Robin Wigglesworth, "Inside the Cult of Crypto," *Financial Times,* September 10, 2021.

10. The literature on Libra (later renamed Diem) that I found most invaluable includes: Hannah Murphy and Kiran Stacey, "Facebook Libra: The Inside Story of How the Company's Cryptocurrency Dream Died," *FT Magazine,* March 10, 2022; David Gerard, *Libra Shrugged: How Facebook Tried to Take Over the Money* (self-pub., 2020); AnnaMaria Andriotis, Peter Rudegeair, and Liz Hoffman, "Inside Facebook's Botched Attempt to Start a New Cryptocurrency," *Wall Street Journal,* October 16, 2019.

11. Libra mission statement, quoted in Leibbrandt and De Terán, *The Pay Off,* chapter 23.

12. CBS News MoneyWatch, "Meet Facebook's Libra, a Digital Currency for the Social Network," June 18, 2019, https://www.cbsnews.com/news/facebook-cryptocurrency-libra-a-digital-currency-for-the-social-network/.

13. Reuters, "France and Germany Agree to Block Facebook's Libra," September 14, 2019.

14. Quoted in Andriotis, Rudegeair, and Hoffman, "Inside Facebook's Botched Attempt to Start a New Cryptocurrency."

15. Andriotis, Rudegeair, and Hoffman, "Inside Facebook's Botched Attempt to Start a New Cryptocurrency."

16. Jemima Kelly, "Suddenly Facebook's Libra Is All about Defending 'the Free World' from China," FT Alphaville, September 20, 2019, https://www.ft.com/content/1bf86023-eb1b-3634-94ac-7adbacee3fde.

17. Interview with the author.

18. Murphy and Stacey, "Facebook Libra."

19. This account of the history and operations of the BIS is heavily drawn from my book *Off Balance,* chapter 2, which in turn is based in part on Toniolo, *Central Bank Cooperation at the Bank for International Settlements, 1930–1973.* The anecdote about the christening of Schacht's grandchild is cited in chapter 22 of Ahamed, *Lords of Finance.*

20. Adam Lebor, *The Tower of Basel: The Shadowy History of the Secret Bank That Runs the World* (New York: PublicAffairs, 2013).

21. Agustín Carstens, "The Future of Money and Payments," 2019 Whitaker Lecture, Central Bank of Ireland, Dublin, March 22, 2019, https://www.bis.org/speeches/sp190322.pdf.

22. Claire Jones, "Central Bank Plans to Create Digital Currencies Receive Backing," *Financial Times,* June 30, 2019.

23. BIS, "BIS to Set Up Innovation Hub for Central Banks," press release, June 30, 2019, https://www.bis.org/press/p190630a.htm.

24. Gillian Tett, "Suits v Hoodies: The Cryptocurrency Battle," *FT Magazine,* January 16, 2020.

25. Interview with the author.

CHAPTER 8

1. Zhou Xin and Cissy Zhou, "China Gets First Glimpse at Sovereign Digital Currency after Screenshot Leaks Online," *South China Morning Post*, April 15, 2020.

2. Jonathan Cheng, "China Rolls Out Pilot Test of Digital Currency," *Wall Street Journal*, April 20, 2020; Nathaniel Popper and Cao Li, "China Charges Ahead with a National Digital Currency," *New York Times*, March 1, 2021.

3. Mark Kruger, "In China, the Digital Renminbi Is Becoming a Reality," Centre for International Governance Innovation, August 21, 2020, https://www.cigionline.org/articles/china-digital-renminbi-becoming-reality/.

4. See Martin Chorzempa, *The Cashless Revolution: China's Reinvention of Money and the End of America's Domination of Finance and Technology* (New York: PublicAffairs, 2022), for a well-informed and insightful account, from which much of the following paragraphs are drawn.

5. Chorzempa, *The Cashless Revolution*, chapter 7.

6. Paul Mozur, "Forget TikTok. China's Powerhouse App Is WeChat," *New York Times*, September 4, 2020.

7. See Chorzempa, *The Cashless Revolution*, chapter 5, for a balanced assessment of China's government surveillance including its "social credit" system. He notes that Western media coverage of this phenomenon has sometimes conveyed the exaggerated impression that Beijing gives each Chinese citizen a "single algorithmic score," or has embarked on plans to do so. At the same time, he calls the social credit system "the world's most ambitious plan to leverage data for governance," and shows that the surveillance net is extraordinarily pervasive.

8. Ann Cao and Tracy Qu, "China's Ambitious e-CNY Plan Faces a Giant Hurdle: Winning Over 1 Billion Consumers at Home," *South China Morning Post*, March 4, 2023.

9. Martha Muir, "Central Banks' Digital Currency Plans Face Public Backlash," *Financial Times*, March 13, 2023.

10. Randal K. Quarles, "Parachute Pants and Central Bank Money," speech at the 113th Annual Utah Bankers Association Convention, Sun Valley, Idaho, June 28, 2021, https://www.federalreserve.gov/newsevents/speech/quarles20210628a.htm.

11. JP Koning, "Are Central Bankers Ready for Payments Theater?" *CoinDesk*, September 10, 2021, https://www.coindesk.com/policy/2021/09/09/are-central-bankers-ready-for-payments-theater/.

12. Reuters, "Fed's Powell: More Important for U.S. to Get Digital Currency Right Than Be First," October 19, 2020, https://www.reuters.com/article/us-usa-fed-powell-digital-currency-idUSKBN2741OI.

13. Federal Reserve Bank of Boston, "The Federal Reserve Bank of Boston Announces Collaboration with MIT to Research Digital Currency," August 13, 2020, https://www.bostonfed.org/news-and-events/press-releases/2020/the-federal-reserve-bank-of-boston-announces-collaboration-with-mit-to-research-digital-currency.aspx.

14. Federal Reserve Board, "Central Bank Digital Currency (CBDC) Frequently Asked Questions," April 11, 2023, https://www.federalreserve.gov/cbdc-faqs.htm.

15. The White House, "Fact Sheet: White House Releases First-Ever Comprehensive Framework for Responsible Development of Digital Assets," September 16, 2022, https://

www.whitehouse.gov/briefing-room/statements-releases/2022/09/16/fact-sheet-white-house-releases-first-ever-comprehensive-framework-for-responsible-development-of-digital-assets/.

16. See these articles for the anti-CBDC quotes that follow: Ben Schreckinger, "The Digital Dollar's Bipartisan Problem," *Politico,* June 13, 2023; Dave Troy, "The New Populist Bogeyman: Central Bank Digital Currencies," *Washington Spectator,* April 11, 2023, https://washingtonspectator.org/new-populist-bogeyman-central-bank-digital-currencies/; Lubomir Tassev, " 'Done, Dead'—DeSantis to Nix Central Bank Digital Currency on Day 1," Bitcoin.com, July 16, 2023, https://news.bitcoin.com/done-dead-desantis-to-nix-central-bank-digital-currency-on-day-1/; Victoria Guida, " 'Tyranny': Trump Vows to Block Any Fed Effort to Launch Digital Currency," *Politico,* January 18, 2024; see also Mike Orcutt, "Is the Digital Dollar Dead?" *MIT Technology Review,* July 21, 2023, https://www.technologyreview.com/2023/07/21/1076645/is-the-digital-dollar-dead/.

17. Many transactions are reported to the US government, to be sure, with no warrant required. As is evident to any American who earns wages or salary income, or who earns interest on a bank account or dividends or capital gains in an investment account, the IRS is informed about those presumably taxable payments. And as noted in chapter 5, government agencies maintain and share records about transfers of ownership of real estate and motor vehicles; and banks are required to file SARs with FinCEN regarding any transaction they suspect of being associated with money laundering, tax evasion, or terrorism, as well as reports of cash deposits or withdrawals greater than $10,000. As Americans living abroad like me know all too well, information about financial accounts held overseas by US citizens—including the maximum amount held during the course of the year—must be reported annually to FinCEN. But those examples are not the same as full government visibility into all of the transactions a person makes using financial accounts, which is what CBDC opponents often suggest would happen if a CBDC were issued.

The question of whether the Fourth Amendment adequately protects Americans' financial privacy is a separate matter. For a libertarian argument that the amendment's protections have been excessively eroded over the past 50 years, see Nicholas Anthony, "The Right to Financial Privacy: Crafting a Better Framework for Financial Privacy in a Digital Age," Cato Institute, Policy Analysis No. 945, May 2, 2023, https://www.cato.org/policy-analysis/right-financial-privacy.

18. Bjarke Smith-Meyer, "Bank of England Deputy Governor: Digital Pound Will Be Private but Not Anonymous," *Politico,* June 15, 2023, https://www.politico.eu/article/boe-deputy-governor-digital-pound-will-be-private-but-not-anonymous/.

19. Blustein, "Can a Central Bank Digital Currency Work?"

20. For an excellent and balanced overview of stablecoins, see Thomas C. Cowan, "The First Wave of Federally Regulated Stablecoins: An Evolutionary, Intermediary-Driven Improvement to Dollar Movement," April 4, 2023, available on Cowan's LinkedIn page, https://www.linkedin.com/in/thomas-c-cowan/.

21. Parma Bains, Arif Ismail, Fabiana Melo, and Nobuyasa Sugimoto, "Regulating the Crypto Ecosystem: The Case of Stablecoins and Arrangements," International Monetary Fund, Fintech Notes, September 26, 2022.

22. Dante Alighieri Disparte, "Is America Losing the Digital-Currency Race?" *Project Syndicate*, July 2, 2021, https://www.project-syndicate.org/onpoint/us-digital-currency-race-private-crypto-sector-secret-weapon-by-dante-alighieri-disparte-2021-07. For updated information on Tether's growing domination of the market, see Krisztian Sandor, "Tether-Issued Stablecoin USDT's Market Share Grows to 75% as Market Cap Tops $118B," *CoinDesk*, September 17, 2024, https://www.coindesk.com/markets/2024/09/17/tether-issued-stablecoin-usdts-market-share-grows-to-75-as-market-cap-tops-118b/.

23. Jake Chervinsky, testimony at hearing titled "Understanding Stablecoins' Role in Payments and the Need for Legislation," House Financial Services Committee, Subcommittee on Digital Assets, Financial Technology and Inclusion, April 19, 2023. https://financialservices.house.gov/calendar/eventsingle.aspx?EventID=408691.

24. @stablekwon, July 1, 2021, https://twitter.com/stablekwon/status/1410491186196795398?lang=en.

25. Caitlin Ostroff, Elaine Yu, and Paul Kiernan, "Cryptocurrency TerraUSD Plunges as Investors Bail," *Wall Street Journal*, May 11, 2022. For an entertaining account of the TerraUSD debacle, see Ben McKenzie with Jacob Silverman, *Easy Money: Cryptocurrency, Casino Capitalism, and the Golden Age of Fraud* (New York: Abrams Press, 2023), chapter 8.

26. The following list includes some of the most illuminating investigative journalism on Tether: Kadhim Shubber and Siddharth Venkataramakrishnan, "Tether: The Former Plastic Surgeon behind the Crypto Reserve Currency," *Financial Times*, July 15, 2021; Zeke Faux, "Anyone Seen Tether's Billions?" *Bloomberg Businessweek*, October 7, 2021, https://www.bloomberg.com/news/features/2021-10-07/crypto-mystery-where-s-the-69-billion-backing-the-stablecoin-tether; David Yaffe-Bellany, "The Coin That Could Wreck Crypto," *New York Times*, June 17, 2022; Ben Foldy, Ada Hui, and Peter Rudegeair, "The Unusual Crew behind Tether, Crypto's Pre-Eminent Stablecoin," *Wall Street Journal*, February 2, 2023; and Ben McKenzie, *Easy Money*, chapter 3.

27. See, for example, J. Austin Campbell, testimony at hearing titled "Understanding Stablecoins' Role in Payments and the Need for Legislation," House Financial Services Committee, Subcommittee on Digital Assets, Financial Technology and Inclusion, April 19, 2023, https://democrats-financialservices.house.gov/uploadedfiles/hhrg-118-ba21-wstate-campbella-20230419.pdf.

28. Dante Alighieri Disparte, "Stablecoins: How Do They Work, How Are They Used, and What Are Their Risks?" testimony before the US Senate Committee on Banking, Housing and Urban Affairs, December 14, 2021, https://www.banking.senate.gov/imo/media/doc/Disparte%20Testimony%2012–14–21.pdf.

29. Gary B. Gorton and Jeffery Y. Zhang, "Taming Wildcat Stablecoins," *University of Chicago Law Review* 90 (2021), https://lawreview.uchicago.edu/sites/default/files/2023-04/03_Zhang%20%26%20Gorton_ART_Final.pdf.

30. Nic Carter, "The Crypto-Dollar Surge and the American Opportunity," *CoinDesk*, September 4, 2020, https://www.coindesk.com/business/2020/09/03/the-crypto-dollar-surge-and-the-american-opportunity/.

31. I am indebted to JP Koning for a blog post that used this case as an illustration of the problems that Tether poses for sanctions. See JP Koning, "Why Do Sanctioned Entities Use Tether?" *Moneyness* (blog), December 5, 2023, https://jpkoning.blogspot.com/2023/12/why-do-sanctioned-entities-use-tether.html. For the federal charges against Orekhov and his confederates, see US Attorney's Office, Eastern District of New York, "Five Russian Nationals and Two Oil Traders Charged in Sanctions Evasion and Money Laundering," October 19, 2022, https://www.justice.gov/usao-edny/pr/five-russian-nationals-and-two-oil-traders-charged-global-sanctions-evasion-and-money.

32. See Zeke Faux, *Number Go Up: Inside Crypto's Wild Rise and Staggering Fall* (New York: Crown Currency, 2023), chapters 18 and 19; Angus Berwick, "The Crypto Exchange Moving Money for Criminal Gangs, Rich Russians and a Hamas-Linked Terror Group," *Wall Street Journal*, October 13, 2023; Ben Foldy, "From Hamas to North Korean Nukes, Cryptocurrency Tether Keeps Showing Up," *Wall Street Journal*, October 27, 2023; and Andy Greenberg, " 'Stablecoins' Enabled $40 Billion in Crypto Crime Since 2022," *Wired,* January 18, 2024, https://www.wired.com/story/stablecoin-sanctions-violations-crypto-crime/.

33. See testimony of Grant Rabenn, director of Financial Crimes Legal at Coinbase, before the US House Committee on Financial Services Subcommittee on Digital Assets, Financial Technology and Inclusion, February 15, 2024, and other testimony at this hearing, https://financialservices.house.gov/calendar/eventsingle.aspx?EventID=409142.

34. Oliver Knight, "Tether Freezes 41 Crypto Wallets Tied to Sanctions," *CoinDesk*, December 10, 2023, https://www.coindesk.com/business/2023/12/09/tether-freezes-41-crypto-wallets-tied-to-sanctions/.

35. See testimony of Carole House before the US House Committee on Financial Services Subcommittee on Digital Assets, Financial Technology and Inclusion, February 15, 2024, https://financialservices.house.gov/calendar/eventsingle.aspx?EventID=409142.

36. For an illuminating explanation of this point, see JP Koning, "The Ramps Killing Bitcoin's Dissident Thesis," *CoinDesk,* March 23, 2022, https://www.coindesk.com/layer2/2022/03/22/the-ramps-killing-bitcoins-dissident-thesis/?utm_medium=referral&utm_source=rss&utm_campaign=headlines.

37. Tim Starks, "U.S. Authorities Go After Another Crypto Mixer," *Washington Post,* November 30, 2023.

38. See "Another Crypto Boss Falls," *The Economist,* November 22, 2023; Emily Flitter, "U.S. Case Details Binance's Knowledge about Criminal Users," *New York Times,* November 22, 2023; US Department of Justice, "Binance and CEO Plead Guilty to Federal Charges in $4B Resolution," November 21, 2023, https://www.justice.gov/opa/pr/binance-and-ceo-plead-guilty-federal-charges-4b-resolution; and John Reed Stark, "Breaking News: A Binance Double Whammy," https://twitter.com/JohnReedStark/status/1733497674110767550.

39. Jesse Hamilton, "U.S. Treasury Campaigning for Amplified Powers to Chase Crypto Overseas," *CoinDesk,* November 30, 2023, https://www.coindesk.com/policy/2023/11/29/us-treasury-campaigning-for-amplified-powers-to-chase-crypto-overseas/.

40. Data in this paragraph can be found in Adam Samson, Scott Chipolina, Eva Szalay, and James Politi, "Crypto Industry Shaken as Tether's Dollar Peg Snaps," *Financial Times,*

May 13, 2022; Shaurya Malwa, "Tether's USDT Stablecoin Drops 3% Below $1 Peg," *CoinDesk,* November 10, 2022, https://www.coindesk.com/markets/2022/11/10/tethers-usdt-stablecoin-slips-from-1-peg/; and Vicky Ge Huang, Hannah Miao, and Caitlin Ostroff, "Circle's USDC Stablecoin Breaks Peg with $3.3 Billion Stuck at Silicon Valley Bank," *Wall Street Journal,* March 11, 2023.

41. Moody's Analytics, "Large Fiat-Backed Stablecoins Depegged 600+ Times in 2023," November 6, 2023, https://www.moodysanalytics.com/articles/2023/moody_launches_new_digital_asset_monitor_to_track_risk. For another related and important problem with stablecoins, see Daniel Neilson's *Soon Parted* blog on Substack, in particular "Tether: On Par," May 18, 2021, https://www.soonparted.co/p/tether-on-par?utm_source=%2Fsearch%2FTether&utm_medium=reader2; and "Stablecoins Are Banks: as Tether Is Demonstrating," May 13, 2022, https://www.soonparted.co/p/tether-breaks-the-buck?utm_source=%2Fsearch%2FTether&utm_medium=reader2.

42. Bank for International Settlements, "The Future Monetary System," in *BIS Annual Economic Report 2022,* chapter 3, June 26, 2022, https://www.bis.org/publ/arpdf/ar2022e3.htm.

43. "Hyun Song Shin on Unified Ledgers, Tokenized Deposits, and Governance," *Fintech Beat Podcast,* July 6, 2023, https://podcasts.apple.com/es/podcast/hyun-song-shin-on-unified-ledgers-tokenized-deposits/id1466867273?i=1000619157161&l=ca.

44. For Shin's presentations in various fora, see the page on the BIS website where his various work is posted, https://www.bis.org/author/hyun_song_shin.htm?videolist=cGFnZT0yJnBhZ2luZ19sZW5ndGg9MTAmc2hvd19ibHVycD1mYWxzZSSzb3J0X2xpc3Q9cHVibGljYXRpb25EYXRlX2Rlc2MmcGVyc29uc04MiZ0YWdzPSSZ0aGVtZT12aWWRlb3MmbGlzdF90eXBlPXZpZGVvvX2xpc3Q%253D. Specifically, see "BIS Media Briefing—The Future Monetary System," June 20, 2022 (BIS video); "The Future Monetary System, Presentation to the BIS Annual General Meeting, June 26, 2022 (BIS video); "After the Crypto Crash: The Future Role of CBDC," webinar, Princeton University Bendheim Center for Finance, June 30, 2022; "Hyun Song Shin-Digital Currencies," roundtable hosted by the University of California, December 7, 2022; "BIS Media Briefing-Blueprint for the Future Monetary System," June 19, 2023 (BIS video); "A Blueprint for the Future Monetary System," presentation to the BIS Annual General Meeting, June 25, 2023 (BIS video); "Crypto, CBDCs and Designing Money," *Fintech Beat* podcast, June 29, 2022; "The Future Monetary System," June 21, 2022 (BIS podcast); and "Improving the Old, Enabling the New," June 20, 2023 (BIS podcast).

45. See BIS, "The Future Monetary System," 93–98; BIS, "Blueprint for the Future Monetary System: Improving the Old, Enabling the New," in *BIS Annual Economic Report 2023,* chapter 3: 89–93, 98–104, https://www.bis.org/publ/arpdf/ar2023e3.htm; and Rodney Garratt and Hyun Song Shin, "Stablecoins versus Tokenized Deposits: Implications for the Singleness of Money," BIS Bulletin No. 73, April 11, 2023, https://www.bis.org/publ/bisbull73.pdf.

46. Anushree Dave, "Jamie Dimon Calls Bitcoin a 'Hyped-Up Fraud,'" MarketWatch, January 19, 2023, https://www.marketwatch.com/livecoverage/stock-market-today-dow-futures-falls-over-200-points/card/jamie-dimon-calls-bitcoin-a-hyped-up-fraud-5leDKuBxDxAtZw0PfEnL.

———

47. For information on J.P. Morgan's ventures into this area and its ideas about future possibilities, see Oliver Wyman and Onyx by J.P. Morgan: "Deposit Tokens: A Foundation for Stable Digital Money," https://www.jpmorgan.com/onyx/documents/deposit-tokens.pdf.

48. Hyun Song Shin, presentation at roundtable hosted by the University of California, December 7, 2022, https://www.bis.org/author/hyun_song_shin.htm?video-list=cGFnZT0yJnBhZ2luZ19sZW5ndGg9MTAmc2hvd19ibHVycD1mYWxzZSSzzb3J0X2xpc3Q9cHVibGljYXRpb25EYXRlX2Rlc2MmcGVyc29ucz04MiZ0YWdzPSZ0aGVtZT12aWRlb3MmblGlzdF90eXBlPXZpZGVvvX2xpc3Q%253D.

49. Interview with the author.

50. The exchange between Waller and Shin can be found here: Federal Reserve Bank of Richmond, Central Bank and Digital Currency Virtual Panel Discussion on "Should Central Banks Issue Digital Currencies?" March 25, 2022, https://www.youtube.com/playlist?list=PLPl7aBTxZbgbrVvi5WXiNghTs0GmR06ch (first video).

51. BIS, "Project mBridge: Connecting Economies through CBDC," https://www.bis.org/about/bisih/topics/cbdc/mcbdc_bridge.htm.

52. BIS, "Using CBDCs across Borders: Lessons from Practical Experiments," June 2022, https://www.bis.org/publ/othp51.htm.

53. See, for example, Robert Murray, "The U.S. Is Facing a Sputnik Moment in the International Economy," Foreign Policy Research Institute, February 11, 2022, https://www.fpri.org/article/2022/02/the-u-s-is-facing-a-sputnik-moment-in-the-international-economy/; Michael J. Casey, "The Real Use Case for CBDCs: Dethroning the Dollar," *CoinDesk,* July 8, 2023, https://www.coindesk.com/consensus-magazine/2023/07/07/the-real-use-case-for-cbdcs-dethroning-the-dollar/.

54. For information on BRICS Bridge, see "Putin's Plan to Dethrone the Dollar," *The Economist*, October 20, 2024; and Charles Clover and Daria Mosolova, "Vladimir Putin's Alternative to 'Weaponised' Dollar Fails to Excite BRICS Partners," *Financial Times*, October 24, 2024.

CHAPTER 9

1. Quoted in Nick Timiraos, *Trillion Dollar Triage: How Jay Powell and the Fed Battled a President and a Pandemic — and Prevented Economic Disaster* (New York: Little, Brown & Co., 2022), chapter 6; and Jeanna Smialek, *Limitless: The Federal Reserve Takes on a New Age of Crisis* (New York: Alfred A. Knopf, 2023), chapter 6. Much of the material in this section comes from these two superb books about the Fed during the late 2010s and early 2020s.

2. Timiraos, *Trillion Dollar Triage,* chapter 6.

3. Jacob Pramuk, "Trump Tweets: 'Who is our bigger enemy,' Fed Chairman Powell or Chinese President Xi?" CNBC, August 23, 2019, https://www.cnbc.com/2019/08/23/trump-tweets-who-is-our-bigger-enemy-fed-chairman-powell-or-chinese-president-xi.html.

4. For information about Powell, see Timiraos, *Trillion Dollar Triage*, chapter 1; and Smialek, *Limitless*, chapter 1.

5. Timiraos, *Trillion Dollar Triage,* chapter 5. Powell's quote was off the record at the time he made it in 2018, but he gave Timiraos permission to use it in his book.

6. Timiraos, chapter 6; Smialek, chapter 6.

7. "Donald Trump Coronavirus Press Conference Transcript March 14," March 14, 2020, https://www.rev.com/blog/transcripts/donald-trump-coronavirus-press-conference-transcript-march-14.

8. Jeffrey Cheng, David Wessel, and Joshua Younger, "How Did COVID-19 Disrupt the Market for U.S. Treasury Debt?" Commentary, The Brookings Institution, May 1, 2020, https://www.brookings.edu/articles/how-did-covid-19-disrupt-the-market-for-u-s-treasury-debt/.

9. Blustein, "Look Who Made It in Wall Street!"

10. Much of this section is drawn from Adam Tooze, *Shutdown: How Covid Shook the World's Economy* (New York: Viking, 2021), chapter 6, which provides a definitive account of the turmoil in financial markets during March 2020 and the Fed's response. Also invaluable are Timiraos, chapters 7–13; Smialek, *Limitless*, chapters 2 and 7–9; Colby Smith and Robin Wigglesworth, "US Treasuries: The Lessons from March's Market Meltdown," *Financial Times,* July 29, 2020; Lev Menand and Joshua Younger, "Money and the Public Debt: Treasury Market Liquidity as a Legal Phenomenon," *Columbia Business Law Review* 224 (2023), https://scholarship.law.columbia.edu/cgi/viewcontent.cgi?article=5111&context=faculty_scholarship; and Younger, "Revisiting the Ides of March, Part I: A Thousand Year Flood," Council on Foreign Relations, July 20, 2020, https://www.cfr.org/blog/revisiting-ides-march-part-i-thousand-year-flood.

11. The quotes in the above two paragraphs can be found in Adam Samson, Robin Wigglesworth, Colby Smith, and Joe Rennison, "Strains in US Government Bond Market Rattle Investors," *Financial Times,* March 12, 2020; Joe Rennison, Phillip Stafford, Colby Smith, and Robin Wigglesworth, " 'Great Liquidity Crisis' Grips System as Banks Step Back," *Financial Times,* March 24, 2020; Karen Brettell and Karen Pierog, "Treasury Liquidity Worsens, Worries Build about Broad Selling Pressures," Reuters, March 12, 2020, https://www.reuters.com/article/usa-bonds-liquidity-idUSL1N2B52JQ; and Jeanna Smialek and Matt Phillips, "Troubles Percolate in the Plumbing of Wall Street," *New York Times,* March 12, 2020.

12. "The Successes of the Fed's Dollar-Swap Lines," *The Economist,* June 18, 2020.

13. Gillian Tett, "Coronavirus Trade Disruption Could Start a 'Dash for Cash,' " *Financial Times,* March 13, 2020.

14. See Tooze, *Shutdown,* chapter 6; Smith and Wigglesworth, "US Treasuries: The Lessons from March's Market Meltdown"; Menand and Younger, "Money and the Public Debt"; and Younger, "Revisiting the Ides of March, Part I."

15. See Tooze, *Shutdown,* chapter 6; Timiraos, chapters 7–13; and Smialek, *Limitless,* chapters 2 and 7–9.

16. Federal Reserve Board, "Federal Reserve Issues FOMC Statement," press release, March 23, 2020, https://www.federalreserve.gov/newsevents/pressreleases/monetary20200323a.htm.

17. Stephanie Segal, "Dollars on Demand: The Fed's New FIMA Repo Facility," Center for Strategic and International Studies, April 1, 2020, https://www.csis.org/analysis/dollars-demand-feds-new-fima-repo-facility.

18. Robert Dohner, "The United States' Stealth Diplomat: The Federal Reserve," *New Atlanticist,* The Atlantic Council, April 2, 2020, https://www.atlanticcouncil.org/blogs/new-atlanticist/the-united-states-stealth-diplomat-the-federal-reserve/.

19. Courtenay Brown, "Trump Says Fed Chairman Is Doing a 'Good Job' amid Coronavirus Crisis," *Axios,* March 23, 2020, https://www.axios.com/2020/03/24/trump-jerome-powell-coronavirus-federal-reserve.

20. Randal K. Quarles, "What Happened? What Have We Learned from It? Lessons from COVID-19 Stress on the Financial System," speech at the Institute of International Finance, Washington, DC, October 15, 2020, https://www.federalreserve.gov/newsevents/speech/quarles20201015a.htm#:~:text=While%20the%20economy%20is%20recovering,the%20strongest%20in%20recorded%20history%2C.

21. Smith and Wigglesworth, "US Treasuries: The Lessons from March's Market Meltdown."

22. William McChesney Martin Jr., "Address before the New York Group of the Investment Bankers Association of America," October 19, 1955, https://fraser.stlouisfed.org/title/statements-speeches-william-mcchesney-martin-jr-448/address-new-york-group-investment-bankers-association-america-7800.

23. Jerome H. Powell, "Monetary Policy and Price Stability," speech at economic policy symposium sponsored by the Federal Reserve Bank of Kansas City, Jackson Hole, Wyoming, August 26, 2022, https://www.federalreserve.gov/newsevents/speech/powell20220826a.htm.

24. See Timiraos, *Trillion Dollar Triage,* chapter 15, and Smialek, *Limitless,* chapters 1 and 12, for detailed accounts of how the Fed's policy review evolved and the thinking behind it.

25. Quoted in Timiraos, *Trillion Dollar Triage,* chapter 15.

26. Material in this section about the rekindling of inflation in 2021–2022 is drawn from Timiraos, *Trillion Dollar Triage,* chapter 17; Smialek, *Limitless,* chapter 15; Peter S. Goodman, "How the Supply Chain Broke, and Why It Won't Be Fixed Anytime Soon," *New York Times,* October 22, 2021; and Anshu Siripurapu, "What Happened to Supply Chains in 2021?" Council on Foreign Relations, December 13, 2021, https://www.cfr.org/article/what-happened-supply-chains-2021.

27. Rich Miller, "Jerome Powell Ditches 'Transitory' Tag, Paves Way for Rate Hike," Bloomberg News, December 1, 2021.

28. See, for example, Thomas J. Sargent and William L. Silber, "Volcker, Powell and the Price of Amnesia about Monetary Policy," *Wall Street Journal,* June 22, 2022; and "Why the Federal Reserve Has Made a Historic Mistake on Inflation," *The Economist,* April 23, 2022.

29. Jeanna Smialek, "Powell Admires Paul Volcker. He May Have to Act Like Him," *New York Times,* March 14, 2022; see also Nick Timiraos, "Jerome Powell's Inflation Whisperer: Paul Volcker," *Wall Street Journal,* September 19, 2022.

30. Colby Smith, "Federal Reserve Under Fire as Slowing Jobs Market Fans Fears of Recession," *Financial Times,* August 3, 2024.

31. See Chelsey Dulaney, Megumi Fujikawa, and Rebecca Feng, "Dollar's Rise Spells Trouble for Global Economy," *Wall Street Journal,* September 18, 2022; and Martin Wolf, "Why the Strength of the Dollar Matters," *Financial Times,* September 28, 2022.

32. Gustavo Adler, Gita Gopinath, and Carolina Osorio-Buitron, "Dominance Currencies and the Limits of Exchange Rate Flexibility," *IMF Blog,* July 20, 2020, https://www.imf.org/en/Blogs/Articles/2020/07/20/currencies-and-crisis-how-dominant-currencies-limit-the-impact-of-exchange-rate-flexibility.

33. "A Double Burden: The Effects of Food Price Increases and Currency Depreciations on Food Import Bills," UNCTAD, Division of International Trade and Commodities, December 16, 2022, https://unctad.org/publication/double-burden-effects-food-price-increases-and-currency-depreciations-food-import-bills.

34. Dulaney, Fujikawa, and Feng, "Dollar's Rise Spells Trouble for Global Economy"; and Joe Rennison and Isabella Simonetti, "A Strong Dollar Is Wreaking Havoc on Emerging Markets. A Debt Crisis Could Be Next," *New York Times,* October 5, 2022.

35. Hélène Rey, *Dilemma not Trilemma: The Global Financial Cycle and Monetary Policy Independence,* Federal Reserve Bank of Kansas City, *Proceedings,* Jackson Hole Conference, 2013, https://www.kansascityfed.org/Jackson%20Hole/documents/4575/2013Rey.pdf.

36. Detailed accounts of these developments can be found in David Beckworth and Christopher Crowe, "The International Impact of the Fed When the United States Is a Banker to the World," chapter 2 in *Rules for International Monetary Stability,* ed. Michael D. Bordo and John B. Taylor (Stanford, CA: Hoover Institution Press, 2017), https://www.hoover.org/sites/default/files/research/docs/rulesforinternationalmonetarystability-ch2.pdf; and in Prasad, *The Dollar Trap,* chapter 7.

37. Mark Carney, "The Growing Challenges for Monetary Policy in the Current International Monetary and Financial System," speech at the Jackson Hole Symposium, August 23, 2019, https://www.bankofengland.co.uk/-/media/boe/files/speech/2019/the-growing-challenges-for-monetary-policy-speech-by-mark-carney.pdf.

38. José Antonio Ocampo, *Resetting the International Monetary (Non)System* (Oxford: Oxford University Press, 2017).

39. See Beckworth and Crowe, "The International Impact of the Fed When the United States Is a Banker to the World."

40. See "The 53 Fragile Emerging Economies," *The Economist,* July 20, 2022; Adam Tooze, "The World Is Seeing How the Dollar Really Works," *Foreign Policy,* August 12, 2022; "Emerging Markets Look Unusually Resilient," *The Economist,* October 13, 2022.

CHAPTER 10

1. The White House, "Press Briefing by Press Secretary Jen Psaki and Deputy National Security Advisor for International Economics and Deputy NEC Director Daleep Singh, February 24, 2022," https://www.whitehouse.gov/briefing-room/press-briefings/2022/02/24/press-briefing-by-press-secretary-jen-psaki-and-deputy-national-security-advisor-for-international-economics-and-deputy-nec-director-daleep-singh-february-24-2022/.

2. Interview with the author.

———

3. US Treasury, "U.S. Department of the Treasury Releases Sanctions Review," October 18, 2021, https://home.treasury.gov/news/press-releases/jy0413; Ian Talley, "Biden Administration to Constrain Use of Sanctions in Foreign-Policy Shift," *Wall Street Journal,* October 18, 2021; Daniel W. Drezner, "Treasury's Promising Start on Reforming Economic Statecraft," *Washington Post,* October 20, 2021.

4. See Ellen Nakashima and Ashley Parker, "Inside the White House Preparations for a Russian Invasion," *Washington Post,* February 14, 2022; and Ian Talley, Daniel Michaels, and Jon Hilsenrath, "How the U.S. and EU Cut Russia Off from the Global Economy," *Wall Street Journal,* March 18, 2022.

5. Demetri Sevastopulo, George Parker, Stephen Morris, and Sam Fleming, "World Leaders Divided on Whether to Eject Russia from Swift Payments System," *Financial Times,* February 25, 2022; Edward Wong, Michael Crowley, and Ana Swanson, "Biden Hits Russia with Broad Sanctions for Putin's War in Ukraine," *New York Times,* February 24, 2022; Rich Noak, Tory Newmyer, and Quentin Airès, "Europe Says It Has a 'Financial Nuclear Weapon' against Russia. But It's Uncertain If It Wants to Use It," *Washington Post,* February 26, 2022.

6. Valentina Pop, Sam Fleming, and James Politi, "Weaponisation of Finance: How the West Unleashed 'Shock and Awe' on Russia," *Financial Times,* April 6, 2022; Justin Ling, "Behind the Push to Freeze Moscow's Foreign Cash," *Politico,* March 1, 2022; and Steve Scherer and Rod Nickel, "With Her Ukrainian Roots, Russian Sanctions Are Personal for Canada's Freeland," Reuters, March 3, 2022, https://www.reuters.com/world/with-her-ukrainian-roots-russian-sanctions-are-personal-canadas-freeland-2022-03-02/.

7. Laurence Norman, Andrew Restuccia, and Tom Fairless, "Behind the Sweeping Russia Sanctions: Zelensky's Plea and a Mounting Crisis," *Wall Street Journal,* February 27, 2022; Benjamin Wallace-Wells, "The Biden Official Who Pierced Putin's 'Sanction-Proof' Economy," *New Yorker,* March 25, 2022.

8. See Robert Fife and Steven Chase, "How Canada Helped Facilitate Support for Banking Sanctions against Russia," *Globe and Mail,* March 4, 2022.

9. Pop, Fleming, and Politi, "Weaponisation of Finance"; "Joint Statement on Further Restrictive Economic Measures," February 26, 2022, https://ec.europa.eu/commission/presscorner/detail/en/STATEMENT_22_1423; US Treasury, "Treasury Prohibits Transactions with Central Bank of Russia and Imposes Sanctions on Key Sources of Russia's Wealth," February 28, 2022, https://home.treasury.gov/news/press-releases/jy0612.

10. Georgi Kantchev, Caitlin Ostroff, and Matthew Luxmoore, "The West's Sanctions Barrage Severs Russia's Economy from Much of the World," *Wall Street Journal,* February 28, 2022; Katie Martin, Tommy Stubbington, Philip Stafford, and Hudson Lockett, "Russia Doubles Interest Rates after Sanctions Send Rouble Plunging," *Financial Times,* March 1, 2022; and Anastasia Stognei and Simon Fraser, "Ukraine Invasion: Russians Feel the Pain of International Sanctions," BBC News, March 1, 2022, https://www.bbc.com/news/world-europe-60558731.

11. Anders Aslund, "Fortress Russia Crumbles," *Project Syndicate,* March 9, 2022, https://www.project-syndicate.org/commentary/russia-economic-collapse-shows-that-sanctions-work-by-anders-aslund-2022-03?barrier=accesspaylog; Anton Troianovski,

"Facing Economic Calamity, Putin Talks of Nationalizing Western Businesses," *New York Times*, March 10, 2022; "Russian Economy Staggers into 1998 'Times Three' with Foreign Exodus," Bloomberg, March 5, 2022, https://www.bloomberg.com/news/articles/2022-03-04/russia-inc-staggers-into-1998-times-three-with-foreign-exodus?embedded-checkout=true; Richard Lough, "French Minister Declares Economic 'War' on Russia, and Then Beats a Retreat," Reuters, March 1, 2022, https://www.reuters.com/world/france-declares-economic-war-against-russia-2022-03-01/.

12. Quoted in Wallace-Wells, "The Biden Official Who Pierced Putin's 'Sanction-Proof' Economy."

13. Sebastian Mallaby, "War in Ukraine Has Created a New Financial Weapon in the West," *Washington Post*, March 1, 2022.

14. See Ivan Nechepurenko, "How Western Goods Reach Moscow," *New York Times*, January 13, 2023; Ana Swanson, "Russia Sidesteps Western Punishments, with Help from Friends," *New York Times*, January 31, 2023; Georgi Kantchev, Paul Hannon, and Laurence Norman, "How Sanctioned Western Goods Are Still Flowing into Russia," *Wall Street Journal*, May 14, 2023; Lazaro Gamio, Leanne Abraham, Ana Swanson, and Alex Travelli, "How India Profits from Its Neutrality in the Ukraine War," *New York Times*, June 22, 2023.

15. See "Russia's Economy Is Back on Its Feet," *The Economist*, May 7, 2022; Valerie Hopkins, "In Moscow, the Fighting Is a World Away," *New York Times*, September 6, 2022; and Jeanne Whalen, Robyn Dixon, Ellen Nakashima, and Mary Ilyushina, "Western Sanctions Are Wounding but Not Yet Crushing Russia's Economy," *Washington Post*, August 23, 2022.

16. See Edward Fishman, "A Tool of Attrition: What the War in Ukraine Has Revealed About Economic Sanctions," *Foreign Affairs*, February 23, 2023; Nicholas Mulder, "Sanctions against Russia Not Slowing War Effort," *New York Times*, February 9, 2023; Peter Harrell, "The Limits of Economic Warfare: What Sanctions on Russia Can and Cannot Achieve," *Foreign Affairs*, March 27, 2023.

17. Alexander Osipovich and AnnaMaria Andriotis, "Russia Built Parallel Payments System That Escaped Western Sanctions," *Wall Street Journal*, March 29, 2022.

18. Interview with the author.

19. Jeffrey J. Schott, "Economic Sanctions against Russia: How Effective? How Durable?" Peterson Institute for International Economics, Policy Brief 23-3, April 2023, https://www.piie.com/publications/policy-briefs/economic-sanctions-against-russia-how-effective-how-durable.

20. Elina Ribakova, Benjamin Hilgenstock, and Guntram B. Wolff, "The Oil Price Cap and Embargo on Russia Are Working Imperfectly, and Defects Must Be Fixed," Peterson Institute for International Economics, *Realtime Economics* (blog), July 13, 2023, https://www.piie.com/blogs/realtime-economics/oil-price-cap-and-embargo-russia-are-working-imperfectly-and-defects-must?utm_source=substack&utm_medium=email; Adam Tooze, "Russia's Long-War Economy," Chartbook No. 236, August 30, 2023, https://adamtooze.com/2023/08/30/chartbook-236/.

21. See Paul Krugman, "Who's Embargoing Whom?" *New York Times*, August 2, 2022.

22. See Austin Ramzy and Jason Douglas, "Booming Trade with China Helps Boost Russia's War Effort," *Wall Street Journal*, August 21, 2023.

23. Nikkei staff, "Special Report: How U.S.-Made Chips Are Flowing into Russia," *Nikkei Asia*, April 12, 2023, https://asia.nikkei.com/Business/Tech/Semiconductors/Special-report-How-U.S.-made-chips-are-flowing-into-Russia.

24. Maxim Chupilkin, Beata Javorcik, and Alexander Plekhanov, "The Eurasian Roundabout: Trade Flows into Russia through the Caucasus and Central Asia," European Bank for Reconstruction and Development, Working Paper No. 276, February 2023, https://www.ebrd.com/publications/working-papers/the-eurasian-roundabout.

25. See Georgi Kantchev, Andrew Duehren, and Joe Wallace, "Russian Oil Is Still Flowing, and That Is What the West Wants," *Wall Street Journal*, February 23, 2023; Anastasia Stognei, "Western Price Caps Cut into Russian Oil Revenue," *Financial Times*, April 26, 2023; and "Russia's Economy Can Withstand a Long War, but Not a More Intense One," *The Economist*, April 23, 2023.

26. For Putin's "diskont" quote, see Craig Kennedy, "Measuring the Shadows," August 23, 2023, in Kennedy's Substack newsletter *Navigating Russia,* https://substack.com/@navigatingrussia. Kennedy's research in *Navigating Russia* provides a treasure trove of information about the successes and shortcomings of efforts by the United States and its allies to deprive Putin of income from Russia's energy resources.

27. See Kennedy, *Navigating Russia,* for detailed information on the "shadow fleet." See also Christian Triebert, Blacki Migliozzi, Alexander Cardia, Muyi Xiao, and David Botti, "Fake Signals and American Insurance: How a Dark Fleet Moves Russian Oil," *New York Times*, May 30, 2023; and Jared Maslin, "The Ghost Fleet Helping Russia Evade Sanctions and Pursue Its War in Ukraine," *Wall Street Journal*, August 18, 2023.

28. David Sheppard, Chris Cook, James Politi, and Anastasia Stognei, "Almost No Russian Oil Is Sold Below $60 Cap, Say Western Officials," *Financial Times*, November 13, 2023; and David Lynch, "With Russian Economy Far from Collapse, U.S. Opts for Tougher Punishment," *Washington Post*, February 23, 2024.

29. See two installments in Kennedy's *Navigating Russia* research: "Dangerous Waters," December 13, 2023, https://navigatingrussia.substack.com/p/dangerous-waters?utm_source=profile&utm_medium=reader2; and "The De-Kastri Mystery," January 15, 2024, https://navigatingrussia.substack.com/p/the-de-kastri-mystery?utm_source=profile&utm_medium=reader2.

30. See Benoit Faucon, Costas Paris, and Joe Wallace, "Russia's Backdoor to the Global Banking System Is Slamming Shut," *Wall Street Journal*, March 19, 2024; "China Banks Tighten Curbs on Russia after US Sanctions Order," Bloomberg News, January 16, 2024, https://www.bloomberg.com/news/articles/2024-01-16/china-banks-tighten-curbs-on-russia-after-us-sanctions-order; JP Koning, "The First Round of U.S. Secondary Sanctions on Russia Is Working," *Moneyness* (blog), February 22, 2024, https://jpkoning.blogspot.com/2024/02/the-first-round-of-us-secondary.html; and "Secondary Sanctions & Russia's Falling Imports," The Bell, May 24, 2024, https://en.thebell.io/secondary-sanctions-russias-falling-imports/.

31. See Kennedy, "Dangerous Waters" and "The De-Kastri Mystery."

32. See Alan Rappeport, "U.S. to Clamp Down on Financial Firms That Help Russia Buy Military Supplies," *New York Times,* December 22, 2023; and Faucon, Paris, and Wallace, "Russia's Backdoor to the Global Banking System Is Slamming Shut."

33. For information on the June 2024 measures, and the arguments that the Biden administration should have taken even tougher steps, see Chris Cook and Max Seddon, "US Unveils Tougher Russia Sanctions for Foreign Banks," *Financial Times,* June 13, 2024; David E. Sanger, Alan Rappeport, Edward Wong and Ana Swanson, "U.S. Expands Sanctions on Russia as G7 Leaders Gather," *New York Times,* June 12, 2024; David Ignatius, "A Wary White House Views Russia Oil Sanctions Through Lens of Inflation," *Washington Post,* June 18, 2024; Anna Hirtenstein, Joe Wallace, Ian Talley, and Costas Paris, "Biden Wants to Be Tough with Russia and Iran—But Wants Low Gas Prices Too," *Wall Street Journal,* June 26, 2024; and JP Koning, "The Intensifying Effort to Isolate Russia's Banks," *Moneyness* (blog), https://jpkoning.blogspot.com/2024/06/the-intensifying-effort-to-isolate.html.

34. Andrea Shalal and Thomas Escritt, "G7 Agrees on Loan Deal to Support Ukraine with Russian Assets," Reuters, June 14, 2024, https://www.reuters.com/world/troubled-g7-leaders-focus-ukraine-war-china-italian-summit-2024-06-13/. Among the most influential articles in the debate over how to use the assets were Lawrence Summers, Philip Zelikow, and Robert Zoellick, "The Moral and Legal Case for Sending Russia's $300 Billion to Ukraine," *Washington Post,* March 20, 2023; Nicholas Mulder, "The West Would Harm Itself with Rash Seizures of Frozen Russian Assets," *Financial Times,* January 4, 2024; and Hugo Dixon, Lee Buchheit, and Daleep Singh, "Ukrainian Reparation Loan: How It Would Work," SSRN, March 19, 2024, https://papers.ssrn.com/sol3/papers.cfm?abstract_id=4733340. An explanation of how the agreed compromise would give Ukraine a "loan" without burdening Ukrainian or G-7 taxpayers can be found in "Russian Roulette: A Sanctions Update with Eddie Fishman and Sergey Aleksashenko," podcast episode by Maria Snegovaya, Center for Strategic and International Studies, June 27, 2024, https://www.csis.org/podcasts/russian-roulette/sanctions-update-eddie-fishman-and-sergey-aleksashenko.

35. Zongyuan Zoe Liu and Mihaela Papa, "The Anti-Dollar Axis," *Foreign Affairs,* March 7, 2022. It should be acknowledged that Liu, an expert on Chinese finance, has subsequently made clear that she does not believe Beijing intends to overthrow the dollar system but rather is seeking to reduce its exposure to the dollar system. See, for example, her remarks in "China's Moves to Create a Dollar Alternative," *Odd Lots* podcast, https://www.youtube.com/watch?v=94Z3XNcjnJo.

36. Rana Foroohar, "China, Russia and the Race to a Post-Dollar World," *Financial Times,* February 27, 2022; Fareed Zakaria, "Russia and China Are Threatening the Power of the Dollar," *Washington Post,* March 24, 2023; George Lei, Tania Chen, and Jacob Gu, "China Takes the Yuan Global in Bid to Repel a Weaponized Dollar," Bloomberg, May 4, 2023, https://www.japantimes.co.jp/news/2023/05/04/business/financial-markets/china-yuan-global-weaponized-dollar/; Michael Stott and James Kynge, "China Capitalises on US Sanctions in Fight to Dethrone Dollar," *Financial Times,* August 24, 2023; Joseph W. Sullivan,

"BRICS Currency Could End Dollar Dominance," *Foreign Policy,* April 24, 2023; Meaghan Tobin, Lyric Li, and David Feliba, "Move Over, U.S. Dollar. China Wants to Make the Yuan the Global Currency," *Washington Post,* May 16, 2023; Reuters, "The Yuan's the New Dollar as Russia Rides to the Redback," November 29, 2022, https://www.japantimes.co.jp/news/2022/11/29/business/economy-business/russia-china-currencies-trade/.

37. See Chelsey Delaney, Evan Gershkovich, and Victoria Simanovskaya, "Russia Turns to China's Yuan in Effort to Ditch the Dollar," *Wall Street Journal,* February 28, 2023; Anastasia Stognei, "Russia Embraces China's Renminbi in Face of Western Sanctions," *Financial Times,* March 26, 2023; Alexander Gabuev, "The Yuan Is an Unlikely Winner from Moscow's Isolation," Bloomberg News, March 14, 2023; and Amy Hawkins, "China's War Chest: How Beijing Is Using Its Currency to Insulate against Future Sanctions," *The Guardian,* May 8, 2023.

38. Summer Said and Stephen Kalin, "Saudi Arabia Considers Accepting Yuan Instead of Dollars for Chinese Oil Sales," *Wall Street Journal,* March 15, 2022; *Global Times,* "China Completes First LNG Cross-Border Yuan Settlement Transaction," March 29, 2023, https://www.globaltimes.cn/page/202303/1288160.shtml.

39. See Carlos Valdez and Daniel Politi, "Bolivia Is the Latest South American Nation to Use China's Yuan for Trade in Challenge to the Dollar," Associated Press, July 28, 2023; and Logan Wright, Agatha Kratz, Charlie Vest, and Matt Mingey, "Retaliation and Resilience: China's Economic Statecraft in a Taiwan Crisis," Atlantic Council and the Rhodium Group, April 1, 2024, figure 6, https://www.atlanticcouncil.org/in-depth-research-reports/report/retaliation-and-resilience-chinas-economic-statecraft-in-a-taiwan-crisis/.

40. See Barry Eichengreen, "Will Geopolitics or Technology Reshape the Global Monetary Order?" *Project Syndicate,* March 10, 2023, https://www.project-syndicate.org/commentary/shift-to-renminbi-reserves-and-payments-not-visible-in-data-by-barry-eichengreen-2023-03?barrier=accesspaylog.

41. See Gerard DiPippo and Andrea Leonard Palazzi, "It's All about Networking: The Limits of Renminbi Internationalization," Center for Strategic and International Studies, April 18, 2023, https://www.csis.org/analysis/its-all-about-networking-limits-renminbi-internationalization.

One exceptional case involves an agreement struck in April 2023 between Bangladesh and Russia to use renminbi for a payment due for a nuclear plant loan. But the plan proved full of snags. See Anant Gupta and Azad Majumder, "Bangladesh to Pay Off Russian Nuclear Plant Loan in Chinese Currency, *Washington Post,* April 17, 2023; Grady McGregor, "The Renminbi's New Role: Sanctions Busting," *The Wire,* April 30, 2023, www.thewirechina.com/2023/04/30/renminbi-new-role-sanctions-busting/; Huamayn Kabir, "RNPP Loan Repayment to Russia in Yuan Falters," *Financial Express,* August 10, 2023, https://thefinancialexpress.com.bd/trade/rnpp-loan-repayment-to-russia-in-yuan-falters.

42. Atlantic Council, "Dollar Dominance Monitor," https://www.atlanticcouncil.org/programs/geoeconomics-center/dollar-dominance-monitor/; SWIFT, "RMB Tracker," https://www.swift.com/our-solutions/compliance-and-shared-services/business-intelligence/renminbi/rmb-tracker/rmb-tracker-document-centre; IMF, "Currency Composition of

Foreign Exchange Reserves (COFER)," https://data.imf.org/?sk=e6a5f467-c14b-4aa8-9f6d-5a09ec4e62a4. See also Maggie Wei, "Progress Check on RMB Internationalization," Goldman Sachs Asia, July 2, 2023, https://www.gspublishing.com/content/research/en/reports/2023/07/02/450c00ac-c2ae-4a96-a5e5-26534e7e493c.html.

43. Maha El Dahan and Aziz El Yaakoubi, "China's Xi Calls for Oil Trade in Yuan at Gulf Summit in Riyadh," Reuters, December 10, 2022, https://www.reuters.com/world/saudi-arabia-gathers-chinas-xi-with-arab-leaders-new-era-ties-2022-12-09/#:~:text=RIYADH%2C%20Dec%209%20(Reuters),dollar's%20grip%20on%20world%20trade.

44. @prchovanec on X, December 10, 2022, https://x.com/prchovanec/status/16015 54753770893312?s=20.

45. See "Russia's Rupee Trap Is Adding to $147 Billion Hoard Abroad," Bloomberg News, June 1, 2023, https://www.bloomberg.com/news/articles/2023-06-01/russia-s-rupee-trap-is-adding-to-147-billion-hoard-stuck-abroad?embedded-checkout=true.

CHAPTER 11

1. This was the view of the great Charles Kindleberger, as cited in the illuminating biography by Perry Mehrling, *Money and Empire: Charles P. Kindleberger and the Dollar System* (New York: Cambridge University Press, 2022), chapter 6.

2. See Associated Press, "Norway Feels the Sting of China's Nobel Anger," May 6, 2011, https://www.ctvnews.ca/norway-feels-sting-of-china-s-nobel-anger-1.640486; Tom Hancock and Wang Xueqiao, "South Korean Consumer Groups Bear Brunt of China's Thaad Ire," *Financial Times,* August 20, 2017; and Richard McGregor, "Chinese Coercion, Australian Resilience," The Lowy Institute, October 20, 2022, https://www.lowyinstitute.org/publica tions/chinese-coercion-australian-resilience.

3. McDowell, conclusion to *Bucking the Buck.*

4. Francisco Rodríguez, "The Human Consequences of Economic Sanctions," Center for Economic and Policy Research, May 2023, https://cepr.net/wp-content/uploads/2023/04/FINAL-The-Human-Consequences-of-Economic-Sanctions-Rodriguez-7.pdf.

5. Chinedu Asadu, Gerald Imray, Farai Mutsaka, and Paul Wiseman, "Emerging Economies Are Pushing to End the Dollar's Dominance. But What's the Alternative?" Associated Press, August 19, 2023, https://economictimes.indiatimes.com/news/economy/policy/emerging-economies-are-pushing-to-end-the-dollars-dominance-but-whats-the-alterna tive/articleshow/102851794.cms?from=mdr.

6. See Stacie Pettyjohn, Becca Wasser, and Andrew Metrick, "War Games: House Committee Simulates Chinese Invasion of Taiwan," Center for a New American Security, April 23, 2023 (with ABC News video), https://www.cnas.org/publications/video/war-games-house-committee-simulates-chinese-invasion-of-taiwan; for the transcript see ABC News, *This Week,* April 23, 2023, https://abcnews.go.com/Politics/week-transcript-4-23-23-sen-mark-warner/story?id=98778375.

7. For the data and examples cited in this paragraph and the next, see Greg Ip, "Biden's Trade Challenge: Kicking the China Dependency Habit," *Wall Street Journal,* June 22, 2023; "China Is Trying to Protect Its Economy from Western Pressure," *The Economist,* May 26,

2022; "Could the West Punish China the Way It Has Punished Russia?" *The Economist*, April 23, 2022; Gerard DiPippo, "Deterrence First: Applying Lessons from Sanctions on Russia to China," Center for Strategic and International Studies, May 3, 2022, https://www.csis.org/analysis/deterrence-first-applying-lessons-sanctions-russia-china; and Wright, Kratz, Vest, and Mingey, "Retaliation and Resilience: China's Economic Statecraft in a Taiwan Crisis."

8. Charlie Vest and Agatha Kratz, "Sanctioning China in a Taiwan Crisis: Scenarios and Risks," The Atlantic Council and the Rhodium Group, June 21, 2023, https://www.atlanticcouncil.org/in-depth-research-reports/report/sanctioning-china-in-a-taiwan-crisis-scenarios-and-risks/.

9. James Crabtree, "The West Is in the Grip of a Decoupling Delusion," *Financial Times*, April 14, 2023.

10. See Richard Baldwin, Rebecca Freeman, and Angelos Theodorakopoulos, "Hidden Exposure: Measuring U.S. Supply Chain Reliance," *Brookings Papers on Economic Activity*, Fall 2023; Caroline Freund, Aaditya Mattoo, Alen Mulabdic, and Michele Ruta, "Is Trade Policy Reshaping Global Supply Chains?" The World Bank Group, Policy Research Working Paper 10593, October 2023; and Han Qiu, Hyun Song Shin, and Leanne Si Ying Zhang, "Mapping the Realignment of Global Value Chains," BIS Bulletin No. 78, October 3, 2023, https://www.bis.org/publ/bisbull78.htm.

11. Gerard DiPippo and Jude Blanchette, "Sunk Costs: The Difficulty of Using Sanctions to Deter China in a Taiwan Crisis," Center for Strategic and International Studies, June 12, 2023, https://www.csis.org/analysis/sunk-costs-difficulty-using-sanctions-deter-china-taiwan-crisis.

12. See Anthony, "The Right to Financial Privacy."

13. Trump's 2019 tweet can be found here: https://x.com/realDonaldTrump/status/1149472282584072192. For his 2021 interview comments, see Suzanne O'Halloran, "Trump: Bitcoin's a Scam, U.S. Dollar Should Dominate," FoxBusiness, June 7, 2021, https://www.foxbusiness.com/markets/trump-bitcoin-a-scam-us-dollar-should-reign; and Talia Kaplan, "Trump Warns Crypto 'Potentially a Disaster Waiting to Happen,'" FoxBusiness, August 31, 2021, https://www.foxbusiness.com/politics/crypto-potentially-a-disaster-waiting-to-happen-trump.

14. For Trump's crypto-related comments that day, see CoinDesk, "In Donald Trump's Own Words—A Partial Transcript of His Bitcoin 2024 Speech," July 27, 2024, https://www.coindesk.com/policy/2024/07/27/in-donald-trumps-own-words-a-partial-transcript-of-his-bitcoin-2024-speech/.

15. Joel Khalili, "Donald Trump's Plan to Hoard Billions in Bitcoin Has Economists Stumped," *Wired*, July 31, 2024, https://www.wired.com/story/donald-trumps-plan-to-hoard-billions-in-bitcoin-has-economists-stumped/.

16. For information about these campaign donations and their impact, see Molly White, "Follow the Crypto," blog post, https://www.followthecrypto.org; David Gerard, "Trump's Crypto Turnaround Heralds an Economic Nightmare," *Foreign Policy*, July 30, 2024, https://foreignpolicy.com/2024/07/30/trump-crypto-2024-election-economic-nightmare/; Jesse

Hamilton, "Democratic Crypto Supporters Call for Crypto-Friendly Party Platform," *CoinDesk*, July 28, 2024, https://www.coindesk.com/policy/2024/07/27/democratic-crypto-supporters -call-for-crypto-friendly-party-platform/; and Jasper Goodman, "A Wave of Crypto-Friendly Lawmakers Is About to Crash Congress," *Politico*, October 22, 2024, https://www.politico.com/ news/2024/10/21/crypto-super-pac-spending-industry-friendly-lawmakers-00183754.

17. For information about Vance and Thiel, see "United States Senate Financial Disclosures, Annual Report for Calendar 2022, Mr. JD Vance," filed 8/14/2023, https://efdsearch. senate.gov/search/view/annual/b19c901b-c566-4c98-9306-a90ea84a77d7/; Ryan Mac and Theodore Schleifer, "How a Network of Tech Billionaires Helped J.D. Vance Leap into Power," *New York Times,* July 17, 2024; Elizabeth Dwoskin, Cat Zakrzewski, Nitasha Tiku, and Josh Dawsey, "Inside the Powerful Peter Thiel Tech Network That Launched JD Vance," *Washington Post,* July 28, 2024; Edward Luce, "Trump and the Politics of Bitcoin," *Financial Times,* July 31, 2024; and Cryptonews, "Peter Thiel's Bitcoin Keynote at Bitcoin 2022," April 8, 2022, https://cryptonews.com/videos/paypal-co-founder-peter-thiel-bitcoin-key note-bitcoin-2022-conference.htm.

18. For information on WLF, see Joe Durbin, "Eric Trump Previews Major Trump Organization Move into Crypto as He Charts the Family Company's Future," *New York Post*, August 14, 2024; David Yaffe-Bellany, Sharon LaFraniere, and Matthew Goldstein, "Trump Rolls Out His New Crypto Currency Business," *New York Times*, September 16, 2024; Sharon LaFraniere and David Yaffe-Bellany, "The `Crypto Punks' Behind Trump's Murky New Business Venture," *New York Times*, October 7, 2024; Nikou Asgari, "Donald Trump Has a New Crypto Venture. The Industry Is Not Impressed," *Financial Times*, October 17, 2024.

19. Economic Club of New York, "Donald J. Trump at the Economic Club of New York," September 5, 2024, https://www.econclubny.org/web/pages/recent-speakers/-/blogs/ donald-j-trump.

20. Paul Krugman, "Donald Trump on the Dollar, in His Own Words," *New York Times*, September 9, 2024.

21. Pierre-Olivier Gourinchas, Hélène Rey, and Maxime Sauzet, "The International Monetary and Financial System," Working Paper 25782, National Bureau of Economic Research, April 2019, https://www.nber.org/system/files/working_papers/w25782/w25782.pdf.

22. Quoted in Tim Sablik, "Is Dollar Dominance in Doubt?" Federal Reserve Bank of Richmond, *Econ Focus*, Second Quarter 2022, https://www.richmondfed.org/publications/ research/econ_focus/2022/q2_feature_2.

23. Information for this and the following paragraph is drawn from the following: Gillian Tett, "Vulnerabilities in the Treasuries Market Aren't Going Away," *Financial Times,* September 7, 2023; Kate Duguid, Costas Mourselas, and Ortenca Aliaj, "The Debt-Fuelled Bet on US Treasuries That's Scaring Regulators," *Financial Times,* September 26, 2023; Daniel Barth, R. Jay Kahn, and Robert Mann, "Recent Developments in Hedge Funds' Treasury Futures and Repo Positions: Is the Basis Trade 'Back'?" Federal Reserve Board, August 30, 2023, https:// www.federalreserve.gov/econres/notes/feds-notes/recent-developments-in-hedge-funds- treasury-futures-and-repo-positions-20230830.html; Darrell Duffie, "Resilience Redux in the US Treasury Market," presentation at Jackson Hole Conference of the Federal Reserve

Bank of Kansas City, August 25, 2023, https://www.kansascityfed.org/Jackson Hole/documents/9726/JH_Paper_Duffie.pdf; Adam Tooze, "Making & Remaking the Most Important Market in the World. Or Why Everyone Should Read Menand and Younger on Treasuries," Chartbook No. 238, September 8, 2023, https://adamtooze.substack.com/p/chartbook-238-making-and-remaking; and Eric Wallerstein, "The $27 Trillion Treasury Market Is Only Getting Bigger," *Wall Street Journal*, March 24, 2024.

24. Paul Krugman, "Does the U.S. Dollar's Dominance Really Matter?" *New York Times*, May 28, 2021.

25. See "Donald Trump Wants a Weaker Dollar. What Are His Options?" *The Economist*, July 25 2024; and "ICYMI: Senator Vance Questions Chairman Powell on the U.S. Dollar's Reserve Currency Status," March 8, 2023, https://www.vance.senate.gov/press-releases/icymi-senator-vance-questions-chairman-powell-on-the-u-s-dollars-reserve-currency-status/?utm_source=npr_newsletter&utm_medium=email&utm_content=20240721&utm_term=9603517&utm_campaign=money&utm_id=11267066&orgid=55&utm_att1=.

26. For insightful analyses on the distinction between the dollar's global dominance and its exchange rate, see Karthik Sankaran, "The Burden of Proof Lies with Proof of the Burden," blog post, Nov. 2, 2023, https://sankaran.substack.com/p/the-burden-of-proof-lies-with-proof?r=r6t&utm_campaign=post&utm_medium=web&triedRedirect=true; and Felix Martin, "Donald Trump May Dent but Not Dethrone King Dollar," Reuters, July 26, 2024, https://www.reuters.com/breakingviews/donald-trump-may-dent-not-dethrone-king-dollar-2024-07-26/.

27. Congressional Budget Office, "An Update to the Budget and Economic Outlook: 2024 to 2034," June 2024, https://www.cbo.gov/publication/60039.

28. See Lawrence H. Summers, opening speech at the Peterson Institute for International Economics, conference on "Rethinking Fiscal Policy – Global Perspectives," May 30, 2023 (video), https://www.piie.com/events/rethinking-fiscal-policy-global-perspectives.

29. Fitch Ratings, "Fitch Downgrades the United States' Long-Term Ratings to 'AA+' from 'AAA'; Outlook Stable," August 1, 2023, https://www.fitchratings.com/research/sovereigns/fitch-downgrades-united-states-long-term-ratings-to-aa-from-aaa-outlook-stable-01-08-2023.

30. See George Selgin, "The Digital Gold Fallacy, or Why Bitcoin Can't Save the US Dollar," Cato Institute, November 29, 2024, https://www.cato.org/blog/digital-gold-fallacy-or-why-bitcoin-cant-save-us-dollar-1.

31. Aime Williams, "Trump Threatens BRICS Nations with 100% Tariffs If They Undermine Dollar," *Financial Times*, December 1, 2024.

32. See, for example, Brad Setser, "The U.S. Has Every Reason It Needs to Drop the Debt Ceiling – Both at Home and Abroad," Council on Foreign Relations, blog post, June 8, 2023, https://www.cfr.org/blog/us-has-every-reason-it-needs-drop-debt-ceiling-both-home-and-abroad.

INDEX

Average Inflation Targeting (FAIT), 206; in Greece, 78; hyperinflation cases, 16–17; in Iran, 143; and oil, 215; in Russia, 217–18, 223

Information, The, 166

Institutional Investor, 51

interest rates: adjustment of, 13, 195, 197, 201–2, 206, 208, 210–11, 246, 248; assault on inflation drives interest rates to record levels, 56–59; kept low in Japan, 88; sky-high in Greece, 78, 83; volatile in the *1970s,* 51–52

International Criminal Court, 145

International Emergency Economic Powers Act (IEEPA), 111

international reserve currency: dollar as, 7–8, 18, 20, 55, 64, 74–75, 100, 105–7, 167, 178, 245, 247; multipolar currency regime better than single dominance, 244, 250; non-dollar alternatives, 74–76, 91, 97, 100, 105, 166–67, 211–12, 225

Iran, 54, 93, 102–6, 130–35, 230, 234; Comprehensive Iran Sanctions, Accountability, and Divestment Act (CISADA), 133; Joint Comprehensive Plan of Action (JCPOA), 134–35; and oil, 103, 105, 130, 133–35, 143; sanctions against, 11, 103–6, 113, 130–35, 143, 234; targeting Iranian banks, 130–34

Iraq, 104, 113–14, 127, 226

Ireland, 82–85, 144

Italy, 83, 85–86, 112, 223

It's a Wonderful Life (movie), 30

Jackson, Andrew, 24, 32

Japan, 38–39, 63, 65; deflation, 89–90; economic miracle, 87; financial repression, 87–88; and SAMA, 49; sanctions against, 112–13; and yen, 86–90, 244; yen bloc, 89

Jay-Z, 82

Jefferson, Thomas, 112

Jin, Renqing, 64

Johnson, Lyndon, 41

JPM Coin, 188

JPMorgan Chase, 188

Juncker, Jean-Claude, 105

junk bonds, 202

Kamp, Jaap, 124

Keatinge, Tom, 140

Kelly, Jemima, 160

Kennedy, John F., 38

Kennedy, Robert F., Jr., 175

Kerry, John, 106

Keynes, John Maynard, 35–36, 38, 45, 73–74, 91, 211; bancor, 36–37, 74, 94; *The General Theory of Employment, Interest and Money,* 35

Khamenei, Ali, 134

Khanna, Parag, 82

Kim, Jong Il, 126, 128

Kindleberger, Charles, 45

Kirshner, Jonathan, 75

Kissinger, Henry, 48

Knickerbocker Trust Co., 32

Koning, John Paul, 173

Korin, Anne, *De-Dollarization,* 18, 138–39

Krugman, Paul, 79, 246

Kublai Khan, 12

Kumar, Aditi, 166

Kunz, Diane, 63, 89

Kwon, Do, 179

KYC (know your customer), 116, 152, 160, 176, 181–84, 239–40

Lagarde, Christine, 97

language, 8, 101

Lavrov, Sergei, 218, 228

law. *See* rule of law

Le Maire, Bruno, 105, 218

League of Nations, 111–12

Lebanon, 121, 190

Lehman Brothers, 68–69, 71–72, 153

Lenihan, Brian, 84

Levey, Stuart, 129–33, 135, 160–61

Lew, Jacob, 106